THE SUPREME COURT REBORN

THE
SUPREME COURT
REBORN

*The Constitutional Revolution
in the Age of Roosevelt*

WILLIAM E. LEUCHTENBURG

New York   Oxford
OXFORD UNIVERSITY PRESS
1995

Oxford University Press

Oxford   New York   Toronto
Delhi   Bombay   Calcutta   Madras   Karachi
Kuala Lumpur   Singapore   Hong Kong   Tokyo
Nairobi   Dar es Salaam   Cape Town
Melbourne   Auckland   Madrid

and associated companies in
Berlin   Ibadan

Library of Congress Cataloging-in-Publication Data
Leuchtenburg, William Edward, 1922–
The Supreme Court reborn : the constitutional revolution
in the age of Roosevelt / William E. Leuchtenburg.
p. cm.   Includes index.
ISBN 0-19-508613-9
1. United States. Supreme Court—History.
2. United States. Supreme Court—
Officials and employees—Selection and appointment—History.
3. Judges—United States—History.
4. United States—Constitutional history.
I. Title.   KF8742.L48   1995
347.73'26'09—dc20   [347.3073509]
94-11840

2 4 6 8 9 7 5 3 1

Printed in the United States of America
on acid-free paper

For

SHELDON MEYER
Editor Nonpareil

Preface

In the late spring of 1962, toward the end of my fellowship year at the Center for Advanced Study in the Behavioral Sciences in California, I began to think about what subject I would take up after I had completed my current commitments. I was in the process of putting the last touches on *Franklin D. Roosevelt and the New Deal, 1932–1940*. Four years earlier, I had published *The Perils of Prosperity, 1914–32*. That spring, I had contracted with Time-Life to write the two final volumes of a projected twelve-volume history of the United States. When I carried out that assignment, I would have written, since the publication of my Ph. D. dissertation, four syntheses in a row, covering all of the period from 1914 to the present. Though I could imagine undertaking other syntheses in the future, I wanted to interrupt that progression to examine a concise question that could be explored in depth but would not be too time-consuming.

It was these considerations that led me to the topic of the "Court-packing" controversy of 1937. I was familiar with the general outlines of that episode (indeed, I had just been engaged in writing several pages about it in my book on FDR and the New Deal), but I wanted to learn more about a time during which Franklin D. Roosevelt became the dominant figure in American political culture and when nothing less than a "revolution" had taken place in the exegesis of the Constitution. I admired the contemporary narrative by two Washington reporters, Joseph Alsop and Turner Catledge, but reasoned that a historian, with access to all of the archives that had opened since that account was published in 1938, and with the added perspective of nearly three decades, ought to be able to improve upon it. One other aspect also attracted me. Since the furor over Court-packing had been short-lived—Alsop and Catledge had entitled their book *The 168 Days*—I anticipated that, though I planned to do thoroughgoing archival research, I should be able to complete the project relatively swiftly and then turn to other things.

Little did I realize how mistaken that last supposition was. The constitutional crisis, I came to realize, could not be comprehended by focusing on 168 days but required an understanding of years, even decades, before and after. Furthermore, I had to teach myself an entirely new and demanding field for which I had no training whatsoever, not even an undergraduate course in constitutional law. And just as I was getting some momentum on research and writing, something happened that every author fears—a book on this very subject was published. That did not lead me to abandon the idea, but it did prove a deterrent. Eventually, I concluded that I might as well take my time, and like a stacked-up plane circling a landing field that loses its priority as other aircraft enter the holding pattern, the book increasingly got displaced by other projects, starting with a revision of Samuel Eliot Morison and Henry Steele Commager's *The Growth of the American Republic*, a magnificent opus but nearly two thousand pages long, and carrying down to books such as *A Troubled Feast, In the Shadow of FDR*, and others *in utero*.

During all these years, however, I continued, whenever I could, to pursue this subject and this new field, with great rewards. That endeavor has led me to teach graduate colloquia in constitutional history, to direct Ph.D. dissertations in the area, and, for a quarter of a century, to offer advanced courses to law students, first at Columbia Law School, where, for a number of years, Benno C. Schmidt, Jr., and I taught a seminar, "The Supreme Court in the Age of Holmes and Brandeis." More recently, following that exhilarating experience, I have had the pleasure of teaching a course at Duke Law School in the very good company of John Hope Franklin and Walter Dellinger.

This interest has also motivated me to give the lectures and to write the essays that compose this book. Five of these nine pieces originated as lectures, in a variety of venues. They were delivered to campus audiences in Chicago and in Arlington, Texas; to a conference of Canadian and American scholars in Montreal; to a gathering of high school teachers in Richmond, Virginia; and in one particularly elegant setting—the French Senate in the Hall of the Medicis in the Palais du Luxembourg in Paris. One of the articles was written for a popular history journal (it is the only one in this volume that is not annotated), and two began as contributions to larger works—an essay for Philip Kurland's *Supreme Court Review* and another in honor of my mentor at Columbia. Only once, in order to create continuity, have I dipped into the manuscript of my ongoing work on the Supreme Court, which has now expanded into a hefty two-volume project for which I have completed a good many chapters totaling hundreds of pages.

In putting together this collection, I have been guided by a few simple precepts. I have not assumed that there was anything sacrosanct about the original text of an essay, and I have, on the contrary, made a point of revising each piece to incorporate more recent research. On the assumption that some readers will want to peruse the book from cover to cover, I have eliminated material that would be repetitious, but, recognizing that other readers may be interested only in a particular essay or essays, I have included enough explanatory material, even at the risk of repetition, so that those readers will understand the context.

In writing these essays, and in assembling them in this volume, I have incurred many debts—to the scholars who have preceded me, to the manuscripts librarians who have catered to my requests, to the students in my courses who have challenged me, but, above all, to my wife, Jean Anne Leuchtenburg, who, yet another time, has devoted days of her life to getting this book to press, who has helped immensely by her astute editorial comments, and who has done it all with inimitable grace and generosity of spirit. I am also grateful for the devoted help of Eric Combest and Lars Golumbic in photocopying materials and obtaining books for me, with good cheer, skill, and imagination, and for the assistance of Harvard Sitkoff in making the resources of the University of New Hampshire Library available to me. I welcome the opportunity to give thanks to the Guggenheim Foundation, the Center for Advanced Study in the Behavioral Sciences, the Wilson Center, and, above all, to the National Humanities Center, where I had the good fortune to be a Fellow in its very first class and then Mellon Senior Fellow.

This book is dedicated to the editor who has, to an astonishing extent, been responsible for the publication of more history books of high quality than anyone else in the annals of publishing and who has never been anything but a constant source of encouragement to me.

Chapel Hill, N. C.   WILLIAM E. LEUCHTENBURG
August 1994

Contents

THE SUPREME COURT REBORN

Mr. Justice Holmes and
Three Generations of Imbeciles

[When Melvin I. Urofsky of Virginia Commonwealth University invited me to give a paper at a conference that he and A. E. Dick Howard of the University of Virginia Law School were organizing on Virginia and the Constitution, I saw the occasion as an opportunity to explore a case that had long fascinated me but that I knew little about. *Buck v. Bell*, I sensed, would provide an unusual perspective on the Supreme Court in the 1920s, a decade in which the Court had a decidedly conservative tilt under Chief Justice William Howard Taft, Edward T. Sanford, and especially "the Four Horsemen"—Pierce Butler, James McReynolds, George Sutherland, and Willis Van Devanter—but was hearing dissenting views from an emerging liberal trio: Louis D. Brandeis, Oliver Wendell Holmes, Jr., and Harlan Fiske Stone. Writing about this case would also, I anticipated, give me a chance to integrate political and social history, which I had recommended in my presidential address to the Organization of American Historians in 1986 ("The Pertinence of Political History: Reflections on the Significance of the State in America," *Journal of American History*, 73 (December 1986): 585–600). The paper was delivered in Richmond in the fall of 1989 at a conference co-sponsored by the Virginia Commission on the Bicentennial of the United States Constitution, Virginia Commonwealth University, and the Virginia Department of Education, and published in a limited edition in A. E. Dick Howard and Melvin I. Urofsky, eds., *Virginia and the Constitution* (Charlottesville, Va.: Virginia Commission on the Bicentennial of the United States Constitution, Center for Public Service, University of Virginia, 1992). I have reworked the paper for *The Supreme Court in the Age of Roosevelt*. As this essay was going to press, I benefited from reading two papers on eugenics presented at the 1994 meeting of the Organization of American Historians by Edward J. Larson and Steven Noll.]

I

Oliver Wendell Holmes has, no doubt, a secure place in the Pantheon of American jurisprudence. Author of the classic *The Common Law*, he served for fully half a century on two of our greatest tribunals—the Massachusetts Supreme Judicial Court, where he became Chief Justice, and the U. S. Supreme Court, on which he was still sitting at the age of ninety. Son of the autocrat of the breakfast-table, he has been widely esteemed as, in the phrase of one admiring author, a "Yankee from Olympus."[1] With his soldierly bearing, his Back Bay Boston manner, his piercing stare above a bristling white mustachio, he seemed, as he looked down from the bench, the very personification of the Anglo-American legal tradition. Indeed, one authority has noted the claim that "no other man of comparable intellect and spirit has been a judge in the United States, or for that matter among English-speaking peoples," while another said, "Like the Winged Victory of Samothrace, he is the summit of hundreds of years of civilization, the inspiration of ages yet to come."[2]

Holmes won this luminous reputation as the magnificent Yankee in good part because of the opinions he wrote in his long service on the Supreme Court. In the field of civil liberties, he is revered as the Great Dissenter who originated the "clear and present danger" doctrine.[3] But he is even better known as the advocate of judicial restraint—the conviction that judges should not deny majorities through their elected representatives the right to enact experimental legislation even when the judge thinks the law that has been challenged is foolish. "I always say, as you know, that if my fellow citizens want to go to Hell I will help them," he once remarked. "It's my job." By deferring to legislatures, even when he harbored doubts about the wisdom of their actions, Holmes, stated Justice Felix Frankfurter, added "cubits to his judicial stature. For he thereby transcended personal predilections and private notions of social policy, and became truly the impersonal voice of the Constitution."[4]

Holmes expressed many of his ideas in pithy sentences that are forever imprinted on our memory. We do not readily forget an apothegm like "The Fourteenth Amendment does not enact Mr. Herbert Spencer's *Social Statics*"; or his observation that the First Amendment does "not protect a man in falsely shouting fire in a theatre."[5] (Perhaps, it has been suggested, Holmes developed his flair for aphorisms because his father rewarded a "bright penny" contribution to breakfast table conversation with an extra dollop of jam.)[6] Commentators have praised him for the inimitable economy of expression with which he punctured the pretensions of conservative judges who flouted majority will. Yet in a 1927 opinion for the Court, Holmes uttered a one-liner that has become as famous as his other contributions but has had very different consequences. It has badly tarnished his reputation and has cast doubt on the virtues of judicial restraint.

II

That 1927 case, *Buck v. Bell*,[7] arose out of a movement for social improvement for which in 1883 the English scientist Francis Galton, cousin of Charles Darwin, coined a word: eugenics. Convinced that intelligence was an inherited trait, little affected by environment, eugenists hoped to better the racial stock by selective breeding of individuals born into families of talent. Even more of their concern came to be directed at averting the depletion of the race's "germ plasm," because, it was thought, the dim-witted bred like rabbits and would eventually outnumber those of sound mind. To prevent that calamity, they advocated segregating the "feeble-minded" during their reproductive years. Some eugenists promoted an even more radical solution: coercive sterilization of the unfit, a proposition favored by no less an authority than Julian Huxley.

This drastic remedy quickly gained a following in America, where eugenics elicited the interest of a variety of prominent individuals, ranging from Alexander Graham Bell to the president of Stanford University, David Starr Jordan, to as improbable a figure as the anarchist Emma Goldman. (Subsequently, Margaret Sanger, the country's foremost advocate of birth control, expressed the desire to weed out the "unfit," and the Socialist Norman Thomas voiced anxiety about the "alarming[ly] high birthrate of definitely inferior stock.") Sterilization also won the support of both the American Association of University Women and the Federation of Women's Clubs. By 1907 the movement had achieved so much momentum that Pennsylvania enacted the country's first coercive sterilization statute. But the idea did not really take off until Mary Williamson Harriman gave it a firm institutional foundation by endowing the Eugenics Record Office in Cold Spring Harbor on Long Island in 1910. "What is the matter with the American people?" she asked at a public meeting in 1915. "Fifteen million must be sterilized!"

Eugenists in the United States embraced coercive sterilization with much greater ardor than their counterparts in Great Britain. Some of their expectations, indeed, were utopian. In 1914 the president of the University of Wisconsin confidently asserted, "We know enough about eugenics so that if the knowledge were applied the defective classes would disappear within a generation." Nor did they have any doubt about the justice of their cause. In an address to the Massachusetts Medical Society in 1912, Dr. Walter E. Fernald declared that "the feebleminded are a parasitic, predatory class [who] are a menace and danger to the community." A series of studies of families such as the Kallikaks, who had a disproportionate incidence of social pathology, reinforced the conviction that heredity determined intelligence. So did the French psychologist Alfred Binet's measurement of cognitive skills which, during mass testing in World War I, was badly misconstrued to correlate intelligence with race and socioeconomic status. [8]

Yet as compulsory sterilization gained advocates, it also met stout resistance. In Indiana, Governor Thomas R. Marshall, who would later be Vice President of the United States and who is usually known for little more than saying, "What this country needs is a good five cent cigar," halted operations. Governors of Pennsylvania vetoed sterilization bills in 1905 and again in 1921, as, in the decade after 1909, did the governors of four more states—Oregon, Nebraska, Vermont, and Idaho. The eugenists were even more troubled by another development. From 1913 through 1921, courts in seven states—New Jersey, Iowa, Michigan, New York, Nevada, Indiana, and Oregon—struck down sterilization statutes because of procedural shortcomings.

To overcome the serious complaints that had been raised, the most important promoter of eugenics, Harry Laughlin, drafted a model sterilization statute he hoped would stand up in the courts. Laughlin, a biologist, has been described as "humorless, intolerant of criticism, and continually afire with dogmatic zeal." In the basic text he published in 1922, he defined the individual targeted for sterilization as "a socially inadequate person . . . who by his or her own effort . . . fails chronically in comparison with normal persons to maintain himself or herself as a useful member of the organized life of the state." An individual would not be at risk, though, if the "ineffectiveness is adequately taken care of by the particular family in which it occurs." Among those grouped in "the socially inadequate classes" were the "wayward," the "tuberculous," the blind, deaf, and deformed, dependents (including orphans), "ne'er-do-wells," paupers, the homeless, and those who, "according to the demonstrated laws of heredity," had the potential for producing offspring at least one-fourth of whom would "most probably function as socially inadequate persons." Neither the eugenists, nor later the courts, appear to have been in any way troubled by the transparent class bias, not to mention the heartlessness toward the handicapped, in this classification scheme. [9]

Laughlin took special pains to meet the objections raised by courts about inadequate procedures, and when in 1924 Virginia enacted a model law for sterilization of "inmates of institutions supported by the State who shall be found to be afflicted with a hereditary form of insanity or imbecility," the statute appeared to give every assurance of procedural due process. The superintendent of an institution was required to petition a special board of directors of his hospital and to file an affidavit with respect to the facts and opinions he presented. The inmate and his or her guardian were to be given notice of this petition and of the time and place of a hearing, and should there be no guardian the circuit court of the county was to appoint one. If the inmate was a minor, his or her parents had to receive a copy of the petition. The inmate had the right to appear at the hearing, and all evidence had to be written down. Once the board had ruled, the inmate and the superintendent each had the privilege of appealing to the county court, which would review the evidence before issuing an order. Lastly, any party could ask to have the order reviewed by the Supreme Court of Appeals.

The Virginia law had been enacted at the behest of hospital officials, in particular the superintendent of the State Colony for Epileptics and Feeble-Minded in Lynchburg, Albert S. Priddy, who had been accused of performing sterilization operations illegally. Scores of women had entered the Lynchburg facility only to depart with their reproductive organs removed because Priddy had diagnosed a pelvic disease. In one instance, while a Richmond man was away from his home, two male family friends called on his wife and their nine children. The police broke in; his wife was charged with prostitution; and she and the two oldest daughters were committed to the Lynchburg colony. There Priddy sterilized the wife, who denied she had any pelvic disorder, and one of the daughters. The Richmond man brought suit, in part to gain the release of the other daughter, and though Priddy prevailed, the judge was said to have admonished him not to perform any more operations until there was a law specifically authorizing them.

Dr. Priddy represented the most odious aspect of the eugenics movement—the determination of men in authority to deny helpless women whom they viewed as their social inferiors the right to bear children because they disapproved of their sexual behavior. In his 1912 address, Dr. Fernald told the Massachusetts Medical Society that "feeble-minded women are almost invariably immoral and if at large usually become carriers of venereal disease or give birth to children who are as defective as themselves." Eighty-eight percent of prostitutes, one study reported, had a mental age below eleven. That finding made it easy for men like Priddy to justify institutionalizing young women as "feeble-minded" when the only evidence of that condition was that they had been sexually precocious. In fact, trapped in circular reasoning, the eugenists never got straight whether women were sexually active because they were feeble-minded, or whether their sexual behavior demonstrated feeble-mindedness. Underlying the conceptions of the eugenists was a strong disposition to penalize lower class young women for giving into "animal emotions" that the middle class was expected to suppress.

Elite groups also had an economic motivation for endorsing eugenics. If the tendency continued "to keep under custodial care in State institutions all females who have become incorrigibly immoral," Priddy explained, "it will soon become a burden much greater than the State can carry."[10] He was far from alone in this belief. Margaret Sanger was one of many who favored sterilization in part because they thought the country was being taxed excessively to support a burgeoning class of morons. Removing Fallopian tubes solved two problems; it freed well-to-do taxpayers from the cost of keeping the "unfit" in institutions for prolonged periods while assuring that suspect sexual traits were not passed on to another generation. (Oddly, it does not seem to have occurred to anyone that sterilized women, liberated from fear of pregnancy, might, after release from an institution, become even more promiscuous.) Priddy's program of coercion served, too, as a form of social control within the hospital. Unless patients agreed to be sterilized, doctors warned them, they would be confined within the hospital walls until their reproductive years were over.[11]

Not coincidentally, the Virginia law came in the very year of two other symptomatic statutes. In 1924 Congress enacted an immigration restriction measure severely limiting newcomers from southern and eastern Europe, a region whose peoples were regarded as "genetically inferior." The House Committee on Immigration and Naturalization which approved the restrictive legislation had earlier taken the extraordinary step of appointing an "Expert Eugenics Agent," none other than the ubiquitous Harry Laughlin, who took pride in forebears he could trace back to the American Revolution and who sneered at more recent arrivals. In 1924, too, under the sponsorship of another enthusiastic eugenist, the Virginia legislature adopted an "Act to Preserve Racial Integrity" forbidding miscegenation so as not to "pollute America with mixed-blood offspring." All three measures shared the aim of keeping pure the racial stock deemed essential to a republican political culture.

If Priddy and Laughlin epitomized the nasty element behind such legislation, the main sponsor of Virginia's sterilization law revealed a different outlook. Aubrey Ellis Strode, whose father had been president of Clemson College, studied law at the University of Virginia and became a prominent member of the Virginia State Senate, where he distinguished himself as an advocate of women's rights, fairer treatment for blacks, penal reform, and aid for the handicapped. Strode thought of eugenics as altogether consistent with his progressive outlook. (His interest in sterilization, however, does have one bizarre aspect: both of his parents died in hospitals for the insane.)

Despite the diversity in their motivations, Priddy and Strode (as well as their allies nationally) shared a common quest—for a test case. The superintendent of the Lynchburg colony needed assurance that he was legally protected when he performed these operations, and Strode, Laughlin, and the national eugenics movement wanted to legitimize the cause. A 1919 effort to get court approval had fizzled when a friendly suit to test Indiana's sterilization law had proved to be flawed because there were not enough hereditary data on the subject, a man who had been institutionalized for incest with his half-sister. A trial judge ruled the act unconstitutional for failing to protect the rights in court of those on whom operations were to be performed, and in 1921 the Indiana Supreme Court affirmed that judgment.[12]

III

The carefully crafted Virginia law, modeled on Laughlin's statute, appeared much more promising, especially when, only three months after it took effect, the state came upon a subject who appeared to have been delivered by Central Casting to personalize a link in a faulty hereditary chain. In 1924, at the age of seventeen, Carrie Buck had been committed to the Lynchburg facility by her foster father, the town's peace officer, because she had become a burden after giving birth to an illegitimate child. Adhering to the provisions of the law, the superintendent at Lynchburg, as the first step in launching what would become *Buck v. Priddy*, asked a three-member special board to order Carrie to be sterilized because she was a "moral delinquent . . . of the moron class." She had been branded as wayward because of her allegedly licentious behavior, though, in fact, she had become pregnant because she had been raped by a relative of her foster parents. Four years earlier, her mother, Emma, who had been convicted of prostitution, and hence was "antisocial," had been committed to the same institution. On the Stanford Binet-Simon test, Carrie had been scored as having a mental age of nine, and her mother, aged fifty-two, a mental age of seven. The eugenists took these marks as proof that feeble-mindedness had been passed on from one generation to the next.

The eugenists' case would be even stronger if they could demonstrate that Carrie's daughter Vivian was mentally deficient too. At a hearing in the attractive white courthouse of the Circuit Court of Amherst County, a Red Cross nurse obligingly testified that when she visited the seven-month-old infant, she discerned a "look" about her that was "not quite normal," adding, "but just what it is, I can't tell." A representative of the Eugenics Record Office also submitted the results of a test for infants he had conducted that, he claimed, showed Vivian was below average. The Buck family, he told the court, revealed a heritage of feeble-mindedness conforming to Mendelian laws. (In truth, Vivian, far from being "slow," made the honor roll when she became a pupil at a public school in Charlottesville, and her second-grade teachers in 1932 regarded her as "bright." Alas, Vivian never got a chance to disprove the diagnosis of the eugenists, for that year, at the age of seven, she died of a childhood ailment, probably measles.) [13]

To buttress their case, Strode and Priddy also secured a deposition from the head of the Eugenics Record Office, Harry Laughlin. Though he had never laid eyes on Carrie, or her family, and though Priddy had apologized to him for not being able to make out "a genealogical tree such as you would like to have" and for giving him "such little data on which to work," he diagnosed her as the product of a line of hereditary feeble-mindedness. Laughlin conceded that "so far as I understand, no physical defect or mental trouble attended her early years," but he asserted that Carrie, rejecting the opportunity she had been given to better herself, had been "sexually very immoral." He rested his assessment of her family on the words of a nurse who had said, "These people belong to the shiftless, ignorant, and worthless class of anti-social whites of the South." Laughlin wound up by praising eugenical sterilization as "a force for the mitigation of race degeneracy." [14]

Given the weight of all this evidence, however spurious, the judgment of the court could hardly be in doubt, especially since, it was claimed, the salpingectomy—excision of the Fallopian tubes—was in Carrie's best interest. If she did not have the operation, the state contended, the prospect was "that both for her protection and the protection of society she must be kept in custody and confinement until her child-bearing age is past." If she were sterilized, she "could leave the Colony and enjoy the liberty and blessings of outdoor life, become self-supporting, and thereby relieve the Commonwealth of Virginia of the burden . . . of her . . . custodial care." She could not anticipate any high-prestige employment, but she could, at a minimum, "help around the house." Furthermore, the Commonwealth pointed out, Carrie had acquiesced in the procedure. When counsel for the hospital had asked her, "Do you care to say anything about having this operation performed on you?", she had replied, "No, sir, I have not, it's up to my people." Unhappily, though, she had no "people" capable of speaking for her. Having heard all this testimony, the judge of the Virginia circuit court upheld the order to cut Carrie Buck's Fallopian tubes.[15] It would have been a moment of gratification for Dr. Priddy, who believed the hospital should serve as a "cleaning house" to take in young women, sterilize them, and send them out into the world, but he had died of Hodgkin's disease before the decision was handed down. Henceforth, *Buck v. Priddy* would bear the name of his successor, Dr. J. H. Bell.

As the law required, the court had appointed a guardian for Carrie, and his attorney, I. P. Whitehead (subsequently chairman of the Virginia Bar Association), dutifully carried her case, now *Buck v. Bell*, to the Commonwealth's highest tribunal. Virginia's Supreme Court of Appeals found that "Carrie Buck, by the laws of heredity, is the probable potential parent of socially inadequate offspring likewise affected as she is," and asserted that the statute "was not meant to punish but to protect the class of socially inadequate citizens from themselves and to promote the welfare of society by mitigating race degeneracy and raising the average intelligence of the people of the state."[16] In short, in affirming the judgment of the Circuit Court of Amherst County, Virginia's appellate court did not content itself with saying that it was respecting the prerogatives of the legislature but unhesitatingly subscribed to the premises of the eugenists.

More than two decades ago, the political scientist Clement Vose contended that *Buck v. Bell* had all the earmarks of a "friendly suit," and we now know, from information that has subsequently surfaced, that he was right. In the circuit court, he points out, there was no "devoted and informed critic of eugenical sterilization," and the eugenists orchestrated both sides of the litigation. Moreover, he writes, "Laughlin's deposition was not subjected to critical examination," for "Carrie Buck's lawyer had neither the resources nor the desire to search for experts who might contradict Laughlin." Whitehead cited only a single precedent in his brief to the Court of Appeals, while his opponent, his boyhood chum Senator Strode, in a masterful presentation, offered many. Afterward, the two attorneys appeared *together* before the hospital board to express their pleasure that as a result of their "victory," the case was "in admirable shape to go to the court of highest resort."[17]

IV

Yet when, on April 22, 1927, the United States Supreme Court heard argument on *Buck v. Bell*, Carrie Buck, inexplicably, had a passionate champion in Whitehead. He claimed that the operation sanctioned by the Virginia legislature violated the due process clause of the Fourteenth Amendment by depriving the plaintiff of her constitutional right of bodily integrity. In 1877, in *Munn v. Illinois*,[18] he noted, the Supreme Court had said of the phrase "deprivation of life": "The inhibition against its deprivation extends to all those limbs and faculties by which life is enjoyed. The deprivation not only of life but whatever God has given to everyone with life . . . is protected by the provision [in the Fourteenth Amendment]."

Carrie Buck's counsel conceded that the law provided for procedural due process, but insisted that "we must look to the substance rather than the form of the law." No procedure could suffice if a person were divested of a constitutional right, he maintained, and "the inherent right of mankind to go through life without mutilation of organs of generation needs no constitutional declaration." He concluded:

> If this Act be a valid enactment, then the limits of the power of the State (which in the end is nothing more than the faction in control of the government) to rid itself of those citizens deemed undesirable according to its standards, by means of surgical sterilization, have not been set.
> . . . A reign of doctors will be inaugurated and in the name of science new classes will be added, even races may be brought within the scope of such regulation, and the worst form of tyranny practiced. In the place of the constitutional government of the fathers we shall have set up Plato's Republic.[19]

In rejoinder, Senator Strode, counsel for Bell—the new Lynchburg superintendent—and, by implication, counsel for the Commonwealth of Virginia, denied that the act imposed cruel and unusual punishment. That prohibition in the Constitution, he insisted, applied only to those actions "of a barbarous character" that had been viewed as beyond the pale at the time of the Founders: "drawing and quartering . . . , burning at the stake, cutting off the nose, ears or limbs, and the like." In one case, he pointed out, the U.S. Supreme Court had ruled that the Eighth Amendment did not apply to the states; and in another, a state court had specifically found that vasectomy was not cruel. He further suggested, drawing on his own experience in a smallpox epidemic in the courthouse town of Amherst where he had begun his practice, that the Virginia statute could be likened to compulsory vaccination laws, "for there, as here, a surgical operation is required for the protection of the individual and of society." To fend off an equal protection claim, he added that compulsory vaccination had been upheld in the courts, even though it was imposed only on public school children and not on society at large.

There was no legal reason why a woman could not decide to have such an operation performed voluntarily, Strode remarked. Hence, it was not *malum in se*. It could only be regarded as illegal if done against the will of a patient or contrary to her interest. But who was to give the consent or make the decision for this particular plaintiff as to whether it was good for her? "She cannot determine the matter for herself both because being not of full age her judgment is not to be accepted nor would it acquit the surgeon, and because she is further incapacitated by congenital mental defect."

"The State may and does confine the feeble minded, thus depriving them of their liberty," Strode went on. Furthermore, the plaintiff was already forbidden by law to procreate. "The precise question therefore is whether the State, in its judgment of what is best for appellant and for society, may through the medium of the operation . . . restore her to the liberty, freedom and happiness which thereafter she might safely be allowed to find outside of institutional walls," he claimed. In sum, this statute, far from being a cruel invasion of her person, was actually to her benefit. [20]

V

Just ten days later, on May 2, 1927, the nation's most celebrated jurist, Oliver Wendell Holmes, delivered the judgment of the Court. [21] His opinion took only five paragraphs, and all but one sentence of the first three paragraphs merely recited the facts in the case, or at least the facts as Holmes understood them. Hence, the substance of his opinion, beyond that one sentence, ran just two paragraphs, constituting barely more than one printed page. Holmes entertained no uncertainty about the facts. He said curtly: "Carrie Buck is a feeble minded white woman who was committed to the State Colony. . . . She is the daughter of a feeble minded mother in the same institution, and the mother of an illegitimate feeble minded child." Nor, he declared, could there be any "doubt that so far as procedure is concerned the rights of the patient are most carefully considered, and as every step in this case was taken in scrupulous compliance with the statute and after months of observation, there is no doubt that in that respect the plaintiff . . . has had due process of law."

The eighty-six-year-old Justice went on to say that the attack was not on procedure but upon the substance of the law. "In view of the general declarations of the legislature and the specific findings of the Court," he responded, "obviously we cannot say as matter of law that the grounds do not exist, and if they exist they justify the result." The thrice-

wounded veteran of the Civil War—who once said that "the faith is true
and adorable which leads a soldier to throw away his life in obedience
to a blindly accepted duty"—then enunciated gruffly what he saw to be
the fundamental principle in the case:

> We have seen more than once that the public welfare may call upon the
> best citizens for their lives. It would be strange if it could not call upon
> those who already sap the strength of the State for these lesser sacrifices,
> often not felt to be such by those concerned, in order to prevent our
> being swamped with incompetence. It is better for all the world, if instead
> of waiting to execute degenerate offspring for crime, or to let them starve
> for their imbecility, society can prevent those who are manifestly unfit
> from continuing their kind.

Holmes wound up this paragraph with two sentences that would engender heated controversy. Taking cue from counsel, he stated flatly,
"The principle that sustains compulsory vaccination is broad enough to
cover cutting the Fallopian tubes." In support of that analogy, he offered
the only citation in his entire opinion—to a ruling upholding compulsory vaccination in Massachusetts.[22] He then concluded the paragraph
with the famous, or infamous, sentence: "Three generations of imbeciles
are enough."

Having dealt with the core of the question, Holmes turned briefly to
consider the argument that the plaintiff had been denied equal protection because the law only applied to the small group inside institutions,
not to the whole population. "It is the usual last resort of constitutional
arguments to point out shortcomings of this sort," he said dismissively.
"But the answer is that the law does all that is needed when it does all
that it can, indicates a policy, applies it to all within the lines, and seeks
to bring within the lines all similarly situated so far and so fast as its
means allow." He ended with the bleak observation: "Of course so far
as the operations enable those who otherwise must be kept confined to
be returned to the world, and thus open the asylum to others, the equality aimed at will be more nearly reached. *Judgment affirmed.*"

Only one Justice entered a dissent, and it came not, as might have
been expected, from either of the prominent liberals, Louis Brandeis or
Harlan Fiske Stone, but from an arch-conservative, Pierce Butler, former
corporation lawyer whom progressives had regarded as a hired gun for
the railroads. Far from being a civil libertarian in his early years, he had
been so contemptuous of academic freedom when a trustee of the University of Minnesota that he had become known as "Bully" Butler.

No one is certain why Butler demurred, for he dissented without
opinion. It seems improbable that he did so out of commitment to the

Bill of Rights because, though he did occasionally reveal such sentiments, notably in a declaration against wiretapping, he was much more often on the side of government repression. Perhaps, it has been suggested whimsically, he thought three generations of imbeciles were not enough. It has always been supposed, though, that he broke away because he was the lone Catholic member of the bench. Proud of his Irish ancestry, he had had the forethought to come into the world on St. Patrick's Day, and no less proud of his faith, he held "the Catholic seat" on the Court that would later be inherited by Frank Murphy and William Brennan. He was quite likely aware that as early as 1895 the Vatican had denounced any "procedure . . . undertaken with the express purpose of sterilizing a woman." "Butler knows this is good law," Holmes had remarked to another Justice. "I wonder whether he will have the courage to vote with us in spite of his religion."[23]

VI

Buck v. Bell gave the imprimatur of the United States Supreme Court to the eugenics movement. "Justice Holmes," one writer said a quarter of a century later, "provided the eugenical sterilization movement with a constitutional blessing and an epigrammatic battle cry. His opinion . . . was regarded by eugenists as the herald of a new day. . . . Holmes . . . was hailed by them as the new Prometheus, and excerpts from his opinion continue to this day to add spice to their literature."[24] Within four years, five more states enacted sterilization laws, and other states revised their statutes to conform with Virginia's. Over the next generation some seventy thousand persons in the United States were sterilized by state order.

A disproportionate number of the operations took place in Virginia, where on the morning of October 19, 1927, Dr. Bell excised young Carrie Buck's Fallopian tubes. In the course of the next generation, the Commonwealth of Virginia, which coercively sterilized more than eight thousand persons, became the second leading state in the country in this procedure, surpassed only by the considerably more populous state of California. The operations were performed at hospitals in Petersburg, Williamsburg, Marion, and Staunton—but predominantly in Lynchburg. It has been surmised that no hospital in the country carried out more of these operations than the one in Lynchburg. (In 1980, by which time operations had ceased, the renamed Lynchburg Training School and Hospital was still the country's largest institution for the retarded, with more than two thousand patients.) As the *New York Times* later reported, "It was as routine as taking out tonsils. Men on Tuesday, women on

Thursday. . . . Over 50 years, thousands of men, women and children diagnosed as mentally retarded were rolled into the operating room."[25]

But the subjects were not only those judged—sometimes, perhaps often, misjudged—to be feeble-minded. Unwed mothers, orphans, poor people who had been dumped into mental hospitals, even unruly children were sterilized too. As an American Civil Liberties Union official later said, "We are talking for the most part about boys and girls ages 12 to 17, who were taken from their homes by the state."[26] So commonplace were these operations on poor white Southerners that they were called "Mississippi appendectomies." (Despite the obsession with racial immaculacy, very few of the compulsory sterilization operations, in Virginia at least, appear to have been performed on blacks, apparently because, ironically, the hospital system was Jim Crow, and blacks fell outside the orbit of social services.)

Of more than six thousand Virginia operations analyzed, 3,600 salpingectomies were performed on women, 2,420 vasectomies on men. Though the law, then, applied to both sexes, it affected women more, and there is a special horror in the thought of a group of male administrators resolving to cut out the procreative organs of a woman.

One particularly graphic transcript gives us a glimpse of how the hearing procedure worked under this "model" law, which ostensibly adhered scrupulously to procedural due process. The patient states: "I say if . . . the social worker . . . let me go home next year for good then I'm going to go home and do what my mama tells me. . . . I do not want to get sterilized either." Her mother and father returned their notice of a hearing with a note saying, "My husband and myself are not going to sign these papers. . . . Send her home to me for good. I am not ruining her life." At the hearing, a letter from her mother was entered into the record: "I do not think [she] should be fix. . . . Put yourself in my place if your daughter or son was to be fix and they wanted to get married someday and the girl or boy could not become a mother or father would you want this to happen to your daughter or son well I don't either I want [her] home for good [she] is a nice girl and a good girl. I am proud of her." The transcript ends with the chilling sentence: "The Board orders that sexual sterilization be performed on this patient no sooner than 30 days from this date."[27]

In his 1933 annual report on the Lynchburg facility, Dr. Bell asserted, "Now is the time to apply the pruning knife with vigor and without fear or favor," and in that same report, he praised Nazi Germany's "elimination of the unfit." There was, in fact, a close tie in the 1930s between the eugenics movement in America and the Nazis. In 1936, at the height of the Hitler era, Heidelberg awarded Laughlin an honorary degree for his work "as the . . . farseeing representative of racial policy in America," a degree Laughlin was "greatly honored to accept," and that year the honorary president of the Eugenics Research Association wrote: "It is unfortunate the anti-Nazi propaganda with which all countries have been flooded has gone far to obscure the correct understanding and the great importance of a German racial policy. . . . No earnest eugenist can fail to give approbation to such a national policy." Under Hitler's Hereditary Health Law, based on Laughlin's model statute, the Third Reich sterilized huge numbers of persons as genetically defective. When that program was condemned at the Nuremberg trials, counsel for the accused Nazis cited in defense Mr. Justice Holmes's opinion on Carrie Buck, a point Stanley Kramer highlighted in his film, *Judgment at Nuremberg.*[28]

VII

The unsavory kinship of the eugenics movement with the Nazis, Holmes's cursory treatment, and objections from scientists to the assumptions of eugenists on which Holmes relied have put *Buck v. Bell* in bad odor in the legal community. In the words of one critic, Holmes's opinion was "astoundingly brief and unusually platitudinous. The jurist is disconcerted by the absence of citations to support its legal principles and the psychiatrist and sociologist are equally surprised by the lack of a thorough understanding of the field of eugenics."[29] Holmes has been raked over especially by Catholic writers who have asserted that he fell into error because he abandoned natural law for positivism and have likened his claims for the primacy of the national state to the viewpoint of Hitler. So infuriated have some critics been that one called Holmes a "monster" for his opinion in *Buck v. Bell,* and another went so far as to say that "it would have been better for the country had he never been born."[30]

At the time, the opinion drew praise for exemplifying the admirable principle of judicial restraint, since Holmes had deferred to "the general declarations of the legislature," but more recently conservative commentators have taken exception. They have made *Buck v. Bell* their text in chiding liberals and radicals for instructing judges to limit their interpretation of the due process clause to ascertaining that proper procedure had been followed. Walter Berns, in particular, has insisted:

> Due process of law *does* require more than certain procedures. . . . There are some things which decent government should not do. One of these is to perform compulsory surgical operations in order to satisfy the racial

theories of a few benighted persons. To reduce the due process clause to a guarantee of prescribed procedures is to permit more than the public control of grain elevators, as libertarians since the *Gitlow* case would be the first to acknowledge. A restricted interpretation of the clause would have prevented the Court from interfering with Mayor Hague's brand of tyranny in Jersey City and with those local school boards which have compelled children to salute the flag. . . . The liberals' quarrel should be with injustice, not with the legal concept of substantive due process. Without the latter it would sometimes be impossible to prevent the former.

Slyly, Berns asks whether Holmes might not better have said that the fundamental issue was which of "two powers or rights shall prevail—the power of the State to legislate or the right of the individual to liberty of person. . . . The mere assertion that the subject matter relates though but in remote degree to the public health does not necessarily render the enactment valid." Carrie Buck's ordeal moves us to applaud these words. But as it happens, they come from the pen of Justice Rufus Peckham in *Lochner*, striking down a law regulating the hours of bakers, an opinion that we have all learned to hiss as judicial activism at its worst and an opinion from which Holmes delivered a memorable dissent. [31]

Holmes's opinion in *Buck v. Bell*, though, should be read less as an instance of deference to the legislature than as an expression of his own deeply felt convictions. Since he had frequently voted to validate social legislation, notably in his dissent in *Lochner*, progressives mistakenly supposed that he shared their enthusiasm when, in fact, he regarded their ideas as "humbugs." The notion that Holmes was a liberal, one writer has said, is a myth as "baseless as the tale of Washington and the cherry tree." He voted as he did only because he wished to acknowledge majority will. "Wise or not," Holmes maintained, "the proximate test of good government is that the dominant power has its way." [32]

Unlike the social welfare measures that he dismissed as "twaddle," however, eugenics was a reform that excited him. As early as 1915, he had written in the *Illinois Law Review*:

> I believe that the wholesale social regeneration which so many now seem to expect, if it can be helped by conscious, co-ordinated human effort, cannot be affected appreciably by tinkering with the institutions of property, but only by taking in hand life and trying to build a race. That would be my starting point for an ideal for the law.

On one occasion, he observed, "I can understand saying, whatever the cost, so far as may be, we will keep certain strains out of our blood," and on yet another: "I believe that Malthus was right. . . . Every society is founded on the death of men. . . . I shall think socialism begins to be entitled to serious treatment when and not before it takes life in hand and prevents the continuance of the unfit."[33]

Far from being, as Frankfurter called him, "the impersonal voice of the Constitution," Holmes in *Buck v. Bell* self-consciously expressed his "personal predilections and private notions of social policy." After delivering his opinion, Holmes told a friend, "One decision that I wrote gave me pleasure, establishing the constitutionality of a law permitting the sterilization of imbeciles." He reported to another frequent correspondent, the leftwing British essayist Harold Laski, "I . . . delivered an opinion upholding the constitutionality of a state law for sterilizing imbeciles the other day—and felt that I was getting near the first principle of real reform." There can be no doubt that Holmes knew exactly what he was doing in employing such bald rhetoric on behalf of his prejudices. He was "amused," he informed Laski, "at some of the rhetorical changes suggested" by his brethren, "when I purposely used short and rather brutal words . . . that made them mad."[34]

In truth, *Buck v. Bell* shows the revered "Yankee from Olympus" at his worst: his disdain for facts (he made a point of never reading newspapers), his contempt for views divergent from his own, his indifference to citing legal precedent, his reliance on quips, and his allegiance to elite attitudes. The opinion reveals an insensitivity to the position of women in a sexist society and to the class prejudice inherent in the legislation. It is hard to imagine that the outcome would have been the same if the subject had been a woman of substance, rather than, in the words of one writer, "a poverty-stricken girl, a nobody's child." Even as ardent an admirer of the Justice's as the philosopher Morris Raphael Cohen came to conclude, "For a thoroughly civilized man, which Holmes was in the best sense of the word, he shows a remarkable absence of sympathy or compassion for the sufferings and faults of mankind." (Perhaps, another writer has suggested, it was "the sight of so many boyhood friends face down in the mud" on Civil War battlefields that "molded Holmes into a form of stoic-callousness.")[35]

A whole regiment of commentators has had no difficulty in demonstrating that *Buck v. Bell* is "a remarkably poorly reasoned opinion." Almost no statement that Holmes made in those few paragraphs will stand up to scrutiny. There was not a shred of evidence linking Carrie Buck to criminal behavior, and, even if there had been, why, it has been asked, did Holmes suppose that "sterilization [makes] the criminally insane fit for society." In drawing his analogy to compulsory vaccination, Holmes ignored what the Massachusetts court had said: "If a person should deem it important that vaccination should not be performed in his case, and the authorities should think otherwise, it is not in their power to vaccinate him by force." The Court added, "The worst that could happen to him under the statute would be the payment of the penalty of $5." Moreover, there is a world of difference between being pricked with a needle and having one's Fallopian tubes excised so that forever after one could not procreate. It has been pointed out, too, that "the suggested analogy with military service in wartime fails. The State, in protecting the public welfare, does not *kill* or *mutilate* its citizens who fight for it in time of war." After painstakingly analyzing the opinion, one representative study concluded: "Respect for Mr. Justice Holmes must not prevent the courts from admitting the fallacious absurdity of his reasoning in *Buck v. Bell.*"[36]

The opinion, with its notorious sentence about three generations of imbeciles, did not, however, merely reflect some Holmesian idiosyncrasy, for the way had been pointed by an imposing figure, the Chief Justice of the United States. After assigning the opinion to Holmes, William Howard Taft wrote him:

> Some of the brethren are troubled about the case, especially Butler. May I suggest that you make a little full your discussion of the care Virginia has taken in guarding against undue or hasty action, the proven absence of danger to the patient, and other circumstances tending to lessen the shock that many feel over the remedy? The strength of the facts in three generations of course is the strongest argument.[37]

Characteristically, Holmes ignored the counsel to be "a little full," but he took Taft's cue in phrasing his problematic epigram.

Holmes's defenders have protested that he has been judged unfairly—by critics who have imposed upon his opinion the standards of a much later day. He cannot be held accountable for the eugenists' ties to the Nazis, for Hitler was not to come to power for some years after *Buck v. Bell.* Nor could he have been aware of many of the specifics of Carrie Buck's life. We cannot expect an appellate court to create a trial record that was not there. Much that was known then was concealed from Holmes, and even more that became known later was not available in 1927. Most important, it has been contended, Holmes should not have been asked to fly in the face of the accepted scientific opinion of his day. Indeed, it has been suggested, *Buck v. Bell* raises the most troublesome questions about how the Justices can establish procedures or mind sets to avoid being taken in by pseudoscientific fads.

Yet, in fact, eugenics had run into a crossfire of criticism well before 1927. Sixteen years earlier, a prominent New York attorney had denounced it in an address to the New York Academy of Medicine, and in 1917 a British scholar who held the Balfour chair in genetics at Cambridge had riddled its statistical assumptions. He estimated that, even if the premises of the eugenists were accepted, it would take seven hundred generations to reduce the incidence of mental deficiency from one in one hundred to one in ten thousand; hence, sterilization was an absurd policy. A year later, in 1918, the once-fanatical Dr. Fernald recanted: "I never lose an opportunity to repeat what I am saying now, that we have really slandered the feebleminded." Fully five years before *Buck v. Bell*, Walter Lippmann, arguably the country's most influential commentator on public affairs, had attracted attention to the weaknesses of the assumptions of the eugenists about intelligence measurement in a well-publicized series of articles in the *New Republic*, and by 1927 only the most sheltered Justice could have failed to know that eugenics had increasingly come into disrepute.[38]

A historian of science, Allan Chase, has declared that a presidential address by Dr. Fernald in 1924, three years before *Buck v. Bell*, repudiating Laughlin's conjectures reflected the conclusions of "the majority of American life and behavioral scientists," and he added:

> The failure of Holmes, and the seven Justices of the Court who voted with him, to be aware as late as 1927 of the fine work and repeated findings of Jacobi, Fernald, Stiles, Morgan, Goldberger, Wallin, and Myerson—to mention but a few of the Americans who scientifically destroyed the myths that mental retardation and shiftlessness and "laziness" were in the genes and not in the growth and development environment; that IQ tests measured innate intelligence; and that most psychoses and other aberrant behavior were the products of bad genes in people of bad stock—represented a major triumph of the previous quarter century of high-powered eugenical propaganda. Instead of heeding the discoveries and the published writings of the men and women whose findings in genetics, psychology, parasitology, clinical nutrition, and psychiatry were earning for American science the admiration of the world's scientists, Holmes and seven of the eight other Justices, including his fellow liberal, Louis Dembitz Brandeis, accepted the validity of the old scientific racism and its dogmas of eugenics and dysgenics.[39]

The ink was hardly dry on *Buck v. Bell* when, in what John M. Conley of the University of North Carolina Law School has called "the most remarkable statement I have ever read in a scientific publication," a highly prominent eugenist, C. C. Brigham, confessed, "One of the most pretentious of these comparative racial studies—the writer's own—was without foundation." As Professor Conley has written, "In subsequent years, much of the most important eugenics research was exposed as sloppy, biased, and, in one famous case, absolutely fraudulent."[40] It has been shown that feeble-mindedness cannot be traced to a single gene in each parent, as in Mendelian theory; that contrary to Holmes's assumption, defective persons do not breed more often than normal persons; and that, even if the suppositions of the eugenists had been correct, a rigorous sterilization program would have yielded the results they sought not, as they claimed, in a brief time but only over millennia.

Chase has summed up the acerbic judgment of scientists on *Buck v. Bell* in one biting sentence:

> This decision, by the son of the great American physician who destroyed one of the hoary tenets of conventional wisdom by publishing the real causes of puerperal fever some five years before Semmelweis, did one thing for genetics; it once again disproved the Galtonian myth that scientific talent and wisdom are unit traits transmitted in the parental genes.[41]

Holmes might still have deduced that scientific opinion was too unsettled in 1927 for the Justices to feel confident about striking down the Virginia law or, in keeping with the precept of judicial restraint, that judges have no business resorting to substantive due process to curb legislatures. If he had been content to limit himself to such reasoning, his opinion would not have become the object of so much disparagement, even though the outcome would have been unchanged.

As recently as 1989, a law professor at Washington University in St. Louis chose *Buck v. Bell* as his text for warning against the evil of substantive due process. He did so deliberately in order to subject his thesis "to maximum stress," for, he acknowledged, "the statute upheld in *Buck v. Bell* was an abomination." Nonetheless, he concluded, "the Court was . . . right to refuse to overturn it. . . . The remedy for a lousy statute is to persuade the legislature to repeal it. While that may not sound like much of a remedy, it is immensely preferable to the alternative of empowering judges to strike down the substance of legislation under the supposed aegis of the Due Process Clause."[42]

In an essay in the *Iowa Law Review*, Mary L. Dudziak has imagined what Holmes might have said had he been willing to abide by his maxim "that if my fellow citizens want to go to Hell I will help them." She writes:

> Given Holmes' central judicial principle of deference to the legislature and his desire to leave room for social experimentation, this case presented the opportunity for a classic Holmes opinion. He might weigh the arguments on one side against the arguments on the other and announce that in this area governed by new and developing scientific principles, the

courts could not clearly say that one answer was right. In such an area of social policy, it was appropriate only to defer to the legislature, to protect social progress through legislative experiments from the dampening hands of the courts.

"But," she adds sadly, "*Buck v. Bell* turned out to be quite a different opinion."[43]

Yet objectionable though the *opinion* is, the *decision* may well have been inevitable. In 1927 the Supreme Court had yet to strike down any state law on the grounds that the liberties protected by the Bill of Rights against federal encroachment also are safeguarded from violation by state governments through incorporation in the Fourteenth Amendment. Though that principle had been recognized two years earlier by the Court, its first application did not come until four years later. Furthermore, the United States Constitution does not specify a right to bodily integrity or even a right to privacy. Subsequently, the Court would tease out of the Constitution a recognition of such rights, but that development lay a full generation ahead. To be sure, the Court was not wholly without precedents had it been disposed to adopt a different course. One state court had struck down compulsory sterilization as "inhumane," and the U. S. Supreme Court itself, in *Meyer v. Nebraska*, had spoken of the right "to marry, establish a home and bring up children."[44] But 1927 was too soon to expect the Court to reverse Virginia's highest court in a case such as *Buck v. Bell*. In sum, if others were to avoid the fate of Carrie Buck, they needed to look not to the U. S. Supreme Court but to the people of the Commonwealth of Virginia, and their salvation was a long time coming.

VIII

In the 1970s the Lynchburg facility got a new director, K. Ray Nelson, a conscientious advocate of the rights of the mentally retarded who was haunted by the memory of *Buck v. Bell*. For six years he sought to locate Carrie Buck, but without success. Then in the summer of 1979 a chance occurrence got him closer. Carrie's sister Doris, who was living in an abandoned motel in Front Royal with her husband, reckoned she might be old enough to qualify for Social Security payments. Having no birth certificate to prove her age, she suggested checking with what she called her "school" in Lynchburg; her request crossed Dr. Nelson's desk. For years, she and her husband had been trying to have children, and when they failed, she had blamed herself. It was only in 1979, at the age of sixty-seven, that she learned for the first time that what she had always thought had been an appendectomy performed on her at sixteen had actually been surgery to excise her Fallopian tubes.

Through her, Dr. Nelson located Carrie, who was, these many years later, still alive. In the decades since her discharge from the hospital, life had not been kind to her. She had returned to the operating table to have a breast removed. She had been compelled, with only five years of schooling, to take jobs so demanding that she weighed barely a hundred pounds. She had washed dishes in a restaurant; had more than once nursed invalids, including a boy who had been born "all twisted"; and had drifted about as a migrant field worker. When the good-hearted Dr. Nelson found her, she was dwelling in a hovel on a dirt road near Charlottesville with her second husband, a crippled alcoholic lost in fantasy—just the sort of ending that Justice Holmes and the eugenists would have predicted for someone with her genes.

Carrie Buck, though, was no "imbecile." As a girl, she had advanced each year with her grade, and before being taken out of school to do chores in her foster home, she had been rated on her final report card as "very good—deportment and lessons." In her later years, she had become actively involved in reading groups and in solving crossword puzzles, and she liked music and dramatics. A social worker spoke of her as an "alert and pleasant lady." It had not been her genes but society and the State that had determined her destiny. After newspaper stories about the discovery of the Buck sisters motivated a number of scholars to restudy the case, the essayist Stephen Jay Gould concluded:

> There were no imbeciles, not a one, among the three generations of Bucks. I don't know that such correction of cruel but forgotten errors of history counts for much, but it is at least satisfying to learn that forced eugenic sterilization, a procedure of such dubious morality, earned its official justification (and its most quoted line of rhetoric) on a patent falsehood. [45]

The revelations about the Bucks reverberated through Virginia and caused authorities elsewhere to reconsider policies toward the retarded, though not without continuing evidence of the persistence of eugenic thinking. The Supreme Court has never found occasion to reverse *Buck v. Bell*,[46] and as late as 1980, compulsory sterilization laws were still on the books in more than twenty states, including Virginia. In 1983, a North Carolina jury took only forty-five minutes to decide that state officials had not violated the rights of a fourteen-year-old black girl when they sterilized her because she was allegedly "promiscuous" and "feeble minded," though at the time of the trial, fifteen years later, she held an associate degree from New York City Technical College and a job in a department store.[47] For a time, Virginia officials, too, continued to defend what had been done, and even tried to silence the people on whom operations had been performed. But in the end, the Commonwealth relented. The operations, which Dr. Nelson had suspended, were, under a 1981 statute, sharply circumscribed.[48]

Vindication, though, came too late for the Buck family. After being institutionalized, Emma Buck spent all the remaining years of her life in the Lynchburg Colony, and there, after nearly a quarter of a century of internment, she died. Carrie Buck, who did not long survive Dr. Nelson's revelations, lies in a Charlottesville grave, separated by a hill from her daughter Vivian some fifty yards away in the same cemetery. And when Doris Buck Figgins learned what had happened to her more than forty years before, she told a reporter: "I broke down and cried. My husband and me wanted children desperate—we were crazy about them. I never knew what they'd done to me."[49]

Mr. Justice Roberts and the Railroaders

[The eight years separating *Buck v. Bell* from the *Rail Pension* case saw considerable alteration in the personnel of the Supreme Court and drastic change in the circumstances under which the Court operated. In 1935 the Chief Justice of the United States was no longer William Howard Taft but Charles Evans Hughes, and Sanford and Holmes had been replaced by Benjamin Cardozo and Owen Roberts. The Wall Street crash of 1929 and the ensuing Great Depression had led to emergency legislation in the states and far-reaching experimentation by Franklin D. Roosevelt and the New Deal that raised stark challenges to the constitutional orthodoxy expounded in the 1920s. In two 1934 cases dealing with state laws, the Supreme Court appeared willing to give wide latitude to legislatures. In *Blaisdell v. Minnesota*, it validated a mortgage moratorium statute, and in *Nebbia v. New York*, price controls on milk. Both of these decisions, though, came by 5–4 votes, with the Four Horsemen in dissent and Brandeis, Cardozo, Hughes, Roberts, and Stone forming a precarious majority. The loss of any one of these five would imperil the New Deal. The Roosevelt administration worried most about Justice Roberts, though in *Nebbia* he had startled the country by saying, "There can be no doubt that upon proper occasion and by appropriate measures the state may regulate a business in any of its aspects, including the prices to be charged." The Court gave the President a jolt in January 1935 by striking down the "hot oil" provisions of the National Industrial Recovery Act in an 8–1 decision, but the following month the *Nebbia* coalition came together once more when, by 5–4, the Court legitimated the government's gold policy, though it made clear that it disapproved of what had been done. It was under these circumstances, with the attitude of the Court toward the New Deal still in question, that, just eleven weeks later, the *Rail Pension* decision was handed down.

This essay has never appeared in print before, but it will be a chapter in a two-volume history of the constitutional crisis of the 1930s to be published by Oxford University Press.]

I

On May 6, 1935, one of the most fateful days in the constitutional crisis of the Great Depression, the Supreme Court handed down yet another 5–4 decision, and this one sent shock waves through the White House and the New Deal agencies. It came on a piece of legislation—the Railroad Retirement Act of 1934—so minor that it is never mentioned in most histories of the period, a measure that the Administration did not regard as one of its own. Indeed, Roosevelt could barely bring himself to sign it into law. Yet the ruling by the Court gravely affected the future prospects of his program, created deep fissures between the executive branch and the Supreme Court and within the Court itself, and left two million railroad workers, past and present, embittered and bereft.

II

In the spring of 1883, a Philadelphia baseball team entirely composed of one-armed men took on a rival club of one-legged players; save for one man whose arm had been severed at Gettysburg, all of the athletes were Reading Railroad employees who had lost a limb in a work-related accident. The life of a railroader was fraught with danger. Casey Jones was not the only engineer who went to kingdom come in a locomotive cab. "You 'roast on one side and freeze on the other' while riding a pitching, rolling monster of heat and steel which must be controlled to the split second and the fraction of a foot," noted one writer; while another declared that the railroad man "never knew when it might be his turn to lose a big toe, an arm, or his life." In 1933 the stunning total of five hundred rail employees were killed while on duty; in 1934 the figure reached 526, with nearly seventeen thousand injured.[1]

Yet many other workingmen, and even some of the middle class, looked at the railroaders with envy. Many held highly skilled jobs, and they were performing a function that both made them seem romantic figures, as they took the Twentieth Century or the Panama Limited on their nightly runs, and indispensable agents of an industrial civilization. In his classic study, W. Fred Cottrell wrote:

> Stories of conquest over sand, fire, sleet and snow, and flood and ava-
> lanche . . . became part of the railroaders' heritage. . . . Stories of . . .
> legendary engineers who set new speed records, brakemen riding runaway
> trains to their deaths, express messengers fighting train robbers, even train
> robbers themselves such as Jesse James—were woven into a mythology

that glorified any man who was part of the great drama. No matter how humble his own role, a railroader long felt himself in some degree superior for being a soldier in so glorious an army. A literature of railroad romance grew up. Railroad men's magazines and novels by the score glorified the knight of the shining rail.[2]

Cottrell also remarked upon why the railroaders were regarded as "the aristocracy of labor":

> The railroad engineer and conductor strutted with all the pomp and dignity of Mark Twain's steamboat pilots. They smoked ten-cent "seegars," drank imported whiskey, captivated the girls with their fine uniforms and their free spending, and outshone the village banker's son. . . . If they go to church, it is more likely to be to the Presbyterian or the Episcopal than to the Methodist or the Baptist. When they drive, it is more likely to be in a Buick or a Chrysler than in a Chevrolet, a Ford, or a Plymouth. They buy strawberries out of season, and porterhouse rather than round steak. They get their hats in the city "shoppes" . . . rather than at Penney's or Sears.[3]

They had the satisfaction of knowing, too, that they could count on powerful unions—the railway "brotherhoods"—to safeguard and advance their interests. Though few factory workers in 1933 had any union at all, or were only taking the first painful steps toward organization, the august brotherhoods could trace their origins to as early as 1863. The "Big Four"—the brotherhoods of Locomotive Engineers, Firemen and Enginemen, and Trainmen, and the Order of Railway Conductors— constituted the elite of the railway workers, to such an extent that they were thought to speak for the entire rail labor force, though they constituted only about one-fourth of union card carriers. Members of the Big Four, one writer noted, were "in a sense 'men of property' who collectively own millions in securities." In 1922 the Brotherhood of Locomotive Engineers built a skyscraper in Cleveland, and they even acquired a coal mine which led them to clash with John L. Lewis when he sought to unionize the colliery.[4] In the 1920s, railroad men accumulated substantial bank accounts, and most owned or were buying their homes. As late as 1932, a commentator could write, "Even in these days of declining glory no other worker, not even the overpaid bricklayer or the forgetful plumber, can show as attractive a job, or, on the average, as good a stipend. And he is immeasurably above the ordinary run of white-collar office workers."[5]

The onset of the Great Depression, though, dealt savagely with the railroad industry. Even before 1929, competition from trucks, intercity buses, pipelines, even the first sign of commercial air travel, was already threatening the supremacy of the railways, and each year at the start of the Depression—1930, 1931, 1932—operating revenues of railroads fell another billion dollars, so that by 1932 income had dropped to under half that of 1929. Over forty thousand miles of track went into receivership or bankruptcy, the greatest total ever. In 1935 the huge Van Sweringen empire, embracing the Nickel Plate, the Chesapeake & Ohio, the Wheeling and Lake Erie, the Missouri Pacific, the Erie, the Kansas City Southern, and the Pere Marquette, collapsed. From 1932 through 1943, at least twelve hundred miles of track were abandoned each year; in 1935, more than two thousand miles. Over the course of the decade, depots went unpainted, locomotives rusted, cabooses went to the graveyard, and prairie weeds overran ties.[6]

Though the Illinois Central, the main artery of America's heartland, never went bankrupt, its experience typifies that of other carriers that survived, but barely. From 1929 to 1933, freight traffic on the I. C. declined by more than half. By 1931 the road was already running in the red; that year it failed to pay dividends on common stock for the first time since 1859. Eventually, I. C. stock, at $136.75 in 1930, slumped to $4.75 a share. On May 28, 1932, the Illinois Central shocked the railroad world by announcing that it was suspending service on the pride of its fleet, the Panama Limited, the elegant liner that accompanied the Mississippi from Chicago to New Orleans. "We could hear the footsteps of the sheriff immediately behind us," said one company official. From 1929 to 1933, the Illinois Central discharged 32,000 employees, many of them heads of families with long records of faithful service. The president of the Illinois Central declared:

> Recently I have been compelled to do what no previous president of our railroad has ever had to do on a large scale— . . . throw thousands of our employees out of work. Having been born and reared in the home of a railroad worker of moderate income, where it was an almost constant struggle to make ends meet, I know what it means when the family income is cut.[7]

From 1929 to 1933, railroads fired more than two out of every five railway workers, and total compensation in 1933 was less than half of what it had been four years earlier. Railroad employment, which had peaked at above two million in 1920, fell to under a million. By the late summer of 1932 more than 760,000 railroad workers had lost their jobs, a decline since 1929 of 54 percent, and thousands of those still employed drew only part-time pay. The very fact that these "aristocrats of labor" had done so well in the past—that they were so much looked up to in their communities—made their decline all the more unsettling.[8]

In recording the impact of the Depression on a number of Americans, the British historian Anthony J. Badger has written:

> Robert Ozment's father was a railroad engineer in Texas. In 1929 the family had a new Overland Whippet car, were buying a home, had money in the bank and plenty of food and clothing. By 1933 all this had gone except the Whippet. They lived in a rent-free house on the edge of the black section of town. They had little to eat except oatmeal. They had no electricity and few clothes. Ozment remembers the house well "because it had no coverings on the splintery old floors. My one pair of shoes had to be saved for winter use, and during the summer my feet were constantly bandaged from the thrust of splinters." As for the car, it sat in a shed because they had no money for either petrol or tyres.[9]

A 1934 government study of one thousand families of railroad employees revealed how hard the depression had hit even those who were not laid off. "Mr. W———," who earned $130 a month as a stationary fireman in 1929, brought home only half as much as a round-house laborer in 1933, and his experience was duplicated by many others. By 1932, two-thirds of railway employees earned less than $1500 a year; one-tenth, less than $500. As income shrank, families could no longer put meat or fruit or vegetables on the table; one family with six children had not had milk for years. Since the breadwinner in the family at least had a job, and the railroad worker made out better than many in other industries, those conducting the study were dismayed to find how constricted family life had become. Many had not seen a movie in four years and had even stopped visiting friends or having them to their home. "If you can't offer your neighbor a bit of refreshment, you don't like to ask him in," one explained.

"The stories they tell are of educational opportunities abandoned and health needs neglected, and of lives stripped bare of even the most inexpensive forms of recreation and social life," the report went on. "Frequently they describe the crowding of families into inferior accommodations, and few fail to record the use of shabby clothing or to note the items of a rough and meager diet." Despite their deprivations, many of these families gave money or groceries to those in greater need, and over one-fifth took relatives or friends who were jobless into their homes. Two-fifths of the families, though, were behind in their mortgage payments, and a good number had already lost their homes. Half of the families had to sacrifice their insurance policies and an even larger proportion was heavily in debt. "For these veteran railway men, then," the report concluded, "the study records a slow retreat from relative security toward destitution."[10]

The railroaders also had a painful sense that the pre-eminence both of their industry and of their social position was eroding. To be sure, railroads were still America's premier industry. Only agriculture had a greater total investment, and the welfare of the roads was vital to banks and a whole array of other investors in rail securities. Most people who traveled any distance went by train, and the railways hauled two-thirds of the nation's freight and provided the market for one-fifth of its coal, steel, fuel oil, and lumber. But as Cottrell pointed out, in contrast to the airline pilot in his dashing uniform, the brass-buttoned conductor was coming to seem a throwback to Prince Albert's day. He added:

> Contraction in employment leaves only old men in the passenger service. Grizzled veterans, often not too heroic as they wrestle with arthritis, are symbols of an old man's game. This hefty veteran of the cab stirs no feminine heart, excites no envy from youngsters, who often pass his train in the cheapest automobile on the road. Even railroad temples have grown shabby, as the station, once the center of civic pride, the acme of local architectural achievement, becomes in contrast to the airport and the streamlined service station, a rococo symbol of an age that is past.
>
> Among railroaders this change is felt keenly.[11]

The aging of the work force, which derived both from the impact of the Great Depression and from the operation of a rigid seniority rule, led the brotherhoods to call upon the federal government to establish a national pension plan. Under the seniority system, the massive layoffs after 1929 drove hundreds of thousands of the youngest men into the ranks of the unemployed, leaving, in the words of one study, a residue with a "very excessive proportion of aged." The carriers had established private pension plans to which employees were not required to contribute, but they were highly unsatisfactory. The amounts of the pensions were small; only a limited number of railroaders at a very advanced age were eligible; and the carriers could abolish the programs at their whim. Some employees had, after many years of work, been denied pensions because they had participated in a strike or were said to have violated some company regulation. The brotherhoods believed that an all-embracing act of Congress would not only provide security for the elderly but also would induce older workers to retire, thereby opening opportunities for the younger men who had been discharged.[12]

Determined to find a long-term solution, the brotherhoods in March 1932 drafted a pension bill for railroad employees that Robert Wagner of New York introduced in the Senate and Robert Crosser of Ohio sponsored in the House. The bill got nowhere in 1932, Hoover's last full year, or in the hectic competition with emergency legislation in the First Hundred Days of 1933, but in 1934 its prospects improved. Opponents objected that the hard-pressed railroads could not afford large sums for a pension fund. They pointed out that railroads had failed to earn enough to offset their fixed charges in 1933, and that the President himself had characterized their situation as "still impaired." It seemed odd, too, at a time when there was not yet a Social Security Act, that railroad workers should be singled out for the first national pension law. But since workers would also have to contribute, Senator Wagner turned that argument around. Railroads, he said, had "a relatively high-paid class of workmen who can afford without self-denial to undergo the charges of compulsory saving." Since Wagner recognized that a challenge would undoubtedly be raised to the constitutionality of the bill, he also maintained that the proposal could be justified as a measure to improve efficiency and safety on the vital arteries of interstate commerce. The railroads, he contended, offered "one of the most dramatic examples" of the perils of "having older and less alert people in charge of operations." Under the force of such arguments, and even more out of respect for the political clout of the brotherhoods, Congress whipped the legislation through in June in the waning hours of the session. The House considered it for only forty minutes before registering its approval. [13]

The Railroad Retirement Act of 1934 required carriers to contribute 4 percent of their payrolls to a common pension pool for more than two million railway workers, past and present, and assessed employees 2 percent of their wages. It made no provision for contributions by the government. Workers would be eligible for pensions on reaching the age of sixty-five, or upon completing thirty years of service on the roads, or if they became disabled. The statute was to be administered by a three-man commission, with the President choosing one from the ranks of labor, one from management, and one to represent the public. It was the first compulsory retirement plan ever imposed by the federal government on private industry. The carriers protested that in the first year the law would double the $35 million the railroads were currently laying out under private pension programs and that by 1953 that sum would nearly quadruple. "Born of the depression," one scholar later wrote, the act "paid lip service to the idea that the plan would promote operational efficiency and safety, but the primary purpose was to ease older men out of their jobs in order that unemployed younger men might have them." [14]

The brotherhoods, though, rejoiced in their success. "The pension act is the finest piece of railroad legislation since the eight-hour day was achieved in 1916," said the leader of the rail unions, A. F. Whitney. "The pension law . . . will permit the retirement of 100,000 men this year alone. Not only will this take care of the men who have broken down in railroad services but it will help the unemployment problem by elevating the young man who is looking for the opportunity to work."[15]

When the measure reached his desk, the President hesitated. As he said tersely in his formal message on the legislation, reaching a decision on whether to sign or veto the bill had been "difficult." He pointed out that the Federal Coordinator of Transportation, "at much public expense," was engaged in a "thorough survey" of the question and had asked that action be deferred until the report could be completed. Furthermore, "the bill, although much improved in its final form, is still crudely drawn and will require many changes and amendments at the next session of Congress." In addition, though the cost to the railroads would not be very large in the first four years, it would rise progressively thereafter, and the legislation made "no sound provision for this increase." Despite all these considerations, he had decided to sign the bill, though a neutral observer might well have thought that he had made a better case for vetoing it.[16]

Roosevelt could not have been too surprised when, after 134 railroads, two express companies, and the Pullman Company filed suit, the Supreme Court of the District of Columbia in October 1934 invalidated the Act and issued an injunction restraining the Railroad Retirement Board from collecting assessments.[17] Chief Justice Alfred A. Wheat explained that the law was unconstitutional because it embraced employees (an estimated two hundred thousand) who were not actually engaged in interstate commerce. He also found that compelling the carriers to pay "huge sums" to men who were no longer employed (though they had been within the past year) and permitting former workers who might subsequently be rehired to qualify for pensions as a result of past years of service violated the due process clause of the Fifth Amendment. "The natural reluctance which a judge feels when compelled to hold an act of Congress unconstitutional is in this case somewhat tempered by the fact that the act seems not to be satisfactory even to some who favor it," he added, quoting from the President's remarks to demonstrate his point. Roosevelt and the New Dealers could take comfort in the fact that Chief Justice Wheat remarked that he was "not prepared to say" that the statute did not fall beyond the commerce power. So long as a compulsory pension program was not unacceptable in principle, any flaws in the legislation could readily be fixed.

Still, Roosevelt, on signing the measure, had also described the law as "in line with sound social policy," and when the Supreme Court decided to hear the case directly, without waiting for an intervening ruling by a circuit court, the Assistant Attorney General of the United States, Harold M. Stephens, spoke in defense of the statute. Even though it had not been a New Deal initiative, the rail pension law could be regarded as, in the words of one publication, "the Administration's only tangible accomplishment to date in the matter of economic-security legislation."[18] Far more important, the law bore so close a resemblance to the pending Social Security bill that the White House had a big stake in the outcome of the rail pension litigation and high hopes that the five-man majority of Hughes, Brandeis, Cardozo, Stone, and Roberts that had sustained earlier measures would once more coalesce to overturn the lower court's decision.

In preparing his brief, Stephens decided to focus his efforts on demonstrating that the law lay within the commerce power. Counsel for the Railroad Retirement Board wanted him to go farther in stressing its "social desirability," but Stephens thought such emphasis would not be necessary for the liberals on the bench and might antagonize the other Justices. "It has been my experience in practice that it is better to show a court a way to decide a case within accepted principles than to ask it to take a new avenue to the desired result," he explained to Felix Frankfurter. "Therefore, I felt it best to concentrate our argument upon the proposition that the Retirement Act is intended and calculated to promote efficiency and economy in railway operations and to improve morale and labor relations and thus to improve and promote interstate commerce." On the eve of the Supreme Court's decision, Professor Frankfurter responded, "I should be really surprised if the Court did not sustain the Railroad Retirement Act."[19]

III

When the Supreme Court convened at noon on May 6, the Chief Justice announced that Owen Roberts would deliver the opinion,[20] and the youngest Justice made the most of his opportunity. A masterful performer, Roberts gave the audience a display of his prodigious powers of recall by reciting large segments from memory. Fully conscious of the drama inherent in the occasion, he fixed his eyes upon the spectators in the semicircular benches about the ancient courtroom as he spoke, at times crossing his arms on his black robes, then putting his elbows on the desk as he leaned forward to add emphasis to his words. When he came to passages of his written opinion he thought his listeners might find tedious, he skipped past them.

The news that Roberts would give the opinion encouraged government counsel to think the *Nebbia* alliance might still be intact, but Roberts quickly dashed these expectations. After treating his brethren to a wooden disquisition on constitutional exegesis that was altogether unnecessary, Roberts turned abruptly to a dissection of the law. So many were the objections he discerned, so far did he reach to find conceivable (and inconceivable) shortcomings in the statute, and so unrestrained was his rhetoric that it was often hard to distinguish his opinion from the brief for the railroads. Roberts added to the impression that he was a combatant, engaged in strife both with the federal government and with several of his fellow Justices, by the vehemence of his oratory.

Roberts began his examination of the law by noting that it provided for annuities for some 146,000 persons who had worked for the railroads within one year prior to enactment of the statute, irrespective of whether they ever would be employed by the carriers again. In a period of mass unemployment, the rationale for this provision was not capricious; the draftsmen of the bill wanted to safeguard those who had been temporarily laid off from having their long years of past service expunged, and to make certain that carriers did not refuse to rehire them in order to escape the burden of pension obligations. Roberts brushed such considerations aside. "It is arbitrary in the last degree to place upon the carriers the burden of gratuities to thousands who have been unfaithful and for that cause have been separated from the service, or have elected to pursue some other calling, or have retired from the business, or have been for some other reasons lawfully dismissed," he declared. "And the claim that such largess will promote efficiency or safety in the future operation of the railroads is without support in reason or common sense."

The Justice moved next to the provision that dealt with the more than one million former employees whose service had ended more than a year before. The law stipulated that if such a worker were rehired, his previous service would count in computing his pension. Once again, Roberts opened the door on a chamber of horrors:

> Such a person may have been out of railroad work for years; his employment may have been terminated for cause; he may have elected to enter some other industry, and may have devoted the best years of his life to it; yet if, perchance, some carrier in a distant part of the country should accept him for work of any description, even temporarily, the Act throws the burden of his pension on all the railroads, including, it may be, the very one which for just cause dismissed him.

This section of the statute constituted "a naked appropriation of private property," Roberts asserted. "The Act denies due process of law by taking the property of one and bestowing it upon another." For the first time, the Court had articulated a specific constitutional objection to the law—that it violated the due process clause of the Fifth Amendment.

Throughout his opinion, Roberts viewed the statute from the perspective of someone seated in a railway board room, never from that of the men on the roads. He acknowledged that counsel had pointed out that the railways could escape the burden of the provision altogether by refusing to hire a former worker. But it was wretchedly unfair, Roberts reasoned, to compel a company to run the danger of unwittingly taking on additional costs merely because it wanted to add to its payroll an experienced "servant." "Must a carrier at its peril exercise, through dozens of employment agencies scattered over a vast territory, an unheard of degree of care to exclude all former railroad workers, at the risk of incurring a penalty of paying a pension for work long since performed for some other employer?" he asked. "So to hold would be highly unreasonable and arbitrary."

Feature after feature of the law, in Roberts's view, gave workers benefits they did not deserve and treated the companies unfairly. Someone might start work for a carrier at twenty, desert the railroad at thirty for "a more lucrative profession," and still qualify for an annuity at sixty-five, albeit one calculated only on a decade of service. Nor was that the only miscarriage of justice that occurred to Roberts. After ten years, a worker might "be discharged for peculation, and still be entitled to a gratuity," he noted. "Or he may be relieved of duty for gross negligence, entailing loss of life or property, and yet collect his pension at 65."

Roberts scoffed at the claim of government counsel that such a program was reasonable because it improved the morale of employees who would know that they would not lose their pension rights if they were discharged. "If 'morale' is intended to connote efficiency, loyalty and continuity of service, the surest way to destroy it in any privately owned business is to substitute legislative largess for private bounty and thus transfer the drive for pensions to the halls of Congress and transmute loyalty to employer into gratitude to the legislature," he stated.

Other aspects of the statute struck Roberts (and presumably the Four Horsemen for whom he also spoke) as no less arbitrary. It was indefensible to make thousands of workers immediately eligible for pensions even though they had made no contribution to the fund, and it was shocking to think that a man who had served for thirty years could elect to retire on an annuity while still in his prime. "Thus many who are experienced and reliable may at their own election deprive a carrier of their services, enter another gainful occupation, cease to contribute to the fund, and go upon the pension roll years before the fixed retirement age of 65," he complained. Furthermore, insofar as the Act based pension rights on past service, it required railroads to dole out money to men who had already been fully compensated. Worse still, pooling discriminated against those carriers (fifty-six in all) who had no employees aged seventy by compelling all railroads to contribute to a common fund. Nor, Roberts contended, was it equable to guarantee the security of workers in their final years by requiring solvent railroads to pay into a fund that would be drawn upon by employees from bankrupt lines.

Justice Roberts made little effort to conceal his contempt both for the legislators who had created this monstrosity and for the attorneys who sought to persuade the Court that it was a legitimate exercise of the powers of Congress. In none of the cases counsel cited did he find any relevance, not even those decisions that sanctioned treating all railroads as components of a single system, or that validated the pooling principle. Roberts could barely contain his exasperation at having to deal with such blather. He did concede that Congress had specified that if the Court found particular sections of the law unconstitutional, the rest of the legislation should still be valid, but he disposed of that point by saying, "Notwithstanding the presumption in favor of divisibility which arises from the legislative declaration, we cannot rewrite a statute and give it an effect altogether different from that sought by the measure viewed as a whole." All of this discussion, filling nearly nineteen printed pages, served to buttress a single conclusion: "The Act is invalid because several of its inseparable provisions contravene the due process clause of the Fifth Amendment."

At this juncture one might have supposed that he had come to the end. Not so. In the very next sentence, Roberts plunged ahead to pursue an altogether different, and far more important, course. He said of the railroad pension statute: "We are of opinion that it is also bad for another reason which goes to the heart of the law, even if it could survive the loss of the unconstitutional features which we have discussed. The Act is not in purpose or effect a regulation of interstate commerce within the meaning of the Constitution."

The claim that the railway annuity scheme was a regulation of commerce, Roberts said, rested on two absurd notions, the first of which was that it promoted efficiency by pensioning off aged employees. As a matter of fact, older workers were superior to younger ones, he declared, but, even if one accepted the government's hypothesis, one could still achieve the aim that was sought simply by firing elderly railroad men. "For these purposes the prescription of a pension for those dropped from the service is wholly irrelevant," he declared. Well aware of this, petitioners were reduced to intruding irrelevant "social and humanitarian considerations," Roberts said. "They assert that it would be unthinkable to retire a man without pension and add that attempted separation of retirement and pensions is unreal in any practical sense, since it would be impossible to require carriers to cast old workers aside without means of support," he noted. "The supposed impossibility arises from a failure to distinguish constitutional power from social desirability."

Roberts thought no better of the second rationale of the petitioners—that the Act was a regulation of commerce because removing anxiety about old-age dependency would improve the morale of those engaged in transportation. To this claim, Roberts replied: If one granted that the federal government could concern itself with "the fostering of a contented mind on the part of an employee," there was no limit to what Washington could impose on business. "Provision for free medical attendance and nursing, for clothing, for food, for housing, for the education of children, and a hundred other matters, might with equal propriety be proposed as tending to relieve the employee of mental strain and worry," he observed. "Can it fairly be said that the power of Congress to regulate interstate commerce extends to the prescription of any or all of these things?" he asked. "Is it not apparent that they are really and essentially related solely to the social welfare of the worker, and therefore remote from any regulation of commerce as such?"

Having completed his exercise in *reductio ad absurdum*, Roberts delivered the most important sentence of his lengthy opinion: "These matters obviously lie outside the orbit of Congressional power." In short, the Court was saying that, wholly apart from any violation of due process because of the deficiencies of this particular statute, Congress had no power to enact any railroad pension law whatsoever, for the subject fell beyond the scope of the commerce clause.

Not content with having disposed of the law on two grounds, Roberts pushed on for six more pages, some of them redundant. He denied that the Railroad Pension Act could be analogized to workmen's compensation laws that the Court had sustained in the past, for the latter derived from common law remedies while the 1934 statute sought "to attach to the relation of employer and employee a new incident, without reference to any existing obligation or legal liability, solely in the interest of the employee, with no regard to the conduct of the business, or its safety or efficiency, but purely for social ends." Nor would he accept as pertinent the statement of the National Industrial Conference Board, even though it spoke neither for government nor unions but for business, that pensions fostered loyalty on the part of workers and promoted efficiency. Once again, he reasoned that it was "axiomatic that the removal of the voluntary character of the pension and the imposition of it in such form as Congress may determine, upon all employers, and irrespective of length of service, or of service for the same employer, will eliminate all sense of loyalty or gratitude to the employer, and remove every incentive to continuance in the service of a single carrier." In sum, the pension plan Congress had enacted, Roberts concluded, was "in no proper sense a regulation of the activity of interstate transportation" but was rather "an attempt for social ends to impose by sheer fiat non-contractual incidents upon the relation of employer and employee."

What many found most striking about Roberts's opinion was precisely his conception of "the relation of employer and employee." His view was almost medieval in nature. He thought of workers as owing fealty and "gratitude" to management. Any benefits they received resulted from the generosity of businessmen who dispensed "largess" or "gratuities" or "bounty" to loyal hands. They were not social rights to which one was entitled in an industrial society. He could express empathy for those engaged in "the conduct of the business," but berated those who raised "humanitarian considerations" or contemplated "purely social ends." If a worker no longer held a job, he presumed that it was because the man had been "unfaithful" or had been dismissed for just cause, quite possibly because he was guilty of "peculation" or of negligence so gross that lives had been lost. He might well, though, in Roberts's perception, no longer be employed by a railroad because he had "elected to pursue some other calling," perhaps "a more lucrative profession." The actual hard lot of the railroad men—more than half of whom had been dismissed in only three years because of the exigencies of the Great Depression—could not penetrate such a frame of mind.

IV

The Chief Justice, who did not hesitate to assign himself the opinion in many of the most important cases, spoke for the four dissenters—Brandeis, Cardozo, Stone, and himself. He wasted no time in getting to the heart of the matter: "The gravest aspect of the decision is that it does not rest simply upon a condemnation of particular features of the Railroad Retirement Act, but denies to Congress the power to pass any compulsory pension act for railroad employees." Had Roberts been content with detailing the deficiencies of the statute, Congress could have adapted itself by re-enacting the measure in a form that took these objections into account, Hughes observed. But "by declaring that the subject matter itself lies beyond the reach of the congressional authority to regulate interstate commerce," the Court had raised a barrier against any railroad pension law, no matter how carefully drafted, no matter how actuarially sound. "That is a conclusion of such serious and far-reaching importance that it overshadows all other questions raised by the Act," he said. "Indeed, it makes their discussion superfluous."

In a powerfully argued dissent, called by one writer "the boldest, frankest, indeed, the greatest opinion of his career,"[21] Hughes assailed Roberts's "unwarranted" reading of the commerce clause as "a departure from sound principles." Chief Justice John Marshall, the fountainhead of all wisdom about that clause, had declared that the commerce power might be "exercised to its utmost extent," Hughes noted, and that power had always been taken to have the widest range with respect to railroads. Since they were vital to the nation, "nothing which has a real or substantial relation to the suitable maintenance of that service, or to the discharge of the responsibilities which inhere in it, can be regarded as beyond the power of regulation." The Court had long acknowledged, Hughes pointed out, that in exercising its sovereign power to regulate railroads, Congress would, as a matter of course, have authority over employee relations. To assure safety and uninterrupted service, Congress could not help but concern itself with "fair treatment" of railroad workers, for efficiency "inevitably suffers from a failure to meet the reasonable demands of justice."

The opinion of the Court not only ignored this history but flew in the face of experience, the Chief Justice contended. "The argument that a pension measure, however sound and reasonable as such, is *per se* outside the pale of the regulation of interstate carriers, because such a plan could not possibly have a reasonable relation to the ends which Congress is entitled to serve, is largely answered by the practice of the carriers themselves," he said, for many years ago railroad companies in Europe and America had adopted pension plans. Nor, he continued, had Roberts come to terms with the expert testimony showing the importance of retiring aged workers, the likelihood that any impairment of pension obligations would "play havoc with railroad labor relations," and the inadequacies of voluntary pension systems.

Roberts had misconceived the situation, Hughes said, because he had the erroneous notion that the relation between railroad companies and their employees was exclusively contractual, and that Congress lacked the authority to impose a non-contractual arrangement—a compulsory pension plan—on the carriers. According to this logic, the government's power in this area was confined to telling railroads to fire elderly workers, "throwing them out helpless." In fact, though, the Chief Justice asserted, there was a wealth of examples of government imposition of non-contractual responsibilities on railroads. In particular, he noted pointedly, there had been a unanimous report elaborating the constitutionality of compulsory workmen's compensation laws by a committee headed by none other than George Sutherland, in the period when the present Justice had been a United States Senator, and the Sutherland committee had approved such enactments in part because of their beneficial effect on the morale of employees. Roberts had failed utterly in his attempt to distinguish compensation laws from pension statutes, Hughes declared, for the fundamental consideration in both types of legislation was that "industry should take care of its human wastage, whether that is due to accident or age." As Charles Beard later noted: "Chief Justice Hughes must have felt himself on familiar ground as he prepared [this] vigorous dissent. . . . He had been Governor of New York when the hot battle over workmen's compensation had been started and had taken a deep interest in the progress of that legislation."[22]

Hughes did not develop this line of reasoning wholly on his own initiative, but had been pointed in that direction by Cardozo and Stone. After the Chief Justice had circulated a draft of his opinion, Cardozo had sent him a lucid memorandum in which Stone joined, and the final version of the dissent revealed that Hughes had taken this memo to heart. The government in its brief had "laid undue stress upon the danger of keeping superannuated men in the service and [on] the resulting loss of efficiency in the operation of the roads," Cardozo said. Both points were valid, but "by emphasizing them overmuch, the Government has given color to the argument of Justice Roberts that the ostensible or professed motive of the statute is not the true one." Besides, there was a better way to defend the law—by analogizing it to a workmen's compensation act, which "is not limited to cases where the employer has been negligent" but is an attempt to require management to assume the risks attendant on employment.

Cardozo concluded:

If that is the rationale of such an act, wherein does it differ from the act in controversy? What is the distinction between compensating men who have been incapacitated by accident (though without fault of the employer), and compensating men who have been injured by the wear and tear of time, the slow attrition of the years? What is the difference between replacing worn out machinery and replacing worn out men? Is not each a legitimate incident of the business? And in that view what is left of the argument of Roberts, J., that the Government should instruct the railroads to dismiss their superannuated workers without payment or pension, throwing them out helpless into the world?[23]

Having disposed of the majority's insistence that the rail pension legislation was an invalid regulation of interstate commerce, Hughes turned to a consideration of Roberts's original contention—that the law violated due process. In only one instance did the Chief Justice, and those for whom he spoke, agree with the majority. The requirement that pensions be paid to those who had been discharged was "arbitrary," Hughes acknowledged. But he quickly added that under the separability clause the Court could nullify that provision and leave the rest of the statute intact. He saw no violation of due process in the other sections to which Roberts had taken such strenuous objection. For example, the principle of pooling, though it unquestionably disadvantaged some railroads, had been validated by the Court a good number of years earlier. He concluded by taking a generous view of legislative prerogatives. "The power committed to Congress to govern interstate commerce does not require that its government should be wise, much less that it should be perfect," the Chief Justice stated. "The power implies a broad discretion and thus permits a wide range even of mistakes."[24]

V

From the beginning of the Roosevelt era, Administration leaders had worried about Mr. Justice Roberts. Their anxiety had eased when Roberts had helped compose the majority in *Nebbia*, *Blaisdell*, and the gold clause cases. But when Roberts joined the Four Horsemen in striking down the Railroad Retirement Act, New Dealers recognized that the conservatives on the Court, for the first time since FDR took office, had gotten the upper hand. Furthermore, the language of Roberts's opinion led them to fear the worst—that this was no temporary defection but a signal that Roberts was permanently lost. In fact, in every important division on the Court for almost all of the next two years, Roberts was to align himself with the Conservative Four. The *Rail Pension* decision, then, loomed as far more important than the particular legislation at issue. May 6 was to be looked back on as the day of a historic shift of power on the highest bench.

Even though the rail pension law was not an Administration measure, commentators interpreted the decision as "the worst defeat the New Deal has suffered in the courts, a defeat which may cripple President Roosevelt's program for social legislation." The essence of the episode, observed *News-Week*, was that "Associate Justice Owen J. Roberts of the Supreme Court of the United States said No to the President of the United States." Moreover, the arch-conservative James M. Beck, a former Solicitor General, noted jubilantly, Roberts had not only split off from the liberal bloc but had "broken rather definitely with the Chief Justice."[25]

Washington speculated about what had caused Roberts to shift allegiance. According to the columnist Drew Pearson, Roberts had started out as a liberal with an affection for Stone. "But," according to Pearson's notes, "Butler [was] constantly putting in a word at psychological moment. A wisecrack." Furthermore, "Roberts mingled with social conservatives. Likes people. Young, gets about." After a while, he came to accept Butler's point of view, in part because of the influence of his wife, who was "avidly" anti-Roosevelt. Once he switched, it was easier for him to remain with the Four Horsemen than to oscillate. Last, Pearson recorded, there was one "inescapable impression: Roberts has eye on Rep[ublican] nomination" for President in 1936.[26]

Gossip about Roberts's political ambitions gained credence from the predicament of the Republican party. The 1932 debacle had eliminated Herbert Hoover as a likely presidential nominee in 1936, and the even worse disaster in the 1934 mid-term elections had not only removed some potential candidates but had signaled to still other hopefuls the imprudence of running against the invincible FDR. In such circumstances, with no obvious GOP choice in sight, some thought the party should turn to the Supreme Court, just as it had persuaded Charles Evans Hughes to step down two decades before. Leonard Baker has written:

> It was a suggestion encouraged by Roberts' friends and members of his family. It was during this time that his philosophy, as expressed in his Court opinions and votes, see-sawed from the liberal to the conservative side. Finally, as the political suggestions grew louder, his philosophy became more in line with what was considered the philosophy of the Republican party.[27]

In one of his 1935 columns, Walter Lippmann alerted his readers to "the fact that there is considerable interest in the idea of going to the Supreme Court for the Republican candidate in 1936." He added, "The idea is that Mr. Justice Roberts, having decided against New Deal measures, is to run as the savior of the Constitution." The boom, Lippmann declared, was "certain to cause acute embarrassment to the Supreme Court as a whole and to Mr. Justice Roberts in particular," for henceforth every vote Roberts cast would be weighed for its electoral impact. "And what could be less edifying than a political campaign in which a justice of the Supreme Court was defending his judicial opinions from the end of a railroad car?" True, Hughes had left the bench in 1916 to run for the presidency. But few thought that a good precedent, and besides, the big question that year had been foreign affairs, not the behavior of the Court. "Now," though, "it is proposed to make the campaign on the very issues which the Court is called upon to decide, and it is nothing less than an outrage to suggest that a member of that Court should be a partisan candidate in such a campaign."[28]

Years later, in testimony before a Senate subcommittee, Roberts offered his own commentary on the episode. The Founding Fathers, he remarked, had done "an extraordinary thing" in insulating the Justices from political pressure by providing for life tenure. Yet there was a "loophole in the Constitution," one that had "appeared over and over again" in the history of the country. "I hope that I will be excused from naming names, but it is a matter of common knowledge that ambition to go from the Court to the Chief Executive of the Government has hurt the work of a number of men on the Court," he declared. Only once had a Justice given in, and Hughes had to be "practically sandbagged." Still, a number of Justices "have had in the back of their minds a possibility that they might get the nomination for President," and that was "not a healthy situation because, however strong a man's mentality and character, if he has this ambition in his mind it may tinge or color what he does, and that is exactly what the Founding Fathers wanted to remove from the minds of the Supreme Court, to make them perfectly free knowing that there was no more in life for them than the work of the Court." Roberts added: "I happen to have a personal knowledge of what that pressure is like, for twice ill-advised but enthusiastic friends of mine urged me to let my name go up as a candidate for President while I was on the Court. Of course, I turned a hard face on that thing. I never had the notion in my mind."[29] In truth, the boomlet for Roberts went nowhere, but he was certainly aware of it, and it may conceivably have had an effect, however indirect, on his behavior on the bench.

If Roberts did have political ambitions—and the evidence for that supposition is slim—he surely did not improve his chances on May 4, for his *Rail Pension* opinion provoked expressions of outrage and contempt. On a day when progressives were mourning the death in an air crash of New Mexico's far-sighted Senator, Bronson Cutting, Felix Frankfurter wrote Justice Brandeis, "Yesterday was a day of two tragedies: (1) Cutting's death; (2) Roberts' opinion." Subsequently, Fred Rodell of Yale Law School wrote that Roberts had "reverted to type as an old railroad lawyer, more comfortable among other old railroad lawyers than among bolder bedfellows"; and Robert H. Jackson, who became Roberts's colleague on the Court, called the opinion "shocking."[30]

Frankfurter made a somewhat more public contribution to demolishing Roberts's opinion in a lengthy unsigned editorial in the *New Republic* entitled "A Dred Scott Decision." In appearance an anonymous expression of the views of the editors of the magazine, it was actually written by Frankfurter and his Harvard Law School colleague Henry Hart. The rail pension ruling, it began, was "another of those tragic misadventures in the work of the Court such as the Dred Scott Case, the Income Tax Case and the Child Labor Case," the latest in a series of those "self-inflicted wounds" that Charles Evans Hughes had warned about. "One wonders how many more such decisions touching the very foundation of national power in a modern industrial society can be absorbed without destroying the very Constitution the odd man on the Court thinks he is preserving," it added.

This slighting reference to Roberts foreshadowed a scorching rejection of the youngest Justice's effort. The editorial continued:

> The consequences of this retrogressive conception of the scope of national power, if adhered to, will be truly paralyzing. Once again we have a dramatic demonstration of the extent to which "petty judicial decisions" can threaten the maintenance of constitutional federalism. Practical considerations bar the states from enacting such legislation; the Court perfects the cul de sac by announcing that the Constitution bars the government.

The writers found incredible Roberts's comment that the railroads could always deal with any problem of superannuated employees by firing them without a pension and his observation that any "supposed impossibility" of such an action arose from a failure to distinguish between what was permissible and what was desirable. "What a bitter dichotomy!" they wrote. "Never within memory has the Court so sharply dissociated the Constitution from social desirability." Roberts, they went on, had treated the issue of voluntary pension systems "with like irresponsibility." Only judges who went into "some mental darkroom of their own" would fail to recognize that railroads had introduced pension plans not out of charity, as Roberts supposed, but because they promoted efficiency.

The editorial concluded with an unbridled assault on Roberts's performance:

> This attitude of taking debaters' points that evoke cheers from the Bar Association gallery while leaving the substance of the matter untouched pervades the opinion. The Court is moved to intellectual frivolity in the presence of some of the gravest issues of contemporary society. One wonders what manifestation of that deep unrest among railroad workers which

prompted the passage of the Railroad Retirement Act last spring will be necessary to convince these judges that economic insecurity is a poignant reality which businessmen and statesmen alike disregard at their peril. Meanwhile, Mr. Justice Roberts has done more than write the most persuasive brief of our times in favor of government ownership of railroads. He has reinforced, as nothing else could, the doubts of those who question the capacity of Court and Constitution to satisfy the needs of our national life.[31]

Not to be outdone by its chief rival, the *Nation,* in an unsigned full-page editorial written by another law professor, Thurman Arnold of Yale Law School, denounced the Court for laying "its paralyzing hand" on the rail pension law and derided Roberts for the "complete lack of common sense" in his theory of government. Roberts's opinion, the *Nation* added, was "a curious document":

> It lacks the fire and moral conviction of the dissent in the gold cases. It is as dry as a common-law pleading, piling up objection after objection without any apparent sense of the relative importance of the points made. . . . It is a combination of pure fantasy and legal syllogisms with little persuasive power, but its bland assumptions that railroads are just little groups of private individuals and that the security of employees has nothing to do with efficient organization must shock any realistic mind.

Though the decision did not appear to rule out pension laws based on the taxing rather than the commerce power, "many informed persons fear that Justice Roberts has revealed such an ingrained hostility to pensions—as undeserved 'bounties' or 'largess'—that he may find a way to dispose even of acts which are based on the taxing power." Hence, it concluded, "the menace of the Supreme Court will continue to hang like an ominous cloud over all legal attempts to solve the social problems that are crowding upon us."[32]

The response in the law journals was more muted, but there, too, Roberts's opinion fared poorly. A compendium by the dean of Yale Law School registered that, of the comments in law journals, fourteen were critical, only one "mildly favorable," and one "neutral."[33] A note writer in the *Columbia Law Review* thought the decision "surprising" in the light of a series of past rulings upholding the constitutionality of statutes dealing with a range of subjects including the wages and hours of railroad workers. Moreover, he found the reasoning of the Court "reminiscent of an approach that was thought to have died in the birth of such cases" as *Nebbia.* A commentator in the *St. John's Law Review* reproached the

Court for overstepping its bounds by concerning itself with the wisdom of the statute despite the fact that "an authoritative body of opinion" sustained the assumptions on which the legislation was based. And a writer in the *Minnesota Law Review* observed drily, "In view of the disagreement among the members of the Court on the question of whether or not a pension system for railroad employees had any reasonable relation to the regulation of interstate commerce, it would seem that this would have been an appropriate case in which to respect the judgment of the members of Congress."[34]

Indeed, the accusation of overreaching has run like a leitmotif through commentary on the document. A later critic, Samuel Hendel, charged that "the blow struck by the majority opinion went far beyond the requirements." He added:

> A cardinal canon of the Court, frequently, to be sure, honored in the breach, is that in constitutional cases it will decide only so much as is necessary to dispose of the case. The majority having reached the conclusion that specific inseparable provisions of the Act offended against due process and that the Act was therefore invalid, there was not legitimate occasion to inquire into . . . whether Congress had exceeded its interstate commerce power. Or, doing so, it might at least have limited its inquiry to whether *this* Act exceeded the . . . commerce power. . . . It went further however by declaring that the subject matter itself lay beyond the reach of Congressional authority. To do this was not merely to condemn the particular plan before it but any plan that might be offered.

At the time, Thomas Reed Powell of Harvard Law School anticipated this judgment by alleging that the Court had given voice to a "condemnation twice removed from all that is necessary to dispose of the case. . . . Lavishly gratuitous was the readiness to declare that a different statute which might or might not later be passed would also fail to be a regulation of interstate commerce."[35]

Above all, commentators scolded Roberts for framing an opinion that was oblivious to the reality of the lives of railroad workers. "The haunting threat of poverty in old age, though perhaps a more subtle factor affecting the fount of action than a violent strike or the physical exhaustion of an overworked body, is viewed with something more than academic aloofness by the wage-earner who fires an engine or operates a switch, and its demoralizing effects upon the vigor and efficiency of work may well constitute just as potent an obstacle to the successful functioning of an enterprise," wrote an observer in the *Fordham Law Review*. "Thus by the narrow margin of one Justice," concluded the *American*

Labor Legislation Review, "the expressed will of Congress was defeated and a million railway workers were deprived of the assurance of security in old age."[36]

In their many harsh words, fault-finders said nothing about the Court that the Justices were not saying about one another. Not only had Roberts expressed contempt for those with whom he disagreed, but Hughes, in his dissent, it was noted, revealed "irritation and chagrin," "outrage," and "bitterness." "The display of extraordinary conviction on both sides tended to bear out the theory that the nine justices have had great difficulty in arriving at their decisions on the disputed law and have indulged in many arguments over it since they took it under advisement more than seven weeks ago," remarked the correspondent for the *New York Times*. The *Herald Tribune*'s reporter discerned even clearer signs of a great fissure. "The majority and minority opinions demonstrated that a serious cleavage exists in the court," he observed. Each was "vigorously presented," and "each undertook to riddle the arguments presented by the other."[37]

It is doubtful that any response matched the fury and disgust of Harlan Fiske Stone's. "The Railroad Retirement Act decision was, I think, about the worst performance of the Court since the Bake Shop case," he wrote Frankfurter in an allusion to the notorious *Lochner* opinion of 1905. He continued:

> The bill, it is true, was a bad one, and if I had been a member of Congress, I am certain I should have voted against it, but to say that it is beyond the range of constitutional power puts us back at least thirty years. A bad matter was made worse by the cocksure assumption that we could determine judicially that there was nothing for the congressional judgment to act upon. How arrogant it must all seem to those unaccustomed to judicial omniscience in the interpretation of the Constitution.

The letter was written only three days after the ruling was handed down, at a time when heated emotions had not had time to cool, but it was not merely a deduction of the moment. That August, Stone was still saying almost word for word what he had told Reed Powell in late May: "The decision in the Railroad Retirement Act was the worst performance of the Court in my time." And in a no less wrathful communication to his sons he wrote: "Constitutionalism has gone mad when it assumes to forbid the federal government from establishing such a system for railroad employees. I fear that it will plague us as long as the famous Bake Shop case did."[38]

VI

Though there had been some muttering about the need to curb the powers of the Supreme Court before, the rail pension case galvanized organized labor, liberal Congressmen, and the Roosevelt administration to take the first serious efforts in that direction. Most of the activity centered on the railway brotherhoods, which had seasoned political operatives on Capitol Hill and excellent connections in the House, who were incensed by the destruction of the legislation they had carefully nurtured. The head of one brotherhood called the ruling "one of the most reactionary decisions handed down by the court," while the president of another proposed a general strike. "Our rail 'boys' dreadfully disappointed," Edward Keating, editor of the brotherhoods' paper, *Labor*, wrote in his diary on the day Roberts spoke. "50,000 would have retired, thus making places for younger men."[39]

"Supreme Ct's decision in Rail Pension case is 'the talk of the town,' " Keating recorded the following day, as progressives ranted against the judiciary and explored how to limit its powers. Roberts, they noted, was spoken of as a possible Republican presidential candidate in 1936, but "Roberts' opinion was so reactionary, he would not get very far." Four days later, David J. Lewis, the pro-labor Congressman from Maryland, sent for Keating. In his hideout in the rotunda of the Old House Office Building, Lewis told the union editor that the time was ripe for action to hamstring the courts. The power of judicial review had been usurped by Marshall, and "today every jackanapes of a judge brushes aside legislative enactments as whim or prejudice may suggest." Lewis did not think that a constitutional amendment was necessary; a simple act of Congress would suffice. When he got back to his office, Keating found the former U. S. Senator from Iowa Smith Wildman Brookhart "hot to go even farther than Lewis." He wanted to re-enact the rail pension law and attach an amendment depriving lower federal courts of jurisdiction and denying the Supreme Court the authority to hear any appeal.[40]

At a meeting in Washington on May 13, leaders of the rail unions gave their approval to not only a new rail pension measure but a proposal to restrict the judiciary. Though Brookhart appeared before them to press his scheme, they decided instead to back legislation introduced by two friends of the unions, Congressmen Robert Crosser of Ohio and Robert Ramsay of West Virginia, to require the vote of at least seven Justices to nullify an act of Congress, an approach that Davy Lewis strongly advocated. An attorney for the Retirement Board had warned earlier that the Court would strike down such a law and "would laugh

at any attempt to curb its powers," but the leadership of the brotherhoods had run out of patience with the Justices.[41]

The rail unions knew that they could count on widespread support
from other labor organizations. The editor of *Black Worker* hoped that
the pension decision would result in a clamor from the country to strip
the Court of the power to invalidate legislation. He added:

> This power in very truth was never delegated to the Supreme Court by
> the Constitution. It was usurped. . . . It is a ridiculous procedure, to say
> the least, that a group of nine old tottering men should be permitted to
> nullify the will of the people where expressed in Congressional acts that
> are unpopular with the social philosophy of erstwhile corporation lawyers.

Once again the solution of Court-packing could be heard. The editor
of the *Hosiery Worker* demanded that the President appoint "added members to the Supreme Court bench, so as to insure a majority whose
minds are not closed to the facts of present-day life."[42]

Roosevelt refrained from any public comment on the decision, but
both he and his aides found Roberts's attitude exasperating. Upon talking to the President two days after the decision, Rexford Tugwell, a
onetime member of FDR's Brain Trust, recorded in his diary that "we
both agreed will probably mean that the Courts will declare the NRA
Act unconstitutional," while the head of the relief program, Harry Hopkins, commenting on an encounter with the author of the *Rail Pension*
opinion at lunch just after it was announced, noted in his diary: "Roberts
is pleasant, tells good stories but his social philosophy comes from Andy
Mellon—pretty dismal to think of Roberts on the Supreme Court for
twenty years more." "The opinion," Stephens reported resentfully to Attorney General Homer Cummings, "was couched in extreme terms and
delivered in a manner which indicated that the majority thought the
viewpoint of Congress as expressed in the statute and of the Government as expressed in its argument and of the minority as expressed in
their opinion was not only beyond law but beyond common sense." At
a meeting at the White House with a delegation from the rail unions,
the President called the decision "rotten," one of the worst ever
handed down.[43]

The Administration worried especially about what Roberts's alliance
with the Four Horsemen implied for other legislation that the Court had
yet to act on, particularly the Social Security bill that was making its
way through Congress. The rail pension ruling, the Denver *Post* was
happy to tell its readers, was "the worst setback the New Dealers have
received," for "it not only junks their scheme for pensioning railroad
employees, but it knocks the props out from under President Roosevelt's

fantastic social-security program and forecasts a judicial death-blow to the NRA."[44]

Business Week shared the pleasure of the commercial world in Roberts's opinion, but it also sounded a cautionary note. Though the social security measure rested not on the commerce clause involved in the rail pension case but on the taxing power, it was "difficult to see how the government lawyers will be able to convince the five frowning justices that the social security legislation is really aimed at raising revenue," it said. In addition, it anticipated that the Court would "rule against some of the provisions of the National Industrial Recovery Act [and] that it may knock out such legislation as the Wagner labor disputes bill." Yet those predictions, it warned, all hinged on a single premise—that the membership of the Court would remain unaltered and thus deny Roosevelt the opportunity to turn a minority into a majority by a single appointment.[45]

The Administration had no intention of waiting passively for a vacancy to develop while Justice Roberts and the Four Horsemen struck down one after another of the New Deal laws. Before the week was out, Cummings had sent a memorandum to Assistant Attorney General Angus MacLean:

> Has any study been made in this office of the question of the right of the Congress, by legislation, to limit the terms and conditions upon which the Supreme Court can pass on constitutional questions? I have seen several memoranda from time to time spelling out a theory by which this result could be achieved without a constitutional amendment. My recollection is that our files will somewhere disclose briefs on the theory that the Supreme Court has no right to pass on constitutional questions at all. Of course, quite a learned document could be prepared dealing with the historical aspects of this matter and the way in which it has developed.
>
> I think it would be well to have this pretty thoroughly covered, but in addition to this it would be well to cover the subject I first above mentioned; namely, the question of legislation which would not cut off the right of the Supreme Court to pass on constitutional questions, but which would limit it somewhere with a view to avoiding 5 to 4 decisions.[46]

The rail pension ruling had indeed been a turning point. The President had not pressed for enactment of the law and had been reluctant to sign it. But he fully understood the peril the decision, and even more the opinion, raised to his program. If the thinking that Roberts revealed on May 6 prevailed, the Welfare State would be stillborn. From that day forward, neither Roosevelt nor his aides would rest until they had found a way to overcome the obstacle to their plans presented by the Court.

The Case of
the Contentious Commissioner

[In the fast-paced course of events in the spring of 1935, the Supreme
Court, which had ruled on the Railroad Retirement Act early in May,
handed down three more decisions on a single day before the month ran
out. One of these rulings was on *Humphrey's Executor v. U. S.*, a case that,
like the rail pension litigation, was more consequential than has often been
appreciated. This essay originally appeared in a somewhat different form
in Harold M. Hyman and Leonard W. Levy, eds., *Freedom and Reform: Essays
in Honor of Henry Steele Commager* (New York, 1967), a Festschrift in honor
of our mentor at Columbia University.]

I

Of the many cases that come before the United States Supreme
Court, some are born to fame and some to obscurity. On the
historic decision day of May 27, 1935, the Supreme Court delivered
three rulings, one of which, concerning some sick chickens, would gain
immediate notoriety as one of the most significant opinions in this century. The first of the three decisions, arising from President Roosevelt's
ouster of William E. Humphrey from the Federal Trade Commission, was
overshadowed by that ruling at the time, and few commentators have accorded it much attention since.[1] Humphrey, so jealous of his reputation,
has had the unhappy fate of having gone down in more than one work of
history, when history noticed him at all, as "Humphries."[2] Yet *Humphrey's
Executor v. U. S.* raised important questions about the prerogatives of the
President and the doctrine of separation of powers, and for Franklin Roosevelt's ultimate confrontation with the Supreme Court it had consequences more far-reaching than its humble reputation would suggest.

52

II

Born in 1862 in rural Indiana, William Ewart Humphrey was to carry into the era of the New Deal the values of a Hoosier farm boy who identified not with the State but with the new industrial order of railway titans and steel barons. After attending Wabash College and practicing law in an Indiana college town, he decided, when the Panic of 1893 struck, to seek his fortune in the Pacific Northwest. In Seattle, Humphrey rose quickly in the ranks of the Republican party; by 1898 he was corporation counsel of the city, and four years later he won election to the U. S. House of Representatives.

From 1903 to 1917, Humphrey represented the business interests of his district and of the country so single-mindedly that progressive Congressmen called him "Jesse James."[3] He was not only a shrill standpatter but a fierce partisan. "If a Democrat is elected," he warned in 1912, when Woodrow Wilson was running for President with FDR's ardent support, "a panic will commence in this country within twenty-four hours after that news is flashed throughout the world."[4] Instead of indulging in the good-natured raillery thought essential for a successful politician, Humphrey was outspoken to the point of rudeness. He wrote one constituent: "I will consider it a personal favor if you will write to the people who wrote to you . . . and tell them that they are making a great nuisance of themselves and doing their cause no good by having people all over this state write me about this matter."[5]

When Humphrey, after losing his bid for a U. S. Senate seat in 1916, demanded that his former associates find him a job as a lobbyist, his attitude and demeanor caused him some difficulty for a time. Humphrey, stated the Tacoma *Times*, which embarrassed his friends by publishing an account of overtures to corporations on his behalf, had been "a noisy, ill-mannered, narrowly-partisan, always-carping critic of the Wilson administration. He was the pet G.O.P. baiter of Wilson, Wilson's policies, Wilson's appointees and Wilson's acts, in Congress and out. It became with him a mania."[6] Some of the groups approached decided not to hire him, but Humphrey was too undeviating a supporter of business interests and had too much influence in Washington to be unconnected for long. Shortly after his term in Congress expired, he was taken on to represent Northwestern lumber companies.

Humphrey, who always had his eye on the main chance, did not propose to spend the rest of his days as a lobbyist. He played an active role in national Republican politics (in the 1922 Congressional elections, he chaired the Speakers Bureau of the Republican National Committee), and he remained a forthright champion of the Grand Old Party

and conservative policies. His years in Washington, he said on one occasion, had given him "a profound distrust of the reformer."[7] Humphrey, in short, offered precisely that combination of economic orthodoxy and party loyalty that should have commended him to Republican
administrations in Washington. Yet not until 1925, though he was aggressive about calling attention to his services, did his search for preferment end. That year, President Calvin Coolidge, seeking just such a
man, named him to the five-member Federal Trade Commission in a
deliberate attempt to force that "independent" agency into line with the
Administration's desires.

The choice of Humphrey proved to be a decisive moment in the
history of the FTC, which had been set up in 1914 to forestall unfair
competition. By placing on the Commission a forceful defender of corporations, it gave those who opposed effective regulation a 3–2 majority. Progressives were appalled. Senator George Norris of Nebraska
cried, "With the greatest reactionary of the country sitting on the Federal Trade Commission, tell me, O God—tell me!—where the toiling
millions of the honest, common people of this country are going to be
protected in their rights as against big business."[8]

Humphrey quickly transformed the FTC into an agency that served
not as an overseer but as a partner of corporations. Only three weeks
after he took office, the Commission voted new rules under which cases
were settled informally with little investigation or publicity. Humphrey
explained: "So far as I can prevent it, the Federal Trade Commission is
not going to be used as a publicity bureau to spread socialistic propaganda." *Outlook* commented: "Business has always hated and has steadily
determined to throttle the Commission." Thanks to "the change in control due to the appointment of Commissioner Humphrey," business was
close to fulfilling its ambition.[9]

Humphrey boasted of his role in the alteration. "I certainly did make
a revolutionary change in the method and policies of the commission,"
he was quoted as stating. "If it was going east before, it is going west
now." Nor was he shy about admitting that he had stacked the FTC's
board of review. "What of it?" he asked. "Do you think I would have a
body of men working here under me that did not share my ideas about
these matters? Not on your life. I would not hesitate a minute to cut
their heads off if they disagreed with me. What in hell do you think I
am here for?" Humphrey recognized that some disapproved of what he
had done, but he dismissed these naysayers as "the vocal and beatific
fringe, the pink edges that border both of the old parties." The FTC,
he announced, would "no longer" serve "as a means of gratifying dema-
gogues."[10]

A bald, round-faced man with a bushy mustache and beard, Humphrey looked the part of the pugnacious autocrat who seemed forever embroiled in controversy. He quarreled not only with his critics in Congress but with his own commissioners. On one occasion his fellow Republican Gifford Pinchot, the head of the Forest Service under Theodore Roosevelt, told him that it was "hopeless" to expect an adequate investigation by the FTC of abuses in the utilities industry "because of long personal experience with you as a bitter enemy of the Roosevelt Conservation policy, an opponent of Federal action and a lobbyist of lumbermen." Humphrey replied: "Your letter of regurgitated filth received. For your own famished sake, and for the infinite relief of the country, have your keeper lead you to a thistle patch." Then, characteristically, Humphrey released both letters to the press.[11]

Under Humphrey, much to the dismay of progressives, the FTC atrophied, in part as a consequence of court decisions, but also because of Humphrey's behavior.[12] Early in 1928, he wrote an Indiana Senator that he objected to "fantastic fishing expeditions" by the Commission which were "doing the administration great harm with the business interests," and he subsequently opposed appropriations for FTC investigations of unfair business practices in a number of industries. When President Herbert Hoover nominated him for another six-year term in 1931, the new Senator from Louisiana, Huey Long, made his maiden speech in opposition, and twenty-eight Senators voted not to confirm. By the time Franklin Roosevelt won election in 1932, Humphrey had become a symbol of all that progressives abhorred in the old order. In January 1933, Congressman Wright Patman of Texas sounded a popular note in voicing the hope that when FDR entered the White House he would "certainly change the policy of the Federal Trade Commission and put it back to its original function or intent."[13]

III

As soon as the First Hundred Days Congress of 1933 concluded its momentous session, President Roosevelt turned toward the task of manning the agencies that had been created that spring or that had been given additional assignments. Among the latter was the Federal Trade Commission, which had been designated by the National Industrial Recovery Act as a court of appeals in trade practices' litigation. Even more important, the draftsmen of the Securities Act of 1933 had decided, surprisingly, to vest authority for administering that new law in the FTC. As James M. Landis, one of the draftsmen, later explained: "Its reputation as an effective regulatory agency during the Harding-

Coolidge-Hoover era had admittedly not been of the highest, but we understood that the administration intended to restaff and reinvigorate it."[14]

As he thought about the enhanced role of the FTC, Roosevelt scrawled his ideas about personnel on a White House pad:

Fed. Trade Comm	10,000
Humphrey—out	F. Murphy?
	La Follette?
March, Minn. ok	
McCulloch—dead	Perk?
Fergusson ok	
Hunt retired[15]	

Anyone acquainted with the Washington scene could readily decipher the scribbling. Of the five positions on the Commission, two were vacant. Not only Edward A. McCulloch, a Democrat, but also the Republican, Charles W. Hunt, listed by Roosevelt as "retired," had died recently. To these places, each of which paid $10,000 a year, Roosevelt decided to name Erwin L. Davis of Tennessee, the brother of Ambassador-at-Large Norman H. Davis, and Raymond B. Stevens of New Hampshire, one of the authors of the original FTC Act of 1914. (Stevens, who wished to return to an assignment in Siam, would serve only briefly. When he stepped down in October, the President picked Jim Landis as his successor. A Brandeisian, Landis was a thirty-four-year-old Harvard Law School professor.) The three remaining members were Humphrey, whose term would not expire until 1937; C. H. March, a liberal Republican from Minnesota whose term ran until 1936; and Garland S. Ferguson, a North Carolina Democrat whose term was about to run out. As his note on the memo pad indicated, Roosevelt resolved to reappoint Ferguson, to leave March undisturbed, but to oust Humphrey and to name someone like Detroit's Democratic mayor Frank Murphy, or Philip La Follette, the progressive Republican from Wisconsin, in his place.

During the month of July 1933, rumors began to circulate about the President's intentions, and on July 19, Will Humphrey, having gotten wind of the disturbing news, wrote the President:

Information comes to me that you are going to ask my resignation. For what reason I do not know.

Senator Dill, who is more responsible for my being in this position and more interested personally and politically in my retaining it, is away and cannot be reached. His return is expected within a few days.

If final action cannot be delayed until his return, then in behalf of the Senator as well as myself, I feel that I should ask for a personal interview. If I have neglected any duty, done anything dishonorable, or discreditable; or have been guilty of disloyalty, it is not necessary for you to ask my resignation. . . .

For the greater part of forty years, I·have been in the public service. I am not aware of anything discreditable in my record, or of any act that I would blot out. If that long service is ended by forced resignation, it would be to some extent a reflection on my career and would greatly injure me in my profession if I should again take up the practice of law. [16]

For half a century Humphrey had been playing the political game of favors and rewards, and in his mind he kept a ledger of good turns he had performed for which he expected payment in full. On July 25, he sent a typically blunt letter to Senator C. C. Dill, a Democrat from his home state of Washington:

I was amazed and shocked at what you said yesterday. If I had known what you told me a few weeks ago, it would have been entirely different, and I could easily have made other satisfactory arrangements.

Naturally, after I left you I got in touch with several of my friends, including Senators and other prominent people, who know about affairs of this kind. Each one said that the President would do whatever you desired in the matter, that he would not ask my resignation unless you acquiesced. . . .

I cannot believe, as I have been informed, and as you seem to believe, that the President is going to ask my resignation without giving me an opportunity to be heard. If it is done in this manner, as you well know, it will smirch my record and greatly handicap me in my profession. I think if he contemplates this, I have the right to insist that you protest such action and that you will arrange an interview. . . .

I shall only add that I have carefully reviewed our many years of friendship. . . . I have found nothing in all those years which I feel does not justify me in thinking I have the right to expect that you will be pleased to comply with the request I have made—and that you will do everything in your power to carry it out. And so I do believe. Nothing but your failure to do so will ever make me believe that you will not.

Dill, who may already have interceded for Humphrey, was quick to follow through, but to no avail. [17]

Even before Dill wrote him, Roosevelt had let Humphrey know that he would not grant him an interview. He continued:

Without any reflection at all upon you personally or upon the service you have rendered in your present capacity, I find it necessary to ask for your resignation as a member of the Federal Trade Commission. I do this because I feel that the aims and purpose of the Administration with respect to the work of the Commission can be carried out most effectively with personnel of my own selection.

May I take this opportunity to tell you that at the earnest request of Senator Dill, I have been withholding this action for some time but have now reached a definite decision to proceed along the lines I have in mind.[18]

By August 1, Humphrey appeared to have accepted that he was about to be fired, and he apparently planned no further overtures to persuade the President to reverse himself. All he asked was a temporary reprieve to allow him enough time to confer with friends in Seattle about returning to private practice. On August 4, Roosevelt wired Humphrey that he appreciated his desire for an interval to make arrangements. Consequently, he was accepting the Commissioner's resignation but not to take effect until August 15.[19]

It was altogether out of character, however, for so combative a man as Humphrey to take being driven out of office this meekly. Sometime in the first two weeks of August, he sought legal advice; he was told that there were strong grounds for doubting that the President had the authority to get rid of him. As he later explained: "While I started out with the belief that the President had the power to remove for any cause he saw fit, fuller examination of the authorities convinces me beyond reasonable doubt that he can remove only for the reasons specified in the statute, and after hearing." He had employed "two of the best Democratic lawyers," and they had confirmed the opinions of counsel he had consulted earlier.[20]

On August 11, Humphrey, in a letter to Roosevelt, denied that he had proffered his resignation. Nor, indeed, did he intend to step down. To do so would be interpreted as an admission that he was guilty of one or more of the failings that would, by statute, justify the President in sacking him: "inefficiency, neglect of duty, or malfeasance in office." Moreover, if he were to quit in order to permit the President to have his way, the independence of all regulatory commissions would be placed in jeopardy. He concluded: "I am fully aware of the great power of the President, and of the dangerous consequences that may follow a refusal of his request, still—

> 'I had as lief not be, as live to be
> In awe of such a thing as I myself'."[21]

A week later, Humphrey once more turned to Dill for help, this time stating his demand even more cavalierly. "I have reason to believe that things are in such shape that if you would send a telegram to the President, urging him—not only on political grounds, but on personal friendship, to stop the whole affair, that it would be done." He went on:

> You will remember when certain parties were insisting upon your being indicted in the matter of the Colville Indian claims, and it accidentally came to my knowledge. While the parties argued that it was impossible for you to escape conviction and that the only course would be to throw yourself upon the mercy of the Court, I argued with them that even if this were true, that such action on your part carried no moral turpitude and that you were innocent of any intentional wrong doing; that you were a young man and it would tend largely to discredit you and would be a disgrace through life—and that I would not consent to it. Just recently I have seen one of the men who attended that conference, and without any prompting from me, when I mentioned the subject, he stated . . . he thought that this plea stopped further proceedings.

He further told the Senator of how he had saved him from "certain unfortunate real estate transactions" and of the political favors he had done. "Under the circumstances," Humphrey said, "I feel fully justified in asking you to send the telegram."[22]

On August 21 from Spokane, Dill replied that he was "deeply grateful" for past favors but pointed out that Humphrey would not have been confirmed on either occasion when he had been nominated to the FTC save for Dill's intervention. Moreover, the Senator noted, he had twice asked Roosevelt not to remove Humphrey. "I did all I could for you this time when I was there, but after all the President is boss and I can't control his appointments," Dill wrote. "I think I have exhausted whatever influence I had in this particular matter." The very next day Dill thought better of his attitude. From a hotel in Ellensburg, Washington, he scribbled a note to Humphrey assuring him that he was interceding with the President yet again. Somewhat mollified, Humphrey nonetheless assumed his familiar role of Republican partisan and threatened the Democratic Senator with reprisals for his party.[23]

If there had ever been a time when Dill might have dissuaded Roosevelt from acting—and that is highly improbable—that time had passed.[24] As soon as the President received Humphrey's letter of August 11, he recognized that the Commissioner might refuse to resign, and he initiated steps to build a case against him. On August 14 he sent a confidential memorandum to Attorney General Homer Cummings requesting him to look into the allegation that Humphrey had favored a cut in funds for the FTC's investigation of utilities. He also asked the newly appointed commissioner, Raymond Stevens, to examine a charge by Samuel Rosenman, one of the original Brain Trusters, that Humphrey had acted improperly in a rayon trust case. On August 17, Roosevelt received word that Stevens had reported that the "matter you asked him to investigate has reached a very critical stage. Anxious to talk with you as soon as Possible."[25]

In the last two weeks in August, reports reached the White House from the Department of Justice and from Stevens, who took advantage of his official position to comb the FTC files for evidence of wrongdoing by Humphrey. Some of the leads failed to prove out. It developed that Humphrey had not advocated a cut in FTC appropriations for the utilities probe, and his relation to the rayon affair was murky. Yet there was ample evidence that he had opposed FTC investigations, had belittled the work of the Commission, and had been guilty of using "intemperate and abusive language."[26]

Bolstered by the communications he had received from Stevens and others, Roosevelt was now ready to move once more. On August 31, in a firm but tactful manner, he requested Humphrey's resignation and asked that he have it in the next week. The President stated: "You will, I know, realize that I do not feel that your mind and my mind go along together on either the policies or the administering of the Federal Trade Commission, and frankly, I think it is best for the people of this country that I should have full confidence."[27]

It is astonishing that as seasoned a politician as FDR would send a letter so ineptly worded. In the spring of 1935 Secretary of the Interior Harold Ickes noted in his diary a Cabinet meeting at which "the President said that he had made a mistake in not preferring charges. He had actual proof of malfeasance in office, but he didn't want to file such charges against Humphreys [sic], believing as he did that he could get rid of him by milder methods." Two years later, Roosevelt expressed similar sentiments in a long conversation with another former Brain Truster, Adolf Berle, who recorded in his diary the President's saying that he "had enough on Humphries [sic] to remove him because he had taken bribes from two rayon companies and a tinning process concern." Out of consideration for the Commissioner's feelings, though, he had consented to base the discharge on difference of outlook. He had permitted his "old kind heart" to let Humphrey outwit him, the President confessed; "he described himself," Berle noted, "both as an ass and a sucker in the whole proceedings." Roosevelt may not have been remembering the course of events accurately, for he appears to have lacked hard evidence in 1933 of malfeasance. But whatever the scenario, the

President's letter had the effect, as Berle said, of giving Humphrey "a certificate of good conduct," and FDR's critics never let him hear the end of the not unreasonable but autocratic-sounding clause, "I do not feel that your mind and my mind go along together."[28]

Even the unmistakably final tone of this letter did not convince Humphrey that Roosevelt truly meant to discharge him. Once again he badgered Dill to wire the President to undertake an investigation. He stated "without reservation" that it was untrue that his mind and FDR's did not go along together. "As I told you before, somebody has been lying to him," Humphrey asserted. Nine days later, he sent a lengthy letter to the President saying that Roosevelt's note of August 31 had gratified him, because for the first time he had been given a reason for his proposed removal. But he immediately added: "You are entirely mistaken as to the facts." He challenged Roosevelt to show where they differed on policies, and contended, strangely, that the FTC had been undivided, and hence that to criticize him was to censure the entire Commission. He was sure that the President had been victimized by "whisperings," "misrepresentations," and "insinuations," some of which may have been the result of "some sinister motive." He asked only for a fair hearing, and, identifying himself with St. Paul, asked: "Is it lawful to scourge a man, an American citizen, and uncondemned?"[29]

The President refused to see Humphrey, but he did ask Charles H. McCarthy, who had served as Roosevelt's secretary during his tenure as Assistant Secretary of the Navy, to telephone the Commissioner. McCarthy explained that the President did not believe that Humphrey agreed with him either on FTC policy or on administration of the Securities Act, and that he wished to name a securities expert to the FTC. Quite apart from "the legal aspect of the matter," Humphrey would be well advised to bow out and avoid being humiliated, McCarthy said. That very day, Associated Press tickers reported the impending ouster. The A.P. story, Humphrey wrote Roosevelt ten days later, had confirmed him in his determination not to resign.[30]

Once the President accepted the fact that he could not persuade Humphrey to leave voluntarily, he proceeded with plans to fire him and to designate a successor. Since Phil La Follette was either unavailable or seemed an inadvisable choice, Roosevelt began negotiations with another progressive Republican from Wisconsin, George Mathews, onetime Wisconsin Public Utilities Commissioner and currently a rate expert for the receivers of the Insull empire. When Mathews was assured that he would not be involved in litigation with Humphrey, the White House arranged to have a wire appointing Mathews sent on the same day, October 7, 1933, that a brisk note was delivered to Humphrey, stating: "Effective as of this date you are hereby removed from the office of Commissioner of the Federal Trade Commission."[31]

For Humphrey, the long struggle to win FDR over had ended, and he did not disguise his fury. He wrote the President:

> For weeks I have known that certain insurgent Republican Senators were demanding my removal, and that you desired my resignation because of reasons assigned by them but concealed from me. . . . I must presume that the charges made were given to you under seal of secrecy and that you feel you are in honor bound to regard them as such. I cannot think of any other justification for your refusal to give me an opportunity to meet these charges. These certain insurgents are cowards. They will not fight like men. . . . They destroy any who trust them. They betrayed the Republican Party. They will destroy the Democratic Party. They will betray you the moment it is to their interest so to do. They are character assassins. They stab only in the back and in the dark. This same collection of political hypocrites tried twice to prevent my confirmation but were defeated each time by a large majority, composed of Democrats and Republicans. These insurgents were too cowardly and dishonest to accept the verdict of an open and honorable fight, and now to accomplish their purpose, they come with slanderous and polluted lips and spew their putrid filth upon you under the pledge of secrecy. The history of American politics does not furnish a more infamous transaction.
>
> These sanctified experts of expediency, who use a party name simply to be elected, are mental perverts who glorify treachery and intellectual dishonesty.[32]

A scrapper to the end, Humphrey now retained William J. "Wild Bill" Donovan, former assistant to the Attorney General, to carry on his battle in the courts, and on advice of counsel, Humphrey acted out a charade of pretending still to be the Commissioner.[33] On October 9, he wrote Mathews:

> You are hereby notified that your appointment as Federal Trade Commissioner is invalid, because there was no vacancy to which you could be appointed, and you are notified that I am still a Member of the Federal Trade Commission, filling the term for which you are supposed to be appointed, and that I claim and shall claim the emoluments of the said office to the expiration of my present term.

That day, when the FTC held its regularly scheduled meeting, Humphrey turned up to hand the Commission a statement disputing the validity of his removal and to sit in silence for two hours while it conducted its business. The commissioners, however, voted to assent to

Humphrey's ouster and validate Mathews's tenure. Humphrey also filed periodic claims for back pay with the disbursing office of the FTC, but these claims were turned down, and the Acting Comptroller General ruled that Mathews's appointment was lawful.[34]

The legal niceties having been attended to, Humphrey turned to pressing his case. On October 20, he wrote Colonel Donovan that he thought "action should be taken soon." (Predictably, he disagreed with his attorney's interpretation of the legal precedents.)[35] On December 28, Humphrey filed suit in the U. S. Court of Claims contesting his removal and demanding $1,251.39 in back salary. (Eventually, interest raised the sum to $3,043.06.)

Humphrey anticipated that his cause would be strengthened by a show of concern on Capitol Hill, since he had been confirmed by the Senate for a full six-year term and believed that Roosevelt's actions would be perceived as an infringement of legislative prerogative. On January 18, 1934, the former Commissioner, once more exploiting his influence with Dill, secured an invitation to appear before the Senate Interstate Commerce Committee, of which Dill was chairman, to challenge the confirmation of Mathews. The committee even postponed the hearing in order to accommodate Humphrey, who had been ill. Yet Humphrey expressed disappointment about one matter. "I doubt if we are going to have any Senator make a speech on our side of the case when the matter of Mr. Mathews' confirmation comes up for consideration," he wrote Donovan.[36] Silence, Humphrey feared, would give the court the impression that the Senate was willing to waive its rights.

Humphrey's concern proved generally well-founded. The Senate—after brief speeches by two Old Guard Republicans criticizing the President's behavior—approved the nomination unanimously. In the House, only one voice was raised in protest, and even Representative Joseph L. Hooper, a Michigan Republican, conceded that it was not absolutely clear that Roosevelt did not have the legal authority to remove Humphrey. Hooper rested much of his argument on the contention that the President was not playing the game of politics squarely. Since the law stipulated that no more than three of the five commissioners could be members of the same party, Hooper reasoned that the other places were reserved not just for Republicans but for bona fide, card-carrying Republicans. If Roosevelt had gone through with his reported intention to replace Humphrey with Phil La Follette, said Hooper, "it would be as though a Republican President had nominated Norman Thomas to the Trade Commission on the theory that he was a Democrat." Furthermore, Hooper warned, there were no limits to how far Roosevelt might go. He might, for example, remove a federal district judge; if he did, it would be "little more violent" an infringement than his ouster of Humphrey. "The law must be the law for magistrate and citizen alike or we are no longer a Republic," he declared. "Those who believe in arbitrary power may take comfort, perhaps, from incidents such as these; but they are big with disaster to democratic ideals and traditions and government." Hooper knew, though, that he was speaking only for the record. His effort was already lost. [37]

On February 14, 1934, four weeks after his testimony before Dill's committee, the seventy-one-year-old Humphrey suffered a stroke and died. His death, however, did not terminate his suit. The executor of his estate, Samuel Rathbun, took over as plaintiff seeking to recover that portion of Humphrey's salary payable from the day of his removal to the day of his death. [38] Humphrey had always been a bare-fisted brawler, and his ghost was to prove an even feistier adversary.

IV

When Stanley Reed became Solicitor General in March 1935, Homer Cummings called him in. "Stanley, you are going to win some cases in the Supreme Court and you are going to lose some," the Attorney General told him between puffs of a cigarette. "For your first case, pick out one that you can win." Sound advice, for there had been a tradition that the government's chief law officer begins in triumph. So, after combing the docket, Reed chose a sure winner: *Humphrey's Executor v. U. S.*, for Humphrey, Reed later reflected, was a case that "couldn't be lost." [39]

Reed's confidence stemmed from a Supreme Court opinion delivered less than a decade before by a Chief Justice of the United States in response to a suit filed by another federal official; like Humphrey, he was from the Pacific Northwest, quarrelsome, and had died before the Court ruled. The postmaster of Portland, Oregon, Frank S. Myers, appointed by President Wilson to a four-year term with the advice and consent of the Senate, had been removed by Wilson in February 1920, without the consent of the Senate, before his term had expired. He filed suit in the Court of Claims for back salary on the grounds that the President needed Senate approval to dislodge him, since an act of 1876 had stipulated: "Postmasters of the first, second and third classes shall be appointed and may be removed by the President by and with the advice and consent of the Senate, and may hold their offices for four years unless sooner removed or suspended according to law." [40] The Court of Claims ruled against Myers, and the case was appealed to the U.S. Supreme Court by Myers's widow.

Until the *Myers* case reached it, the Supreme Court had been circumspect about passing judgment on the President's removal power. The Court appeared to be willing to accept the precedent set by the "Legislative Decision of 1789," when the First Congress, somewhat ambiguously, had recognized the right of the President to dismiss the Secretary of Foreign Affairs without its consent. Understandably, the Justices were reluctant to meddle in so "political" a question. On the few occasions the Court had spoken, it had construed the removal power liberally. In *Shurtleff*, upholding President William McKinley's dismissal of a minor official, the Court had stated: "The right of removal would exist if the statute had not contained a word upon the subject. It does not exist by virtue of the grant, but it inheres in the right to appoint, unless limited by Constitution or statute." Yet the opinion in the *Shurtleff* case was open to more than one interpretation, and the Court had still not defined the exact scope of the removal power.[41]

Myers, however, came to a court led by William Howard Taft, a Chief Justice who had no hesitation about intervening in matters that some of his predecessors would have shied away from. Stung by the many verbal barbs flung at him by insurgent Congressmen during his term as President, Taft seized on this suit as a way to strike a blow for the authority of the chief executive. "I am very strongly convinced that the danger to this country is in the enlargement of the powers of Congress, rather than in the maintenance in full of the executive power," he confided. "Congress is getting into the habit of forming boards who really exercise executive power, and attempting to make them independent of the President after they have been appointed and confirmed. This merely makes a hydra-headed Executive, and if the terms are lengthened so as to exceed the duration of a particular Executive, a new Executive will find himself stripped of control of important functions, for which as the head of the Government he becomes responsible, but whose action he cannot influence in any way."[42]

Taft quickly found that a majority of the Justices shared his conviction that the ouster of Myers was a legitimate exercise of the President's authority, but he was not content to confine himself to the issue at hand. He wished to establish the widest possible latitude for the removal power. To that end, he called a rump meeting of the Justices who supported him, and, to meet their objections, worked and reworked the draft of his opinion. Not until a year and a half after arguments had been completed was Taft satisfied, but he regarded his labors as time well spent. "I agree with you that we have not had a case in two generations of more importance," he told Justice Stone.[43]

On October 25, 1926, almost seven years after Myers had been dumped, the ruling on *Myers v. United States* finally came. For a Court divided 6–3, Taft, in a sixty-one page opinion, sustained the decision of the Court of Claims. The section of the 1876 Act requiring Senate concurrence in the removal of a postmaster was unconstitutional, he announced. Devoting almost half his opinion to the "Legislative Decision of 1789," the Chief Justice found ample precedent for the view that the President's removal power was illimitable. The President's exclusive power of removal, he maintained, derived from his authority to appoint and his obligation to execute the laws. Even more far-reaching was Taft's contention that this prerogative was inherent in the executive power granted by Article II of the Constitution, and could not be circumscribed by Congress. All "executive officers of the United States" were subject to removal by the President at will.

Not satisfied with enunciating this sweeping doctrine, the Chief Justice went on to offer a brief obiter dictum asserting that the President's removal power extended even to members of independent regulatory commissions. Taft declared:

> There may be duties of a quasi-judicial character imposed on executive officers and members of executive tribunals whose decisions after hearing affect interests of individuals, the discharge of which the President can not in a particular case properly influence or control. But even in such a case he may consider the decision after its rendition as a reason for removing the officer, on the ground that the discretion regularly entrusted to that officer by statute has not been on the whole intelligently or wisely exercised. Otherwise, he does not discharge his own constitutional duty of seeing that the laws be faithfully executed.[44]

That night, having at long last been delivered of his weighty opinion, the hefty Chief Justice wrote his brother that he felt "like a woman who has given birth to a large Child."[45]

Taft, who prided himself on his ability to mass the Court, suffered the affliction of three separate dissents. Justice Oliver Wendell Holmes required only three paragraphs to state his disapproval of the "spiders' webs" the Chief Justice had woven. Affirming his belief in legislative authority, Holmes said: "We have to deal with an office that owes its existence to Congress and that Congress may abolish tomorrow. Its duration and the pay attached to it while it lasts depend on Congress alone."[46]

Justice James McReynolds prepared a dissent which ran to sixty-two pages, but instead of reading it, he gave an acrid extemporaneous speech from the bench as he was later to do in the Gold Clause Cases.[47] "The decision of the majority of the court is revolutionary, and the sooner the thinking people of the country understand it the better,"

McReynolds said. "Yesterday we supposed we had a government of definitely limited and specified powers. Today no one knows what those Powers are."[48]

The most trenchant dissent came from Justice Brandeis, who distrusted concentrated power whether exercised by a business monopoly or by the state. James Landis, who was Brandeis's law clerk at the time, later called the dissent "as thorough a piece of historical research as you would find in the Supreme Court reports anywhere." He explained:

> It started out with a page and a half. It ended up with, oh, I would say approximately 35 pages. Months were spent on that. . . . I paged, literally paged, every one of the Senate journals from the time of the passage of the Tenure of Office Act. . . . Just in order to determine what the practice was. After all, practice is the important thing in determining constitutional law.[49]

A detailed, learned statement of objections to Taft's arguments, Brandeis's dissent ran fifty-six pages. Mortified by its length, Brandeis offered to pay the cost of printing it, but Taft would not hear of it, though he deeply resented the opinion.[50] In his dissent, Brandeis disputed Taft's claim that the removal power was inherent in the authority of the Executive. Such power, he argued, came from Congress, and the Founding Fathers had opposed granting the President an unlimited removal prerogative. "The conviction prevailed then that the people must look to representative assemblies for protection of their liberties," Brandeis wrote. "And protection of the individual, even if he be an official, from arbitrary or capricious exercise of power was then believed to be an essential of free government." Moreover, he pointed out, the principle of separation of powers had been adopted "not to promote efficiency but to preclude the exercise of arbitrary power. The purpose was not to avoid friction, but, by means of the inevitable friction incident to the distribution of the governmental powers among three departments, to save the people from autocracy."[51]

The *Myers* decision stirred up a storm. For the first time since the *Insular Cases*[52] a quarter of a century earlier, a Supreme Court ruling won front page coverage in the morning newspapers. Taft's opinion met a volley of criticism from a political spectrum ranging from liberals such as Robert M. La Follette, Jr., to conservatives such as Senator George Wharton Pepper, who, at Taft's invitation, had represented the Senate as *amicus curiae*. Thomas Reed Powell found the logic "lame," the language "inconclusive," and the history "far from compelling," while Senator Hiram Johnson sneered that the opinion gratified those who thought the country needed a Mussolini.[53]

So disturbed was the National Municipal League by the possible consequences of *Myers* for local as well as national officials that it invited
Edward S. Corwin, McCormick Professor of Jurisprudence at Princeton
University, to write an analysis. Corwin's monograph, published in
1927, assailed Taft's reasoning and his handling of historical data. The
Constitution, as interpreted by Taft, Corwin protested, "permits congress to vest duties in executive officers in the performance of which
they are to exercise their own independent judgment; then it permits
the president to guillotine such officers for exercising the very discretion
which congress has the right to require of them!" The power of removal,
Corwin concluded, should vary with the nature of the office.[54]

Though such widespread objections might well have made Roosevelt
more hesitant about ousting Humphrey, he did not act capriciously.
Stevens, who had known the FTC from its infancy, advised that, on the
basis of *Shurtleff* and *Myers*, the President could get rid of Humphrey
for whatever reason he wished. He suggested to him that, in removing
Humphrey, he adopt the very language of the order dismissing Shurtleff, and the final order did follow closely the form of McKinley's
edict.[55]

There appeared to be good grounds for Roosevelt, and for lieutenants
such as Stevens and Reed, to feel sanguine. If Taft's opinion had been
raked over, it had also elicited considerable support, particularly in law
journals.[56] Not only commentators who approved of the opinion but
some who deplored it stated that it was now the law of the land that
FTC members were removable by the President at will.[57] A Chicago
attorney, writing in the *American Political Science Review*, applauded the
recognition by the Court of "the untrammeled control by the President
of his subordinates, including . . . the Federal Trade Commission."[58]
Furthermore, no amount of adverse commentary meant as much as the
fact that only nine years had passed since a Chief Justice of the United
States, supported by a majority of his brethren, had found the President's power to be plenary and had, albeit as dictum, validated the application to the kind of agency at hand.

There was one final reason for optimism. The White House had con-
sulted Jim Landis, and the former law clerk, though sympathetic to
Brandeis's dissent, had assured the President of his authority to fire
Humphrey. Landis later told an interviewer:

> I'm not sure who asked me, but I was asked by someone in very close
> connection with the White House as to what I thought about the Presi-
> dent's power to remove a member of the Federal Trade Commission. I
> said I doubt whether there is anybody in the United States that can an-

swer that question better than I can, because I went through the whole Myers controversy, and I know how insistent the Chief Justice (that was Taft) and the majority of the Court was, in placing in that opinion, even though it dealt with a fourth-class postmaster . . . , statements to the effect that the President's power of removal extended to members of various independent commissions. I said, "That was deliberately put there. If that had not been put in there, I doubt whether some of the dissents would have been as bitter as they were."

So indirectly I advised Mr. Roosevelt that there was no question about his power to remove Humphrey.[59]

On May 1, 1935, Solicitor General Reed, comforted by such counsel, came before the Supreme Court to argue the matter in combat against his well-publicized adversary, Colonel Donovan. The suit of Humphrey's executor had been certified to the Supreme Court by the Court of Claims which, instead of ruling, had posed two questions. Both centered on the provision of the FTC statute of 1914 which stipulated: "Any commissioner may be removed by the President for inefficiency, neglect of duty, or malfeasance in office."[60] The Court of Claims asked: Did this section restrict a President's power to discharge commissioners to one of these specific causes? If so, was such a limitation on a President's removal authority constitutional?

The joust between Reed and Donovan took a predictable form. Reed insisted that *Myers* and *Shurtleff* offered sufficient precedent for Roosevelt's action, and he contended that a study of the Act showed that the FTC was "predominantly administrative" with only parts of one section of the 1914 law revealing "legislative agency character." In addition, he maintained that the duty to carry out faithfully such novel legislation as the Securities Act of 1933 "may presuppose wholehearted sympathy with the purposes and policy of the law, and energy and resourcefulness beyond that of the ordinarily efficient public servant. The President should be free to judge in what measure these qualities are possessed and to act upon that judgment." Donovan countered that *Shurtleff* was not relevant because it dealt with an official whose tenure had not been stipulated by statute, and that *Myers* was inapplicable because a postmaster belonged to a different category from a member of a regulatory commission, a type of agency whose independence must be safeguarded from executive domination.[61] The arguments concluded, both sides awaited the verdict of the U. S. Supreme Court on *Humphrey*, a case that, to most of the country, seemed considerably less compelling than the lively controversy over the constitutionality of the National Industrial Recovery Act, one of three important cases docketed for the same day.

V

On May 27, the Supreme Court gathered for the next to the last time in the old Senate chamber. That October, it would reconvene in the marble edifice across the Capitol Plaza. Shortly after noon, the nine black-robed justices filed in, with six of the nine judges who had taken part in *Myers* marching in the procession. Without ceremony, they proceeded to read the day's decisions. First came Pierce Butler's opinion for the Court in an insignificant life insurance suit; as Butler read, spectators in the crowded courtroom squirmed in their seats. They had come expecting more momentous events, and their boredom with this first opinion was transparent.[62]

Attention quickened as the Chief Justice nodded to Justice George Sutherland, and Sutherland, in an indistinct murmur, began to read his fourteen-page opinion in the case of *Humphrey's Executor v. U. S.*[63] For some minutes, as Sutherland recited the terms of the Federal Trade Commission Act, the thrust of his opinion was not apparent. In an orderly fashion, he dealt in turn with each of the questions posed by the Court of Claims. Did the FTC law restrict the power of a President to remove a commissioner except for cause? Of that, there could be little doubt. Nor could one dispute that Roosevelt had not removed Humphrey for cause; instead of charging him with some dereliction like malfeasance, he had indiscreetly written that their minds did not go along together.

The crucial question was the second asked of the Court: Was the restriction on a President's removal power set forth in the FTC law valid? Here the Court came squarely up against the *Myers* precedent. Though Sutherland had joined in Taft's opinion, he now denied its relevance to the Humphrey matter. All that *Myers* had settled, he declared, was that a President could dismiss a postmaster, but "the office of a postmaster is so essentially unlike the office now involved that the decision in the Myers case cannot be accepted as controlling." But had not the Chief Justice said a good deal more than that in *Myers*? Sutherland remarked breezily: "In the course of the opinion of the court, expressions occur which tend to sustain the government's contention, but these are beyond the point involved, and therefore, do not come within the rule of *stare decisis*. In so far as they are out of harmony with the views here set forth, these expressions are disapproved." Without ever joining issue with Taft directly, Sutherland noted that "dicta . . . may be followed if sufficiently persuasive but . . . are not controlling."

Sutherland then sought to explain how the office of a postmaster differed from that of a federal trade commissioner. "A postmaster is an executive officer restricted to the performance of executive functions," Sutherland stated. "He is charged with no duty at all related to either legislative or judicial power." *Myers*, he insisted, applied to "purely executive officers," not to "an officer who occupies no place in the executive department and who exercises no part of the executive power vested by the Constitution in the President."

Justice Sutherland continued:

> The Federal Trade Commission is an administrative body created by Congress to carry into effect legislative policies. . . . Such a body cannot in any proper sense be characterized as an arm or eye of the executive. Its duties are performed without executive leave and . . . must be free from executive control. In administering the provisions of the statute . . . the commission acts in part quasi-legislatively and in part quasi-judicially. . . . To the extent that it exercises any executive function—as distinguished from executive power in the constitutional sense—it does so in the discharge and effectuation of its quasi-legislative or quasi-judicial powers, or as an agency of the legislative or judicial departments of the government.

After noting that if a President were conceded unlimited power to remove members of the FTC, he would, in principle, be able to remove at will almost all civil officers, including judges of the Court of Claims, Sutherland declared:

> We think it plain under the Constitution that illimitable power of removal is not possessed by the President in respect of officers of the character of those just named. The authority of Congress, in creating quasi-legislative or quasi-judicial agencies, to require them to act in discharge of their duties independently of executive control, cannot well be doubted; and that authority includes, as an appropriate incident, power to fix the period during which they shall continue, and to forbid their removal except for cause in the meantime.

The doctrine of illimitable power of removal, Sutherland contended, did violence to the principle of the separation of powers. "Its coercive influence," he observed, "threatens the independence of a commission, which is not only wholly disconnected from the executive department, but which . . . was created by Congress as a means of carrying into operation legislative and judicial powers, and as an agency of the legislative and judicial departments." He conceded that the Court might be bequeathing a "field of doubt" between the two rulings, but he added: "We leave such cases as may fall within it for future consideration and determination as they arise."

Only when Sutherland ended his reading and no dissents were announced did the full import of the decision become clear. By a unanimous 9–0 verdict, the Court had ruled that Roosevelt had exceeded his authority, and, by implication, it had instructed the Court of Claims to award Humphrey's estate back pay. Sutherland had adroitly put together an opinion which caused a minimum of embarrassment for the Court, whatever other failings it might have. There was not a suggestion that he, as well as three of his brethren—Van Devanter, Butler, and Stone—had gone along with Taft's sweeping opinion in *Myers* or that the President had ample grounds for believing that *Myers* represented the Court's view of the scope of his powers in 1933.[64] For Franklin Roosevelt, it was but the first of the rebuffs he would receive that afternoon. For Will Humphrey, it was a posthumous triumph, the old crosspatch's final victory.

VI

The "field of doubt" the Court had left was far more extensive than Sutherland suggested: no one has yet measured its metes and bounds. Even commentators who approved of the *Humphrey* decision found Sutherland's discussion of executive power confusing. Analysts familiar with the operation of the Federal Trade Commission were startled by his contention that an FTC member occupied "no place in the executive department." Nor could commissions like the FTC be categorized as "arms of Congress" in any meaningful sense, since they performed executive and judicial functions which Congress could not perform constitutionally. Besides, as Robert E. Cushman of Cornell has noted, "No task has been given to an independent regulatory commission which could not, with equal constitutional propriety, be given to an executive officer."[65]

Corwin, while generally in accord with the *Humphrey* result, later observed:

> The truth is that some of Justice Sutherland's dicta are quite as extreme in one direction as some of Chief Justice Taft's dicta were in the opposite direction; and especially does he provoke wonderment by his assertion that a member of the Federal Trade Commission "*occupies no place in the executive department.*" . . . The dictum seems to have been the product of hasty composition, for certainly it is not to be squared by any verbal legerdemain with more deliberate utterances of the same Justice. . . .
> Moreover if a Federal Trade Commissioner is not in the executive department, where is he? In the legislative department; or is he, forsooth, in the uncomfortable halfway situation of Mahomet's coffin, suspended

"'twixt Heaven and Earth?" . . . . Nor is Justice Sutherland's endeavor to make out that [Federal] Trade Commissioners are any more "agents of Congress" than is a postmaster at all persuasive. Both officials get their powers—such as they are—from an exercise by Congress of its constitutionally delegated powers; there is no other possible source.[66]

Sutherland's implication that the FTC was in the legislative branch had first been enunciated during the debates on the FTC bill in 1914. Most lawmakers expressed no interest in the question whether the new commission was a direct agent of Congress, but when the measure was amended to expand the agency's powers, Senator Albert Cummins explained: "The trade commission . . . is purely an executive or administrative tribunal. It exercises no legislative function whatever." Alone of all the Senators, Sutherland persisted in describing the proposed agency as a "legislative commission." Strangely, in light of the *Humphrey* opinion, it was Senator Sutherland who delivered the main argument against the constitutionality of the FTC bill; in particular, he objected that the new commission was being vested with judicial powers. As Cushman has observed drily, in 1914 Sutherland had not yet "discovered the possibilities of the terms quasi-legislative and quasi-judicial."[67]

In 1937, a colloquy took place that raised doubts about whether Sutherland understood the implications of what he had said in *Humphrey* two years earlier. During oral argument, James W. Ryan, an attorney for a shipping company, stated that the Shipping Board was not in the executive branch. Cushman has described what ensued, as reported to him by someone who had observed the proceedings:

Justice Sutherland, who had been sitting back in his chair and asking occasional questions during the course of the argument, leaned forward quickly when he heard this.

"Did you say that the Shipping Board was not in the executive branch of the government?" He spoke as though he did not believe he had heard correctly, and several other Justices smiled condescendingly at counsel as though he were making a far-fetched proposition.

"Yes, your Honor," Mr. Ryan replied.

"What makes you think that? Where do you find any legal basis for such a conclusion?" the Justice wished to know.

"Why in your Honor's opinion in the Humphrey case, this Court held that the Federal Trade Commission and similar regulatory agencies were not in the executive branch of the government. The Shipping Board fell within the same general category as the Federal Trade Commission and the Interstate Commerce Commission." Mr. Ryan then proceeded to read certain portions of that opinion.

"What branch of the Government do you think the Shipping board was in, if it was not in the executive branch?" the Justice wanted to know.

"In the legislative branch, your Honor."

Justice Sutherland shook his head, as though he disagreed, and seemed to be thinking the question over as the discussion went on to other points.[68]

In ruling out any kind of role for a President in the functioning of independent commissions, Sutherland never troubled to look at the actual history of the FTC and similar tribunals. One would not gather from the Court's opinion that any of Roosevelt's predecessors had ever tried to influence the Commission. Yet Wilson had secured inclusion in the FTC law of a clause authorizing the President to direct the Trade Commission to make investigations, and he had used that power frequently. As "weak" a President as Calvin Coolidge had made clear that he viewed these commissions as subordinate to the will of the chief executive. Coolidge, indeed, had gone far beyond anything Roosevelt later did in the Humphrey affair when, in offering an appointment on the Tariff Commission to David J. Lewis, he stipulated that Lewis submit an undated resignation that Coolidge could use at any time he saw fit.[69]

Though Sutherland insisted that the FTC was a creature of Congress and must be kept independent of the executive, Congress had, on more than one occasion, indicated its belief that the President had various kinds of authority over the Commission, and it had even scolded the President for the FTC's deficiencies. "In short," Cushman has written, "the commission was very definitely an agent of the executive branch and was recognized by Congress as being so." He summed up the situation at the time Roosevelt took office: "Throughout the discussions of this whole period there runs an underlying assumption that the commission's policy, if not actually directed from the White House, at least conforms to the President's wishes, that the President cannot escape responsibility for the commission's policy, and that an incoming President objecting to such policy should change it, if not by the actual issuance of orders to the commission, at least by the making of suitable appointments." In removing Humphrey, Cushman concluded, "the President was apparently doing in this situation what Congress assumed that he would and should do."[70]

Congress, perceived to be one of the beneficiaries of the *Humphrey* ruling, found the implications of the opinion perplexing. In 1938, when Congress faced the question of drafting legislation to regulate the aviation industry, Representative Clarence Lea explained the measure that he was sponsoring: "It is the belief of the committee that we have written a bill in harmony with the Humphrey decision. We limit the power of the President to remove the members of the authority. We leave him unlimited authority to remove the members of the safety board and the administrator, because those officers are manifestly executive officers, concerning whom the President has the right of removal." Yet the matter remained confusing:

MR. BOREN. Under the Humphrey decision, the Federal Trade Commission is made an orphan child, so far as the three constitutional branches of the Government are concerned?

MR. HESTER. That is correct. [71]

Sutherland's exegesis bypassed the very difficult issue of how the fused functions of the independent tribunals may be reconciled with the doctrine of separation of powers. The Interstate Commerce Commission, for example, has been variously described as "an executive body," "wholly legislative," and "in essence a judicial tribunal." Sutherland's opinion gave most comfort to those who thought of the three branches as warring sovereignties and who aligned themselves with Congress against the President. The Detroit *Free Press*, in criticizing the removal of Humphrey, had referred to Congress and "the rival establishment centered in the White House."[72]

For those who believed that commissions must be kept free of "political control," *Humphrey* was a thrilling triumph. The decision, said one jurist, "echoed down the corridors of the independent tribunals and administrative bodies of the government. . . . It throws a mantle of protection over a large group of public officers who are called upon to exercise independent judgment without fear of political reprisal."[73] In a confidential interview a month after the decision, Justice Brandeis, pleased by the outcome, warned that if such commissions could not act autonomously, the country would have, in effect, a dictatorship. "What would happen to us if Huey Long were President and such a doctrine prevailed?" he asked.[74]

Felix Frankfurter, who endorsed virtually everything Roosevelt did to the point of sycophancy, must have surprised the editor of the *New Republic* when he told him that he hoped the *Humphrey* ruling would be commended. He asserted:

That really is a right decision from any point of rightness. You must remember that in that case the Court sustained the power of Congress. A contrary decision would really make impossible ever building up a decent

Civil Service in the technical fields in this country. The Meyers [sic] case decided less than ten years ago was the one that was mischievous.

Quite apart from his assessment of the merits of the case, Frankfurter may, in this instance, have found the tug of his allegiance to Brandeis, the dissenter in *Myers*, stronger than his affinity for FDR.[75]

VII

Of the many misconceptions surrounding the *Humphrey* case, none is so striking as the misunderstanding of Franklin Roosevelt's aims. Many criticized the ouster as an attempt by the President to create another opportunity for patronage. Humphrey himself wrote Senator Dill: "The truth about it is that the action of the President is about the boldest act to restore the spoils system that has occurred since the days of Andrew Jackson." Several weeks later, he protested to Senator Norris: "When I remember that during all the time I have been in this office, I have not written a political letter, or made a political speech, or made a political contribution . . . I feel exasperated that I should be removed for purely political reasons." Humphrey's defenders repeatedly castigated Roosevelt for trying to "Tammanyize" the national government. "The deduction is a simple one, that Mr. Humphrey being a real Republican was therefore objectionable to the President," asserted Congressman Hooper. "If Mr. Hoover had removed a Democrat for *purely political reasons* from an office such as this, the country would have rung with denunciations."[76]

Those who attributed Roosevelt's removal of Humphrey to "political" motivations quite missed the point; the President fired Humphrey not because he was a Republican but because the obstreperous Commissioner might sabotage an important New Deal operation. At first glance, it appears surprising that Roosevelt would run the risk of discharging Humphrey when he already had enough vacancies on the FTC to control the agency. Yet Humphrey was an adamant conservative. When a friend, in jest, called him a "standpatter," he replied: "When I think of the 'brain trust,' the progressives and the other fanatics and reformers, I think the word 'standpatter' is a badge of distinction and honor."[77] It seemed highly likely that Humphrey, as the senior member of a commission which now had added duties under the National Industrial Recovery Act and the Securities Act, would create dissension within the government.

Roosevelt viewed that prospect with particular alarm because of his determination to alter the balance of power between business and the State. Any new administration must be prepared to tolerate the presence of holdovers in such tribunals, but FDR was impatient because he regarded his coming to power in the crisis of March 1933 as no ordinary changing of the guard. If the New Deal did not mark a "revolution" in American government, it did represent, in areas such as regulation of Wall Street, a significant departure. Roosevelt was unwilling to leave a man of the old order in charge of administering the legislation of the new order.

When the incoming President sought to rebuild the government to enable it to cope with the catastrophe of the Great Depression, he quickly recognized that the Federal Trade Commission cried for attention. If his administration was to have coherence, he could not permit the FTC to move in opposite directions from the National Recovery Administration in policies toward business. Furthermore, though it was no doubt a mistake to turn the administration of the Securities Act over to the FTC, once that had been done Roosevelt could not afford to maintain the fiction that the Commission was a tribunal which should be altogether "independent" of executive influence.

The Trade Commission demanded executive leadership for other reasons as well. Born of high hopes, it had proven a painful disappointment. A former commissioner remarked that the chief function of the FTC had come to be "preventing false and misleading advertising in reference to hair restorers, anti-fat remedies, etc.—a somewhat inglorious end to a noble experiment." Called on to carry out a policy on the trusts about which no one could agree, the FTC had not only been hampered by the courts but assaulted by interest groups speaking through Congressmen. One Commissioner recalled: "Senators who would not think of seeking to influence a court in the decision of a case pending before it have no compunction about stalking the halls of the Commission and offering *ex parte* arguments and representations concerning cases pending before it." If the FTC was to maintain its independence against the claims of such interests, it needed strong backing from an administration that would take responsibility for its actions. Roosevelt thought he could give that kind of support only if he had officials sympathetic to his program. As early as 1926, Senator Norris had stated: "It seems to me that if the Commission is to function, if it is to continue to perform the work that the law designed it to perform, its personnel must be of men who believe in that kind of law."[78]

FDR's removal of Humphrey constituted not an isolated episode but one skirmish in a well-coordinated campaign to reshape the national government. When the President took office, he found most of the commissions manned by Republican appointees hostile to the New Deal. "We stood in the city of Washington on March 4th," Roosevelt's adviser Raymond Moley recalled, "like a handful of marauders in a hostile territory." Pendleton Herring has explained:

> When President Franklin D. Roosevelt embarked upon his plans for national recovery, he gathered into his hands every strand of authority that might lead toward his objectives. At the level of the presidential office, a greater degree of integration was introduced into the federal administrative organization than has ever been witnessed in peacetime experience. And the reach of the President did not falter before the independent commissions. The problems of these bodies were regarded as presidential responsibilities as well. The tasks of the Federal Trade Commission, the Tariff Commission, or the Interstate Commerce Commission could not be separated from the rehabilitation of trade and industry. Yet how could these establishments participate in a national recovery program and still remain administrative agencies? The President got around this difficulty in his characteristically adroit fashion. Placing his key men in the departments was a simple matter but bringing the independent establishment within his control required more ingenuity. The judicial calm of the Interstate Commerce Commission was left undisturbed, but the most able and aggressive commissioner was created federal coordinator of transportation. The Tariff Commission was reduced to a harmless position through the passage of the reciprocal tariff act. The Radio Commission was abolished outright and a New Deal commission took its place. The President secured the resignation of Hoover's chairman of the Power Commission and added two appointees of his own. [79]

The ouster of Humphrey represented only one step in that march of events.

VIII

The *Humphrey* decision stunned the Roosevelt administration. "Today was a bad day for the Government in the Supreme Court," Cummings noted in his diary. "It lost the Humphrey case much to the surprise of most everyone." He added: "In order to decide against the Government, the Supreme Court had to reverse itself and attempt to make distinctions which, I must admit, do not exist. The significance of this decision, however, lies in the disposition of the Court to curb the executive powers of the President." [80]

The President and his circle thought that Sutherland had malevolently subjected Roosevelt to a public humiliation by making it appear that he had been willfully violating the Constitution. Had the Court admitted that it was modifying *Myers,* and had it conceded that FDR might have been acting in good faith in being guided by that earlier opinion, the

Court's ruling in *Humphrey* would not have aroused so much resentment. Though Frankfurter approved of the *Humphrey* decision, he wrote subsequently:

> Of all the silly things, one of the silliest is to charge F. D.'s dismissal of Humphreys [sic] as an act of lawlessness. No lawyer with proper respect for the Supreme Court would have advised the President otherwise than he was advised— . . . that in view of the *Myers* Case he was free to terminate Humphreys' services without charges. . . . It was almost indecent, and certainly not judicial-minded, the way in which the Court swallowed the weighty and deliberate scope of Taft's opinion in the *Myers* Case.

In like manner, Robert H. Jackson commented:

> Within the Administration there was a profound feeling that the opinion of the Court was written with a design to give the impression that the President had flouted the Constitution, rather than that the Court had simply changed its mind within the past ten years. The decision could easily have forestalled this by recognizing the President's reliance on an opinion of Chief Justice Taft. But the decision contained no such gracious acknowledgment. What the Court had before declared to be a constitutional duty of the President had become in Mr. Roosevelt a constitutional offense.

The White House deduced that "the Court was applying to President Roosevelt rules different from those it had applied to his predecessors" and that there was a "touch of malice" in Sutherland's opinion.[81]

Of Roosevelt's anger at the opinion, there could be no doubt. Sutherland's objection to presidential supremacy in 1935 when he had accepted Taft's assertion of that very doctrine in 1926 raised the suspicion that the main difference in the two cases lay less in their nature than in the fact that FDR was now in the White House. The *Humphrey* ruling went far to persuade the President that, sooner or later, he would have to take bold action against a Court that, from personal animus, was determined to embarrass him and to destroy his program. Jackson commented afterward: "I really think the decision that made Roosevelt madder at the Court than any other decision was that damn little case of *Humphrey's Executor v. United States.* The President thought they went out of their way to spite him personally and they were giving him a different kind of deal than they were giving Taft."[82]

Rexford Tugwell has suggested not only that Roosevelt's eventual effort to curb the Court may have come from irritation at the *Humphrey* decision, but also that his vexation at this opinion determined the character of the particular plan he submitted, a plan doomed to defeat. Tugwell observed:

> If Franklin, who not only had a vivid sense of presidential prerogatives but who by election and reelection was the chosen leader of the American people, felt that the obstructions of the Court constituted an impertinent denial of his right to act as leader, there was certainly justification. It has been suggested that the Humphries [sic] case constituted an affront to the presidency. It may very well have been that case, even more than the other decisions of 1935, which provided the motive for the post-election attempt to humiliate the Court in turn; for of all the ways open to him, Franklin does seem to have chosen the one most upsetting to judicial dignity. And it was this more than anything else—more even than the attempt to reduce the judicial power—which created reaction of a violence he hardly anticipated. [83]

Joseph Alsop and Turner Catledge, authors of the earliest account of the subsequent Supreme Court battle, have offered a similar interpretation:

> The President's character was the deciding element in the struggle. . . . Essentially the fight's course was decided by the fact that the Court had wantonly offended every strongest trait in the President.
>
> Perhaps the most immediate of the Court's offenses was its denial of satisfaction to the President's taste for power. The President regards great powers as his prerogative. . . . It is significant that those close to him have said that he was most angered by the decision in the comparatively trivial Humphries [sic] case. . . . The President saw in the decision the most direct of all possible trespasses on his powers as Chief Executive; he was completely infuriated. [84]

When, in February 1937, Roosevelt precipitated the historic controversy over his endeavor to "pack" the Supreme Court, a number of his opponents traced the conflict back to *Humphrey*. On the very next day, Representative Earl C. Michener, Michigan Republican, commented on Roosevelt's message:

> The President used a lot of words and indulged in a lot of argument to tell Congress something the Congress already knew, to wit, that the President is convinced that if the mind of the Supreme Court, the mind of the Federal Trade Commission, as in the Humphrey case, or the mind of any other government agency does not run along with the President's mind, then the agency should be changed. [85]

The following month Dr. Edmund A. Walsh, S. J., vice-president of Georgetown University, stated that future historians would find the origins of the controversy between Roosevelt and the Court in the summary removal of Commissioner Humphrey, and Ray Lyman Wilbur, who had been Hoover's Secretary of the Interior, wrote a friend: "In my judgment you are quite right in going back to the Humphrey decision. That was the first knock-out blow from the Court and no doubt was an offense to the idea that the Tammany system could be made national."[86]

Roosevelt, who had been frustrated by the Court in *Humphrey*, was to meet defeat on the Supreme Court measure in no small part because many liberals who shared his annoyance at a Court which had invalidated so much social legislation did not agree with the President's conception of executive power. Tugwell has written:

> They feared an indefinitely strengthened executive. They were highly sensitized to dictatorship by Hitler and Mussolini; and Franklin had shown signs, they thought, of suggestive impatience. . . . They . . . wanted . . . the legislative branch to regulate business in the interest of public welfare. . . . But they did not want, as Franklin did, to reconstitute the Court so that on no issue could it oppose the other branches. Decidedly, this was too much. They felt, for instance, that the Court was right in the matter of Humphries [sic], which had so incensed Franklin.[87]

From his first communication to Humphrey, Roosevelt had displayed that indifference to public sensitivity about unchecked presidential power that was to cause him so much grief in the Court-packing scheme. If his critics were sanctimonious, the President himself was careless about quieting uneasiness regarding the vast power concentrated in his hands and about the threat that was perceived to the civil service and the capacity of officials to render disinterested judgments. Roosevelt's action in removing Humphrey was not an arbitrary deed but a rational attempt to enable the President to shape the economic policy for which he would be held responsible. But it did not seem to be—and that made all the difference.

The Origins of Franklin D. Roosevelt's "Court-packing" Plan

[The adverse decisions in *Rail Pension, Humphrey,* and close to a dozen other cases, conspicuously those in which the National Industrial Recovery Act and the Agricultural Adjustment Act were struck down, turned Roosevelt's thoughts toward altering either the Constitution or the judiciary, a course that culminated in the controversial "Court-packing" bill of 1937. I first explored the origins of that legislation in an essay published in the *Supreme Court Review 1966,* edited by Philip B. Kurland. I have considerably altered that article to reflect research I have done in sources opened since it appeared, notably the Homer S. Cummings papers at the University of Virginia. Work in these manuscripts results in a markedly different account from that set forth in the standard version of Joseph Alsop and Turner Catledge.]

I

No event of twentieth-century constitutional history is better remembered than Franklin D. Roosevelt's ill-fated "Court-packing" scheme of 1937; yet the origins of the plan remain obscure and are often misstated. The proposal has been variously attributed to Felix Frankfurter, who had nothing at all to do with it; to "two brilliant young brain-trusters," Benjamin Cohen and Thomas Corcoran, who favored a different remedy and had almost no hand in shaping this one; and to Samuel I. Rosenman, who played only a minor role after the decision had already been made.[1] Among those who have been said to have helped frame the plan were James M. Landis, who had heard only rumors of it before it was announced, and Robert H. Jackson, who first learned of the legislation when he read about FDR's message of February 5 in a Philadelphia newspaper. The project has been described either as an impulsive act born of the *hubris* created by FDR's landslide victory in 1936 or as a calculated plot hatched many months before in angry resentment at the *Schechter* decision striking down the National Industrial Recovery Act. A widely circulated columnist wrote that the scheme resulted from the influence on the President of a "junta" of radicals, some of them "sympathetic to theories from Russia." Roosevelt himself never said anything to clear up the confusion. Three weeks after the President launched the proposal, Senator Hiram Johnson of California wrote a friend: "He has been beaten from pillar to post upon when he conceived the brilliant idea, and how he conceived it."[2]

II

The constitutional crisis of 1937 had been brewing for a long while. Franklin Roosevelt began his political career at the time when his distant cousin Theodore was assaulting the sanctity of the courts and the air was loud with cries for the recall of judges and judicial decisions. In the 1920s, mounting progressive animus toward the Taft Court manifested itself in such ways as the Robert M. La Follette platform of 1924, which called for empowering Congress to override the Supreme Court. In the Hoover years, progressives had waged fierce contests against the confirmations of Supreme Court nominees John J. Parker and Charles Evans Hughes. Increasingly, liberals believed that a majority of the Justices spoke for the interests of the rich and well-born, and FDR agreed with that criticism.[3]

Even before Roosevelt took office, he had aroused speculation over whether his presidency would result in a confrontation with the Court. In a campaign speech in Baltimore on October 5, 1932, he blurted out: "After March 4, 1929, the Republican party was in complete control of all branches of the government—the Legislature, with the Senate and Congress; and the executive departments; and I may add, for full measure, to make it complete, the United States Supreme Court as well." This last clause had been interpolated in the original text of the address, but the next day Roosevelt told Senator James F. Byrnes: "What I said last night about the judiciary is true, and whatever is in a man's heart is apt to come to his tongue—I shall not make any explanations or apology for it!" Republicans, though, hopped on FDR's statement as a warning that, if elected President, he might, in Herbert Hoover's words, "reduce the tribunal to an instrument of party policy."[4]

Roosevelt, who was right in thinking that the composition of the federal courts was heavily Republican,[5] found an even greater source of concern in the doctrines pronounced by the Supreme Court in decisions as recent as 1932,[6] but he hoped that the aged Justices would recognize the Depression to be an emergency justifying unprecedented government action. In his inaugural address on March 4, 1933, the new chief executive stated: "Our Constitution is so simple and practical that it is possible always to meet extraordinary needs by changes in emphasis and arrangement without loss of essential form."[7]

Roosevelt, however, eyed the Court warily in his first two years in the White House. The Administration put off tests of the constitutionality of the legislation of the First Hundred Days as long as possible; as a result the Supreme Court did not have the opportunity to rule on a New Deal statute until 1935. Meanwhile, the President was heartened by two 1934 decisions in *Blaisdell* and *Nebbia*, which, though only by 5–4, appeared to indicate that the emergency might be the occasion for governmental restrictions on property rights. Especially encouraging was Justice Roberts's statement in *Nebbia*: "This court from the early days affirmed that the power to promote the general welfare is inherent in government."[8]

Such a pronouncement served, for the moment, to dispel the conviction that a collision between Roosevelt and the judiciary was inevitable and that steps must be taken to revamp the Supreme Court, ideas that emerged remarkably early. In January 1933, some seven weeks before FDR took office, Homer Cummings, who subsequently became Attorney General after Roosevelt's original designee died, recorded in his diary a conversation with William G. McAdoo, U. S. Senator from California:

> [McAdoo] also discussed the possibility of changing the law with regard to the Supreme Court so as to get the antiquated judges off the bench. He was wondering if a law could be drawn that would be constitutional. . . . He thought perhaps a bill could be drafted that would stand a constitutional test if it provided, for instance, that the judges become emeritus as it were after they became 70 or 72 . . . , that their salaries would go on, and that they could sit with the Supreme Court when requested by the Chief Justice but no more than one at a time. He suggested I have the matter briefed in my office and said that if it could be worked, he would be glad to introduce such a bill. He said he had talked to Governor Roosevelt about it and the latter liked the idea. McAdoo said that this would get rid of some of the "old fossils" though he would regret to see Brandeis go.[9]

Advocates of change sometimes accompanied the idea of ridding the Court of Methuselahs with the notion of expanding the size of the bench by adding younger, more liberal Justices. Almost two years before the Court had invalidated the first New Deal law, an Illinois man wrote the President: "Sometimes I get thinking about the many millions who are unemployed, and I wonder, if we really can get them back to work, and retain our social order. . . . If the Supreme Court's membership could be increased to twelve, without too much trouble, perhaps the Constitution would be found to be quite elastic." As early as January 1934, the *Literary Digest* reported: "In the intimate Presidential circle the idea of reconstituting the Supreme Court has been considered. . . . In the conversation within the Roosevelt circle, a court of fifteen, instead of the present nine, has been mentioned." The *Digest* added that the *Blaisdell* decision sustaining the Minnesota mortgage moratorium law, which indicated a liberal majority on the Court, had caused such talk among the New Dealers to subside.[10]

Yet conservatives remained uneasy. The following month, Henry Prather Fletcher, soon to be chosen Republican national chairman, wrote the columnist Mark Sullivan: "You seem to rely on the Courts for relief in the last analysis. Let us hope the Supreme Court will not bend before the storm—but even if it does not, it is the weakest of the three coordinate branches of the Government and an administration as fully in control as this one is can pack it as easily as an English Government can pack the House of Lords."[11]

III

At the start of 1935 the period of nervous calm abruptly shattered. On January 7, 1935, in its first ruling on a New Deal law, the Court invalidated the "hot oil" provisions of the National Industrial Recovery Act, with only one Justice dissenting.[12] The Republican New York *Herald Tribune* commented:

> In the skylarking days of 1933-34, the happy administrators of the New Deal brushed aside the Supreme Court as they brushed aside Congress and the Constitution. . . . The President paid perfunctory lip-service to the nation's charter of liberty. Behind the scene the whispers were loud enough to be beyond misunderstanding. Let the Supreme Court try to halt the march of the new order, according to F. D. R., an Act of Congress would be passed adding to its membership and packing it with enough Tugwellian jurists to overturn any conservative decision overnight.

Now, the *Herald Tribune* exulted, the emphatic 8-to-1 split had thrown "this revolutionary nonsense into the Potomac where it belongs."[13]

The New Dealers actually found the "hot oil" decision, which rested on procedural defects that might be corrected, much less alarming than the tests of the constitutionality of gold legislation making their way relentlessly toward the Supreme Court. A ruling for the plaintiffs would deny Congress the right to regulate the currency at a time of national economic disaster and would create financial chaos by increasing the country's debt by nearly $70 billion. Washington officials, observed Arthur Krock of the *New York Times*, were more absorbed with the question of how the Court would decide than by any subject since the bank holiday of March 1933. In contemplation of that opinion, cold shivers "chase up and down their spines when they waken in the night."[14]

At a Cabinet meeting on January 11, 1935, Attorney General Homer S. Cummings reported on the *Gold Clause Cases*, which he had just finished arguing. Secretary of the Interior Harold L. Ickes noted in his diary:

> The Attorney General went so far as to say that if the Court went against the Government, the number of justices should be increased at once so as to give a favorable majority. As a matter of fact, the President suggested this possibility to me during our interview on Thursday, and I told him that that is precisely what ought to be done. It wouldn't be the first time that the Supreme Court had been increased in size to meet a temporary emergency and it certainly would be justified in this case.[15]

Many in the Administration had an almost apocalyptic sense of inevitable conflict. After the Cabinet session on January 11, Ickes reported:

> I told the President yesterday that only a few years ago I had predicted that sooner or later the Supreme Court would become a political issue as the result of its continued blocking of the popular will through declaring acts of Congress unconstitutional. During the discussion today the Vice President said that he had read a pamphlet which had been written about a hundred years ago in which the author advanced the theory that sooner or later, through the aggrandizement of power by the Supreme Court, a political crisis of major magnitude would be precipitated in this country.[16]

Close observers anticipated that the President would not permit the Court to disrupt his attempts to achieve recovery, even if his resolve led to a constitutional crisis. In his Kings Feature Syndicate column, Arthur Brisbane created a stir when he questioned whether there was any constitutional authority for the practice of judicial review. Brisbane wrote:

As a matter of constitutional law, as actually written by the constitutional convention, if the Supreme Court should say to the President of the United States "We find unconstitutional, and ask you to revoke, your law abolishing the gold clause," the President might reasonably reply, "I have your message and respectfully request that you show me what part of the Constitution authorizes you to nullify a law passed by the Congress of the United States and signed by the President."

If he sent that message, the Supreme Court would be puzzled, for it could show nothing in the Constitution.[17]

Roosevelt was, in fact, ready to act much as Brisbane suggested. A month earlier, in response to an inquiry from the President, Robert H. Jackson, general counsel of the Bureau of Internal Revenue and a future Supreme Court Justice, had suggested that the government might withdraw its consent to be sued. Accordingly, a message to Congress was drafted recommending the withdrawal of the right to sue the United States for more than the face value of government bonds and other obligations. In the event of an adverse decision, Roosevelt was prepared with a proclamation of national emergency to regulate currency transactions; for ninety days, no payment on any contract would be permitted save at the rate of $35 for an ounce of gold, the rate fixed by the President on January 31, 1934, under authority of the Gold Reserve Act.[18]

If the Supreme Court ruled against the government, Roosevelt was prepared to deliver a defiant radio address in which he would declare that the decision, if enforced, would result in "unconscionable" profit to investors, bankruptcy for almost every railroad and for many corporations, default by state and local governments, and wholesale mortgage foreclosures on farms and in cities. It would not only increase the national debt by a staggering sum but would catapult the nation "into an infinitely more serious economic plight than we have yet experienced." He did not seek a quarrel with the Supreme Court, but he did think it appropriate to quote from Lincoln's First Inaugural Address:

> The candid citizen must confess that if the policy of the government, upon vital questions affecting the whole people, is to be irrevocably fixed by decisions of the Supreme Court, the instant they are made, in ordinary litigation between parties in personal actions, the people will have ceased to be their own rulers, having to that extent practically resigned their government into the hands of that eminent tribunal.

Neither the President nor Congress, Roosevelt planned to say, could "stand idly by and . . . permit the decision of the Supreme Court to be carried through to its logical, inescapable conclusion," because that would "imperil the economic and political security of this nation." He sought only to carry out the principle that "For value received the same value should be repaid," a doctrine "in accordance with the Golden Rule, with the precepts of the Scriptures, and the dictates of common sense." "In order to attain this reasonable end," the President intended to announce, "I shall immediately take such steps as may be necessary, by proclamation and by message to the Congress of the United States."[19]

On February 18, as word reached the White House that the Justices had assembled, Roosevelt took his place at the Cabinet table to await word. Minutes later, the tension broke, as it became clear that in each of a series of cases, the government had won.[20] On the following day, the President sent a saucy note to Joseph P. Kennedy, chairman of the SEC:

> With you I think Monday, February eighteenth, was an historic day. As a lawyer it seems to me that the Supreme Court has at last definitely put human values ahead of the "pound of flesh" called for by a contract.
>
> The Chairman of the Securities Exchange Commission turns out to be far more accurate than the Associated Press in that he reported the decisions accurately. How fortunate it is that his Exchanges will never know how close they came to being closed up by a stroke of the pen of one "J. P. K."
>
> Likewise, the Nation will never know what a great treat it missed in not hearing the marvelous radio address the "Pres" had prepared for delivery to the Nation Monday night if the cases had gone the other way.[21]

Roosevelt and his followers knew, though, that it had been a near thing. "In spite of our rejoicing," he wrote, "I shudder at the closeness of five to four decisions in these important matters!" Congressmen began to talk more seriously about the need to find some way to restrain the Court. Senator George Norris protested: "These five to four Supreme Court decisions on the constitutionality of congressional acts it seems to me are illogical and should not occur in a country like ours."[22]

Three months later, the New Dealers got news of yet another 5-to-4 decision, and this one gave them a bad jolt, for, with Justice Owen Roberts joining the majority, the Court invalidated the Railway Retirement Act of 1934.[23] The implications of the ruling carried well beyond its effects on railroad workers. Many believed that if Justice Roberts disposed of other cases as he had this one, the pending social security bill, when enacted, would also be invalidated. "Congratulations to rail carriers over pension decision yesterday," the general attorney for the

Cudahy Packing Company wired a spokesman for the railroads. "That monumental decision so parallels our necessities in connection with Social Security legislation that we owe you a debt for fight now vindicating constitutional interpretation upon which all American business stands for future welfare all citizens." The ruling, wrote *Business Week*, indicated that the Court "would smash any social security legislation that may be passed by Congress."[24]

For the first time since Roosevelt took office, the Court had delivered an opinion that impelled an important interest group to demand restrictions on the Court's powers.[25] The president of one railroad brotherhood called the decision, which affected a million railroad workers, a "bitter disappointment." From Wichita Falls, Texas, one man wrote Roosevelt: "I Had an idea they would turn Down that Railroad Pension. I told you the Rich Men always Run to the Supreme Court to Beat Our Laws. . . . The Supreme Court is a Public Nuisance."[26]

Prodded by the *Rail Pension* decision, which raised the alarming likelihood that Justice Roberts had joined the conservatives to create a permanent 5-to-4 majority against the New Deal, the Roosevelt administration began to explore possibilities of counter actions. Before the week was out, Cummings sent a memorandum to his Assistant Attorney General asking him to look into "the question of the right of the Congress, by legislation, to limit the terms and conditions upon which the Supreme Court can pass on constitutional questions."[27]

IV

On "Black Monday," May 27, 1935, in three 9-to-0 decisions, the Court invalidated the National Industrial Recovery Act and the Frazier-Lemke Act on mortgage moratoria and, in *Humphrey's Executor v. United States*, circumscribed the President's power to remove members of independent regulatory commissions.[28] Roosevelt was incensed by the overturning of the NRA, the keystone of his industrial recovery program.[29] The Court's language in denouncing the delegation of powers and its narrow construction of the commerce clause appeared to place other New Deal laws in jeopardy and to bar the way to new legislation.[30] He was also outraged by the *Humphrey* ruling, for, given the broad language Chief Justice Taft had used in *Myers*[31] less than a decade earlier, he had strong grounds for believing he had acted properly.[32] He found the unanimity of the Court in all three cases bewildering. "Well, where was Ben Cardozo?" he asked. "And what about old Isaiah?"[33]

For four days, while the country speculated about what he would do, the President said nothing, but on May 31, reporters were summoned

to the White House. As they filed in, they saw on FDR's desk a copy
of the *Schechter* opinion and a sheaf of telegrams. For the next hour and
a half, as the press corps listened intently, Roosevelt, in an unusually
somber mood, discoursed on the implications of the Court's opinion in
Schechter. Thumbing a copy of it as he spoke, the President argued that
the Court had stripped the national government of its power to cope
with critical problems. "We are facing a very, very great national non-
partisan issue," he said. "We have got to decide one way or the other
. . . whether in some way we are going to . . . restore to the Federal
Government the powers which exist in the national Governments of
every other Nation in the world." Of all the words the President spoke
at the extraordinary conference, newspapermen singled out one sentence which headline writers emblazoned on late afternoon newspapers:
"We have been relegated to the horse-and-buggy definition of interstate
commerce."[34]

FDR's "horse-and-buggy" conference created a furor. The next day,
Raymond Clapper wrote in his Scripps-Howard column:

> Within an hour after President Roosevelt held his press conference yester-
> day, you could almost feel the electric excitement about Washington.
>   Gossip travels with lightning speed through the National Capital. . . .
> Long before the first newspapers reached the street corners . . . , the
> whole city knew that something of unusual importance had occurred.

Most commentators upbraided the President severely. The *Washington
Post* typified much of the press response with an editorial bluntly titled,
"A President Leaves His Party." Henry Stimson, who had been Secretary
of State in the Hoover administration, wrote Roosevelt a long letter in
which he protested that the "horse-and-buggy" observation "was a wrong
statement, an unfair statement and, if it had not been so extreme as
to be recognizable as hyperbole, a rather dangerous and inflammatory
statement." Senator Arthur Vandenberg, Michigan Republican, declared: "I don't think the President has any thought of emulating Mussolini, Hitler or Stalin, but his utterance as I have heard it is exactly what
these men would say."[35]

Roosevelt's remarks did not please all liberals either. The Tennessee
editor George Fort Milton told the President that his target should be
not the Court but the Constitution. After all, Milton pointed out, men
such as Cardozo, Stone, Hughes, and Brandeis had joined in the
Schechter judgment; given our Constitution, they had had no other
choice. Milton counseled:

Take the lead in a great program of constitutional reform. That is what we need to have done. Let the Constitution be amended so that the Congress will be given power to control indirect as well as direct effects of Interstate Commerce. Let the Constitution be amended to provide for an intelligent measure of delegation. I believe that you will get a very important and effective support from progressives all over the country on a program such as this. But I do not believe that there would be nearly so much support and strength for a program bottomed on a criticism of the Court itself.[36]

Despite his lengthy press conference, Roosevelt never stated directly what he proposed to do. When reporters asked him in what manner the question might be resolved, he replied: "We haven't got to that yet." Nor did he intend prompt action: "I don't mean this summer or winter or next fall, but over a period, perhaps of five or ten years."[37]

From both within and outside the Administration, he heard calls to act immediately. In the confusion after the horse-and-buggy conference, Raymond Moley, one of the original members of the Brain Trust, called Vice President John N. Garner and Senators James F. Byrnes, Jr., of South Carolina, and Robert M. La Follette, Jr., together and found that they, like he, favored a constitutional amendment. Encouraged by the meeting, Moley, who had become a magazine editor, wrote an editorial advocating this course, and Byrnes spoke in support of it in Charleston, South Carolina. In Congress, displeasure with Black Monday produced a freshet of new proposals. Some legislators wanted to amend the Constitution to make explicit grants of additional power to Congress; others, such as Senator Norris, advocated requiring at least a 7-to-2 vote by the Supreme Court to invalidate legislation.[38]

Those in Washington who wished to move right away found encouragement in a growing anti-Court sentiment in the country that they might tap. To the forces arrayed against the Court by the *Rail Pension* opinion, the *Schechter* decision had added both beneficiaries of the NRA and people who resented any setback to FDR and the New Deal. A Memphis man advised the President to balk the Court by declaring martial law, and a Kentucky attorney wrote: "I should think that you and Congress were as tired of the Supreme Court stunts as the people are."[39]

But Roosevelt decided against taking the initiative at once. For a moment, Moley recalls, the President showed a "flicker of enthusiasm," but a flicker it was. Roosevelt sensed that the time was not yet ripe. The NRA had its supporters, but its detractors were more numerous; he could not go to the country with an appeal on its behalf. The clamor raised by the horse-and-buggy conference indicated that the Court would have to antagonize a much larger portion of the nation before it would be politically safe to challenge it. The difficulties in the way of winning approval for a constitutional amendment were daunting. Norris conceded: "It looks now as though it would be an absolute impossibility to pass it through the Senate or the House by the necessary two-thirds majority in order to submit it to the states." Nor had the explorations in the Department of Justice proceeded far enough so that the President was ready with a specific recommendation. [40]

For the next year, Roosevelt tread water. He made no public reference to the Supreme Court even when additional adverse decisions appeared to require some sort of response. He left the impression that he was accepting the Court's verdicts without complaint and that, having had his knuckles rapped for his horse-and-buggy remarks, he proposed neither to say nor to do anything further. In fact, though, as his biographer Rexford Tugwell has written, "If open battle was not at once joined, a kind of twilight war did begin." [41]

In June 1935, Roosevelt spoke freely about the course he would pursue to the American ambassador to Italy, Breckinridge Long, who, when he returned to the United States for a brief visit, found "one thing . . . uppermost on the minds of political America": the *Schechter* decision. At lunch alone with Long on the White House porch, Roosevelt confided that he intended to move other cases up to the Supreme Court to give it an opportunity to modify its interpretation of the commerce clause. If the Court did not do so, then it might be necessary to propose an amendment. Long noted in his diary:

> The amendments are not yet in specific or concrete form but might be broached under three headings: first, to define Inter-State Commerce with authority to Congress to legislate on the subject; second, to define certain phases of Inter-State Commerce; and third, taking a page from Lloyd George, to give authority to the Congress to pass over the veto of the Supreme Court legislation which the Court held unconstitutional. [42]

If and when the time came to act, the amendment route seemed the most promising path, although not everyone agreed about this. Some thought that the difficulty lay not in the Constitution but with the Court; hence, they reasoned either that the composition of the Court needed to be altered or that the Court must, and perhaps could, be persuaded to change its views. The Felix Frankfurter cadre, which had always disliked the NRA anyway, opposed the amendment approach. From a different standpoint, Homer Cummings, angered by the *Schechter* ruling, said: "I tell you, Mr. President, they mean to destroy us. . . .

We will have to find a way to get rid of the present membership of the Supreme Court." Yet the unanimity of the Court on "Black Monday" made it seem unlikely that the New Deal could win a majority, and it argued against solving the problem by appointing a few additional judges. After the *Schechter* opinion was handed down, Raymond Clapper wrote: "Talk of blackjacking the court by enlarging its membership collapsed when all nine justices joined in the decision. That subterfuge of packing the court, a weak and uncertain one at best, becomes ridiculous to think of now."[43]

Both Roosevelt and Cummings agreed that the Justice Department should continue to seek out solutions for the impasse. A week after the horse-and-buggy conference, one of the Attorney General's aides, Alexander Holtzoff, who was to be a central figure in the search for a plan, sent Cummings a memorandum responding to the suggestion that the Court might be stripped of most or all of its appellate jurisdiction. When Holtzoff explained that such a proposal would encounter too much opposition and still not eliminate all the problems confronting the Administration, Cummings was not satisfied and told him to develop his point "a little more fully." On June 22, Holtzoff came up with another five-page memorandum on the question, but the matter did not end there. On August 15, W. W. Gardner at the Justice Department prepared a fourteen-page study for the Solicitor General in which he, too, looked into whether "the power of the Supreme Court to pass upon the constitutional validity of congressional legislation might be abolished or restricted by an Act of Congress." But he also found objections, and the quest continued.[44]

The President displayed a lively interest in these inquiries. In July he sent Cummings a memorandum calling to his attention "two extremely interesting articles by Harold Laski" in the Manchester *Guardian*. Roosevelt also corresponded with critics of the Court outside the government. In August, Charlton Ogburn, counsel for the American Federation of Labor, informed the President that he had submitted a proposed constitutional amendment to the executive council of the Federation for approval. That same month, Roosevelt told Charles E. Wyzanski, Jr., solicitor of the Department of Labor: "Of course, if the Supreme Court should knock out the AAA, then the constitutional amendment would be the real issue. It probably will be anyway, and there will be less difficulty in phrasing it than many people think."[45]

In addition to seeking a feasible plan, Roosevelt sought to build popular support for altering the Constitution. The horse-and-buggy conference had been one move toward that end. In August the President took another step when he met at the White House with George Creel. In collaboration with Creel, the head of the government's propaganda agency in World War I and subsequently a magazine writer, Roosevelt sometimes used the pages of *Collier's* to launch trial balloons. For an article entitled "Looking Ahead with Roosevelt," the President now dictated to Creel:

> In the next few months, the Supreme Court will hand down fresh pronouncements with respect to New Deal laws, and it is possible the President will get another "licking." If so, much will depend on the language of the licking. In event that unconstitutionality is found, perhaps the decisions will point the way to statutory amendments. If, however, the Constitution is construed technically; if it is held that one hundred and fifty years have no bearing on the case, and that the present generation is powerless to meet social and economic problems that were not within the knowledge of the founding fathers, and therefore not made the subject of their specific consideration, then the President will have no other alternative than to go to the country with a Constitutional amendment that will lift the Dead Hand, giving the people of today the right to deal with today's vital issues.

He told Creel grimly: "Fire that as an opening gun."[46]

Contrary to Roosevelt's expectation, the trial balloon attracted almost no notice. Most of the nation in 1935 was still either indifferent to the Court question or outrightly opposed to tethering the Court. To the query: "As a general principle, would you favor limiting the power of the Supreme Court to declare acts of Congress unconstitutional?" the Gallup Poll in the autumn of 1935 received the following replies: yes, 31 percent; no, 53 percent; no opinion, 16 percent. The most articulate anti-Court feeling came from those who felt they had been hurt by specific decisions. A Virginian objected: "The Supreme Court turned down my railroad pension." But many more thought the Justices wise, the system of checks and balances sacred, and Congress mercurial, although their conception of these institutions was sometimes primitive. Asked his view, an Ohio relief recipient said: "If they didn't know more than the other courts, they wouldn't be called the Supreme Court."[47]

Despite this discouraging response, the President pushed quietly ahead. At a long lunch at the White House on November 12, 1935, Roosevelt and Harold Ickes palavered about the Court. The President remarked that he did not think that any Justices would retire and permit him to make new appointments, and he made use of an analogy that was to crop up frequently in succeeding months in discussions of the judiciary crisis. Secretary Ickes wrote in his diary:

The President's mind went back to the difficulty in England, where the House of Lords repeatedly refused to adopt legislation sent up from the House of Commons. He recalled that when Lloyd George came into power some years ago under Edward VII, he went to the King and asked his consent to announce that if the Lords refused again to accept the bill for Irish autonomy, which had been pressed upon them several times since the days of Gladstone, he would create several hundred new peers, enough to outvote the existing House of Lords. With this threat confronting them, the bill passed the Lords. [48]

Roosevelt's recollection was faulty—the episode actually concerned Herbert Asquith and the attempt to reform the House of Lords—but the British analogy was clearly important for him. He returned to it once more on December 27 at a Cabinet meeting during which the Supreme Court question was again reviewed at length. This time he alluded not only to the Irish Home Rule Bill, but also to Lloyd David George's success in pushing through a social security act by the threat to create three hundred new peers. [49]

After the Cabinet session, Ickes made a new entry in his diary:

Clearly, it is running in the President's mind that substantially all of the New Deal bills will be declared unconstitutional by the Supreme Court. This will mean that everything that this Administration has done of any moment will be nullified. The President pointed out that there were three ways of meeting such a situation: (1) by packing the Supreme Court, which was a distasteful idea; (2) by trying to put through a number of amendments to the Constitution to meet the various situations; and (3) by a method that he asked us to consider very carefully.

The third method is, in substance, this: an amendment to the Constitution conferring explicit power on the Supreme Court to declare acts of Congress unconstitutional, a power which is not given anywhere in the Constitution as it stands. The amendment would also give the Supreme Court original jurisdiction on constitutional questions affecting statutes. If the Supreme Court should declare an act of Congress to be unconstitutional, then—a congressional election having intervened—if Congress should repass the law so declared to be unconstitutional, the taint of unconstitutionality would be removed and the law would be a valid one. By this method there would be in effect a referendum to the country, although an indirect one. At the intervening congressional election the question of the constitutionality or unconstitutionality of the law would undoubtedly be an issue. [50]

In essence, the President's strategy left the power of decision to the Supreme Court. If the Court upheld New Deal statutes, the issue would fade away. But if all the legislation were thrown out, Roosevelt warned, there would be "marching farmers and marching miners and marching workingmen throughout the land." For almost half a year, while the Court was recessed, the conflict between the President and the Court had simmered on a low flame. But during those months, as Roosevelt was keenly aware, such significant matters as challenges to the Agricultural Adjustment Act processing tax—the lever of FDR's farm program— had been making their way through the lower courts; the Supreme Court could be expected to render decisions on these cases early in 1936. "If the Court does send the AAA flying like the NRA," the President had told Wyzanski, "there might even be a revolution."[51]

V

On January 6, 1936, the Supreme Court, in *U. S. v. Butler*, handed down its long-awaited ruling on the AAA processing tax. Divided 6 to 3, the Court held the tax unconstitutional, thus overturning the second of Roosevelt's two most important recovery programs. In an opinion that earned him scorching comments from the law journals, Justice Roberts held the levy to be an illegitimate use of the taxing power, "the expropriation of money from one group for the benefit of another."[52]

The *Butler* decision aroused acrimonious criticism of the Court.[53] Coming on top of the 1935 opinions, the *Butler* verdict appeared to indicate a determination by the Court to wipe out all of the New Deal. "Is Poe's Raven who croaked 'Never More' their model?" asked one man. An Oklahoman penciled a letter to the Attorney General stating that he wanted to impeach every judge who had declared the AAA invalid, and another man wrote the President: "I'm in favor of doing away with the Constitution if it's going to interfere with the general welfare of the people." The head of a Chicago advertising agency asked: "Are you aware that the people at large are getting damned tired of the United States Supreme Court, and that, if left to a popular vote, it would be kicked out?"[54]

A nation of tinkerers, the country flooded Washington with home-made inventions to improve the government machinery. Many of the contrivances stressed either the age of the Justices or the device of packing the Court, or both. A South Carolina attorney wrote: "We are hoping and believing that you and the Congress of the United States will not allow six old men to destroy this Country." A Minnesota lawyer urged compulsory retirement at 65 or 70, "whichever would retire the majority of the present members of the Court." A Los Angeles man questioned the fitness of "that body of nine old hasbeens, half-deaf, half-blind, full-of-palsy men. . . . That they are behind the times is very plain—all you have to do is to look at Charles Hughes' whiskers."[55]

From different parts of the nation, Roosevelt heard calls for additional Justices "with younger minds." Some wanted four more Justices, like the Memphis businessman who pointed out: "Business does not accept an applicant with twelve gray hairs on his head." Others thought six new Justices would have to be added to "reverse this infamy." An Arizona attorney recommended: "In order to avoid the impending seizure of this government by the special interests it is incumbent on you to increase the membership of the Supreme Court to fifteen; and appoint the new membership from the Frankfurters, Olsons, and other men who place human rights above the rights of predatory wealth." From Richmond, Virginia, came a demand for a Court of "at least twenty or more members. Nine OLD MEN, whose total age amounts to about 650 years, should have additional help." A member of the Kansas House of Representatives had an even more radical suggestion: add sixteen new members, "the new members to be not over thirty-five years of age, and retired at forty. This would put men on the court that are in step with TO-DAY."[56]

A number of correspondents seemed to believe that Roosevelt was unaware of the Court's infamy or that he needed to be stiffened to oppose the Court. A Seattle woman wrote:

> I have just this minute heard the decision of the U. S. Supreme Court on the A.A.A.
>
> Mr. Roosevelt, are you going to sit back and let these few men, controlled by the selfish elements of our country, control the destinies of intelligent, thinking and country-loving people, who really make this great country of ours?

A Kansan maintained: "One who is really a man will resist to the end being governed by men who lived one hundred and fifty years ago"; and a Miami attorney assured the President: "If you, as the Executive, and Congress will make the Supreme Court an issue in this country it will not fail. Jackson did not fail, Grant did not fail, and the Dred-Scott decision was treated with contempt."[57] A Mississippi editor wired Roosevelt:

> On behalf of farmers and workers urge that you set aside Supreme Court decision and destroy their assumed right to declare laws of Congress unconstitutional. . . . President Andrew Jackson, our greatest Democrat, defied Supreme Court on this very point. Hope you will do the same. Sincerely believe that future of Democratic government hinges on

whether you will take the bull by the horns. Drastic action is imperative. America is depending on you. Perhaps civilization and its perpetuity is involved in your acts. God grant that you have the courage to do right.[58]

FDR's strategy of watchful waiting seemed to be paying off. The Court, which had antagonized groups such as railway employees in 1935, had now angered farmers who would be denied more than two billion dollars in AAA benefit checks in the next year. Edward A. O'Neal, president of the American Farm Bureau Federation, warned: "Those who believe the American farmer will stand idly by and watch his program for economic justice fall without a fight are badly mistaken. The fight is on—and this time it will be with the gloves off."[59] O'Neal laid plans to meet with the A.F. of L.'s Charlton Ogburn to forge a farmer-labor alliance.

Yet none of this agitation moved Roosevelt to act. Despite constant prodding, he refused even to comment on the *Butler* decision. An election year, he believed, was not the propitious moment to give the opposition, which was bereft of issues, an opportunity to stand by the flag. Nor had the coalition against the Court yet reached full strength. If O'Neal denounced the *Butler* opinion, other farm leaders hailed it, and a Gallup poll, which appeared the day before the decision was rendered, showed a majority of the country disapproved of the AAA. Nor had opponents of the Court reached agreement on a proposal. Ogburn, for one, thought that nothing should be done at present save to make the amending process easier.[60]

The Administration itself had not yet come up with a tenable approach. Shortly after the *Butler* verdict was rendered, Assistant Attorney General John Dickinson wrote:

The way in which the high command has apparently decided to treat the AAA decision has been to smother its effect as much as possible. I am not at all sure that this is a wise strategy, but apparently the feeling is that there is a widespread readiness, throughout the country, to blaze up against the Supreme Court and that this state of mind must be wet-blanketed, for fear that otherwise it would drive the Administration into the position of either attacking the Court, or calling for an amendment, which they are not yet prepared to do.[61]

While maintaining public silence, though, Roosevelt was indicating privately that he was getting set for a faceoff with the Court. At the Cabinet meeting on January 24, 1936, Ickes recorded:

The President said that word is coming to him from widely separated parts of the country that people are beginning to show a great deal of interest in the constitutional questions that have been raised by recent Supreme Court decisions. . . . The President made the point, based upon some statement by Harold J. Laski, that the Supreme Court, in its decisions on New Deal legislation, was dictating what it believed should be the social philosophy of the nation, without reference to the law or the Constitution. . . . It is plain to see, from what the President said today and has said on other occasions, that he is not at all averse to the Supreme Court declaring one New Deal statute after another unconstitutional. I think he believes that the Court will find itself pretty far out on a limb before it is through with it and that a real issue will be joined on which we can go to the country.

For my part, I hope so. Here is an issue that must be faced by the country sooner or later, unless we are prepared to submit to the arbitrary and final dictates of a group of men who are not elected by the people and who are not responsible to the people: in short, a judicial tyranny imposed by men appointed for life and who cannot be reached except by the slow and cumbersome process of impeachment.[62]

That same day, Roosevelt prepared a memorandum for the files, with a copy to Raymond Moley, stating:

It has been well said by a prominent historian that fifty years from now the Supreme Court's AAA decision will, in all probability, be described somewhat as follows:

(1) The decision virtually prohibits the President and Congress from the right, under modern conditions, to intervene reasonably in the regulation of nation-wide commerce and nation-wide agriculture.

(2) The Supreme Court arrived at this result by selecting from several possible techniques of constitutional interpretation a special technique. The objective of the Court's purpose was to make reasonableness in passing legislation a matter to be settled not by the views of the elected Senate and House of Representatives and not by the views of an elected President but rather by the private, social philosophy of a majority of nine appointed members of the Supreme Court itself.[63]

Roosevelt continued to explore ways to deal with the Court. A week after the *Butler* decision, he wrote Cummings: "What was the McArdle case . . . ? I am told that the Congress withdrew some act from the jurisdiction of the Supreme Court." The Attorney General replied: "The case of ex parte McCardle . . . is one of the classic cases to which we refer when considering the possibility of limiting the jurisdiction of Federal Courts. This whole matter has been the subject of considerable study in this Department, and, in view of recent developments, is apt to be increasingly important."[64]

That exchange between the President and the Attorney General suggests the crucial development in the early weeks of 1936: loss of faith in the amendment solution and rising belief that the Court could be curbed by an act of Congress. The most important influence on this change of attitude was the division of the Court in *Butler* and Harlan Fiske Stone's ringing dissent, less because the minority voted to sustain the processing tax than because of Stone's vigorous assault on judicial usurpation. Cummings wrote Stone:

> Your dissenting opinion is on a high plane—sound, constructive and human.
>
> It may not be the law *now*—but it will be the law later, unless governmental functions are to be permanently frozen in an unescapable mold.
>
> You spoke at a great moment and in a great way. Congratulations.[65]

The split in the Court confirmed those who had been arguing that the source of the problem was not the Constitution but the composition of this particular tribunal, and Justice Stone's dissent made it easier to argue that Congress must act to regain powers the Court had usurped. The amendment route was not abandoned, but the search for a suitable amendment now concentrated for the first time on compelling the retirement of Justices, thus altering the makeup of the bench. In addition, the Administration gave increasing attention to resolving the predicament by statute.[66]

On January 29, 1936, Cummings wrote the President:

> The real difficulty is not with the Constitution but with the Judges who interpret it. As long as a majority of those who have the final say in such matters are wedded to their present theories, there are but two courses open to us. We must endeavor, with all the ingenuity at our disposal, to find a way to bring helpful national legislation within the explicit terms of their decisions, or we must frankly meet the issue of a constitutional amendment.
>
> For the present, at least, I think our proper course is along the former line rather than the latter. The hand has not yet been played out. If we come to the question of a constitutional amendment, enormous difficulties are presented. No one has yet suggested an amendment that does not either do too much or too little, or which does not raise practical and political questions which it would be better to avoid.

But the Attorney General then said, in a sentence that, as Roosevelt read it, quite possibly leaped off the page: "We might well be giving some serious thought to an amendment to the Constitution (should we find we are forced to that point) which would require the retirement of all Federal Judges, or, at least, all Supreme Court Judges, who have reached or who hereafter reach the age of seventy years." Cummings added: "Such an amendment would probably encounter less opposition than almost any other I can think of. It would have the advantage of not changing in the least degree the structure of our Government, nor would it impair the power of the court. It would merely insure the exercise of the powers of Court by Judges less likely to be horrified by new ideas."[67]

That same day, perhaps before receiving the communication from Cummings, the President, after talking over the Court issue at lunch with Senator Norris, continued the discussion with Ickes. He told the Interior Secretary that he had concluded he could achieve Court reform without resort to an amendment; he had also confided this to Norris. Roosevelt's thinking continued along much the same lines he had sketched out in November authorizing Congress to re-enact a statute which the Court had struck down, thereby making it the law of the land. Ickes noted:

> I made the obvious remark that the Supreme Court would declare unconstitutional such an act as the President had in mind and he said that of course it would. To meet that situation his plan would be somewhat as follows: Congress would pass a law, the Supreme Court would declare it unconstitutional, the President would then go to Congress and ask it to instruct him whether he was to follow the mandate of Congress or the mandate of the Court. If the Congress should declare that its own mandate was to be followed, the President would carry out the will of Congress through the offices of the United States Marshals and ignore the Court.

After their talk, Ickes reflected:

> There isn't any doubt at all that the President is really hoping that the Supreme Court will continue to make a clean sweep of all New Deal legislation, throwing out the TVA Act, the Securities Act, the Railroad Retirement Act, the Social Security Act, the Guffey Coal Act, and others. He thinks the country is beginning to sense this issue but that enough people have not yet been affected by adverse decisions so as to make a sufficient feeling on a Supreme Court issue.
>
> I told the President that I hoped this would be the issue in the next campaign. I believe it will have to be fought out sooner or later, and I remarked to him that the President who faced this issue and drastically curbed the usurped power of the Supreme Court would go down through all the ages of history as one of the great Presidents.[68]

Two days later, at a Cabinet meeting, Cummings asked whether the government should appeal a lower court decision denying the federal government the right to condemn property for a low-cost housing project. Tommy Corcoran and Ben Cohen were but two of the President's advisers who thought the government should drop the case, in part because they feared an adverse opinion from the Supreme Court that might wipe out the Public Works Administration. Ickes noted:

> The President was firmly of the opinion that we ought to go ahead with the case. He scouted the idea that anyone could draw an act which would pass the scrutiny of the Supreme Court in its present outlook on New Deal legislation. He thought that if all PWA projects should be suspended as the result of an adverse decision by the Supreme Court, it would be all to the good. . . . It is clear that he is willing to go to the country on this issue but he wants the issue to be as strong and clear as possible, which means that he hopes the Supreme Court will declare unconstitutional every New Deal case that comes before it.[69]

Yet, while blithely accepting this prospect of a constitutional Armageddon, the President continued to say nothing publicly. Early in February, George Fort Milton wrote one of FDR's friends:

> I thought a month ago that the Court and the Constitution were very definitely going to be in this year's presidential debate. But everything in Washington is of the hush, hush attitude. . . . What I am feeling is that maybe he is depending too much on his resourcefulness and that he could do some thinking on what would be the usefulness of being re-elected if he was going to have to go into a second term denied the essential powers of nationality. Wouldn't he be all dressed up and have nowhere to go?[70]

Roosevelt's silence, which some interpreted as acquiescence in the Court's decisions, left the initiative to Congress. "The years 1935–1937," Michael Nelson has noted, "saw more Court-curbing bills introduced in Congress than in any other three-year (or thirty-five-year) period in history." In the 1936 session, Congressmen introduced more than a hundred proposals to alter the balance of power. Some measures, such as the "Human Rights Amendment," aimed to expand the power of Congress to enact social legislation. Others sought to strip the courts of the prerogative of judicial review. Still others resorted to enlarging the bench. In January 1936, Representative Ernest Lundeen, Minnesota Farmer Laborite, filed a bill to increase the Supreme Court by two Justices so that the Court could handle more work and because "new blood will mean a more liberal outlook on constitutional questions." Lundeen pointed out that after his bill had been adopted, and Justice Willis Van Devanter carried out his purported plan to retire, the President would be able to name three new Justices and thus assure a liberal majority. A week earlier, Representative James L. Quinn, Pennsylvania Democrat, had gone even further; he had introduced a measure to expand the Court to fifteen Justices.[71]

On February 12, 1936, George Norris delivered a major address on the floor of the Senate denouncing the Supreme Court as a "continuous constitutional convention." To the contention that the processing tax was invalid because agricultural production was not mentioned in the Constitution, Norris retorted: "Nowhere in that great document is there a syllable, a word, or a sentence giving to any court the right to declare an act of Congress unconstitutional." The Nebraska Senator expostulated: "The members of the Supreme Court are not elected by anybody. They are responsible to nobody. Yet they hold dominion over everybody." Rejecting the amendment procedure he had once favored as "impracticable," Norris asked Congress to have the "courage" to enact legislation requiring a unanimous decision to invalidate an act of Congress.[72]

The columnist Robert S. Allen wrote Norris:

I have been wondering for weeks what the hell this session was for. Your matchless speech on the Supreme Court this afternoon cleared up the mystery. The session was solely so you could deliver this superb exposition—so it could go into the *Record* for all history to read—so you could say what everybody was thinking, but no other leader had the guts to say out loud.

It was a grand and unequaled job, Senator. And what was no less significant was the tremendous response it is being accorded. It is really amazing the extraordinary press coverage it has received. Even the filthy Hearst jackals carried almost a column of your remarks. It was also amazing to me how deeply moved the press gallery was. Reactionary old bastards who haven't had an intelligent idea in decades spoke respectfully of your views.[73]

Norris's concern over the Court question was long-standing, but it was heightened during these weeks by foreboding over the fate of the Tennessee Valley Authority, of which he was acknowledged to be the "father." In January, Norris had written: "Up to the time this decision was rendered in the AAA case, I had no doubt whatsoever that the Supreme Court would sustain the TVA Act. . . . Since the AAA decision, however, I would not be surprised if the Court would hold the TVA Act unconstitutional."[74] On February 17, the Court, by an unexpectedly lopsided 8-to-1 vote with only McReynolds in dissent, diminished these anxieties by validating the power of the TVA to dispose of power generated at Wilson Dam.[75]

Although some critics pointed out that the Court still had not rendered a decisive judgment on the constitutionality of the TVA and had set a bad precedent in agreeing to hear the case at all, friends of public power expressed delight. "I had completely resigned myself to a bad decision, only holding out hope that we would have some crumb of comfort in that unlike AAA and NRA we would not be swept completely out to sea, bag and baggage," wrote the TVA director David Lilienthal. "The decision, clearing away so many of the clouds hanging over us, makes me feel very humble. We are given an almost incredible grant of power."[76]

The decision, despite its limitations, served, for the moment, to quiet demands for renovating the judiciary. By showing the fairness of the Court, the ruling, observed the *Washington Post*, "should do more than anything else to end the campaign for limitation of the Court's authority." From Chattanooga, George Fort Milton wrote gleefully:

> Well, after TVA, I think we ought to start talking about "one old man and the eight young men." . . .
>
> I suspect that some of the members of the Court set themselves forward deliberately to show that they could render other than a Tory decision. Would you call this modernizing Mr. Dooley, so that the Supreme Court precedes the election returns?[77]

The respite provided by the TVA decision proved short-lived. Six weeks later, the Court sternly rebuked the Securities and Exchange Commission,[78] and on May 18, 1936, it went out of its way in the *Carter* case[79] to strike down the Guffey Coal Act, the "little NRA" for the coal industry, in an opinion that appeared to doom the National Labor Relations Act as well as any attempt by act of Congress to control wages and hours.

The *Carter* decision set off a new round of condemnations of the Court and demands for restrictions. Once more, the age of the Justices and the possibilities offered by "packing" were pointed out. "We permit old men 90, probably as childish as boys of 9, to sit on the Supreme Court bench and in case of a 5 to 4 vote one old man controls the affairs of the nation," a critic wrote the President. "In reviewing the Constitution of the United States," noted a Pennsylvania man, "it comes to my attention the fact that there is no limit to the Personell of the Supreme Court." A Los Angeles man urged the President to name four more Justices. He added helpfully: "For these four positions I nominate

Senator Hiram Johnson of California and Senator Geo. W. Norris of Nebraska. Now you name two." Yet Roosevelt not only would not heed such advice but when newsmen pressed him for a statement on *Carter* brusquely closed off that line of questioning.[80]

The *Carter* ruling turned out to be only the first in a series of rapid-fire blows the Court delivered. On successive Mondays in the spring of 1936, the Court handed down *Carter*, overturned the Municipal Bankruptcy Act,[81] and, in the most consequential event of all, invalidated the New York state minimum-wage law in the *Tipaldo* case.[82] Each decision came from a divided bench.

For critics of the Supreme Court, *Tipaldo* was the last straw. Before that ruling, even some New Dealers hoped to avoid a direct confrontation with the Court. After it, Tugwell has written, liberals agreed that "something must be done." Not since the *Dred Scott* disaster had the Court inflicted on itself so deep a wound. As Alpheus T. Mason has observed: "At any time up to June 1, 1936, the Court might have retreated and thus avoided a showdown. The New York Minimum Wage opinion, handed down that day, convinced even the most reverent that five stubborn old men had planted themselves squarely in the path of progress."[83]

Tipaldo produced a national outcry against the Court. Ickes noted angrily: "The sacred right of liberty of contract again—the right of an immature child or a helpless woman to drive a bargain with a great corporation. If this decision does not outrage the moral sense of the country, then nothing will." But it was not only New Dealers who objected. The Court had embarrassed Administration opponents who had been arguing that protection of the rights of labor should be left to the states. "Hereafter," wrote Franklyn Waltman in the *Washington Post*, "whenever New Dealers are taunted with trying to break down the rights of the States to manage their own affairs, the taunters will have this decision tossed in their faces." The *Post* labeled the opinion "An Unfortunate Decision," and Herbert Hoover called for an amendment to restore to the states "the power they thought they already had."[84]

Once more, Roosevelt felt pressure to act. From California, the head of the Stockton Democratic Club wrote him: "By another 4 to 5 decision on the part of JUDOCRACY, *one man* has been able . . . to nullify the progress of half a century along humanitarian lines, exposing the Motherhood of America to further exploitation on the part of unscrupulous employers. If this be Democracy—may God save the mark!" A telegram from Brooklyn demanded: "Increase number of justices in Supreme Court with men in their fifties." The head of a New York printing firm warned the President that it would be "useless" for him to pursue his program unless he pushed through an amendment. "You can't side-step the issue," he scolded. "The people who will re-elect you will expect you to have something to say about this matter."[85]

At a press conference on June 2, 1936, Roosevelt broke his silence. For the first time since the "horse-and-buggy" meeting, he commented on a ruling by the Court. Of *Tipaldo*, he said:

> It seems to be fairly clear, as a result of this decision and former decisions, using this question of minimum wage as an example, that the "no-man's-land" where no Government—State or Federal—can function is being more clearly defined. A State cannot do it, and the Federal Government cannot do it.

But when a reporter asked, "How can you meet that situation?" the President replied, "I think that is about all there is to say on it."[86]

Roosevelt was no less circumspect about drafting the 1936 Democratic platform. Both he and Senator Robert Wagner of New York, chairman of the Resolutions Committee, were urged to incorporate commitments to specific proposals, such as requiring a 7-to-2 majority to invalidate a law, or amending the Constitution to empower Congress and the states to enact minimum-wage laws.[87] But the Administration was determined to keep the platform ambiguous, not only because it wanted to remove the Court issue from the campaign, but also because it still had not decided on a particular remedy.

In putting together their platform, the Democrats had to cope with the fact that the Republicans had already pledged themselves to an amendment to overcome the *Tipaldo* decision. Cummings warned the President that if the Democrats sought to outbid the Republicans they ran the risk of going so far as to shift the whole emphasis of the campaign to the constitutional question. The Attorney General hoped to avoid any specific plank, but if one was required, he favored a statement so vaguely worded that it would leave the door open "to the thought that perhaps, after all, an amendment may not be necessary." Four days earlier, Donald Richberg, who had been a prominent labor attorney and chairman of the National Industrial Recovery Board, had also submitted a draft which was adroitly phrased to escape any definite obligation.[88]

On the Sunday before the 1936 Democratic convention, Roosevelt, Wagner, and several others met after dinner in the White House to frame the platform. When they encountered difficulties, the conferees asked two of the participants, Samuel I. Rosenman, a member of the original Brain Trust, and Stanley High, a skillful phrase-maker, to try their hands after the meeting broke up. They worked all night at a typewriter, and by morning the President had the results on his break-fast tray, but the Supreme Court plank was still missing.

After breakfast, Rosenman and High went into FDR's bedroom, where they found Richberg, whom the President had called to the White House to help out. Richberg turned up with a carbon of his proposed plank in his pocket, and after going over it, Roosevelt whistled softly and said, "I think this is it." The others gathered in the President's bed-room agreed, and, with minor changes, Richberg's approach was incor-porated in the platform. Purposely opaque, it proposed to achieve a "clarifying amendment" only "if these problems cannot be effectively solved by legislation."[89]

In the 1936 campaign, Roosevelt maintained a studied silence on the question despite counsel from different sides that he urge action to alter the federal judiciary or that he assure the country that he would not pack the Court. The President wanted the campaign to center not on the Constitution but on the many achievements of the New Deal and the past iniquities of Herbert Hoover. In retrospect, it has seemed to a number of commentators that Roosevelt fumbled away the opportunity to create a mandate for judiciary reform in his second term by not mak-ing an issue of the behavior of the Court in the 1936 campaign, which, since he was so decisively ahead, he could have done. That reasoning, though, reads back into the experience of 1936 knowledge that was not there at the time. The newly established Gallup poll gave FDR only a five-point margin during the summer, and the *Literary Digest* survey, which had never been wrong and had predicted Roosevelt's victory in 1932, foresaw an overwhelming defeat for the President. Under these circumstances, deliberately raising the Court question seemed fool-hardy. Within the Roosevelt circle, Felix Frankfurter and Secretary of Labor Frances Perkins opposed belaboring of the Court, and even Ickes conceded that the groundwork had not been laid. One correspondent advised the President to leave the Court matter "till after the campaign, so as not to supply ammunition to the 'constitution cryers.' When the campaign is over, Congress could proceed in a calm mood and adopt certain changes. . . . Congress could suggest to the President to add to the present Tribunal two, four or six justices to make the number 11, 13, or 15."[90]

Nonetheless, the constitutional question surfaced at times. In differ-ent parts of the country, conservatives warned that if FDR won, he would pack the Court. Conceivably, a few votes may have been swung by such concerns. One man wrote: "In my opinion any man who sneered at the United States Supreme Court like he did in May 1935, when they ruled against N.R.A., is not worthy of my vote though I have been voting the Democratic Ticket since 1884." Yet Roosevelt's restraint made it possible for Stephen Duggan, director of the Institute of International Education, to write a long letter, which the *New York Times* published, urging support of the President, who "has given no evidence that he wants to 'pack' the court," and for the conservative Senator Josiah Bailey of North Carolina to defend Roosevelt on his intentions. Enlarging the Supreme Court, wrote Frederick Lewis Allen of *Harper's* shortly before the election, "need hardly be regarded as a serious possibility in the immediate future: it would be too obviously a cowardly move."[91]

VI

In November 1936, Franklin Roosevelt rolled up the greatest victory in the history of two-party competition by capturing the electoral votes of all but two of the forty-eight states. His political opponents routed, his policies vindicated, he could now give full attention to the challenge posed by the Supreme Court. Time was short. In just two more months the Court would reconvene; awaiting it were tests of the validity of the Social Security Act, the National Labor Relations Act, the Railway Labor Act, the Commodity Exchange Act, and state minimum-wage and unemployment compensation laws, as well as of the powers of the PWA, the SEC, and the Federal Communications Commission. Even the gold clause resolution faced another contest.

In view of this prospect, what was Roosevelt to do? He might just wait for vacancies to develop. The laws of nature were on his side, for never in the history of the republic had a Court been so elderly. Moreover, Justices Willis Van Devanter and George Sutherland had talked of stepping down. Yet Roosevelt had seen nearly four years go by without one opportunity to make an appointment, a situation that had occurred in no other full presidential term. (In contrast, William Howard Taft, in just one term, had named six Justices; in only two and a half years, Warren Harding had chosen four.) Anyone familiar with the conversation of Justices knew enough to place a high discount on muttering about retiring, and these particular Justices seemed determined to stay on the bench so long as Roosevelt was in the White House. In the final week of the campaign, one of FDR's aides noted in his diary: "[Roosevelt] frequently returns to a discussion of the Supreme Court—wonders how long some of its ancient judges will hold out. Tom [Corcoran] said the other evening: 'I just saw Van Devanter. He looks very bad.' We all laughed." At the first Cabinet meeting after the election, the President, in a spirit of gallows humor, said that Justice McReynolds would still be on the tribunal when he was 105.[92]

Still, Roosevelt might wait to see whether the Court would follow the election returns. The switch of even one Justice could be decisive. It might be anticipated that the emphatic outcome of the election would startle some Justices who had believed that they were speaking for a nation outraged by the New Deal. In July, Justice McReynolds had written his brother, "There seems a growing feeling that Roosevelt may be defeated," and as late as the beginning of November, Van Devanter thought the election would be close.[93]

The President ran risks, though, in biding his time. The Court had behaved so arrogantly in the spring of 1936 that prospects for an alteration of views seemed slim. Not only did the Court's reasoning in its last term leave little hope for supposing that the Court would not strike down such landmarks as the Wagner Act and the Social Security law, but it barred the way to new legislation. Returned to office with a tremendous vote of confidence, the President might be denied by the Court the opportunity to use the renewal of power. If he tarried too long, he might find himself with his past achievements obliterated and the momentum for future change dissipated.

Roosevelt had a strong sense of his own place in history. He would not countenance being written off in the history books as a man who had been frustrated in his attempts to lead the country out of the Depression and to create a more humane social order. "When I retire to private life on January 20, 1941," he later remarked, "I do not want to leave the country in the condition Buchanan left it to Lincoln."[94] Nor did he wish to be known as a President who had permitted judicial usurpers to impair the office of the Executive. Finally, it should be noted, the Court, by such decisions as that in the *Humphrey* case, had wounded his self-esteem, and by other acts had convinced him that it was personally hostile to him.[95] He sought a way not merely to liberalize the Court but to chastise the Justices for past misdeeds.

If he did act, what method should he choose? The most obvious was some form of constitutional amendment, but he had become distrustful of the amendment route many months before—for a number of reasons. In the first place, he thought an amendment would be difficult to frame. Two years of study in the Justice Department had not yielded a satisfactory draft, and liberals outside the government were far from a consensus. Some of those who advocated a constitutional amendment found that, on examining the various proposals, they liked none of them. When the National Consumers' League, which had spearheaded the drive for minimum-wage legislation, polled legal experts after the *Tipaldo* decision on whether a campaign for an amendment should be launched, the results were discouraging. Half of those surveyed—including Frankfurter—opposed agitation for an amendment, and the other half were so far apart on what kind of amendment should be sought that the League decided against doing anything at all.[96]

Even if an amendment could be drafted, and approved by two-thirds of each house of Congress, it would have to run the gauntlet of ratification by three-fourths of the states. If ratification was by state legislatures, as seemed most likely, it would require an adverse vote by only one house in thirteen legislatures to defeat an amendment, and the malapportioned state legislatures overrepresented conservative interests. Nor did Roosevelt have much faith in the probity of these assemblies. He wrote a prominent New York lawyer three months later:

> If you were not as scrupulous and ethical as you happen to be, you could make five million dollars as easy as rolling off a log by undertaking a campaign to prevent the ratification by one house of the Legislature, or even the summoning of a constitutional convention in thirteen states for the next four years. Easy money.

In a conversation with Ickes, Tommy Corcoran had no trouble in ticking off the thirteen states "that would naturally be against a broadening amendment or in which money could be used to defeat it."[97]

At best, ratification would take a long time, and time was priceless. Conscious of the brief span allotted to reform movements, Roosevelt wanted to exploit his landslide to drive through legislation such as a wages and hours bill while Congress still felt the full force of his popular endorsement. To be sure, the Norris lame-duck amendment had been adopted quickly, but that, he thought, was because it had not been opposed by any strongly entrenched interest. A constitutional amendment affecting the courts would not only be rejected by big business but would encounter state legislatures largely composed of lawyers, who would be more disapproving of tinkering with the judiciary than would other groups.[98]

The President was especially influenced by the tiresomely long, unsuccessful saga of attempting to win ratification for the child-labor amendment, a struggle then in its thirteenth year. As La Rue Brown, formerly Assistant Attorney General under Wilson, told the National Consumers' League:

> My personal experience with the Child Labor Amendment leads me to view with great dubiety the prospect of ratification of an amendment increasing federal power. Our side is at so tremendous a disadvantage as to resources and so many truly liberal folk are so questioning as to the ultimate intendments of increasing the federal authority that I fear we should simply wear our hearts out in another hopeless fight.[99]

Subsequently, Stephen Early, FDR's press secretary, summed up the objections for Raymond Clapper, who set down in his diary:

> Steve said that the president had given him sidelight this morning on court proposal that he thought he would pass on to me to use or not as I saw fit. It was this—that people who talked about an amendment either didn't realize difficulties in that method or else did realize them and for that reason advocated this course. Steve said that to seek an amendment meant getting two-thirds of both houses and then submitting it to states where 3/4 needed. He said suppose 13 governors refused to submit amendment. It dead then. He said all of us who ever been around legislatures know how easy be for moneyed interests to buy up enough legislatures to prevent action. Said this not like prohibition—here are vast and powerful groups determined to prevent action. Said another reason would be that to follow amendment course would make this an issue in 1938 campaign and might lose a number of "our congressmen." Might cost them their seats. [100]

Even if an amendment went through, success would not eliminate all objections to relying on that process. Any legislation enacted under authorization of such an amendment would still be subject to review in the courts unless such an amendment was purely procedural. "In view of what Mr. Justice Roberts did to a clause as broad and sweeping as 'the general welfare,' " wrote the historian Charles A. Beard, "I can see other justices of his mental outlook macerating almost any clarifying amendment less generous in its terms. If there is any phrase wider than providing for the general welfare, I am unable to conjure it up in my mind." Besides, if the President should sponsor an amendment enlarging federal powers, it might seem tantamount to conceding that he had been wrong and the Supreme Court right in their dispute over the constitutionality of New Deal measures, and this, especially after his bracing election triumph, Roosevelt was less willing than ever to do. [101]

Not until almost the very end did Roosevelt and Cummings wholly discard the thought that they might wind up proposing some kind of amendment, but for many months they had been more inclined toward a statutory answer, though a number of the suggestions needing only an act of Congress seemed no more promising than an amendment. An act requiring more than a majority of Justices to invalidate a law, a solution a number of legislators favored, did not bear scrutiny. Roosevelt believed that the Supreme Court would be justified in holding such a requirement unconstitutional. "From the days of Queen Elizabeth or Henry the Eighth, for all we know, the rule of the old English common law has been that the majority of a court could determine the action of that court," he told reporters. Richberg later observed: "A mere statute to this effect would either be disregarded by the court, or have the result that Justices anxious to preserve the prestige of the court would join unwillingly with the majority so as to make a decision of the court effective." Moreover, such a law would limit the Court's role as a protector of civil liberties. An alternative proposal that emerged very early was an act of Congress withdrawing appellate jurisdiction, but it had two disadvantages—the Court would still have original jurisdiction, especially in cases involving conflicts among states, and, much more important, the lower courts would retain their powers. [102]

While Roosevelt at his New York home contemplated what to do, one recommendation that had been a recurrent drumbeat throughout his first term found its way into print yet again. In its post-election editorial, New York's high-circulation tabloid, the *Daily News*, under the banner "What Next?" wrote:

> There was one issue which was more or less soft-pedaled during the campaign by both sides, for reasons of strategy. Yet it was and is, we believe, the most important issue facing us today.
>
> That issue is the Supreme Court of the United States. . . . The power of the nine men whose average age is 71 must be curtailed somehow, or the will of the people as expressed in their return of the New Deal to power will be thwarted. . . . The power the Supreme Court has taken to itself—to nullify any laws it does not like—must be taken from it if our progress is to continue.

"What the best way to do this may be, we do not know," the *News* said, but the very first thought that came to mind was "by packing the Court with additional justices friendly to the New Deal." [103]

The uninvited counsel the President received in the aftermath of the election, too, though it indicated that opinion was still unsettled, also expressed a favorable view of Court-packing and distress over the age of the Justices. A Baltimore lawyer wanted "a law to be enacted at once that the personnel of the Supreme Court be increased to not less than two more judges"; and a Memphis man wrote: "I think you the grandest President we have ever had, and I think God will give you a hand. . . . Mr. President, the labor people want you and Congress to curb the Supreme Court. You all know just 9 old men should not rule this grand country." [104]

Of the many correspondents Roosevelt heard from in the aftermath of the election, one had far more influence on the quest for a judiciary bill than any other: William Denman of the Ninth Circuit Court in San Francisco. He had been a cowpuncher in Nevada; had scaled Mt. Shasta; had saved the fortune of the murdered president of Guatemala for his widow; had, as head of the mayor's committee to rid the City on the Bay of graft, filed the well-publicized "Denman Report" on corruption in 1910; had chaired the U. S. Shipping Board under Wilson; and, in association with Brandeis, had successfully defended an eight-hour law for women.

Even before taking his seat on the Ninth Circuit, Denman had voiced dismay with the state of the federal judiciary, and in 1936 he made a series of trips to Washington to press for reform. "It was rather a bold venture for a green judge," Denman acknowledged, "but I put aside my native shyness with the thought that since nobody else seemed to be doing it, I would assume the initiative—very much as Mr. Wells, with literary reluctance, assuming the writing of the history of the world." Denman at the outset concentrated on persuading Congress and Attorney General Cummings to add at least fifty new federal judges. He later confessed that he originally proposed so many judgeships in the hope that "if I got all those balls flying in the air, I might snake out two" for the Ninth Circuit. But the more he studied the matter the more he became convinced that fundamental change was required.

Over the course of 1936, Denman made his mark. He lobbied the Chief Justice, won the approval of Brandeis and Stone for some of his views, and especially caught the attention of the President. He had known FDR since childhood and addressed him as "Franklin." On one visit to the White House, he told Roosevelt that delays in litigation were scandalous and that the Judicial Conference was doing nothing meaningful about them. Denman favored both adding judges to relieve congestion and appointing an official, eventually called a "proctor," to monitor the behavior of the courts.

Denman found an attentive listener in the President, who had been troubled for some time by the problem of crowded dockets and impediments to appeals. In the spring of 1934, the attorney for the Southern District of New York had told him that there was an urgent need for more federal judges. "It now takes thirty-five months to get an admiralty case to trial, or one month under three years," he pointed out. Later that year, Roosevelt had written Cummings, "Will you speak to me about . . . percentage of certiorari applications by the Government being denied by the Supreme Court?" In March 1936, Denman wrote FDR's secretary, "As usual, I was again astonished at the mass of detail the President carries in his mind. There is complete justification for his plan to staff up the federal courts to a point where the federal administration of justice will approximate the pace of our industrial life." Roosevelt, in turn, told Denman to "keep up the good work" and instructed Cummings to heed the judge's recommendations.

In the critical days after the election, Denman wrote "Franklin" once more to warn him that people "mistrust the federal courts" because "their delays deny justice," adding, "I do hope you are to make the reform of the Federal Courts a part of your Inaugural." Denman never advocated Court-packing, but he strongly reinforced Roosevelt's growing conviction—that the federal judiciary was in urgent need of "reform" and that an essential element in any plan was a large increment of younger judges. [105]

VII

Six days after the election, the President returned to Washington, where two hundred thousand admirers gave him a rousing welcome, and on his very first night in the capital he summoned the Attorney General to the White House to find out what progress the Justice Department had made on coming up with a solution for him. Cummings began by reporting on Judge Denman's concern about crowded dockets, a matter Roosevelt had asked him to look into, but the discussion soon moved on to larger issues. They "talked . . . . over at great length," Cummings recorded in his diary, "the constitutional implications involved in such legislation as might be necessary at the incoming session . . . weighing pro and con the question of constitutional amendments of one kind or another, or possibly changes in the Supreme Court or *additions thereto.*" The ambiguous final phrase suggests that they might have been giving some attention to Court-packing as a remedy. The tenor of most of Cummings's summary, though, does not indicate that a specific course was agreed upon at this meeting or that immediate action was contemplated. Legislation would be framed that would spell out the constitutional authority for enacting new laws, and, if the Court proved unresponsive, *"perhaps* Congress *may* have some right to reassert itself as against judicial usurpation." Cummings added cautiously: "The path to an amendment to the Constitution is a thorny one and would necessitate a delay of at least two years before anything tangible could be done." When, on November 18, Roosevelt set sail for southern waters, nothing had been resolved, and the capital continued to wonder what he would do with his election victory. "Washington is practically paralyzed with inaction when the vital personality of FDR has been withdrawn," reported one observer. "It looks like an empty glove." [106]

During the four weeks Roosevelt toured South America, Cummings and his aides canvassed the possibilities for judicial reform, but when the President returned on December 15, they still had not found a formula. The main result of their labors was an exhaustive sixty-five-page report W. W. Gardner submitted to Reed, and the Solicitor General forwarded to Cummings. ("This matter has been handled confidentially," Reed assured him, "and I have my copy of the memorandum under lock.") Scholarly, shrewd, carefully written, the report was more valuable for warning of the pitfalls in various proposals than in pointing out what should be done. [107]

Gardner's memo examined several plans, including one "that Congress might increase the number of Supreme Court justices, in order to obtain a judiciary more of whose constitutional views are attuned to the contemporary development of the society which is governed by the Constitution." He explained: "It would be necessary to add either three or perhaps as many as nine or ten new justices, according as one evaluates the likelihood of antagonizing the present liberal justices to a point where they would retaliate by voting against the constitutionality of legislation."

The young attorney underscored no fewer than six formidable objections to this solution, including "the superficial character of the remedy" and "the paradoxical character of a cure for personal incapacity by appointing other judges who almost certainly will be subject . . . within a short time to a similar inability to reconcile innovation with the Constitution." (Many years later, he wrote wryly, "At the age of 27 it is axiomatic that senility settles in from the 70th year forward, a conclusion I find dubious in my 80th year.") In a fair-minded way, Gardner balanced these considerations by noting that, of the many propositions, this was "the only one which is certainly constitutional and . . . may be done quickly and with a fair assurance of success." In sum, he thought "that the choice must be made between a constitutional amendment and increasing the size of the court," but "only the former of these alternatives would seem to offer a lasting solution." [108]

Meantime, Cummings was carrying on a much more fruitful exchange with Edward S. Corwin. In late October, Thurman Arnold, a Yale Law School professor who sometimes served the New Deal, had written home:

> Professor Corwin of Princeton who is retained to consult with me on the social security case brief was with me when court opened the other day. He says that they ought to change the invocation from "God save the Government of the United States *and* this Honorable Court" to "God save the Government of the United States *or* this Honorable Court." He insists that God can't possibly do both, and He should not be asked even to try. He should be given his choice and let it go at that.

The author of numerous articles and books excoriating the infringement by the Court on the prerogatives of the other branches, Corwin had developed a close relationship with the Justice Department. Like other constitutional authorities, he had, for a time, put his faith in the hope that the conflict between the President and the Court could be resolved by the judges correcting their own errors.[109]

Corwin's thinking may have been turned in a new direction by Charles E. Clark, dean of the Yale Law School. In August 1936, Clark had written him to say that he admired his book *The Commerce Power versus States Rights*,[110] but questioned his "arguing against any attempted constitutional amendment." Early in September, he wrote again, and this time one sentence, pregnant with implications for the future, stood out: "I do think that the possibility of increasing the size of the Court ought to be more considered in Congress than apparently it has."[111]

After the election, Corwin put together a set of newspaper pieces on the Court question, and on December 3, Cummings wrote the President in South America:

> Professor Corwin of Princeton has prepared a series of articles dealing with some of our Constitutional difficulties. These articles will shortly be published in the Philadelphia Record. They are especially pertinent to the last discussion I had with you on this subject. I have just received from Doctor Corwin the proof sheets of the articles, which I enclose herewith. I am very sure that you will find them well worth reading.[112]

Corwin's series turned out to be a curious performance. With corrosive wit, he derided the record of the Court during the New Deal. In exposing the inadequacies of the panaceas that had been offered, he wrote brilliantly. But his own remedies were murky and even contradictory. After showing with devastating clarity why the Administration should not resort to amendments, he stated that some amendments might be needed. He called on the Court to reform itself, yet conceded that this particular tribunal could not be expected to do so. One sentence in the final article, though, emerged boldly: "No reform could be better adopted than the requirement, to be laid down by an act of Congress, or, if necessary, by constitutional amendment, that no Judge may hold office under the United States beyond his seventieth birthday."[113]

The columns evoked a variety of responses. Corwin got an encouraging letter from Cummings, who said he hoped to be able to talk to him soon, but Stanley Reed, to whom advance sheets had been sent, wrote him: "I wonder whether you over-emphasize the possibility of requiring retirement at seventy. It seems too small a thing to justify a constitutional amendment." More detailed criticism came from colleagues in his field. The Harvard political scientist Fritz Morstein Marx cautioned him:

"To expect voluntary resignations in the face of 'issues' is, I think, Utopian. I am afraid that most of the gentlemen concerned would act on the assumption that theirs is the mission to stem the tide. And to press for resignations would be tantamount to a move toward 'packing' the Court." Corwin himself was, at this very time, appearing in print in opposition to Court-packing. The disadvantage of such a scheme, he said in the December issue of a Princeton periodical, "is obvious on the face of it. The operation is one which might be repeated indefinitely until the Court, loaded with superfluous members and become the football of politics, would have lost all semblance to a judicial tribunal and all claim upon popular regard."[114]

On December 7, however, Arthur Holcombe, professor of government at Harvard, pushed Corwin, whose thinking was rapidly evolving, considerably farther along the path on which Clark had started him in late summer. Holcombe wrote Corwin that after reading his series, he had a suggestion designed to accomplish their common objective of "maintaining the supply of young men, that is to say, men under the age of 70, on the Court." He went on:

> What would you say to an act of Congress providing that judges under the age of 70 should always comprise a majority of the Court and giving the President power to make additional appointments to the Court whenever the number of members above 70 years of age should be equal or should outnumber the members of the Court under 70? At the present time six judges are over 70, and if no resignations of older judges should take place and such an act as I propose were adopted, the President would have power to make four additional appointments of judges under the age of 70. That would bring the total membership of the Court up to thirteen, but as older judges retired the number would automatically fall again to nine before further appointments would be in order. If, however, two of the older members of the present Court could be persuaded to resign, it would be possible to replace them with two judges of less than 70 years and establish a majority for the younger members of the Court without bringing the total membership above nine.
>
> My feeling is that the threat of such an act of Congress might perhaps persuade some of the older judges to resign without the necessity of making additional appointments, but if not, I believe the public would support the general proposition that the majority of the total number of the Court, whatever the total number might be, should be not more than 70 years of age.

Corwin responded that the scheme was "*most* ingenious, devilishly so. . . . I'm going to pass the idea along, and we'll see what comes of it."[115]

On December 16, Corwin, prompted by these communications and even echoing their language, wrote Cummings:

> It is probably utopian to hope that the Court will supply the needed remedy for a situation which it has itself created. Hence we must turn either to constitutional amendment or Congressional action.
>
> As to the latter, I did not care to go on record as favoring a *tour de force*: yet it is essential to face the fact that Congressional action may be necessary.

Nor, he added, had his articles exhausted the possibilities. Corwin continued:

> A friend of mine has made this ingenious suggestion: that the President be authorized, whenever a majority of the Justices, or half of the Justices, are seventy or more years old, to nominate enough new Justices of less than that age to make a majority. This, too, would require only an act of Congress, and something of a legislative precedent for such a measure is furnished by § 375 of title 28, of the U. S. Code.
>
> Mr. Reed appears to think that I put too much emphasis on my age-limit proposal, but I'm not so sure. A 70-year age-limit would secure more rapid replacement of justices. Furthermore, it might serve to draw the attention of the appointing power more frequently to the faculties of our great Law schools where superior talent emerges at an earlier age than in practice at the Bar.[116]

Since Corwin had pointed out in his series the folly of enlarging the Court, this suggestion marked an important departure. For the first time, compulsory retirement at seventy was linked to the appointment of new Justices. On the very next day, Cummings replied to Corwin:

> Of course, I realize that there is a good deal of prejudice against "packing the Court." I have been wondering to what extent we have been frightened by the phrase.
>
> Quite apart from immediate consideration, and as a mere matter of general policy, I have often thought that much was to be said for a constitutional amendment requiring retirements when the age of 70 is reached. I am wondering if there would be much opposition to such an amendment if it were so framed as not to affect the present judiciary by making it apply to future appointments only.[117]

Corwin's contribution reached Cummings at a propitious moment. Both the Attorney General and the President had been attracted to "Court-packing" for a long time, but they recognized that the proposition violated a taboo and that some principle would have to be found to legitimate it. Corwin offered such a formula by relating new appointments to the ages of Justices. If Corwin's suggestion (or, more precisely, that of Corwin's "friend" Holcombe) was adopted, Cummings could exploit growing popular resentment at the age of the bench.

By now, it had become commonplace to refer to the Justices as "the nine old men." A. A. Berle, a member of the Brain Trust, had used the term in passing in 1933, and a column in a Kentucky newspaper reflected a popular notion when it referred to the Court as "nine old back-number owls (appointed by by-gone Presidents) who sit on the leafless, fruitless limb of an old dead tree." But it was the publication on October 26, 1936, of *The Nine Old Men* by the widely circulated columnists Drew Pearson and Robert S. Allen that made the phrase a household expression. Allen later said there were "just scores, if not hundreds, of antiquated and senile federal judges. In the history of the court, when we wrote *The Nine Old Men*, I discovered instances of judges who were moribund, actual cadavers, walking derelicts." The book touched a nerve, for there had, in the recent past, been instances of Justices who had stayed on beyond their time. William Howard Taft's biographer later noted that when Taft became Chief Justice he found, among others on his bench, Justice Mahlon Pitney, overwhelmed by a nervous breakdown, and the seventy-nine-year-old Joseph McKenna, who "continued on until 1925, a cantankerous old man, as obdurate and senile as Judge Robert C. Grier had been fifty years before."[118]

The Pearson and Allen book quickly climbed onto the best-seller lists, and it was serialized in newspapers across the country. Even critics of the Justices were disturbed by the book's tone and by its inaccuracies, but this exposé helped concentrate popular attention on both the age and the viewpoint of the Court as a more sober account might not have done. The Wisconsin Progressive, Representative Thomas Amlie, while regretting the book's innuendoes, thought "that Pearson and Allen have done a particularly good job on the Constitutional law angle," and Senator Joseph Guffey called for a Senate investigation of the allegations the authors made. The Pennsylvania Democrat called the volume "the most disturbing—I would say shocking book on public officials I have ever read. Its purported disclosures are sensational."[119]

After receiving Corwin's letter, Cummings was close to the end of the trail. Yet Corwin still had not shown him the precise route he was seeking, and the Attorney General's reply suggests that he was still thinking that an amendment might be required and that the present Justices might be exempted. Once Corwin had blazed the path this far, however, it did not take Cummings long to trace out the rest of the way.

At some point in the next five days, Cummings found his answer. It is not certain how he did, but one scenario seems the most likely. While carrying on his other duties, he had also been writing a history of his department, in collaboration with his aide Carl McFarland. One passage in *Federal Justice*, which was about to be published, may now have stood out from the pages as it would not have before, an innovation that McReynolds, when serving as Wilson's Attorney General and not long before being named a Supreme Court Justice, had advocated in 1913. His recommendation stated:

> Judges of the United States Courts, at the age of 70, after having served 10 years, may retire upon full pay. In the past, many judges have availed themselves of this privilege. Some, however, have remained upon the bench long beyond the time that they are able to adequately discharge their duties, and in consequence the administration of justice has suffered. . . . I suggest an act providing that when any judge of a Federal court below the Supreme Court fails to avail himself of the privilege of retiring now granted by law, that the President be required, with the advice and consent of the Senate, to appoint another judge, who would preside over the affairs of the court and have precedence over the older one. This will insure at all times the presence of a judge sufficiently active to discharge promptly and adequately the duties of the court.[120]

Cummings may now have reasoned that McReynolds's prescription, which had been limited to the lower courts, might also be applied to the Supreme Court. Once the principle of retirement was adopted, any age might be stipulated, but seventy seemed especially compelling. It had been the age that, on different occasions, McReynolds, Cummings, and Corwin had all hit upon, and it had the not inconsiderable advantage of Biblical sanction. That summer, an Oklahoma newspaper had proposed to retire Supreme Court Justices at seventy, "as set out in Holy Writ as the reasonable span of human life."[121] With the retirement age fixed at seventy, the President would be able to name six new Justices, thus practically assuring a bench that would approve New Deal legislation.

If the McReynolds precedent is indeed the source of the final version of the proposal, it is puzzling that Cummings did not mention it to Roosevelt until January 17, but so closely did Cummings's final formula parallel that offered by McReynolds that this explanation has the highest probability. No other script seems as plausible, and there is no doubt that Cummings learned of the earlier recommendation at precisely, or almost precisely, this time. Robert Jackson later remarked that the fact that McReynolds had once been identified with the notion "seems to have been given great weight"; and, more than half a century later,

Warner Gardner, who claimed to have written the first draft of the bill (and may well have done so), thought it possible that he might have developed the basic idea because his "attention had been drawn" to the earlier statement of McReynolds.[122]

The President, for his part, on hearing about it, savored the irony that the proposition originated with none other than his relentless foe, Justice McReynolds. Cummings noted: "He was very much interested and amused." Roosevelt's repeated digs at McReynolds suggest that the crabby Justice had become his *bête noire*. According to one account, word reached the President right after the election, just as he was contemplating what to do with his big victory, that Justice McReynolds had said, "I'll never resign as long as that crippled son-of-a-bitch is in the White House."[123]

On December 22, Cummings penciled a note to the President: "I am 'bursting' with ideas anent our constitutional problems; and have a plan (of substance & approach) I would like to talk over with you when you have the time."[124] He may not have fully realized how receptive FDR would be. By this point, Roosevelt was already disposed toward "packing" the Court. He did not yet know how to carry it off, and he still thought of the idea as a birch rod to be taken out of the closet only if the Court did not mend its ways in the new term, but the idea was uppermost in his mind even before Cummings came to see him.

The President had invited George Creel to the White House once more to prepare an article, this one to be called "Roosevelt's Plans and Purposes." During the afternoon and evening they worked together, the President told Creel that the social objectives he cherished would all be challenged in the Supreme Court. But his face brightened as he said: "I've thought of a better way than a constitutional amendment stripping the Court of its power to nullify acts of Congress. The time element makes that method useless. Granted that Congress could agree on such an amendment for submission to the several states, it would be two, three, or four years before the legislatures could or would act. What do you think of this?" From a drawer in his desk, he extracted a heavily marked copy of the Constitution and riffled the pages as he read off passages and commented on the powers of Congress to act for the general welfare.

After reading Article III, § 1, he asked: "Where is there anything in that which gives the Supreme Court the right to override the legislative branch?" As the President talked, Creel wrote afterward:

> I was amazed by his reading on the subject and by the grip of his mind on what he conceived to be essential facts. For example, he quoted at

length from Madison's *Journal* and Elliot's *Debates*, citing them as his authority for the statement that the framers of the Constitution had voted on four separate occasions against giving judges the power to pass upon the constitutionality of acts of Congress.

If Congress was to reclaim the powers that had been usurped from it, Roosevelt reasoned, it should add a rider to each bill at the next session *charging* the Supreme Court to remember that the Constitution vested *all* legislative power in Congress and explicitly authorized it to provide for the general welfare. Suppose this proved ineffective? Creel related: "'Then,' said the President, his face like a fist, 'Congress can *enlarge* the Supreme Court, increasing the number of justices so as to permit the appointment of men in tune with the spirit of the age.'" The total could grow to as many as fifteen. When *Collier's* published this article on December 26, with three columns discussing the Supreme Court, Creel expected an explosion. Yet, once again, the President's explicit words were ignored.[125]

VIII

On the same day that Creel's article appeared, Cummings, who had had a sketch of the plan in hand two days earlier, went to the White House to report to Roosevelt. Although December 26 was the day after Christmas, he could not wait for the end of the holiday season. That morning he went to his office to go over some papers on the chance that the President might be willing to see him, and when he phoned the White House, Roosevelt gave him an appointment for five o'clock that very afternoon, the start of what turned out to be "one of the longest and most interesting conferences I have had with him in a long time," the Attorney General noted in his diary.

Cummings, who may well have been torn between pride of parenthood and anxiety about how his offspring would be viewed, asked Roosevelt to promise not to laugh when he told him he thought he had the solution. That sentence only resulted in their both breaking up in laughter, but thereafter the discussion was much more serious. The Attorney General explained that he had been studying prayerfully the whole question, and he had read everything he could get his hands on, only to find that there were powerful objections to all of the suggestions they had been considering.

So he had concluded that it was necessary to go back to the beginning and figure out what the precise problem was before coming up with a remedy, a deduction that directed him to an examination of constitutional history. If Oliver Wendell Holmes's dissent in the first child labor case[126] had been the holding of the Court, he observed, almost none of the subsequent problems would ever have arisen. Similarly, the New Deal would have had all it ought to have expected if the reasoning of the minority on the bench in the past year had been adopted. So the real problem was not with the Constitution but with the way it had been misconstrued.[127] "Go on, you are going good," Roosevelt responded. "I wish I had a stenographer present so that this could be taken down."

The performance of the Court, the Attorney General continued, led to one inescapable conclusion—that they should put out of their minds any thought of amending the Constitution. Why tamper with the Constitution when the trouble lay with judges who were out of step with the rest of the country? Amendments should be resorted to only as an extreme resort. Furthermore, there were practical difficulties. It had taken years to undo the damage wrought by the *Dred Scott* and income tax decisions,[128] and the child labor amendment, which had been bounced around for more than a dozen years, was still unlikely to be ratified. The loudest cry for an amendment solution, he added, came from those who thought that through money and propaganda they could defeat any amendment that was proposed. Hence, the President ought to be turning his thoughts instead to what to do about the personnel of the Court, a conclusion Roosevelt had no difficulty in accepting.

The President broke in at this juncture to say he had been told confidentially by someone close to McReynolds that at the end of this term of Court, McReynolds and quite probably Sutherland and Van Devanter might all retire, but he was not disposed to count on those prospects, and the word that reached him did not come with any promises. Cummings retorted that by the time the Court recessed Congress would have gone home, there would be additional delays, and before they knew it the 1938 Congressional campaign would be under way and the fat would be in the fire. The President should not wait, the Attorney General said; he should strike right away. Roosevelt heard this counsel with a lively interest that quickened as the discussion went on.

Instead of proceeding directly to his solution, Cummings took a side route. Judge Denman and others, he noted, had stressed the need for additional judges in the lower federal courts, and the Attorney General agreed, for many people were dissuaded from bringing suit because they feared they would die of old age before their cases were decided. In sum, "speedy justice was the crying need of the day, and the present situation was a reproach to our standard of civilization, and brought about all kinds of collateral demoralization." It was difficult, though, to solve the problem along the lines Denman had proposed "because of the competing interests of various districts." Without indicating why he was doing so, Cummings then jumped to a very different matter. William Howard Taft, he remarked, had once pointed out that there was a defect in the Constitution because it did not stipulate that federal judges must retire at seventy, a deficiency the former Chief Justice had thought could be met only by a constitutional amendment.

That observation led Cummings to some reflections on packing the Court. He thought that, though "we were probably unduly terrified by a phrase," there was "substantial objection in the country to a deliberate addition to the Supreme Court for the purpose of meeting the present situation." But if the entire federal judiciary were expanded, there was no reason that the Supreme Court should not be included, especially given the widespread criticism of the Court for refusing to grant certiorari in important cases. Strangely, Cummings did not record in his diary any mention of FDR's final response, but the Attorney General's subsequent behavior indicates that Roosevelt gave his assent. [129]

Buoyed by this exchange, Cummings turned his hand to sketching the remaining details. He wanted not only to liberalize the Court but to improve the entire judiciary. By presenting "Court-packing" in the guise of judicial reform, he would make the plan more palatable. Yet the Attorney General's interest was not just expedience. He had long cherished the aim of overhauling the structure of the courts, and Roosevelt shared some of his ardor. Once they launched what they knew would be a historic fight, they wanted it to be remembered for bettering the whole judicial system as well as for overcoming the intransigence of the Supreme Court. In particular, Cummings resolved to relate Court-packing to Judge Denman's persistent recommendations not only for more lower court judges, but also for appointment of a proctor to supervise lower tribunals and creation of "roving judges" to clear up congestion. All of these ideas he now tied together into a single package. [130]

The bill went through many drafts and numerous minor revisions, embracing four proposals: (1) that when a judge of a federal court who had served ten years did not resign or retire within six months after his seventieth birthday, a President might name another judge as coadjutor; (2) that the Supreme Court should not have more than six added Justices, nor any lower-court bench more than two additions, nor the total federal judiciary more than fifty; (3) that lower-court judges might be assigned to exceptionally busy courts; and (4) that the lower courts should be supervised by the Supreme Court through a proctor. [131]

Roosevelt and Cummings decided it would be helpful to accompany the bill with both a message from the President and a letter from the

Attorney General. Instead of concentrating on the desirability of a more liberal court, both documents would stress the incapacity of aged judges and the need for additional appointments to get the Court abreast of its work. By emphasizing the need for greater efficiency, they hoped the plan would be accepted as a project for judicial reform rather than being viewed simply as a stratagem to pack the Court. Once again, Cummings parceled out assignments within the department so that men were called on to supply statistics on denial of certiorari or the ages of judges without ever being told why this information was wanted or being given enough to do to be able to piece together what was happening.

When all three documents were taken to the White House, Roosevelt offered little comment on the bill, but he gave the letter, to which Alexander Holtzoff at the Justice Department had made important contributions, a thorough going-over, and Cummings had to revise it before he would approve. Even more care was lavished on the President's message. Roosevelt wanted it to be regarded as a magisterial state paper, and, not certain that Cummings was up to the task, he decided, once more, to summon Donald Richberg to contribute his skills.

On learning of what the President was about to do, Richberg, one young Department of Justice employee later reported, reacted with "extreme political fear and shock." The aide added: "As McFarland told me, he was 'scared to death.'" Furthermore, like Reed, Richberg questioned the emphasis on crowded dockets. According to his later account, which may have been self-serving, Richberg delayed the plan for forty-eight hours, and, for a moment, thought he had nearly won the President over. But once Richberg realized he had lost, he told Ray Clapper a year later, he "confined self to fighting to get message revised and fony stuff about congestion, etc. out of it and made presentation more simple and direct." In the end, though, he fell into line and did what was asked of him. It was later said of the message, "Cummings prepared the first draft—but Richberg added the venom."[132]

On the night of January 30, when Judge Rosenman arrived at the White House for the President's birthday party, Roosevelt asked his favorite speech-writer and faithful friend to contribute his talents also. It was the first Judge Rosenman had heard of the plan, even though he had helped write both the State-of-the-Union message and the Inaugural Address that month. When Rosenman told Corcoran, who had also been kept in the dark, what was happening, the President agreed that Corcoran, too, should be asked to go over the final draft of the message. But he instructed Rosenman not to let Cummings know that Corcoran was involved.[133]

The last stages of the drafting process proved remarkably time-consuming. On Saturday, January 30, Cummings, Reed, and Richberg went to the White House for a late lunch with the President and Rosenman that lasted three hours, then returned to the Justice Department where they worked the rest of the afternoon. On Sunday, the trio spent a couple of hours more on the documents at the Attorney General's home, and on Monday, between lunch at the White House and John Gielgud's performance in *Hamlet* that evening, Cummings was, as he noted tersely in his diary, "busy working on matter affecting the judiciary." Late the following afternoon, February 2, Cummings, Reed, and Richberg once more closeted themselves with Sam Rosenman at the White House to debate whether the increase in judges was to be temporary or permanent. Cummings, who insisted that the feature should be permanent, met resistance from Richberg, and the matter was not resolved until the next day when the four men took part in a session with the President that lasted nearly five hours. At this gathering, the Attorney General was relieved to find that Richberg had come around to his way of thinking and that the President held the same view. Even that lengthy session did not suffice, for the draftsmen returned to the White House at 8:30 that night and remained until 11 p.m., when they scheduled yet another meeting for the following day.[134]

Not until the afternoon of February 4, over a stretch of three hours at the White House, did Cummings, Richberg, and Rosenman put the finishing touches on FDR's message, and even then, Clapper later recorded in his diary, Cummings "didn't know until last minute whether Rvt would go through with it or not." As Rosenman worked on the documents in the waning days, he thought he detected some anxiety in the President's manner. "It was the only time I can recall," he wrote subsequently, that Roosevelt "seemed worried after deciding upon a course of action." But when on the night of February 4 the President went over the final draft of his message one more time with his press secretary, Stephen Early, and his son James, who was on the White House staff, his son noted in his diary, "All of us emitted war whoops."[135]

Though the number of consultants had been growing, Roosevelt continued to demand secrecy, an insistence that combined fear of premature disclosure that might promote bickering with his love of the dramatic. A few days after the plan was announced, Steve Early told Ray Clapper that "reason Rvt didn't talk it over with more people was that he was afraid of a leak which would tip off opposition and enable them to start hostile build up before he got his plan out." Save for Cummings, no one in the Cabinet, not even the ubiquitous Ickes, knew of the plan. Indeed, Roosevelt, at one Cabinet meeting in January, deliberately misrepresented what was going on. Nor was any member of Congress told. Some of the men who would soon bear the burden of defending it were busy drafting quite different proposals, and Henry Fountain Ashurst, the Democratic Senator from Arizona who would shortly be called on to move the proposal through the Senate Judiciary Committee, was publicly denouncing Court-packing as "the prelude to tyranny." On the morning of February 5, the House Minority Leader told an ailing Republican Congressman, "No one even on the Majority side seems to know what the program of legislation etc. is going to be."[136]

Through all of this, the President gave little indication of the surprise he was about to spring. As Moley later observed, "Roosevelt's pronouncements in the course of his good-will trip to South America would not have frightened the birds of St. Francis." Despite some shafts aimed at the Supreme Court, FDR's State-of-the-Union message was praised for its good-tempered restraint, and he made no mention at all of the judiciary in his Inaugural Address. Informed observers predicted that the President would wait to see how the Court disposed of the Wagner Act cases before taking any action. On January 24, Dean Dinwoodey, editor of *United States Law Week*, wrote that "last week it was made plain that he does not at the present time have in mind any legislation directed at the Court."[137]

IX

As the final details of the bill, the letter, and the message were hammered out, only one question remained: when to launch the plan. It was conceivable that Roosevelt might wait until the Wagner Act cases had been decided, but if he had any such intention, he felt compelled to abandon it. The situation in Congress, where more and more members were committing themselves publicly to divergent proposals, was getting out of hand. Outside the government, progressives had called a national conference to reach agreement on an amendment. Most important, word of FDR's plan had begun to leak out, and speculation about what the President intended was getting closer and closer to the mark.[138]

Not everyone had thought that Roosevelt's State-of-the-Union address signaled inaction. Breckinridge Long noted in his diary:

> After I heard the speech I went home and read the printed speech twice. It is rather mysterious in that it is enshrouded somewhat in mystery in that he makes no intimation of his specific plan, but it is very plain that he has something definitely in mind. I say it is very plain, but I mean that

it is very plain to those who read with a discriminating eye the words of his message and use as a background his whole history in connection with the Supreme Court.[139]

The conservative Republican Congressman from Minnesota, Harold Knutson, also found the address unsettling. He wrote: "I rather thought the President's message contained one or two disquieting features and the question that is bothering me is, will he attempt to 'pack' the Supreme Court. There is no limit on the number of judges that may be appointed to the Supreme Court and by adding two or three he could easily secure control of the judiciary. Will he go that far?"[140]

In divining FDR's intentions, Long had an advantage. On the same day that Roosevelt gave his address, Long had lunched with Cummings. Afterward, he set down in his diary:

> Homer has devised a means and has a specific draft to carry out the provisions intimated. It contemplates a large treatment for the whole judicial system and is not confined to the Supreme Court alone. He thinks the President has the matter definitely in mind. Procedure along that line would permit the drafting of a bill to disqualify members of the judiciary over the age of 70 years, if they have not retired voluntarily within six months after they have passed that age, and the appointment of a successor. More than that, it makes various changes in the structure of the judiciary and mobilizes the framework of the system. Whether anything will come of it is to be determined only in the future, but in the light of the President's Annual Message to the Congress it seems to my mind clearly that he has some definite proposal in mind, and after my conversation today I am of the opinion that it is this proposal.[141]

FDR's speech-writers were no more discreet than his Attorney General. Over cocktails on January 20, Donald Richberg let slip what was going on. Ray Clapper noted in his diary:

> Richberg says Rvt has a number of bombshells ready to shoot which will astound country—says Rvt is in audacious mood and is even thinking of proposing to pack Supreme Court by enlarging it. R seems favor instead compulsory retirement. He says Rvt is determined to curb the court and put it in its place, and will go ahead even if many people think it unwise.[142]

Curiously, considering his emphasis on secrecy, Roosevelt had offered the St. Louis *Post-Dispatch* an exclusive on his attitude toward the Supreme Court in December and sometime in the fourth week in January had let both the leader of the CIO, John L. Lewis, and Charlton

Ogburn of the A.F. of L. in on the secret. Lewis said that he thought the plan better than the amendment route. Tommy Corcoran also agreed that it was workable, when he, too, was told of the proposal.[143]

Before the month was over, the Senate had begun to sniff out what was happening. On January 24, Irving Brant, who as head of the editorial page of the St. Louis *Star-Times* had often written on constitutional subjects, wrote the President: "Several senators have told me that you expect to make a statement about the Supreme Court within a few days." On February 2, in a speech that seemed to imply more than it said, Senator William Borah, the Idaho Republican, deprecated the "purloining" of state powers by the federal government and lauded the Supreme Court as the shield of individual liberties. Alert Washington columnists knew that something was in the wind, but they had not yet discovered exactly what it was. "Strange things are being said in Congress," Paul Mallon noted in his column of February 4. First there had been a speech by Ashurst, then one by Congressman Samuel Pettengill, now Borah. But what were they aiming at? Borah, he pointed out, "left the definite impression he was attacking something Mr. Roosevelt was going to propose, but he did not say what."[144]

The President could wait no longer. Since the Court was scheduled to begin hearings on the constitutionality of the Wagner Act on Monday, February 8, he wanted to submit the message before then so that it would not be interpreted as a direct threat to the Court. On February 2, he was scheduled to entertain the judiciary at dinner at the White House, so he could not very well present the plan before then. Richberg later recalled that Roosevelt had said impishly that "his choice should be whether to take only one cocktail before dinner and have it a very amiable affair, or to have a mimeographed copy of the program laid beside the plate of each justice and then take three cocktails to fortify himself against their reactions." The President thus felt limited to the interval between February 3 and February 6. On February 3, the Senate recessed until February 5; so Friday, February 5, became the day he chose.[145]

In the week following announcement of the plan, Cummings called in Clapper for a talk, and the columnist asked him why the plan had been sprung on February 5. There were several reasons, the Attorney General answered. They wanted to make the announcement early in the session simply because it would take a while to get the bill through. Furthermore, they needed to leave time for nominations of new Justices to be approved. Launching the proposal right away also had the advantage of signaling advocates of dozens of other solutions that they could drop what they were doing. Finally, the administration anticipated that by getting the plan enacted reasonably early in the session, it would permit Congress to go ahead with substantive legislation confident that it would be interpreted by a Court behaving in the spirit of Brandeis, Cardozo, and Stone, which was all, Cummings added, the government sought.[146]

The real ending of the odyssey of the search for the Court plan came not on February 5, however, but three days earlier when the guests assembled in the East Room of the White House for the judiciary dinner. It was a gala evening. Among the ninety guests were most of the Supreme Court Justices, Mrs. Woodrow Wilson, Senator Borah, and the Gene Tunneys. In the room sat men such as Reed, who the Justices did not suspect would soon be their colleague, and Cummings, who was told by Rosenman that he had the lean and hungry look proper to a conspirator. Two of those present, Senator Ashurst and Representative Hatton Sumners, chairmen of the Senate and House Judiciary Committees, would in three more days be handed a bill to blunt the power of the honored guests of the evening. As the guests filed out of the dining room, Roosevelt, in high spirits, remained seated talking to Justices Hughes and Van Devanter. Borah, seeing them together, remarked: "That reminds me of the Roman Emperor who looked around his dinner table and began to laugh when he thought how many of those heads would be rolling on the morrow."[147]

X

To put together the complete puzzle of the origins of the Court plan, one still needs a few pieces. But it is clear that many of the men alleged to have been its authors either knew nothing of it or played quite minor roles. The main operation, from beginning to end, involved a very few, most of them concentrated in the Justice Department. Within that small band, Stanley Reed was, as he later said, no more than "lukewarm" toward the idea. Moreover, he felt uncomfortable, as Solicitor General, about conspiring to pack a Court that he would be appearing before.[148] Of those who exerted influence from outside the department, Corwin, a department consultant, was more important than such putative architects as Corcoran. First and last, Homer Cummings was the principal author, though the President was intimately involved throughout. Five days after the proposal was announced, Jimmy Roosevelt noted in his diary that the Attorney General "made it quite plain that he resented the newspaper stories that Ben Cohen and Tommy Corcoran had anything to do with it!!"[149]

Though few, understandably enough, have found much good to say about the plan, its presentation was not a capricious act but the result of a long period of gestation in which it seemed sensible to conclude that the problem lay not in the Constitution but in the composition of the Supreme Court; that a confrontation with the intractable Justices was some day going to be unavoidable; and that a solution must be found not in a constitutional amendment but in a statute. During this time, other options were carefully examined, favored for a while, and then discarded on not unreasonable grounds. Throughout this period, Roosevelt was called on repeatedly to take action, and it appeared, in particular, that he would have a sizable following for a recommendation that would justify the appointment of additional Justices by stressing the infirmity of the Hughes Court and the need to reform the entire judiciary. In retrospect, it appears that the President misjudged the state of opinion and underestimated the resiliency of the Court, but, at the time, the plan seemed to have an inherent logic and even inevitability.

F I V E

FDR's "Court-packing" Plan

[Several of the essays in this volume deal with aspects of FDR's "Court-packing" plan of 1937, but this is the only one that encapsulates the entire episode. It draws upon the Walter Prescott Webb Lecture I delivered at the University of Texas at Arlington, subsequently published in Harold M. Hollingsworth and William F. Holmes, eds., *Essays on the New Deal* (Austin: University of Texas Press, 1969), but I have changed and enlarged upon that lecture to assimilate nearly a quarter of a century of more recent scholarship and research. In particular, I have integrated material from an address delivered on May 14, 1984, to the Supreme Court Historical Society in the Restored Court Chamber of the John Marshall era. Usually that room in the Capitol is roped off, but once a year it is opened to invited guests of the Society for an annual lecture, followed by a formal banquet with the Justices at the U. S. Supreme Court. The lecture was published with minor revisions in the *Duke Law Journal* in 1985.]

I

Franklin Roosevelt's proposal to pack the Supreme Court in 1937 bore the mark of a proud sovereign who after suffering many provocations had just received a new confirmation of power. In November 1936, the President had won the biggest electoral victory in the annals of the two-party system, but his sense of triumph was flawed by the realization that it was incomplete. Even though he controlled the Executive office and could expect to have his way with Congress, where he had led his party to a smashing victory, the third branch, the Supreme Court, seemed intractable. Four of the Justices—James McReynolds, Pierce Butler, Willis Van Devanter, and George Sutherland—were such staunch conservatives that almost every time either the Solicitor General, Stanley Reed, or the Attorney General, Homer S. Cummings, went into court, he knew he had four votes against him; if he lost even one of the remaining five, he would be beaten. Three judges—Louis Brandeis, Harlan Fiske Stone, and Benjamin Cardozo—would approve most of the New Deal laws. But if either of the two Justices in the center—Chief Justice Charles Evans Hughes or Owen Roberts—moved into the camp of the "Four Horsemen," FDR's program would perish in the courtroom.

Early in the New Deal, the Supreme Court had appeared willing to uphold novel legislation, but in the spring of 1935 the roof had fallen in. Justice Roberts joined the Four Horsemen to invalidate a rail pension law, and thereafter Roberts voted consistently with the conservatives.[1] Later that same month, on "Black Monday," May 27, 1935, the Court, this time in a unanimous decision, demolished the National Industrial Recovery Act.[2] In the next year, the Court, by a 6–3 vote in *Butler*, struck down the Agricultural Adjustment Act with an opinion by Justice Roberts that provoked a blistering dissent from Justice Stone; took special pains to knock out the Guffey Coal Act in the *Carter* case; and in *Tipaldo* invalidated a New York State minimum wage law.[3] "Never in a single year before or since," Max Lerner later wrote, "has so much crucial legislation been undone, so much declared public policy nullified." Of all the wounds the Court inflicted on itself, the *Tipaldo* decision cut deepest. It appeared to create, as Roosevelt said, a "no-man's-land," in which neither the federal government nor any state government could act to protect the worker.[4]

The President said nothing more about the Court publicly for all the rest of 1936, and after his great victory in November he went off on a cruise to South America without intimation that he had any notion of taking action affecting the Court in his second term. In January he gave his inaugural address without indicating that he had any particular plans. The new Congress convened, and more days passed, and still he did not let on what he intended. Then, abruptly, without warning, the President, on February 5, 1937, dropped a bombshell. Instead of calling for new social legislation, he caught the nation, his Congressional leaders, and his closest friends by surprise with a bold, quite unexpected proposal—to alter the composition of the United States Supreme Court.

Roosevelt sent his scheme for reorganizing the judiciary up to the Hill in a special message. He claimed that insufficient personnel had resulted in overcrowded federal court dockets and had occasioned great delay and expense to litigants. "A part of the problem of obtaining a sufficient number of judges to dispose of cases is the capacity of the judges themselves," he stated. "This brings forward the question of aged or infirm judges—a subject of delicacy and yet one which requires frank discussion." He continued:

In exceptional cases, of course, judges, like other men, retain to an ad-vanced age full mental and physical vigor. Those not so fortunate are often unable to perceive their own infirmities. . . .

A lower mental or physical vigor leads men to avoid an examination of complicated and changed conditions. Little by little, new facts become blurred through old glasses fitted, as it were, for the needs of another generation; older men, assuming that the scene is the same as it was in the past, cease to explore or inquire into the present or the future.

Life tenure for judges, the President declared, "was not intended to cre-ate a static judiciary. A constant and systematic addition of younger blood will vitalize the courts."

To achieve this end, he recommended that when a federal judge who had served at least ten years waited more than six months after his sev-entieth birthday to resign or retire, a President might add a new judge to the bench. He could appoint as many as six new Justices to the Supreme Court and forty-four new judges to the lower federal tribu-nals.[5] Even though it was conceivable that if the legislation was enacted, the superannuated Justices, sensing a national will, would choose to re-sign, thereby leaving the bench at nine members, the plan was per-ceived to be an attempt to enlarge the Court.

II

FDR's message generated an intensity of response unmatched by any legislative controversy of this century, save perhaps for the League of Nations episode. "No issue since the Civil War has so deeply split fami-lies, friends, and fellow lawyers," wrote one columnist. Day after day for the next half-year, stories about the Supreme Court conflict rated banner headlines. One diarist noted: "Roosevelt's alteration plan of Su-preme Court stirs America. Addresses, talks, arguments for and against it, everywhere." The question was debated at town meetings in New England, at crossroads country stores in North Carolina, at a large rally at the Tulsa courthouse, by the Chatterbox Club of Rochester, New York, the Thursday Study Club of La Crosse, Wisconsin, the Veteran Fire Fighters' Association of New Orleans, and the Baptist Young Peo-ple's Union of Lime Rock, Rhode Island. In Beaumont, Texas, a movie audience broke out in applause for rival arguments on the plan when they were shown on the screen.[6]

Constituents inundated members of Congress with communications on the Court bill. Senator Hiram Johnson of California reported, "I receive some hundreds of letters a day, all on the Court,—sometimes some thousands." Senator Charles O. Andrews of Florida acknowledged:

"We are receiving hundreds of letters regarding the Supreme Court and they have not been answered because it has been impossible to even read one-third, much less answer them. We have, however, answered many by working nights and Sundays." Snowed under by thirty thousand letters and telegrams, Senator Royal Copeland of New York said his office was "quite disorganized," and he pleaded for "some relief." He added drily, "I feel fully informed of the wishes of my constituents."[7]

No sooner was the message read in the House than the San Antonio Congressman, Maury Maverick, raced down the aisle and dropped the bill in the hopper. But the Administration decided to concentrate not on the House but on the Senate, in part because it wished to avoid a clash with another Texan, Hatton Sumners, the hostile chairman of the House Judiciary Committee, and with Speaker William Bankhead of Alabama, who resented Roosevelt's failure to take Congressional leaders into his confidence. Even opponents of the plan conceded, however, that the bill would be approved in the House, where the Democrats had a nearly 4–1 advantage, with many votes to spare.[8]

The situation in the Senate seemed almost as promising. The President had so overwhelming a majority in the upper house that several Democrats could find seats only across the aisle in the Republican section. He figured to lose a few conservative Democrats, but he might make them up with progressive Western Republicans such as Hiram Johnson of California and Gerald Nye of North Dakota, the Farmer-Laborite, Henrik Shipstead of Minnesota, and the independent, George Norris of Nebraska.[9] Yet Roosevelt was unlikely to need these, for there were enough Democratic Senators who owed their election to him to provide a comfortable margin. If every one of the sixteen Republicans rejected the measure, the opponents would still need to persuade more than twice that many Democrats to desert the President just to draw even.

In the first week, numbers of Democratic Senators announced themselves for the bill, including a phalanx of influential legislators: the forceful Majority Leader Joseph T. Robinson of Arkansas; the chairman of the Judiciary Committee, Henry Fountain Ashurst of Arizona, though he disliked it; and such potent allies as Pat Harrison of Mississippi, James F. Byrnes, Jr., of South Carolina, and Key Pittman of Nevada. Men of rather conservative disposition, they received the plan with varying degrees of unenthusiasm but supported it out of loyalty to the President and the Democratic party. More ardent backing came from New Deal liberals such as Hugo Black of Alabama and Sherman Minton of Indiana, both future Supreme Court Justices. After assessing the situation, the White House concluded that no more than fifteen Democrats would oppose the bill in the Senate, and *Time* reported: "Newshawks who immediately made surveys of Congressional sentiment agreed that the bill would be passed without serious difficulty."[10]

Greeted in the press with anguished cries of outrage, the plan also elicited no little approbation, especially from FDR's admirers. They argued that the proposal was designed not to pack the Court but to "unpack" it, since the Court had been "stuffed" with corporation lawyers in previous Republican regimes.[11] The whole machinery of American government, they asserted, lay at the will of a single Justice, Owen Roberts, who, by combining with the Four Horsemen, could nullify the wishes of the people.[12] A number of the bill's proponents charged that the Court had usurped its powers; some even denied that there was any constitutional sanction for judicial review. Moreover, they found ample historical precedent for altering the size of the bench. Nor would they concede that Roosevelt was politicizing the Court; Representative Thomas R. Amlie, a Wisconsin Progressive, contended: "The fact is that the Supreme Court has always been in politics up to its ears."[13]

Many shared Roosevelt's concern about the age of the Justices. One man wrote Chief Justice Hughes: "Seems to me if I were 75 I would be glad to enjoy life instead of working and taking a job away from some young family man."[14] Some Tennessee lawyers pointed out that a Justice of seventy was an adult "before the telephone was invented, he was 35 before the automobile became of importance, and was over 40 before the airplane became a factor in national life. The golden age of gasoline, electricity, chemistry, mass production, radio and education had not in the main begun when the man of 70 had reached the age of 45." A Wisconsin man declared:

> Take it in my own case. I am assured by my acquaintances that I do not look any older than I did fifteen or twenty years ago. That may be true as to looks and mentality, but at my age (seventy-seven), any sane man must know that physically I can not measure up to fifteen or twenty years ago. I could not possibly put in working hours that I did when serving in the State Senate eighteen years ago.[15]

Supporters of the plan scoffed at the reverent attitude opponents took toward the Constitution and the Court. "A constitution is not an idol to be worshipped; it is an instrument of government to be worked," maintained Senator Robert J. Bulkley of Ohio. Many doubted the sincerity of the Constitution-worshippers. A South Carolinian observed: "If I got up tomorrow and advocated rigid adherence to the 14th and 15th [Amendments] of the Constitution, the same folks who are yelling 'Constitution' loudly now would fight among themselves for priority in applying the tar and feathers."[16] Henry M. Hart of the Harvard Law School contested the notion that a Supreme Court opinion was like the pronouncement of a Delphic oracle, and Donald Richberg, former chairman of the National Industrial Recovery Board, asserted: "We need to be disillusioned of the idea that putting a black robe upon a man makes him a superior variety of human being." Secretary of the Interior Harold Ickes protested:

> To listen to the clamor, one would think that Moses from Mount Sinai had declared that God Himself had decreed that if and when there should be a Supreme Court of the United States, the number Nine was to be sacred. All that is left to do now is to declare that the Supreme Court was immaculately conceived; that it is infallible; that it is the spiritual descendant of Moses and that the number Nine is three times three, and three stands for the Trinity.[17]

III

Although such sentiments strengthened the hand of the Administration Democrats in the Senate, the bill also encountered vigorous opposition, far more than had been anticipated. Roosevelt must have expected the defection of anti-New Deal Democrats such as Carter Glass of Virginia and Josiah Bailey of North Carolina. Much more serious was the rebellion of party regulars like Tom Connally of Texas and of the liberal Democrat Burton K. Wheeler of Montana. The loss of Wheeler was a stunner. After all, in 1924 Wheeler had been the vice-presidential nominee on the Progressive ticket headed by Robert M. La Follette, Sr., who charged the federal judiciary with usurpation and wanted to authorize Congress to override Supreme Court rulings. Since no one could dispute his credentials as a liberal, Wheeler, by denouncing the plan, made it difficult for the President to claim that his adversaries were the same bunch of economic royalists who had fought him in 1936.[18]

In fact, it quickly became apparent that FDR's antagonists enjoyed widespread support. Marshaled by the publisher Frank E. Gannett's National Committee to Uphold Constitutional Government, they bombarded Congressmen and newspaper editors with remonstrances comparing Roosevelt to Stuart tyrants and European dictators. "Our President evidently has noted the apparent success of Hitler and is aiming at the same dominance," wrote a Saginaw, Michigan, businessman. Opponents pointed out that Roosevelt had failed to suggest in his 1936 campaign either that the country faced a crisis or that he planned to remold the Supreme Court.[19] They argued that he should seek to amend the Constitution, and emphasized that it had taken only ten months to ratify the Twenty-first Amendment.[20] Above all, they protested that Roosevelt was not showing proper regard for the judiciary. "As a boy I was taught to honor and revere the Supreme Court of the United States above all things," wrote a New Orleans insurance man. "It seems strange to hear the Supreme Court discussed like a business, a going concern needing new capital to expand," commented a Charleston publisher. "We always were taught to think of it, with reverence be it said, as like the Church, where men selected for their exceptional qualifications presided as Bishops should." A prominent Catholic layman compared the Court's authority to that of the Pope and added: "To all intents and purposes our Supreme Court is infallible. It can not err."[21]

Many also took exception to the President's stress on the age of the Justices. Even friends of the proposal fretted about the deviousness of his contention that he was putting it forward out of concern that senescent judges were responsible for crowded dockets, for it seemed obvious that Roosevelt wished to pack the Court with Justices of a liberal persuasion. Congressmen over seventy were not entranced by the assertion that men's faculties are impaired when they reach seventy, and other older people objected that the scheme assaulted the elderly, who deserved respect, not opprobrium. One man counseled a Florida Congressman:

> If you think youth is more competent and reliable than the aged, remember Clemenceau who led France to victory, Chauncey Depew who died at 94 active to the last; Justice Holmes who at 90 gave a Supreme Court decision.
>   Reflect how at 84 Hindenburg headed Germany; at 83 Edison was active, and at 86 Elihu Root was doing good work at his office.[22]

Another opponent wrote the *Washington Post*:

> Between the ages of 70 and 83, Commodore Vanderbilt added one hundred million dollars to his fortune. . . . At 74 Immanuel Kant wrote his "Anthropology," the "Metaphysics of Ethics," and "Strife of the Faculties." . . . Marcus Portius Cato began the study of Greek when a youthful Roman of 80! Goethe at 80 completed "Faust." . . . Tennyson wrote his divinely impressive farewell, "Crossing the Bar," at 83. . . . At 98 Titian painted his historic picture of the "Battle of Lepanto." . . . Can you calculate the loss to the world if such as these had been compelled to retire at 70?[23]

The strategy of the crowded dockets—advanced age rationale turned out to be a blunder, and in March, the President virtually abandoned that line of argument and came out with his primary reason: that the Court was dominated by conservative Justices who were making it impossible for a national government to function. This emphasis appealed to FDR's New Deal followers, but others bristled at any attempt to tamper with an institution established by the Founding Fathers. Although the number of Justices had been changed several times before, many believed that the Constitution specified nine. One writer encountered an elderly lady who protested, "If nine judges were enough for George Washington, they should be enough for President Roosevelt. I don't see why he needs fifteen."[24] In vain, supporters of the bill retorted that the Founding Fathers had been revolutionaries and that the opponents were attempting to escape modern problems by evoking nostalgia for a mythical past.

Still other critics such as the historian James Truslow Adams believed that "the sole bulwark of our personal liberties" was the judiciary. "If a President tries to take away our freedom of speech, if a Congress takes away our property unlawfully, if a State legislature, as in the recent case of Louisiana under the dictatorship of Huey Long, takes away the freedom of the press, who is to save us except the Courts?" he asked. "If I were a Hebrew I would be scared green," asserted a Detroit businessman. "If I were a Negro I'd hate to have my precious amendment taken away from me—the one that put me on an equal footing with whites, thanks to Mr. Lincoln."[25]

On the other hand, Southerners frequently warned that the Court was a bastion of white supremacy. "Our very social and racial integrity rests behind these 'checks and balances,' " a constituent wrote the Louisiana Senators. "Voices cry from every Confederate grave," declared another.[26] (Polls, however, showed support for the plan greatest in the South, largely because, as a consequence of loyalties created in the era of Reconstruction, it was, by far, the most Democratic section of the country.)

So boisterously did opponents voice their objections that a number of Democratic Senators searched desperately for some device that would free them from the need to commit themselves. In particular, the freshman Democrats who had been swept into office in the Roosevelt tidal wave in 1936 looked for a way that would save them from voting for a scheme they found repugnant and that they knew outraged many of their constituents, if they could do so without breaking openly with the President. Typical of these freshman Democrats in the Senate were Prentiss Brown of Michigan, who took a resolutely circumspect stance; Charles O. Andrews of Florida, who told his son: "It will be my policy, right on, not to commit myself to any particular course with regard to the Courts"; and John H. Overton of Louisiana, who raised straddling to an art.[27] Overton's standard release stated: "The importance of the subject, its many aspects, the high source of the recommendation and the contrariety of opinion throughout the United States suggest to me that the proper course is to with-hold any definite conclusion until the matter has been more thoroughly investigated, discussed and considered." To one constituent, Senator Overton explained: "You state that you note that I am following Polonius' advice to 'reserve thy judgment.' I am going farther than this and, to paraphrase another precept of his, I am with respect to this matter, giving every man my ear and none, as yet, my voice."[28]

With the Democrats divided, the Republicans, at the urging of the canny Minority Leader, Charles McNary of Oregon, resolved to keep quiet and thus avoid offering an occasion that might reunite the Democrats. On the day after the President sent his message, Republican Senator Arthur Vandenberg of Michigan recorded in his diary:

> This morning ex-President Hoover phoned me from the Waldorf-Astoria in New York, eager to jump into the fray. . . . Now here is one of the tragedies of life. Hoover is still "poison"—(the right or the wrong of it does not matter). [William] Borah, McNary and I had a conference at 11 o'clock. Borah is prepared to lead this fight; but he insisted that there is no hope if it is trade-marked in advance as a "Hoover fight" or a "Republican fight." McNary emphatically agreed. As a matter of fact, this already was my own attitude.

Men such as Vandenberg, McNary, and Borah (Senator from Idaho) had some success in getting national GOP leaders to abide by the strategy of silence, though Hoover would not go along and others soon spoke out.[29] While the Republicans, by their relative restraint, were encouraging Democratic dissension, they held their own lines. Although the Administration had expected the support of some progressive Republicans, in the end every one of the sixteen Republican Senators, including Johnson and Nye, rejected the bill.

The opponents made the most of the opportunity offered by the public hearings before the Senate Judiciary Committee. They led off with their most important witness, Senator Wheeler, who began with a discursive, disarming statement that gradually worked around toward the Administration's contention that aged Justices were unable to keep abreast of their work. With a dramatic flourish, Wheeler then unfolded a letter from Charles Evans Hughes. The Chief Justice denied that the Court was behind in its business or that more Justices would increase efficiency. Instead, he asserted, "there would be more judges to hear, more judges to confer, more judges to discuss, more judges to be convinced and to decide."[30] Hughes's unanticipated contribution not only effectively rebutted the President's crowded dockets argument, but also suggested that henceforth Roosevelt, in pushing his proposal, would encounter not just the wily Wheeler but the formidable figure of the Chief Justice.

The Administration made the mistake of presenting its case briefly, and most of the hearings served to publicize the views of the opposition. The President's former aide Raymond Moley, clergymen, law school deans, and journalists all testified against the measure. Professor Erwin Griswold of Harvard Law School protested that "this bill obviously is not playing the game." "There are at least two ways of getting rid of judges," he observed. "One is to take them out and shoot them, as they are reported to do in at least one other country. The other way is more genteel, but no less effective. They are kept on the public payroll but their votes are canceled."[31]

Despite all the antagonism, though, it still seemed highly likely in the last week of March that FDR's proposal would be adopted. Many of those who were skeptical nonetheless did not want the Court to continue to invalidate liberal legislation, and if faced with a choice between Roosevelt's plan and the strangling of the New Deal, they would be likely to go along with the President. Roosevelt was certain to win unless Democratic Senators, especially the freshmen, abandoned him in droves, and it did not seem well-advised to break with a man who had been given so emphatic an endorsement just a few months before. Senator Andrews's son scolded his father:

> I have noticed a decided dissatisfaction among the laymen for your straddling attitude regarding the Supreme Court. . . . I do not see how you can stand to go against the President and his Supreme Court proposal. Your being in Washington you cannot realize the absolute necessity of patronage and you have not gotten one little bit and you have got to have it. This Supreme Court proposal is the first test that will be placed upon your loyalty to the Democratic party. A year from now you might afford to "bolt," but right now I do not see how you can afford to have them place you on the first go-round as a "bolter."[32]

A Michigan voter stated even more bluntly:

> I had never heard of Prentiss M. Brown until the last election, when I learned that a man by that name had been nominated for the United States Senate on the Democratic ticket.
>
>   So I voted for Brown, not because he was Brown, but because he merely happened to be the candidate on the Roosevelt ballot, and I

wanted to send to Washington every man possible to aid our President. . . .

Now I read with amazement . . . this Senator Brown as saying that he has not made up his mind regarding just how he'll vote on the proposal to change the Supreme Court.

Why does Senator Brown think we made him Senator Brown and sent him to Washington? We sent him there to support Roosevelt. Brown as Brown doesn't have to do any thinking or make any decisions. If he merely follows the policies outlined by our President he will be doing all the voters who voted for him will require.[33]

Men such as Brown and Andrews continued to probe for an acceptable compromise, but when it came to showdown, they figured to be on FDR's side. At the end of March, *Time* wrote: "Last week the stanchest foes of the President's Plan were privately conceding that, if he chose to whip it through, the necessary votes were already in his pockets."[34] The undecided Senators might not like the scheme, but they could not justify frustrating the President while the Court persisted in mowing down legislation.

IV

The Court itself, however, had some big surprises in store. On March 29, by 5–4 in the *Parrish* case with Justice Roberts joining the majority, the Court upheld a minimum wage statute from the state of Washington that to most people seemed identical to the New York law it had wiped out in *Tipaldo* less than a year before.[35] Two weeks later, Roberts joined in a series of 5–4 decisions finding the National Labor Relations Act constitutional.[36] On May 24, the Court validated the Social Security law.[37] These rulings marked a historic change in constitutional doctrine. The Court was now stating that local and national governments had a whole range of powers that this same tribunal had been saying for the past two years these governments did not have.

The crucial development was the switch of Justice Roberts, which converted a 5–4 division against New Deal legislation to 5–4 in favor. Some have argued that Roberts did not change at all. They explain that his vote against the New York minimum wage law in *Tipaldo* resulted from his unwillingness to rule on questions not properly brought before the Court, a contention that is unpersuasive. More important, if the Social Security opinions are contrasted to the *Rail Pension* ruling and to *Butler*, and the Wagner Act opinions are set against the *Carter* decision, it is clear that the Court, and specifically Mr. Justice Roberts, had shifted ground.[38]

Many observers, especially supporters of the plan, did not question that the Court had altered its views, and that it had done so because it had been baptized "in the waters of public opinion." After the *Parrish* decision, one correspondent asked: "Didn't the Welshman on the Supreme Court do a pretty job of amending the Constitution yesterday?" George Fort Milton, the Tennessee editor and historian, remarked: "The Supreme Court thing is quite amazing. Mr. Roberts changed his mind and so a law unconstitutional for New York is constitutional for the State of Washington." Justice Roberts, said a national Democratic leader, "performed that marvelous somersault in mid-air. One day Mr. Roberts is at one side of the tent—the next day he grasps the trapeze, makes a far swing, turns a double somersault and lands on the other side of the tent. But there [is] no telling when he will swing back again."[39]

Commentators differed, too, about why Justice Roberts joined the liberal majority. Some believed that he had been brought in line by Chief Justice Hughes with the deliberate intent of defeating the President's plan by removing its main justification. A columnist asserted: "No insider doubts that the whole change of trend represented in the decisions was solely the work of Mr. Hughes. Everyone gives Mr. Hughes credit for arguing Associate Justice Roberts into position." Others thought that Roberts had merely followed the election returns. FDR's Court proposal could not alone have been responsible, for the *Parrish* decision was reached before the President sent his message to Congress, although it was not handed down until afterward. The threat of Court-packing, however, may well have affected Roberts's vote in later cases.[40]

The switch by Roberts had ironic consequences. On the one hand, it gave Roosevelt the victory he wanted, for the Court was now approving New Deal legislation. In the middle of May 1937, Justice Stone told a friend, "It looks as though I should get through this term of Court without writing a single dissenting opinion, which hasn't happened for a long time," and Thurman Arnold confided, "Roosevelt has already accomplished his objectives and we are rewriting all our briefs in the Department of Justice in terms of the new definition of the commerce power." FDR's success brought to mind for one wag a line from Fielding: "He . . . would have ravished her, if she had not, by a timely compliance, prevented him."[41] But, on the other hand, Roberts's "somersault" gravely damaged the chances of the Court plan. By eliminating the critical need for recasting the membership of the bench, it erased the most important justification for the bill. Why change the Court now that you had the kind of decisions you desired?[42]

This argument became even more compelling when on the morning of May 18, while the President was breakfasting in bed, a messenger arrived at the White House with a letter from one of the Four

Horsemen, Justice Willis Van Devanter, announcing his resignation from the bench. Van Devanter's action was widely believed to have been the result of counsel from Senators Borah and Wheeler. Borah lived in the same apartment house on Connecticut Avenue; the two were on "Hello, Bill" and "Hello, Willis" terms.[43] The "conversion" of Roberts had given Roosevelt a 5–4 majority; soon he would be able to name someone to take Van Devanter's place and have the opportunity for a 6–3 advantage.

Since it appeared that the President had won substantially what he sought, he was now urged to call off the fight. "Why," it was asked, "shoot the bridegroom after a shotgun wedding?" The *Parrish* and Wagner Act decisions turned some Senators against the plan and encouraged others to press for compromise. Prentiss Brown stated that the switch of the Court took "a good deal of the ground work from under the arguments for the court bill and I believe it will open the way for friends and opponents to re-approach the issue." By the end of April, the two sides were roughly even. One poll showed forty-four Senators in favor, forty-seven opposed, four doubtful, with one seat vacant. The Social Security opinions and Van Devanter's resignation tipped the balance against the six-judge bill; thereafter, opponents held a narrow edge.[44]

Several in the FDR circle wanted to drop the whole project, but others argued that Justices who could switch so easily in his favor could just as easily jump back once the pressure was off. One of the President's aides said: "No man's land now is Roberts land." The Scripps Howard columnist Raymond Clapper noted in his diary that Roosevelt's press secretary had told him "that president is going ahead with fight—that don't know how long Hughes can keep Roberts liberal or how long Hughes will stay so."[45] Others reasoned that the switch of the Court had proven what the President had been saying all along: there was nothing wrong with the Constitution, only with the Court. And if enlightenment was such a good thing, why not have more of it?[46] Senator Theodore Green of Rhode Island declared: "Again we learn that the Constitution is what Mr. Justice Roberts says it is. So what we need is not amendments to the Constitution, but a sufficient number of judges to construe it broadly, lest one man's mistaken opinion may decide the fate of a nation."[47]

Furthermore, Roosevelt believed the country was with him. Only half a year had gone by since his decisive victory at the polls. "Why compromise?" the Democratic party chairman, Jim Farley, asked. "The Democratic senators were elected on the basis of supporting the President's program. It is up to them to back it now." To be sure, mail ran heavily against the bill, but since attitudes toward the plan divided sharply on class lines, and upper income groups were more articulate, that was not surprising. Members of Congress noted that opponents of the proposal often wrote on lithographed and embossed stationery, and when they analyzed their mail, they frequently found, too, that adverse letters came overwhelmingly from Republicans who in the recent campaign had been noisy but outnumbered.[48] If the press denounced the plan, 80 percent of editorial writers had been against FDR in 1936, and look what had happened on Election Day. True, by now the polls also showed a small margin unfavorable to the bill, but remember how wrong the *Literary Digest* canvass had been a few months before. Only one significant election had been held since the President sent his message, and in that race a Congressional seat in Texas had been won by a candidate committed to the plan, a newcomer named Lyndon B. Johnson.

Still another reason compelled Roosevelt to push ahead. Although he could name a new judge to the Van Devanter vacancy, it was understood that he had promised the next opening on the bench to Senator Robinson. He could hardly avoid choosing the Majority Leader without inciting a Senate uprising. On the day that Van Devanter made his announcement, Robinson's colleagues surrounded him on the Senate floor to congratulate him on becoming the next Supreme Court Justice. Three days later, a reporter, tongue in cheek, drew guffaws at a White House press conference by asking the President whether he intended to confirm the Senate's nomination of Robinson. Yet the Arkansan was a 65-year-old conservative. If appointing Joe Robinson was to be the climax of his effort to bring young, liberal men to the Court, the enterprise would end in a fiasco. It seemed more necessary than ever to balance the expected Robinson appointment by creating vacancies for liberal Justices.

Well before the end of May, however, FDR's lieutenants in Congress had to face up to the fact that they simply did not have the votes. One leader confided that five polls of the Senate had all come out with the same result: defeat. On Capitol Hill, the debonair chairman of the Senate Judiciary Committee, Henry Fountain Ashurst, who covertly opposed the legislation, was heard humming an old tune: "Massa's in the Cold, Cold Ground."[49]

With his plan foundering, Roosevelt got still more dismaying news: the Vice President was skipping town. At the end of a Friday afternoon Cabinet meeting, John Nance Garner, who was counted on by the President to hold party regulars in line, revealed abruptly that he was going home to Texas that very weekend and that he would be away for quite a while. When FDR's message was being read in February, the Vice

President had allegedly held his nose and pointed thumbs down. He was no idolater of the judiciary, though, and he was apparently more upset about relief spending and labor violence than he was about Court-packing. His behavior, however, sent a message to other Democrats in Washington—that one did not any longer have to put up with FDR's exotic ideas and even more exotic advisers, that it was perfectly all right, good for the country and even good for the party, to turn one's back on the White House.[50]

Two days after Garner took French leave, Roosevelt received a much bigger jolt: the long-awaited adverse report of the Senate Judiciary Committee. Of the ten Senators who signed the document, seven came from FDR's own party, but almost from the opening word the report showed the President and his proposal no mercy. The plan, it said, revealed "the futility and absurdity of the devious." An effort "to punish the Justices" whose opinions were resented, the bill was "an invasion of judicial power such as has never before been attempted in this country." If enacted, it would create a "vicious precedent which must necessarily undermine our system."

Without ever directly saying that Roosevelt was another Hitler, the authors called attention to "the condition of the world abroad" and maintained that any attempt to impair the independence of the judiciary led ineluctably to autocratic dominance, "the very thing against which the American Colonies revolted, and to prevent which the Constitution was in every particular framed." Consequently, the report concluded, "It is a measure which should be so emphatically rejected that its parallel will never again be presented to the free representatives of the free people of America." The columnist Ray Clapper noted in his diary: "Bitter document, extremely rough. . . . It reads almost like a bill of impeachment."[51]

Delighted by all this evidence of internecine bickering, Roosevelt's hard-core adversaries believed that, at long last, they had him on the run. A new Gallup survey found that support for judicial reform had been sliding at the rate of about 1 percent a week down to a new low of 41 percent. FDR's opponent in the 1936 campaign, Alf Landon, wrote: "His right wing is smashed and in retreat; his center is confused and wavering; his left wing advanced so far it is out of touch with his center"; and Ray Clapper jotted in his diary: "This seems most serious ebb of Rvt sentiment since he took office." As adjournment fever swept Capitol Hill, the Administration feared it could not withstand the movement to table the Court legislation and pack up and go home.[52]

To many observers, it seemed improbable that Roosevelt could salvage anything from the debris. The report, wrote the Kansas editor

William Allen White, "delivered the coldest wallop that the President has had to take. He can't stand another one." Five thousand miles away in London, Foreign Secretary Anthony Eden received what appeared to be the final verdict. His Majesty's ambassador at Washington, Sir Ronald Lindsay, informed him:

> Seven Democratic Senators have committed the unforgivable sin. They have crossed the Rubicon and have burned their boats; and as they are not men to lead a forlorn hope one may assume that many others are substantially committed to the same action. One can only assume that the President is fairly beaten.[53]

V

But at precisely this point, when his fortunes had sunk to their lowest, Roosevelt brought about an astonishing recovery that breathed new life into the apparently moribund idea of Court-packing. On June 16, while Washington continued to hum with talk of the Judiciary Committee critique filed two days before, the President, as he had so often in the past, diverted attention to the White House by announcing to surprised Democratic Congressmen that all 407 were invited to picnic with him on an island in Chesapeake Bay, a former bootleggers' hideout that had become a Democratic fish and game club. The Jefferson Island frolic proved to be an inspired idea. Almost everyone agreed, noted a correspondent for the *New York Times*, "that the President had done himself a 'world of good.'" Roosevelt, the Cleveland *Press* had remarked before the picnic, "is a gambler for small gains. That is, he never overlooks the slightest chance when engaged in a big legislative battle, as he has often demonstrated. Who can tell . . . that out of his three-day family party he might not clinch the few votes needed to put over a compromise on his court plan?" By many accounts, that is just what the President did.[54]

After the camaraderie of Jefferson Island, not a few Democratic Congressmen began to have second thoughts about the Senate Judiciary Committee's diatribe. Foes of the President had been picturing him as a man consumed by rancor and determined on revenge. Instead, the lawmakers had found a jolly innkeeper who radiated geniality. He had greeted the authors of the vitriolic report magnanimously and had given every impression of "a large soul rising above contumely." The Washington columnist Arthur Krock commented:

> The dramatization was perfect; the hero played his role flawlessly; and the audience began to forget his faults and indignantly to recall his aspersed virtues.

"It reminded me," said a cynical spectator today, "of what happens in the gallery when, on the stage, a long-suffering son slaps the face of his father. Forgetting the provocation the father gave, remembering only instinct and precept, the audience turns on the son for going too far."[55]

No longer was the opposition boasting of an early victory. At Whitehall, Anthony Eden now received very different intelligence from His Majesty's envoy at Washington. In a follow-up dispatch, Sir Ronald Lindsay informed him:

The meeting of the Democratic Congressmen on Jefferson Island . . . had rather surprising results, for the Roosevelt charm was turned onto them as through a hose pipe and they have returned to the Capital in a far more malleable spirit. . . . The feelings which induced seven Democratic Senators to sign the adverse report . . . are no longer in fashion.[56]

This newfound euphoria heightened prospects for a revised Court bill that had been put together earlier in June. The revamped legislation authorized the President to appoint an additional Justice per calendar year for each member of the Supreme Court who remained on the bench after the age of seventy-five. (Originally, the age had been seventy, and they could be named all at once.) Since there were currently four Justices seventy-five or over, the bill would empower him to name four new Justices, as well as a Justice to fill the Van Devanter vacancy, but the total of five could not be reached until the beginning of 1940.[57] Under this so-called "compromise," FDR lost very little. The most immediate effect of the measure would be to permit Roosevelt by the beginning of January 1938—only six months away—to add three Justices to the Court: one for the 1937 calendar year, one for the 1938 calendar year, and one to fill Van Devanter's slot. The principle of Court enlargement was still very much alive.

The prospects for enacting this new bill appeared very promising. All through the month of June, Joe Robinson had been piecing together a majority. At his direction, his chief lieutenants—Sherman Minton, Hugo Black, and Alben Barkley—worked the Senate corridors, buttonholing their Democratic colleagues; and when they sensed someone was weakening, bringing him to the Majority Leader's office to see if a commitment could be extracted. Robinson and his aides found that a number of Senators were not so hostile to this new version as they had been to the original bill, and the White House brought pressure on others. "Wait until the heat is turned on," FDR's agent on Capitol Hill, Tommy Corcoran, told a Senator in the troubled days after the Judiciary Committee report was released. "What do you mean by turning on the heat?"

the Senator asked. With a disarming grin, Corcoran replied, "The heat of reason."[58]

In the final days of June, the Majority Leader held three caucuses, each attended by some fifteen Senators, at which he explained in detail the nature of the new legislation, which was nearing finished form, and implored his fellow Democrats not to desert the leader of their party. He ended each session by stating that he would regard every man in the room as pledged to vote for the revised measure unless someone spoke up on the spot. Only one man did, and he indicated simply that he wanted more time. When the process was completed, Robinson was able to give the President the news he most wanted to hear: he had his majority.[59]

Most independent observers agreed. Though the press was over-whelmingly antagonistic to the proposal, Capitol Hill correspondents credited Robinson with fifty or more commitments. Under the headline "F. D. GIVEN EDGE ON REVISED COURT BILL," the Washington Daily News ran the subhead:

> Senate Poll Shows
> Administration Has
> Upper Hand in Fight.

"The best guessing here," wrote Raymond Clapper in his column, "is that the new . . . court enlargement bill . . . will get thru," while the Washington bureau of the Portland Press Herald in rock-ribbed Republican Maine reported: "General opinion is the substitute will pass, and sooner than expected, since votes enough to pass it seem apparent, and the opposition cannot filibuster forever."[60]

Privately, FDR's foes conceded that these reckonings were correct. On July 7, the morose Republican Senator Hiram Johnson informed a friend: "They have the votes at present to put it over." A confidential tally sheet set numbers on that conclusion. In an estimate prepared for the leading lobbyist against the Court plan, Frank Gannett, the Nebraska Senator Edward Burke revealed that if the roll were called right away, FDR would wind up the winner, 52–44.[61]

To be sure, the opposition, with its estimated forty-four votes, might well mount a filibuster, but many doubted that stalling tactics would succeed. Roosevelt's opponents, who had been charging him with perverting the democratic process, would be in an embarrassing position if they sought to deny the people's representatives in Congress an opportunity to vote and thereby contrived the triumph of the will of a minority. Nor did no-holds-barred hostilities appeal to party moderates.

"Among the conciliatory Democrats," remarked the *New York Times*, the filibuster was "losing favor. They have apparently come to the conclusion that the party would not present a pretty spectacle to the country by engaging in that kind of warfare."[62]

A national periodical that had been single-mindedly hostile to Court-packing from the start summed up the melancholy predicament of its cause. *Business Week* lamented: "Too many of them are not willing to run a real, organized filibuster. Too many of them are uncertain whether they would be justified in the eyes of their constituents." At no time in the history of successful filibusters could the foes of a piece of legislation count so many Senators in their ranks as were aligned against the Court bill, it observed. Unhappily, though, the measure still might be adopted. It explained:

> Despite the size of the opposition, and the ease with which they could prevent a vote being reached by Christmas, were they anything like as determined as were the much smaller number who fought Woodrow Wilson on the Versailles treaty, no one [can] be sure of the outcome.[63]

Analysts who concluded that Joe Robinson had put together a winning combination attributed much of the advantage to the Majority Leader. An important figure in his party, he had been chosen Democratic vice-presidential nominee in 1928, and, in his many years on the Hill, had put a number of men in obligation to him. In addition, so overbearing was his manner, he might intimidate some of the freshman Senators into going along. Besides, as *Time* noted: "Just as an expectant mother commands a certain ethereal prestige above other women, so Joe Robinson, as an expectant Justice of the Supreme Court, has become since Justice Van Devanter's retirement a sort of Super-Senator with a prestige all his own among his colleagues." Through the sheer strength of his personality, the Majority Leader might be able to get Roosevelt those few uncommitted votes that could mean the difference between victory and defeat. Without Robinson, the President would be undone.[64]

Robinson knew that a very difficult struggle lay ahead, and he concluded that there was only one way he could prevail—by turning the Great Debate that finally opened in July, a full five months after FDR's original message, into an endurance contest. Despite the forecasts of victory, he could not be sure of his own ranks; many of the freshman Democrats seemed especially shaky. On July 10, the Associated Press found seventeen votes still in doubt, and the Majority Leader realized that he did not have anything close to the two-thirds of the Senate required to impose cloture. But he surmised that there were limits to the price his Democratic colleagues would pay to balk the President, and he was determined to keep pushing those limits. He could do so by insisting on strict adherence to the rules, moving to Saturday sessions, and requiring evening and all-night meetings. Although the words were never spoken, the assumption behind Robinson's maneuvers was that if Senators continued to be obstinate, they would do so at the risk of their lives. Yet no one could be certain that Death was a friend of Court-packing. Two Senators were undergoing treatment at Washington's Naval Hospital, and both were counted on the Administration side of the ledger. There were even grounds for concern about Robinson himself, though few knew how serious they were.[65]

To hold the waverers in line, Robinson ran the debate with a whip hand. He invoked seldom used rules to ward off the possibility of a filibuster and even threatened continuous sessions, although members protested that such an ordeal would take its toll of the Senate, for more than a third of the body was over sixty. Tempers grew short in the murderous Washington heat. Senator McNary wrote home: "We are having a hot spell and the weather is just as hot as _ _ _ _, at least as hot as I think it is."[66]

On the opening day of the Great Debate, Robinson made an aggressive two-hour speech that carried the fight to the enemy. His face an angry purple, his voice bellowing, his arms pawing the air, both feet stamping the floor, Robinson gave the appearance of an enraged bull. When the opposition Senators, like so many *banderilleros*, tormented him with pointed questions, he roared all the louder and charged around the floor as though it were a *plaza de toros*. Throughout the afternoon, Robinson, though finding it hard to choke off his wrath, appeared ready to go round after round with his antagonists, but, altogether unexpectedly, came to a precipitate end in a curious, even shocking, fashion. After talking for some two hours, the Majority Leader reached into his pocket for a cigar and struck a match to light it. Since striking a match on the Senate floor was, as one writer noted, "frowned upon almost as severely as striking a senator," his colleagues stared at him in disbelief. His face, usually florid, turned ashen, and he seemed not to know quite where he was. He spoke a few words with the match in his hand, but, as it began to burn his fingers, he flung it to the floor and stamped it out. When Burke tried to ask him yet another question, Robinson said abruptly, "No more questions today. . . . Good-bye."[67]

That odd note of farewell signaled what was to come. Over the next several days, Robinson had a hard time enduring both the enervating weather and the relentless assaults on his bill not only in the Senate chamber but also in the House, where Hatton Sumners, the powerful chairman of the House Judiciary Committee, was cheered lustily when he denounced the advocates of Court-packing and cried, "We must give Nature—Nature—God Almighty—a chance," presumably by creating a vacancy for Roosevelt to fill by striking down some aged Justice. Little more than a week after the Great Debate began, the Majority Leader left the Capitol at the end of the day's proceedings to make his way through the suffocating heat to his apartment in the Methodist Building across the plaza. The next morning, his maid entered the apartment and came upon Senator Robinson sprawled face forward on the floor. He had been dead since midnight.[68]

The demise of Joe Robinson doomed all hopes for FDR's plan. "The Court issue went with Joe," concluded a Florida Congressman. "I think the death of Robinson will have a marked effect upon the Congress," wrote a prominent Southerner, "and I do not think that Robert E. Lee sustained a greater loss in the death of Stonewall Jackson than Roosevelt has . . . in the death of Robinson." A Minnesota editor reflected: "It is not unlikely that the death of Senator Robinson will be the turning point in the President's career."[69] To apprehensive Senators, already on edge from the strain of the long session, Robinson's death sounded a warning gong. A Washington column reported: "The sudden passing of Robinson has brought the pressure of wives, families and physicians on many senators to hasten their departure from the sweltering capital."[70] Two members of the upper house had died in the brief period since the session began, and Senators could readily imagine what prolongation of the dispute might bring.

Determined to exploit this anxiety to the fullest, foes of the judiciary bill accused the President and his New Deal cronies of nothing less than manslaughter. "Joe Robinson was a political and personal friend of mine," declared Senator Wheeler. "Had it not been for the Court Bill he would be alive today. I beseech the President to drop the fight lest he appear to fight against God." Wheeler's statement revealed the poor judgment that was to characterize other of his public utterances. "Your bad taste," a Massachusetts mayor wired him, "is surpassed only by your conceit in assuming the role of God's spokesman."[71]

But Wheeler's "ghoulish" comments reflected a widespread conviction. A reader of the *Washington Post* wrote: "The death of Senator Robinson, chief advocate of Roosevelt's court packing scheme, indicates that the Divine Power which spread the fogs to cover the movements of the hard pressed colonial army of the Revolution is still guarding the three-pillared edifice which those heroes built." Not everyone found these florid deductions persuasive. "I do not take much stock in the contention that God was taking a hand in this Court controversy," remarked a former governor of North Carolina. "If He were, I think probably He would have struck in another direction."[72]

That mordant remark revealed what many Senators had come to feel—that the acrimony was getting altogether out of hand. One morning Senator Minton found a bullet in the mail wrapped in a two-foot-long piece of white scrap paper with the printed penciled message: "SEN. SHERMAN MINTON. DON'T MISTAKE. I AM EDUCATED. IF YOU SUPPORT ROOSEVELT'S COURT BILL WE WILL GET YOU—YOU DIRTY RUBBER STAMP." The communication ended with an obscenity. That same day, Congressmen received a mimeographed flier asking, "What will be gained by the passage of this bill, should thousands of citizens, with blood in their eyes, converge upon the Capital of Our Nation, and exact the retribution which is rightfully and justly theirs?"[73]

On the train returning from Robinson's funeral in Little Rock, every compartment housed a caucus. In one of them, three of the freshman Senators decided that the game was over. They were alarmed, in particular, by how the fight was tearing the Democrats apart. Even Roosevelt's successor in Albany, Governor Herbert Lehman, had come out against the plan, though his intervention infuriated the White House circle and party leaders. When Prentiss Brown returned to Washington, he called together eight freshman Democrats, including Senators Overton and Andrews, who held the balance of power. After a two-hour conference, they marched across the hall in the Senate Office Building to Vice President Garner's office to announce that they would vote to recommit the bill. That did it. "After the self-delivery of the freshmen Senators, we had fifty or fifty-one votes," Hiram Johnson confided, "but we did not have them until then." Shortly afterward, Homer Cummings reflected:

> There was no moment during the controversy when we did not have the battle won up to the time of the death of Senator Robinson. It must be confessed, however, that our strength gradually diminished so that when the Senator's death occurred the margin was too small to stand the shock. It is also clear that there never was a moment when we could not have compromised advantageously.[74]

On July 22, the Senate unceremoniously returned the legislation to committee, from which it never emerged. The President and his supporters could claim that Congress never actually voted down the measure, but no amount of obfuscation could disguise the reality: Roosevelt had suffered a severe setback, and his proposal had drawn its last breath. The Court-packing scheme, declared a Mississippi paper, was as "dead as a salt mackerel shining beneath the pale moonlight," and, as if that were not final enough, added, "as dead as the ashes of Moses, world's first law giver." "The Senate today 're-committed' the ill advised and dangerous bill to 'pack' the U. S. Supreme Court," a Colorado Congressman wrote in his diary. *"Requiescat in pace."*[75]

VI

But for FDR, all was not lost. Not only did he have a Court that was ruling in favor of the constitutionality of New Deal laws, but also he had the right to appoint someone to the Van Devanter vacancy. Moreover, in astonishing contrast to his experience in his first term, other opportunities rapidly came his way. Within two and a half years after the defeat of the Court proposal, the President was able to choose five of the nine Justices, including his Solicitor General, Stanley Reed, and his adviser, Felix Frankfurter. Indeed, as one historian has pointed out, in less than four years after the end of the legislative struggle, Roosevelt "had named more Justices than any President since George Washington." Before he was done, he had filled eight vacancies and had elevated Harlan Fiske Stone to the Chief Justiceship. "Roosevelt," another historian has written, "succeeded more than any other President in packing the court."[76]

This new Court—the "Roosevelt Court" as it was called—ruled favorably on every one of the New Deal laws whose constitutionality was challenged. It expanded the commerce power and the taxing and spending power so greatly that it soon became evident that there was almost no statute for social welfare or the regulation of business that the Court would not validate. Though the Court had once held that the national government lacked power over even major industries, because, it said, those industries were not in interstate commerce, the Court now permitted Washington to reach into the most remote enterprises. In one case, it ruled that a farmer was engaged in interstate commerce even when he grew wheat wholly for his own consumption on his own farm.[77]

Since 1937 the Court has not struck down a single piece of Congressional legislation constraining business. Although before 1937 legal realism influenced only a few Justices, thereafter the old doctrines of constitutional fundamentalism lost out. Whereas the beneficiaries of the Court before 1937 had been businessmen and other propertied interests, after 1937 they became less advantaged groups. As early as the first week of June 1937, *Business Week* was complaining: "The cold fact is that, for all practical purposes, the reorganization of the Court, sought by legislative process, has been accomplished by the ordinary process of court decision." Eight months later, Frank Gannett wrote: "Since the President now controls the Supreme Court, our only hope lies in influencing the members of Congress."[78]

Early in 1940, a holding company attorney, Wendell Willkie, who later that year would be FDR's opponent in the presidential contest, wrote resignedly:

> Mr. Roosevelt has won. The court is now his. . . . Mr. Roosevelt has accomplished exactly what he would have accomplished if he had won the court fight. . . . When a series of reinterpretations overturning well-argued precedents are made in a brief time by a newly appointed group of judges, all tending to indicate the same basic disagreement with the established conception of government, the thoughtful observer can only conclude that something revolutionary is going on. And that is what has happened here.
>
> During the past three years the American people have had a series of majority opinions from the Supreme Court that substantially change their form of government. On almost every occasion on which the court has been called upon to decide, it has wiped out state and local lines, and has relentlessly extended Federal authority to every farm, every hamlet, every business firm and manufacturing plant in the country.[79]

Then and later, Willkie's lament became a common theme in board rooms and among well-paid counsel. "The doctrine of stare decisis went into the discard," grumbled the official historian of a prestigious Manhattan law firm. In the fall of 1940, John W. Davis, the country's leading corporation lawyer, reported: "I grind away day by day in my office, reaching out occasionally to cast a few pearls before judicial bodies— who are not always as receptive as they should be. This last is peculiarly true of the strangely altered Supreme Court at Washington." Four years later, Davis was still grousing: "Like small boys with their hands on a great machine, they take pleasure in casting aside the wisdom of the ages. To say that a question has been settled by previous decisions is a fatal mistake by an advocate. It almost guarantees him defeat."[80]

No one, though, could match Justice McReynolds in expressions of outrage. In the fall of 1937 he griped: "The court starts off about as I expected. There is not much to be expected of it by sensible people of the former order." From 1937 through 1941 he dissented 119 times. One by one, his comrades-at-arms among the Four Horsemen vanished—Van Devanter during the Court fight, then Sutherland, then Butler. "With the death of Mr. Justice Butler in the fall of 1939," wrote a political scientist in his annual review of Supreme Court cases, "Mr. Justice McReynolds stands like the boy on the burning deck amidst what obviously appears to him to be the imminent destruction of the old constitutional system." Each passing year, he became more sour. He refused to show up for the President's annual state dinner for the Supreme Court, and when the Justices, at the opening of the 1939 term, paid their traditional courtesy call at the White House, McReynolds was nowhere to be seen. He had only one frosty aspiration left—to outlast Franklin Delano Roosevelt in Washington. But when FDR won election to an unprecedented third term, even that consolation was denied him. "Now his nightmare had come true," *Time* noted. "'Nero' was in for a third term." McReynolds stayed away from the inauguration, then two days later wrote out his resignation in two stiff sentences. Stepping down did nothing to mellow his view of Roosevelt. "A war with a fool at the top is not a pleasant prospect," he wrote his brother that fall. "He is acting like a crazy man." Three years later, still unreconciled, he asked his fellow Wilsonian Democrat, John W. Davis: "I wonder how great the megalomania will grow. Or is there room for any further growth?" Little wonder then that, with his arch enemy so thoroughly discountenanced, Roosevelt claimed he had lost the battle but won the war. [81]

VII

There were other respects, though, in which FDR lost the war. Never again would he be as predominant, either on Capitol Hill or at the polling places, as he was when 1937 began. To be sure, a number of Congressmen were probably determined to split with him anyway, and simply used the controversy as an excuse, although even that consideration assigns some importance to the Court fracas. As the historian Robert Maddox has shrewdly noted, "The political significance of the Court battle is not so much that it created opposition, which it certainly did, but that it provided a rallying point around which so much latent opposition could coalesce." In like manner, another historian has observed, "On the defensive in the 1936 elections, with no firm intellectual foothold from which to launch an effective political attack, the miscellaneous clusters of resistance to the New Deal were suddenly given an unexpected opportunity." [82] Granted, Roosevelt's diminished authority resulted, in part, from other developments: dismay at the harsh recession of 1937–1938, anxiety over relief spending, and resentment at sitdown strikes. But to attempt to explain the erosion of 1937 and ignore the Supreme Court donnybrook is like accounting for the coming of the Civil War without reference to slavery.

The Court struggle had a number of disruptive aspects:

1. It helped blunt the most important drive for social reform in American history and squandered the advantage of Roosevelt's triumph in 1936. A Scandinavian commentator has pointed out: "The fight had begun as an incident between the White House and the judiciary. It ended as a full-scale war between the executive and its former congressional partner in which the New Deal experiment in pragmatic liberalism became the ultimate victim." In the spring of 1937, one observer noted, "Congress has been completely addled by the President's court proposal." The controversy, he added, had resulted "in the sidetracking of much useful legislation that otherwise might have been put through." By the time the session sputtered to an end in "spasms of bitterness" in late August, it had been, the *New York Times* commented, the "stormiest and least productive in recent years." At the close of the "sock-Roosevelt" session, one reporter wrote: "Tonight the political 'master minds' of the capital gathering over their cups in relaxed reminiscence of the historic events of the last seven months, were mulling over one question: 'How did the President slide so far—so fast?' "[83]

The Court controversy helped weld together a bipartisan coalition of anti-New Deal Senators. Roosevelt's plan, noted one White House correspondent, had resulted in a "novel development": "the unity which has linked Republicans of all economic and political shadings for the first time in years. Certainly there has been nothing like it since the World War." The GOP legislators found an unexpectedly large number of Democratic defectors at their side. The historian George Tindall has written:

> Roosevelt later claimed he had lost the battle but won the war. If so, it was a pyrrhic victory that divided the Democratic party and blighted his own prestige. For the first time Southern Congressmen in large numbers deserted the leader and the opposition found an issue on which it could openly take the field. Things were never again quite the same.

This bipartisan anti-New Deal coalition proved to be enduring. As its foremost chronicler, James T. Patterson, has observed:

> Senators from both sides of the aisle at first opposed the plan as individuals; within a few weeks they had organized a conservative bloc strong

enough to deal Roosevelt his first serious setback in four years. The bloc was composed of the irreconcilable Democrats, Republicans, and, most important, previously loyal moderate Democrats.[84]

This conservative coalition handed Roosevelt a series of rebuffs at the special session of Congress in the autumn of 1937 and at the regular session the following year. In June 1938, the British commentator Denis Brogan remarked that since his 1936 landslide triumph, "Mr. Roosevelt has failed to get any serious part of his legislative programme enacted into law, and a legislator has only to vote against an administration bill to acquire the stature of a new Cato." He noted that, after the hostilities over the Supreme Court, a "witch-fever" had arisen, most conspicuously evident in the defeat of the President's bill for executive reorganization, though "this measure did not seem, to the outsider, a Trojan horse from whose interior Goering or Vyshinsky was liable to pop out at any moment." Prospects for reform had diminished perceptibly, and for the next quarter of a century the advocates of social change would rarely win anything but minor successes in Congress. Years later, Henry Wallace reflected: "The whole New Deal really went up in smoke as a result of the Supreme Court fight."[85]

2. The Court squabble deeply divided the Democratic party. In state after state, it precipitated factional wars. In Massachusetts, the governor opposed the plan; his auditor and his attorney general favored it. In Florida, the Democratic party was split asunder when FDR's followers denounced the state chairman as a toady of the utilities for opposing the Court plan, and in Montana, the struggle triggered a primary contest between Senator Wheeler and a rival. In numerous states—Indiana, Missouri, New Jersey, North Carolina, Ohio, Rhode Island, South Carolina, Tennessee, Texas, Utah, West Virginia—each of the two Democratic Senators pursued a diametrically opposite course on the bill. The fight also led to a series of later episodes, notably the purge campaign of 1938, that rubbed brine in the wounds. "The defeat of the court-enlargement bill," a *New York Times* reporter noted, "left President Roosevelt with quite a long son-of-a-bitch list," and a generation after the struggle ended, the chairman of the House Judiciary Committee, Emmanuel Celler, said of FDR: "He could be crafty and vindictive. I opposed his court-packing and he never forgave me."[86]

Some of the Congressmen who broke with Roosevelt in 1937 were never to give him the same degree of loyalty they had in his first term. In April, the North Carolina Democrat Senator Josiah Bailey, observed blandly: "I feel that the President made a mistake, but I am not disposed to criticise him or complain of him. He is on one side and I am on another, but the whole thing will pass." Less than four months later, Bailey was writing:

> We are engaged in a great battle in America. Do not be deceived about this. The lines are drawn. The issues are clear. Those who are not with us are against us. . . . Men must stand up now. The fight is not over. We have broken down the first big attack, but the attack will be made on many lines and ultimately there will be another attack on the Court. The socialistic forces of America are not confined to the Socialistic Party.[87]

3. Because of the Court dispute, the middle-class backing Roosevelt had mobilized in the 1936 campaign ebbed away. Discord over his plan, coupled with other events, ended the brief era of great Democratic majorities. One historian has summed up the conclusion of a *Fortune* poll in July 1937: "The Supreme Court struggle had cut into the President's popularity as no other issue ever had." A man who claimed to have started the first "Roosevelt for President Club" and the first "Reelect [Roosevelt] Club of the United States" resigned his government position to signify his disapproval of the President's Court plan. "I have been a firm supporter of the New Deal and President Roosevelt," declared a Memphis attorney early in March. "I feel now that the President has not only destroyed the Democratic Party but has betrayed his oath to uphold the Constitution, which he took no longer than last January 20." An attorney from Lake Charles, Louisiana, wrote: "I voted for President Roosevelt in both elections but would not have done so had he announced his intention to destroy the independence of the judiciary. These are the sentiments of everyone in this City that I have spoken to." A Miami woman protested to a Florida Congressman: "Neither I, nor any of my friends who voted for him, gave him a mandate to destroy the independence of the court, nor of congress. I have actually lost faith in his honesty." A trade-unionist from New York confided: "As a member of the Newspaper Guild of America, I have supported the President in the past, because of his humanitarian aims and his attitude toward organized labor. But his present effort to undermine the independence of the Judiciary has destroyed my confidence in his judgment." In North Carolina, a former law school dean told Senator Bailey: "I was an enthusiastic supporter of Roosevelt last November. If an election was held tomorrow, I would not vote for him."[88]

4. The Court issue produced divisions among reformers of many types. It separated Senator Wheeler from labor supporters in Montana and resulted in a breach between Wheeler and the Administration that was never closed. One of FDR's lieutenants observed, "I've always granted to every man the right to his own opinions. . . . But to find

Burt in the front ranks of those who were piously upholding the sanctity of the Supreme Court . . . well, that was really a sight to make the angels weep!" In Minnesota, the controversy sundered the Farmer-Labor Party; many Farmer-Laborites were angered by Senator Henrik Shipstead's opposition to the bill. The president of an organization of "independent" Minnesota lawyers wrote him: "Fake liberals are through, Shipstead; so is Burton K. Wheeler. Wait and see." It alienated the publisher of *The Nation* from his editors; split Dr. Francis Townsend from officers of his old age pension organization; and cut off veteran reformers such as John Haynes Holmes and Oswald Garrison Villard from the main body of the New Dealers.[89]

5. It undermined the bipartisan support for the New Deal. Many of the Republican progressives had become growingly disquieted about the men around Roosevelt. The Court issue confirmed them in their suspicions that something alien, something fundamentally illiberal, had been introduced into the reform movement by the New Dealers—that, in the guise of solicitude for the common man, they were actually seeking self-aggrandizement. The President, too, seemed disturbingly eager to concentrate power in Washington. William Allen White, who admired much that the New Deal had achieved, wrote during the Court fight: "I fear him as I fear no other man in our public life." The Court fracas, the former Bull Mooser Hiram Johnson told Raymond Moley, "has forced me into a position of opposition to him, which will widen as the days pass."[90]

6. The Court dispute affected Roosevelt's conduct of foreign affairs. At a minimum, it proved distracting. In February 1937, A. A. Berle recorded in his diary: "The President seems interested in furthering the European matter; though not until the court fight is over." More important, the controversy gave hostages to opponents of his foreign policy. As the Fascist powers grew ever more menacing, the British believed that the greatest contribution the United States could make would be to amend the neutrality legislation so that the President would have greater flexibility in dealing with aggressors. But, as Robert Dallek has noted, the President accepted a mandatory law in good part because he wished "to avoid a congressional debate that could forestall action on judicial reform." Dallek added:

> For Roosevelt, Court reform had implications ranging beyond social change in the United States; it was also tied to the question of whether democracy was a more effective system than Fascism or Communism. . . . To continue to make democracy work in the United States, Roosevelt believed that he must curb the Court. And to do this, he felt com-

pelled temporarily to put . . . foreign affairs on the shelf. . . . Roosevelt had no intention of asking for more than the congressional bills gave. In the midst of his "bitter" all-consuming Court fight, in which opponents styled him "a remorseless dictator" out to destroy the Constitution and the courts, Roosevelt was in a weak position to ask for Executive control over foreign affairs.[91]

The British viewed these developments with dismay. Three days before the end of the Court battle, the British ambassador reported to Foreign Secretary Eden:

> Mr. Roosevelt's struggle with his Congress has now again reached an acute stage, and I find it unpleasantly reminiscent of the battle Mr. Wilson waged eighteen years ago over the Treaty of Versailles, though, thank heaven, Mr. Roosevelt has not displayed all the uncompromising severity of his predecessor. I cannot forecast the outcome of the present contest, but it makes me very uneasy; for it is certainly not in the interest of the outside world that the President's prestige in his own country should be severely impaired.[92]

As the British envoy feared, the controversy had long-range reverberations. Commentators frequently likened the Court ruckus to the League of Nations hostilities and compared Hiram Johnson's stand, especially, to that of the battalion of death. The President's proposal fortified men such as Johnson and Burton K. Wheeler in their misgivings about FDR's attitude toward external matters, for it seemed to reveal what they deplored about his foreign policy—that it was devious, and that it sought too much power for the executive. Many years later, Wheeler recalled, "Because I had licked Roosevelt on the Court issue, a lot of people thought I should lead the fight to keep us out of the war."[93]

VIII

These multifold misfortunes exacted an enormous toll for the gains Roosevelt achieved, but they should not obscure the President's one huge success in the Court fight—the legitimation of a vast expansion of the power of government in American life. Ten days after the legislative contest ended, at the close of a lengthy, searching analysis in his diary of his experiences, Homer Cummings concluded:

> We managed to reverse the constitutional trends of twenty-five years. We cast off the chains that have imprisoned the American people in their attempts to deal with national problems on a national scale. All these

struggles and ferments are the growing pains of a young and somewhat disintegrated nation toward more unified and effective Democracy. This is a great achievement and fifty years from now, when this era is discussed by historians, it will be apparent that whatever mistakes of tactics were made, and whatever immediate details were lost, nevertheless the war for greater reform was achieved. The final verdict may safely be left to historians.[94]

Four years after the tumultuous controversy of 1937, the political scientist Edward S. Corwin summed up the changes that had been wrought:

The Court has discarded the idea that the *laissez-faire*, noninterventionist conception of governmental function offers a feasible approach to the problem of adapting the Constitution to the needs of the Twentieth Century. Rendered into the idiom of American constitutional law, this means that *the National Government is entitled to employ any and all of its powers to forward any and all of the objectives of good government*. This fundamental point being established, . . . the principal doctrines of American constitutional theory, those which have furnished the matrix of the vastly extended judicial review which developed after 1890, have become largely otiose and superfluous.[95]

The Court struggle speeded the acceptance of a substantial change in the role of government and in the reordering of property rights and also had the probably unanticipated result of the appointment of Justices much more solicitous of civil liberties and civil rights. Not only would the Court over the next generation absorb virtually all of the Bill of Rights into the Fourteenth Amendment, but its expansive reading of the commerce clause would make it possible in the 1960s for the government to tell even the most obscure fried chicken shack that it could not discriminate against African-American patrons because, in the eyes of the judiciary, its two-bit, off-the-beaten-track operation was an enterprise in interstate commerce.[96] It is not surprising, then, that historians speak of "the Constitutional Revolution of 1937," for in the long history of the Supreme Court, no event has had more momentous consequences than Franklin Roosevelt's message of February 1937.

S I X

The Case of
the Wenatchee Chambermaid

[When my former Columbia University colleague John A. Garraty asked me to suggest some Supreme Court cases that might be included in a revision of his book, *Quarrels That Have Shaped the Constitution,* I put foremost on my list *West Coast Hotel v. Parrish* because in the history of the Court it marked a historic divide. In addition, that ruling had a not inconsiderable impact on the fate of FDR's Court-packing plan. For the expanded version of his volume, Garraty invited me to contribute the article on the Elsie Parrish case. Before being included in the new edition of *Quarrels,* which was published by Harper and Row in 1987, it appeared in the December 1986 issue of *American Heritage.* In neither instance was it annotated, and it has been left in that form—a piece written for a popular audience. I have, though, altered it slightly, mostly in order to incorporate some new material.]

When on a spring day in 1935 Elsie Parrish walked into the office of an obscure lawyer in Wenatchee, Washington, to ask him to sue the town's leading hotel for back pay, she little realized that she was linking her fate to that of exploited women in a Brooklyn laundry a continent away. Still less did she think that she was setting off a series of events that would deeply affect President Franklin D. Roosevelt's plans for his second term. Least of all did she perceive that she was triggering a constitutional revolution that, even today, remains the most significant chapter in the two centuries of existence of the U. S. Supreme Court. All Elsie knew was that she had been bilked.

Late in the summer of 1933, Elsie Lee, a woman of about forty who would soon be Elsie Parrish, had taken a job as a chambermaid at the

163

Cascadian Hotel in Wenatchee, entrepôt for a beautiful recreation area reaching from the Columbia valley in Oregon to the Cascades and the country's foremost apple market. "Apples made Wenatchee and apples maintain it," noted the WPA Guide to Washington. "It is surrounded by a sea of orchards, covered in spring with a pink foam of blossoms, mile upon mile, filling the valleys and covering the slopes; the air of the town is sweet with the fragrance." Here, in the land of Winesaps and Jonathans, where "in summer and fall the spicy odor of apples is everywhere," Parrish worked irregularly over the next year and a half cleaning toilets and sweeping rugs for an hourly wage of twenty-two cents, later raised to a quarter. When she was discharged in May 1935, she asked for back pay of $216.19, the difference between what she had received and what she would have gotten had she been paid each week the $14.50 minimum mandated for her occupation under state law. The Cascadian, which was owned by the West Coast Hotel Company, offered to settle for $17, but she would not hear of it. Instead, she and her husband Ernest brought suit for what she insisted was due her.

The Parrishes rested their case on the provisions of a statute that had been enacted by the state of Washington a quarter of a century before when, catching the contagion of reform from neighboring Oregon, it had taken steps to wipe out sweatshops. The 1913 act declared it "unlawful to employ women or minors . . . under conditions of labor detrimental to their health or morals; and . . . to employ women workers in any industry . . . at wages which are not adequate for their maintenance." To safeguard the welfare of female employees, the law established a commission that was authorized, after investigation, to call together employers, employees, and representatives of the public to recommend a wage standard "not detrimental to health and morals, and which shall be sufficient for the decent maintenance of women." On receiving that recommendation, the commission was to issue an order stipulating the minimum wage that must be paid. For chambermaids, the weekly minimum was set at $14.50. Twice the statute had been challenged in the courts, and on both occasions the Washington Supreme Court had validated it. Elsie Parrish appeared to have an airtight case.

Alas, any law student in the land could have told her that her case was hopeless, for twelve years before, the U. S. Supreme Court had ruled, in a widely reported decision in *Adkins v. Children's Hospital*, that a minimum wage act for women was unconstitutional because it violated the liberty of contract that the Court claimed was guaranteed by the Constitution. Though the opinion by Justice George Sutherland commanded only five votes and elicited vigorous dissents, it reconfirmed a notion incorporated in constitutional doctrine only a generation before: that a great corporation and its employee—even someone as powerless as a chambermaid—each had an equivalent right to bargain about wages, a fantasy that Justice Holmes dismissed as "dogma" and the renowned commentator Thomas Reed Powell of Harvard Law School called "indefensible."

Adkins, said one commentator, "makes forever impossible all other legislation along similar lines involving the regulation of wages." The case involved an act of Congress rather than a state statute, but there was no difference in principle. Any law that transgressed the due process clause of the Fifth Amendment would, if enacted by a state, be held to violate the due process clause of the Fourteenth Amendment. Though the Washington law remained on the statute books, it was presumed to be null and void. Hence, it startled no one when in November 1935, after hearing Elsie Parrish's case, the presiding judge of the superior court of Chelan County ruled against her, explaining that *Adkins* bound every court in the nation.

Surprisingly, the Supreme Court of the state of Washington took a different view. On April 2, 1936, it overturned the lower court's decision. To get around the huge obstacle of *Adkins*, the court pointed out that the U.S. Supreme Court had never struck down a *state* minimum wage law, which was true but irrelevant. The decision gave the Parrishes a moment of euphoria, but it hardly seemed likely that this opinion would survive a test in the U.S. Supreme Court, given the *Adkins* ruling and the manifest hostility of Justices such as Sutherland to legislation of this nature.

Only eight weeks later, the Court settled any doubt on the matter by a decision on a case that, three thousand miles from Wenatchee, had begun to wend its way through the judicial system while Elsie Parrish was still making beds in the Cascadian Hotel. It arose out of the hope of social reformers in New York, especially women active in the Consumers' League, that the Court, despite *Adkins*, might look favorably on a minimum wage law for women and minors if wage setting was related not just to the needs of women but to the value of the services they rendered. To that end, Felix Frankfurter of Harvard Law School and Benjamin Cohen, a former Brandeis law clerk who was to be a prominent New Dealer, crafted a model law. New York State adopted it in 1933, the fourth year of the Great Depression, which had reduced some young women, living on starvation wages, to sleeping in subways; and other states copied the New York act. Frankfurter warned that it was "foolish beyond words" to expect the Court to reverse itself, but he hoped that the Justices might be willing to distinguish this statute, with its added feature of "value of services," from the one struck down in *Adkins*. "Every word of the New York law," explained a prominent woman reformer, was "written with the Supreme Court of the United States in mind."

In accordance with the provisions of the model legislation, New York State obtained an indictment against Joseph Tipaldo, manager of the Spotlight Laundry in Brooklyn, who had been brutally exploiting his nine female employees, first by paying them far below the minimum wage and then by pretending to pay the minimum but forcing the laundresses to kick back the difference between what the state required and what he actually intended to pay. When Joe Tipaldo went to jail to stand trial on charges of disobeying the mandatory wage order and of forgery, the hotel industry (the same business that would be involved in the Parrish case) rushed to his side with an offer to bankroll a test of the constitutionality of the New York law. Since hotels were working their employees twelve hours a day, seven days a week, they had a high stake in the case. In fact, the state had already begun minimum-wage proceedings against them. Consequently, each hotel put money in a kitty to finance Tipaldo's petition for a writ of habeas corpus to compel Frederick L. Morehead, warden of Brooklyn's city prison, to release the laundry manager from custody. While his case was being prepared, Tipaldo renamed his sweatshop the Bright Light Laundry and made a big investment in expanding his business. Utterly shameless, he explained, "I expect to get it back eventually on what I save in wages."

On June 1, 1936, the U. S. Supreme Court appeared to justify his optimism when, in a 5–4 decision in *Morehead v. New York ex rel. Tipaldo*, it struck down New York's minimum wage law. In a sweeping opinion written by Pierce Butler, the Court found no meaningful difference between the New York statute and the District of Columbia act that had been invalidated in *Adkins*. Both, it said, violated the liberty of contract that safeguarded equally the rights of employer and employee to bargain about wages. After quoting from *Adkins* with obvious approval, the Court declared, in language that shocked champions of the exploited, "The decision and the reasoning upon which it rests clearly show that the State is without power by any form of legislation to prohibit, change or nullify contracts between employers and adult women workers as to the amount of wages to be paid." Those words all but doomed Elsie Parrish's cause, and gave cocky Joe Tipaldo the victory of a lifetime.

That victory, however, turned out to carry a very high price. "After the court decision, business looked good for a while," Joe told a reporter three months later. "I was able to undercharge my competitors a little on what I saved in labor costs." But then business started to fall off, then fell some more. "I think this fight was the cause of my trouble," he said. "My customers wouldn't give my drivers their wash." Before the summer was over, the Bright Light Laundry had folded, and Joe Tipaldo was one of the army of unemployed. "I'm broke now," he confessed. "I couldn't stand the gaff."

Elsie Parrish was made of sterner stuff. She was determined to carry on her struggle, though her prospects seemed bleak indeed. Given the precedent of *Adkins*, her case had never been promising. When the attorney for the West Coast Hotel Company asked the judge who had written the opinion of the Supreme Court of Washington sustaining that state's minimum wage law in *Parrish* how he could possibly have done so in view of what the U.S. Supreme Court had said in *Adkins*, he replied, "Well, let's let the Supreme Court say it one more time." Now, in *Tipaldo*, the Court had "one more time" stated unequivocally that minimum wage laws for women were invalid. So gloomy was the outlook that, on the advice of Ben Cohen and Felix Frankfurter, the Consumers' League did not even file a brief in *Parrish*. "We are both rather pessimistic regarding its outcome," Cohen confided. Elsie Parrish had every reason to expect the worst.

The *Tipaldo* decision, though, engendered a powerful backlash, not least from some of the members of the Supreme Court. In a strongly worded dissent, Chief Justice Charles Evans Hughes upbraided the majority for failing to acknowledge either that the New York law could be distinguished from the act of Congress struck down in *Adkins* or that the state has "the power to protect women from being exploited by overreaching employers." Far more biting was the separate dissent filed by Justice Harlan Fiske Stone on behalf of himself and Justices Louis Brandeis and Benjamin Cardozo. In one of the most scathing criticisms of fellow jurists ever uttered from the bench, Stone accused the majority of indulging its "own personal economic predilections." He found "grim irony in speaking of the freedom of contract of those who, because of their economic necessities, give their service for less than is needful to keep body and soul together." In an impassioned warning to his brethren to exercise more self-restraint, Stone wrote: "The Fourteenth Amendment has no more embedded in the Constitution our preference for some particular set of economic beliefs than it has adopted, in the name of liberty, the system of theology which we may happen to approve."

Much of the nation shared Stone's sense of indignation about *Tipaldo*. People of the most diverse political views were appalled by a ruling that seemed to deny government, state or federal, any kind of authority over working conditions. New Dealers were irate, and a Republican newspaper in upstate New York declared, "The law that would jail any laundryman for having an underfed horse should jail him for having an underfed girl employee."

Apart from business interests, only two groups applauded the decision. One was the press in a scattering of cheap-labor towns undismayed by the fact that, following the ruling, the wages of laundresses—mostly impoverished blacks and Puerto Rican and Italian immigrants—were slashed in half. The other was a small faction of advanced feminists centered in Alice Paul's National Woman's Party. "It is hair-raising to consider how very close women in America came to being ruled inferior citizens," one of them wrote Justice Sutherland. Most women activists, though, were horrified by that view, which they believed reflected the dogmatism of upper-class ladies who had no familiarity with the suffering of workers. They were as devoted as Alice Paul to equal rights, and they must have shuddered at the paternalism implicit in earlier opinions sustaining separate treatment for women on the grounds that they were wards of the state. But they were sure that female employees required protection, and they knew that insistence on the principle of equal rights meant no minimum wage law whatsoever, since the Court, as constituted during FDR's first term, would never sanction social legislation for men. "Thus," the historian Mary Beard wrote Justice Stone, Alice Paul "plays into the hands of the rawest capitalists."

Stone himself had no doubt of the implications of *Tipaldo.* "We finished the term of Court yesterday," he wrote his sister, "I think in many ways one of the most disastrous in its history. . . . Our latest exploit was a holding by a divided vote that there was no power in a state to regulate minimum wages for women. Since the Court last week said that this could not be done by the national government, as the matter was local, and now it is said that it cannot be done by local governments even though it is local, we seem to have tied Uncle Sam up in a hard knot."

Tipaldo, handed down on the final day of the term, climaxed an extraordinary thirteen months in which the Court struck down more important socioeconomic legislation than at any time in history, before or since. During that brief period, it turned thumbs down on a number of New Deal laws and state reforms and cavalierly rebuked the President and his appointees. Most of the rulings had come from a split court, with the "Four Horsemen," Pierce Butler, James McReynolds, George Sutherland, and Willis Van Devanter, a quartet of adamantly conservative judges whose ideas had been molded in the heyday of laissez-faire in the late nineteenth century, voting in the negative. From the spring of 1935 on, they were often joined by the youngest member of the bench, Owen Roberts. At the end of the term, a nationally syndicated columnist wrote, "After slaughtering practically every New Deal measure that has been dragged before it, the Supreme Court now begins its summer breathing spell, ending a winter's performance which leaves the stage, as in the last act of a Shakespearean tragedy, strewn with the gory dead."

Despite the enormous setbacks the New Deal had sustained, Roosevelt gave every indication through the fall of 1935 and most of 1936 that he was accepting his losses virtually without complaint. While Elsie Parrish's feeble case was advancing toward its final reckoning in the U. S. Supreme Court, the President gave not the slightest indication that he had any plans whatsoever to make the Justices any less refractory, for it seemed altogether inadvisable in the 1936 presidential campaign to hand his opponents, who were hard put to find an issue, an opportunity to stand by the Constitution.

On February 5, 1937, however, the President stunned the country by sending a special message to Congress that constituted the boldest attempt a chief executive has ever initiated to remold the judiciary. He recommended that when a federal judge who had served at least ten years waited more than six months after his seventieth birthday to resign or retire, the President could add a new judge to the bench. Since this Court was the most aged in history—its members were referred to as "the nine old men"—Roosevelt would be able to add as many as six new Supreme Court Justices.

Though FDR's scheme provoked fierce protests, political analysts anticipated that it would be adopted. By winning in a landslide in 1936, Roosevelt had carried so many members of his party into Congress that the Republicans were left with only sixteen of the ninety-six seats in the Senate and fewer than one hundred of the more than four hundred seats in the House. So long as the Court continued to strike down New Deal reforms—and such vital legislation as the Social Security Act was still to be decided on—it was highly unlikely that enough Democrats would desert their immensely popular President to defeat the measure. The very first evidence of the attitude of the Court would come with its decision on Elsie Parrish's case, and there was every expectation that, acting not many months after *Tipaldo*, the Court would render an adverse ruling that would improve Roosevelt's already excellent chances of restructuring the Court. On the very day the *Parrish* decision was handed down, March 29, 1937, the president of the National Women's Republican Club declared, "I don't see how the President's bill can fail to get a majority."

March 29 came during the Easter holidays, always a gala season in Washington, D. C. On that bright Monday morning, a host of camera-toting tourists and children carrying Easter baskets crowded the steps of the recently opened Supreme Court building and queued up in record numbers to enter the marble palace. The unusually protracted time of 103 days had elapsed since Elsie Parrish's case had been argued, and some twelve thousand visitors flocked to the building in the belief that this would be journey's end for the suit that had begun nearly two years earlier. An hour before the session was scheduled to start at noon, four thousand visitors had already been admitted to the building, where many lined up two abreast from the courtroom doorway almost to the suite of Justice Stone in the idle hope of getting a peek at the activity.

For some minutes it appeared that the spectators who had been fortu-nate enough to get into the courtroom were also to be frustrated, for the proceedings began with a recital of an opinion on another case by one of the Four Horsemen that left the audience nearly numb with bore-dom. But no sooner had he finished than the Chief Justice leaned for-ward in his chair, picked up some sheets of paper, and announced, "This case presents the question of the constitutional validity of the minimum wage law of the State of Washington." It was to be Elsie Parrish's day after all, and the spectators stirred in anticipation. Hughes, fully aware of the effect he was having and surely conscious of his mag-nificent appearance (with his patrician manner, sparkling eyes, and well-groomed beard, he was often likened to Jove), raised his voice to over-come the bustle, then paused and peered out over the crowded chamber for a moment before returning to his written opinion.

Anxious minutes passed as Hughes labored through a reprise of the facts in the case. When he finally took up one of the arguments of Elsie Parrish's attorneys, he did so only to reject it disdainfully. It was "obvi-ously futile," he said, for counsel to claim that the present case could be distinguished from *Adkins* on the ground that Mrs. Parrish had worked for "a hotel and that the business of an innkeeper was affected with a public interest." As it happened, he noted, one of the cases *Adkins* had disposed of had dealt with a hotel employee. If the state of Wash-ington law was to survive the day, it would need a better justification than this rickety effort. The Court was going to have to meet *Adkins* head on.

It took only a moment more for Hughes to reveal that the Court was prepared to do just that. In *Tipaldo*, the U. S. Supreme Court had felt bound by the ruling of the Court of Appeals of New York that the New York minimum wage act could not be distinguished from the statute in *Adkins* and hence was invalid; *Parrish*, the Chief Justice declared, presented a quite different situation. Here the highest tribunal of the state of Washington had refused to be guided by *Adkins* and had sanctioned the law in dispute. "We are of the opinion that this ruling of the state court demands on our part a reexamination of the Adkins case," he continued. "The importance of the question, in which many States having similar laws are concerned, the close division by which the decision in the Adkins case was reached, and the economic conditions which have supervened, and in the light of which the reasonableness of the exercise of the protective power of the State must be considered, make it not only appropriate, but we think imperative, that in deciding the present case the subject should receive fresh consideration." To do so properly, he observed, required careful examination of the doctrine of freedom of contract that had bulked so large in *Adkins*.

"What is this freedom?" Hughes inquired, his voice rising. "The Constitution does not speak of freedom of contract." Instead, the Constitution mentioned liberty and forbade denial of liberty without due process of law. The Constitution did not recognize absolute liberty, however. "The liberty safeguarded is liberty in a social organization," he declared. "Liberty under the Constitution is thus necessarily subject to the restraints of due process, and regulation which is reasonable in relation to its subject and is adopted in the interests of the community is due process." Hughes's delivery of the opinion in "a clear, resonant voice," noted one correspondent, "electrified and held spellbound the spectators who crowded every corner of the majestic Supreme Court chamber." As the Chief Justice spoke, members of the bar in the choice seats near the bench followed his every word as though transfixed.

The Court had long since established that the state had especial authority to circumscribe the freedom of contract of women, the Chief Justice continued. In *Muller v. Oregon* (1908), he pointed out, the Court had fully elaborated the reasons for accepting a special sphere of state regulation of female labor. In that landmark case, the Court had emphasized, in the words of Justice David Brewer, that because a woman performs "maternal functions" her health "becomes an object of public interest and care in order to preserve the strength and vigor of the race." Hence, Brewer had gone on, a woman was "properly placed in a class by herself, and legislation designed for her protection may be sustained even when like legislation is not necessary for men and could not be sustained." The state could restrict her freedom of contract, the Court had determined in *Muller*, not merely "for her benefit, but also largely for the benefit of all."

The precedents established by *Muller* and several later rulings had led the dissenters in *Adkins* to believe that the District of Columbia minimum wage law should have been sanctioned, and with good reason, Hughes asserted. The dissenting Justices had challenged the distinction the majority in *Adkins* had drawn between maximum hours legislation (valid) and minimum wage statutes (invalid), and that challenge remained "without any satisfactory answer." The state of Washington law was essentially the same as the Washington, D. C., act that had been struck down in *Adkins*, he acknowledged, "but we are unable to conclude that in its minimum wage requirement the State has passed beyond the boundary of its broad protective power." In that sentence, however convoluted, Hughes had in effect said what for some minutes it had been clear he was going to say: the Supreme Court was sustaining Washington's minimum wage law. Against all odds, Elsie Parrish had won.

Lest anyone miss the implication of the Court's reasoning, the Chief Justice spelled it out: "The *Adkins* case was a departure from the true application of the principles governing the regulation by the State of the employer and employed." In short, *Adkins*, written by Sutherland and carrying the votes of several of Hughes's other brethren, was being put to death in its fifteenth year. One could not possibly reconcile *Adkins*, Hughes maintained, with "well-considered" rulings such as *Muller*. "What can be closer to the public interest than the health of women and their protection from unscrupulous and overreaching employers?" he asked. "And if the protection of women is a legitimate end of the exercise of state power, how can it be said that the requirement of the payment of a minimum wage fairly fixed in order to meet the very necessities of existence is not an admissible means to that end?"

With an eloquence, even passion, few thought him capable of, the Chief Justice added:

> The legislature of the State was clearly entitled to consider the situation of women in employment, the fact that they are in the class receiving the least pay, that their bargaining power is relatively weak, and that they are the ready victims of those who would take advantage of their necessitous circumstances. The Legislature was entitled to adopt measures to reduce the evils of the "sweating system," the exploiting of workers at wages so low as to be insufficient to meet the bare cost of living, thus making their very helplessness the occasion of a most injurious competition.

Since many states had adopted laws of this character to remedy the evil of sweatshops, the enactment of such legislation by the state of Washington could not be viewed as "arbitrary or capricious, and that is all we have to decide," Hughes said. "Even if the wisdom of the policy be regarded as debatable and its effects uncertain, still the legislature is entitled to its judgment." Delighted at what they were hearing, the New Deal lawyers in the chamber smiled broadly and nudged one another.

In his closing remarks, the Chief Justice advanced "an additional and compelling" reason for sustaining the statute. The exploitation of "relatively defenceless" employees not only injured those women, he asserted, but directly burdened the community, because "what these workers lose in wages the taxpayers are called upon to pay." With respect to that reality, he said, the Court took judicial notice of the "unparalleled demands" the Great Depression had made upon localities. (That comment revealed how far he was reaching out, for the state of Washington had submitted no factual brief about any added responsibilities, and the statute in question had been enacted long before the Wall Street crash.) Hughes did not doubt that the state of Washington had undergone these tribulations, even if it had not troubled to say so. That deduction led him to declare, again with unexpected acerbity: "The community is not bound to provide what is in effect a subsidy for unconscionable employers. The community may direct its law-making power to correct the abuse which springs from their selfish disregard of the public interest." Consequently, the Chief Justice concluded, "The case of *Adkins v. Children's Hospital* . . . should be, and it is, overruled," and the judgment of the Supreme Court of Washington on behalf of Elsie Parrish "is affirmed." Some two years after she had changed sheets in the Cascadian Hotel for the last time, the Wenatchee chambermaid was to receive her $216.19 in back pay.

It would require some time for Court-watchers to grasp the full implications of Hughes's opinion in *Parrish*—to write of "the Constitutional Revolution of 1937"—but George Sutherland's dissent revealed that the Four Horsemen understood at that very moment that their long reign, going all the way back to *Adkins* and even before, with only slight interruption, had abruptly ended. When he had spoken the final words, the Chief Justice nodded to Justice Sutherland seated to his left. The author of *Adkins* surveyed the chamber silently, almost diffidently, then picked up the sheaf of papers in front of him and began to read. Sensing his day had passed, Sutherland—who, with his pince-nez, high collar, goatee, and hair parted in the middle, seemed never to have left the nineteenth century—appeared barely able to bring himself to carry out his futile assignment. He started off speaking in a curiously toneless murmur, and even those near the dais had trouble at first catching his words. On the rear of the room, all was lost.

As a consequence, not a few missed altogether Sutherland's first sentence, and even those who did hear it needed a moment to take in its full import. "Mr. Justice Van Devanter, Mr. Justice McReynolds, Mr.

Justice Butler and I think the judgment of the court below should be reversed," Sutherland began. A commonplace utterance. Yet that sentence signaled a historic shift in the disposition of the Supreme Court. Once again, the Justices had divided 5–4, but this time, Owen Roberts had abandoned the Conservative Four to compose a new majority that on this day, and in the days and months and years to come, would legitimate the kind of social legislation that in FDR's first term had been declared beyond the bounds of governmental authority. The loss of Roberts did not go down easily. In the course of the afternoon, noted one captious commentary, "the Four Horsemen of Reaction whom he had deserted looked glum and sour."

After no more than a cursory paragraph maintaining that all the contentions that had just been advanced in *Parrish* had been adequately disposed of in *Adkins* and *Tipaldo*, Sutherland delivered a dissent that for several minutes constituted less a reply to Hughes and the majority in *Parrish* than to Justice Stone's 1936 calls for judicial restraint in cases such as *Tipaldo*. Undeniably, a Justice was obliged to consider the contrary views of his associates, Sutherland acknowledged, "but in the end, the question which he must answer is not whether such views seem sound to those who entertain them, but whether they convince him that the statute is constitutional or engender in his mind a rational doubt upon that issue." He added:

> The oath which he takes as a judge is not a composite oath, but an individual one. And in passing upon the validity of a statute, he discharges a duty imposed upon *him*, which cannot be consummated justly by an automatic acceptance of the views of others which have neither convinced, nor created a reasonable doubt in, his mind. If upon a question so important he thus surrender his deliberate judgment, he stands forsworn. He cannot subordinate his convictions to that extent and keep faith with his oath or retain his judicial and moral independence.

Though Sutherland had been directing most of his barbs at Stone (Hughes's opinion had been all but forgotten), these last words may well have had a different target. His remarks, one writer conjectured, must have been intended as a rebuke to Owen Roberts. Perhaps so, for the minority opinion did appear to be irritating Roberts. The San Antonio Congressman Maury Maverick, who was sponsoring the Court-packing bill in the House of Representatives, reported:

> A murmur, something of a titter, went up in the courtroom among the lawyers. Justice Roberts flushed and looked with evident displeasure in the direction of Sutherland. He looked his usual part—the big football hero,

angry at the other side, and as though he should like to start a free-for-all. He pulled out his handkerchief and wiped his face and showed evident marks of disapprobation.

Sutherland, for his part, had hit full stride. After sipping some water he seemed to gain strength, and his voice resounded throughout the chamber. Indeed, the *Washington Post* characterized the reading by "the usually mild-mannered Sutherland" as nothing less than "impassioned." The elderly judge, described in another account as "pale, grim-lipped," even went so far as to rap his knuckles on the bench as he took issue with the President, though never by name; with Roberts, no longer his ally; and even more vigorously, again without mentioning him directly, with Stone. ("A flicker of a smile came over Justice Stone's face," Maverick noted.) In rebuttal to the Chief Justice's assertion that the case before the Court required a fresh examination, in part because of "the economic conditions which have supervened," Sutherland stated bluntly, "The meaning of the Constitution does not change with the ebb and flow of economic events."

When, having read nearly five pages of his opinion, Sutherland finally turned to the case before the Court, he said little more than that *West Coast Hotel* replicated the situation in *Adkins.* In every important regard, the two statutes involved had identical "vices," Sutherland maintained, "and if the *Adkins* case was properly decided, as we who join in this opinion think it was, it necessarily follows that the Washington statute is invalid." It was beyond dispute, he asserted, that the due process clause embraced freedom of contract, and Sutherland remained convinced, too, that women stood on an equal plane with men and that legislation denying them the right to contract for work was discriminatory. "Certainly a suggestion that the bargaining ability of the average woman is not equal to that of the average man would lack substance," he declared. "The ability to make a fair bargain, as everyone knows, does not depend upon sex."

If anyone thought that those last sentences had a hint of jocularity, they quite misperceived Sutherland's mood. The *Parrish* decision blew taps for the nineteenth-century world, and Sutherland, born in England in 1862 and reared on the Utah frontier, knew it. Having had his say, he understood that there was no point in going on any longer. Wearily, he concluded, "A more complete discussion may be found in the *Adkins* and *Tipaldo* cases cited *supra.*" Then he carefully laid his opinion on the dais and, stern-visaged, settled back in his chair.

When news of the momentous decision, relayed swiftly to every part of the nation over press association wires, reached Sutherland's supporters, they shared his sense of dismay. Conservatives were outraged. If FDR wanted a political court, said a disgruntled Senator, he had one now, for the decision was blatantly political, a transparent effort to kill the Court-packing bill by demonstrating that the judges would no longer misbehave. Ardent feminists were no less incensed. One of them wrote Sutherland: "May I say that the minority opinion handed down in the Washington minimum wage case is, to me, what the rainbow was to Mr. Wordsworth? . . . You did my sex the honor of regarding women as persons and citizens."

Most reformers, though, women as well as men, hailed the *Parrish* ruling as a triumph for social justice and a vindication for FDR, who had been accorded an altogether unexpected victory in the least probable quarter. One outspoken progressive, the columnist Heywood Broun, commented: "Mr. Roosevelt has been effective not only in forcing a major switch in judicial policy, but he has even imposed something of his style upon the majority voice of the court. There are whole sections in the document written and read by Chief Justice Hughes which sound as if they might have been snatched bodily from a fireside chat."

Partisans of the President jeered at the Court for its abrupt reversal of views on the validity of minimum wage legislation. Because of "the change of a judicial mind," observed Attorney General Homer Cummings sardonically, "the Constitution on Monday, March 29, 1937, does not mean the same thing that it meant on Monday, June 1, 1936." The head of one of the railway brotherhoods carried that thought a step further in noting, "On Easter Sunday, state minimum wage laws were unconstitutional, but about noon on Easter Monday, these laws were constitutional." It was "the Greatest Constitutional Somersault in History," Maverick concluded. "For Owen Roberts, one single human being, had amended the Constitution of the United States by nodding his head instead of shaking it. The lives of millions were changed by this nod."

That development perturbed some longtime critics of the Court— "What kind of respect do you think one can instill in law students for the process of the Court when things like this can happen?" Felix Frankfurter asked—but gave others no little satisfaction. A former United States Senator from West Virginia wrote:

Suppose you have noticed that the untouchables, the infallible, sacrosanct Supreme Court judges have been forced to put upon the record that they are just a bundle of flesh and blood, and must walk upon the ground like the rest of human beings. I got quite a "kick" out of reading that the Supreme Court said, right out loud in meeting, that it had been wrong.

Like most of the wrongs done in life, there is no compensation for the great wrongs which that old court has been doing the country; but like all democrats, I am forgiving.

The performance of the Court proved especially embarrassing for the Chief Justice. Commentators, observing that Hughes had once said of a nineteenth-century decision that "the over-ruling in such a short time by one vote, of the previous decision, shook popular respect for the Court," pointed out that "Now, within a period of only ten months, the Supreme Court has reversed itself on minimum wages, again by one vote." To be sure, Hughes did not admit that the Court had shifted, and years later Roberts claimed that he had voted with the Four Horsemen in *Tipaldo* only because New York had not presented the issue in the right manner. Furthermore, we now know that Roberts in *Parrish* was not responding to the Court-packing threat since he cast his vote before the plan was announced. Nonetheless, scholars, despite their access to information not generally available in 1937, find Roberts's contention that he did not switch unpersuasive.

At the time, no one doubted that the Court, and more particularly Mr. Justice Roberts, had crossed over. "Isn't everything today exciting?" wrote one of the women who led the National Consumers' League. "Just to think that silly Roberts should have the power to play politics and decide the fate of Minimum Wage legislation. But, thank God he thought it was politically expedient to be with us." In a more whimsical vein, *The New Yorker* remarked: "We are told that the Supreme Court's about-face was not due to outside clamor. It seems that the new building has a soundproof room, to which justices may retire to change their minds."

Yet notwithstanding the ridicule directed at the Court, Hughes read the opinion in Elsie Parrish's case with an unmistakable note of exultation in his voice, for by being able to show that he had won Roberts to his side in *Parrish*, he had gone a long way toward defeating the Court-packing scheme. Once Roosevelt had a 5–4 majority for social legislation, there no longer appeared to be an urgent need for so drastic a remedy. Not for nearly four months would FDR's proposal be finally rejected, and it would retain substantial backing almost to the very end, but never was it as formidable a proposition as it had been on the eve of the ruling on Elsie Parrish's suit. Within days after the decision was handed down, Washington insiders were regaling one another with a saucy sentence that encapsulated the new legislative situation: "A switch in time saved nine."

The Court's shift in *Parrish* proved to be the first of many. On the very day the case was decided, "White Monday," the Court also upheld a revised farm mortgage law (the original one had been struck down on "Black Monday" in 1935) as well as other reform statutes. Two weeks later, once more by 5–4 with Roberts in the majority, it validated the Wagner Act (the National Labor Relations Act) and in the following month it turned aside challenges to the Social Security Act. Indeed, never again did the Supreme Court strike down a New Deal law, and from 1937 to the present, it has not overturned a single piece of significant national or state socioeconomic legislation. Many commentators believe that the Court has forever abandoned its power of judicial review in this field. Hence, they speak of "the Constitutional Revolution of 1937."

Battle-scarred veterans of the minimum wage movement found themselves in a universe remade. The seventeen states with minimum wage statutes on their books now took steps to enforce them, and New York made plans to enact new legislation to replace the law struck down in *Tipaldo*. Even more consequential were the implications of *Parrish* for the national government. Late in 1936, President Roosevelt had told newspapermen of an experience on the streets of New Bedford when his campaign car was mobbed by enthusiastic well-wishers, twenty thousand of them crowded into a space intended to hold a thousand:

> There was a girl six or seven feet away who was trying to pass an envelope to me and she was just too far away to reach. One of the policemen threw her back into the crowd and I said to my driver, "Get the note from that girl." He got it and handed it to me and the note said this: "Dear Mr. President: I wish you would do something to help us girls. You are the only recourse we have got left. We have been working in a sewing factory . . . and up to a few months ago we were getting our minimum pay of $11 a week. . . . Today the 200 of us girls have been cut down to $4 and $5 and $6 a week. You are the only man that can do anything about it. Please send somebody from Washington up here to restore our minimum wages because we cannot live on $4 or $5 or $6 a week."
>
> That is something that so many of us found in the Campaign, that these people think that I have the power to restore things like minimum wages and maximum hours and the elimination of child labor. . . . And, of course, I haven't any power to do it.

Now, thanks to the Constitutional Revolution that the Wenatchee chambermaid had detonated, Congress was able to give Roosevelt that power, and when the Fair Labor Standards Act of 1938, which set minimum wages and maximum hours for both men and women, was challenged in the courts, a reconstituted Supreme Court found no difficulty in validating it.

Long before then, Elsie Parrish had faded into the anonymity from which she had risen. She had remained in the public eye only long enough to comment on the Court's decision in 1937. News of it had reached her in Olympia, Washington, where she was now employed—ironically enough, in the light of Joe Tipaldo's trade—in a laundry. "I am happier over what it will mean to the working women of the state than over the money I will receive," she said. "There have been thousands of girls and women working for whatever they could get in this state, and now they will get a break."

When more than thirty-five years later Adela Rogers St. Johns, a reporter who had won renown as the "sob sister" of the Hearst press, tracked her down in Anaheim, California, Mrs. Parrish expressed surprise that anyone would pay attention to her. Surrounded by grandchildren, looking much younger than her years, "dressed in something pink and fresh-washed and ironed," she said that she had gotten little notice at the time "and none of the women running around yelling about Lib and such have paid any since." But she was quietly confident, she indicated to the author of *Some Are Born Great*, that she had accomplished something of historic significance—less for herself than for the thousands of women scrubbing floors in hotels, toiling at laundry vats, and tending machines in factories who needed to know, however belatedly, that they could summon the law to their side.

A Klansman Joins the Court

[I first discussed the Hugo Black appointment in the second annual William Winslow Crosskey Lecture in Legal History at the University of Chicago Law School on February 28, 1973. An augmented version of that talk appeared in the *University of Chicago Law Review* in its Fall 1973 issue, and I have expanded it yet again, drawing upon recently opened archives, for this book.]

I

On August 12, 1937, Franklin Delano Roosevelt, rebounding from the worst setback of his long Presidency, took the first of a series of steps toward creating what historians would one day call "the Roosevelt Court." Galling defeat had come less than a month before when the Senate had killed his "Court-packing" scheme, amid loud rejoicing from his opponents. The President was not finished yet, however, for one legacy of the protracted struggle was the creation of a vacancy on the Supreme Court, and it was FDR's prerogative to nominate a successor. The choice he finally made would trigger an acrimonious controversy and would have a momentous impact on the disposition of the Court.

The vacancy may have resulted from FDR's Court-packing plan. Roosevelt had advanced his bold proposal in February because he was frustrated by the performance of the Supreme Court, particularly the "Four Horsemen," Willis Van Devanter, Pierce Butler, James McReynolds, and George Sutherland. In May, during the heated Congressional battle, Van Devanter had announced his retirement in what some thought was a well-timed move to dispose of the plan, though his action may instead have come in response to more favorable retirement legislation or other considerations. The President, though, had not been able to exploit this advantage by selecting a liberal to replace Van Devanter, for he was widely understood to have promised the very first opening on the bench

180

to Joseph T. Robinson, the loyal but conservative Majority Leader. Robinson's death in July, at a critical point in the Great Debate, had doomed the Court-packing bill, but it had also had the ironic conse- quence of freeing Roosevelt from his presumed pledge to Robinson and leaving him with an opportunity that his opponents had hoped to deny him—naming the first Justice of his own choosing.

The battle over the Court plan, Joseph Alsop and Turner Catledge have written, "conferred a strange, almost a lurid, importance on the President's choice for the Supreme Court vacancy." As he had done in February while preparing his Court-packing message, Roosevelt acted in a covert fashion that put Washington on edge. Each day it was expected that he would send a name up to the Hill, but July ran its course without a decision and Congress, more particularly the Senate, which had hoped to go home in June, found itself in the sultry capital in August with adjournment near and still no word from the White House.[1]

In early August, a *New York Times* correspondent noted that "an unusu- ally fierce attack of nervous irritability has seized the 529 legislators." He added: "You have to see the shaking hands and the quivering facial muscles, hear the rage-quavers of the voices" of Congressmen to ap- preciate "the violence of the nerve tension." They "snap at each other over trifles in floor debates" and bite the heads off secretaries, causing "a new high in headless . . . secretaries," he continued. One secretary remarked, "Yesterday morning I had to phone six Senators, all of them my friends, and remind them of a subcommittee meeting. Five of them bawled me out for it, and the sixth hung up on me." Another secretary said: "The boss came back from a subcommittee row over a technicality the other day so ill that I had to nurse him and dose him for an hour and then call a doctor. It's the first time I've ever known him to be sick without a hangover for eleven years."[2]

Roosevelt had added to this anxiety when, at a press conference on July 27, he said that he was exploring the possibility of filling the va- cancy after the Senate had adjourned. Mutinous legislators were in- censed at the prospect of not having a chance to act on the selection until after the nominee had donned the black robes of a Justice and taken part in the Court's deliberations. The President's declaration also indicated that he might be contemplating a particularly offensive choice, making it desirable for him to bypass the Senate. "I hope F. D. will make soon a wise appointment to the Court," a worried Justice Brandeis wrote Felix Frankfurter. "A bad one—or any recess appoint- ment—would be serious."[3]

On August 2, over lunch at the White House, Homer Cummings, noting the strong resistance to a recess nomination, asked the President bluntly, "What is the objection to making the appointment now while the Senate is in session?" No objection, so long as they could agree upon the man, he was told. That would be easy, the Attorney General retorted, once they established the qualifications. One requirement, he said, was that the person could be confirmed without a fierce fight. Roosevelt did not regard that feature as essential. Cummings persisted. The President, he said, ought to choose someone, a Democrat presumably, who had the respect of the legal profession. Roosevelt kidded him about what he meant by such a phrase; was it conceivable that he could name a man the leading Republican organ, the New York *Herald Tribune*, would accept? He did not mean a reactionary, Cummings countered, but someone who would put an end to accusations about FDR's intentions. Furthermore, with five Easterners on the Court, the nomination should go to someone to the west of the Atlantic seaboard. A number of names surfaced, notably that of Solicitor General Stanley Reed, but the conversation ended inconclusively. [4]

Although Roosevelt may have been needling his Attorney General and the Senators with his talk of a recess appointment, he did have a valid reason for delay. On August 4, Stephen Early, the White House press secretary, reviewed the situation for the Scripps-Howard columnist Raymond Clapper. Early explained that the President did not know how long Congress would remain in session, and he needed two to four more weeks to make up his mind. It had not been clear until the Senate killed the Court bill in late July that he would have only one seat to fill. It might be supposed, Early said, that Roosevelt could easily come up with one name since he had originally sought six, but in fact it was harder to pick one, because he could not submit a balanced group and had to "make it a bull's eye." Clapper summarized the President's position in his diary: "been sixty to 75 names recommended since Robinson died. All have to be carefully investigated. Is serious matter and Rvt would be in bad spot if he sent up a name and then the opposition dug out some dumb chapter in his record. . . . Opposition which has been complaining that Rvt is slapdash would leap on him and say this is the kind of dumb[b]ell or bad actor he would have given us six of." [5]

As the tension mounted, Congressmen and reporters made book on whom the President would pick, but they had little to go on. Although it was expected that Roosevelt would try to close the breaches within his party and the Senate by making an especially judicious choice, he gave no sign of where his favor might light. Even veteran Administration Senators remained in the dark. "I haven't the slightest idea who will be appointed to the Supreme Court, nor has anybody in Washington other than the President," James F. Byrnes wrote a South Carolina friend on August 10. "The President certainly has not consulted anybody in the Senate about it. The only information we have is that contained in the Press; namely, that Sam Bratton of New Mexico, now a Judge of the Circuit Court of Appeals and formerly a member of the Senate, is receiving serious consideration. It may be that it is because the Senators have such a high opinion of Bratton that they think he has a good chance."[6]

On the morning of August 11, Cummings called at the White House to go over the list of possibilities. First, they eliminated all of the U.S. District Court judges. They then discarded all the U.S. Circuit Court prospects, though they both thought very highly of John J. Parker. They gave a good amount of time to considering Chief Justice Walter P. Stacy of North Carolina, but passed him by too. In the end, they got down to a group of four: Senator Hugo Black of Alabama, Solicitor General Stanley Reed, Senator Sherman Minton of Indiana, and Lloyd Garrison, dean of the University of Wisconsin Law School, roughly in that order. Roosevelt remarked that he had talked to no one but Cummings about the vacancy, save for Barkley who was pushing Reed. The Attorney General noted in his diary that he had "told the President that in many ways . . . Mr. Reed was the best qualified of the available candidates and had had intimate contact with all of the New Deal cases and, in a way, had been through the fire." Reed, though, Roosevelt noted, came from a circuit already represented on the Court, whereas Black did not. "I think also, from something he said, that he would regard the Black appointment as a little more significant in view of everything that has gone on," Cummings recorded. "On the other hand he would be reluctant to lose Black from the Senate. The matter, therefore, is in suspense and will remain so at least until tomorrow, and perhaps longer."[7]

When Roosevelt finally made his decision, he moved in the same furtive manner he had adopted in preparing the Court plan. That very night, August 11, the President startled the man he had chosen by summoning him to the White House after dinner and, upon informing him of the honor in store for him, swore him to silence. Only Cummings was informed, but not until the following morning when the deed was already done. Not even the White House staff knew what had taken place. The next morning, Early indicated that Roosevelt was still considering a list of sixty or seventy names and that a selection might not be made during the current session. Two hours later, the President sent a courier to Capitol Hill with a notice of appointment that he had written in his own hand. He kept the secret almost to the very end, but it became too much for him. Like "a small boy waiting for his surprise to be revealed," as Virginia Hamilton has written, he had to blurt out the news to someone. Before the messenger reached the door of the Senate chamber, Roosevelt told Early the name of the nominee. "Jesus Christ!" Early exploded. FDR grinned.[8]

II

The words "I nominate Hugo L. Black . . ." sent the Senate into a state of shock. Black, who had not let on at any point that he knew what the message contained, slouched in his seat, white-faced and wordless, and nervously shredded a stack of papers. A few liberal colleagues came over to congratulate the Alabama Senator, but other legislators did not try to hide their unhappiness. The House of Representatives responded more volubly. One reporter noted, "From the House press gallery it was quite a show to watch the reactions of the Congressmen as the news swept across the floor. A great buzzing as the name of Black was passed from lip to lip."[9]

Roosevelt may well have anticipated immediate acquiescence from the Senate. Henry Fountain Ashurst, the grandiloquent chairman of the Judiciary Committee, rose on behalf of the Administration to ask the lawmakers to confirm instantly the appointment of this "lawyer of transcendent ability, great, industrious and courteous in debate, young, vigorous, of splendid character and attainments." Ashurst contended that there was "an immemorial rule of the Senate that whenever the Executive honors this body by nominating a member thereof, that nomination by immemorial usage is confirmed without reference to a committee for the obvious reason that no amount of investigation or consideration by a committee could disclose any new light on the character or attainments and ability of the nominee, because if we do not know him after long service with the nominee no one will ever know him."[10]

But any expectation of easy confirmation reckoned without the diehards. For a few minutes, the Senate appeared to be willing to let the appointment of a colleague slip through without a hearing. When, as presiding officer, Vice President John Nance Garner, increasingly unhappy with FDR and his New Deal, inquired whether there were any objections, he heard none. Dissatisfied, he asked a second time. Again, silence in the chamber. Not until he raised the question a third time did Hiram Johnson of California and Edward Burke of Nebraska finally take the cue. When the Republican and the renegade Democrat spoke up, Ashurst was compelled to name a subcommittee to consider the nomination. Not since 1888, when President Grover Cleveland named Lucius

Quintus Cincinnatus Lamar to the Supreme Court, had a proposed appointment of a Senator or former Senator been sent to committee.[11]

The President could hardly have made a choice that would have disconcerted his opponents more. Black was an ardent New Dealer and had been a strong supporter of Court-packing; indeed, it was said that he was one of the few Senators who actually believed in the plan.[12] Most people had expected that Roosevelt would take pains to choose someone like a seasoned federal judge, but Black's judicial career was limited to eighteen months as a police court magistrate in Birmingham. Senator Peter Gerry of Rhode Island explained to Canada's prime minister, "His legal experience was not considered sufficient and he hasn't a judicial attitude of mind. He is a prosecutor and not a judge."[13] Little about him suggested the judicial temperament, and he had especially incensed conservatives by his performance as a no-holds-barred interrogator on Senate committees. As a Congressional inquisitor, Black, William O. Douglas later wrote, "was as relentless as a terrier pursuing a rat." One of Black's biographers acknowledged, "The paths of his investigations had been lurid with charges and countercharges, *subpoenas duces tecum*, searches and seizures, and contempt proceedings," and a political scientist later noted that "Senator Black in 1936 was the kind of legislator Justice Black had no use for twenty years later."[14]

A year before the nomination, Newton D. Baker, a onetime progressive leader who had become a prominent corporation attorney, had written a friend:

> I heard last week that the incredible Senator Black with his eavesdropping, peeping-Tom committee had secured from the Western Union Telegraph Company all the telegrams sent out of my office in a year. As I run a law office and not a criminal conspiracy, I am entirely indifferent as to what he discovered from the telegrams, but the oftener I permit myself to reflect on this outrage, the more violent I become. Man of peace as I am, I am quite sure I could not keep my hand off the rope if I accidentally happened to stumble upon a party bent on hanging him.[15]

Conservatives outdid themselves in expressions of indignation. "His appointment of Black," asserted an Oregon editor, "was the grossest insult to the Supreme Court and the American people that we have ever been called upon to accept." "I was disgusted," an editor of *Life* jotted in his diary. "If Black is a Roosevelt choice, thank God the country was saved five more like him under the court bill." A number of commentators came out independently with the same judgment. "If the President had searched the country for the worst man to appoint, he couldn't possibly have found anyone to fill the bill so well," grumbled a Senator, while the columnist David Lawrence wrote, "Mr. Roosevelt could not have made a worse appointment if he had named John L. Lewis." In like manner, the Chicago *Tribune* declared: "If Mr. Roosevelt wanted to degrade the Supreme Court he has made a good effort. If he wanted the worst man he could find he has him."[16]

In *News-Week*, FDR's onetime close adviser Raymond Moley observed:

> There have been worse appointments to high judicial offices; but, with Rodgers and Hart, I can't remember where or when. Like the late Huey Long, Senator Black is an able man. His sympathies, again like those of the Kingfish, lie with the socially and economically dispossessed of the country. But Huey's fundamental weaknesses, his passion for short cuts, his tendency to oversimplify complex problems, his gullibility where plausible crackpot economic schemes were concerned, his use of reckless methods to attain his ends, all characterize Hugo Black. Huey's chief redeeming feature was a constructive effort which gave the poor of his State better schools, cheaper books, good roads. Black looms only as a destroyer, an attacker, an inquisitor. . . .
>
> If this is the Presidential conception of "new blood" on the Supreme Court, I can only offer up profound gratitude that the country escaped six such appointments.[17]

A former high-ranking official of the Hoover administration noted in his diary: "All Washington is disgusted at the nomination of Senator Hugo Black to the Supreme Court. He is a snarling, obstreperous, narrow minded and unintelligent bounder. . . . More than anything that has passed before, the appointment makes me wonder as to Roosevelt's sanity." A day later, he was still fuming. "People . . . talk of nothing except the appointment of Black and certainly nobody has a good word to say about him," he recorded. "He is a low creature. Moulton of the Brookings . . . said this afternoon that he has seen a good deal of him and had always considered him the worst in character and in intellect in the Senate."[18]

The most devastating critique appeared on the editorial page of the *Washington Post*:

> Men deficient in the necessary professional qualifications have occasionally been named for the Supreme Court. And qualified men have sometimes been put forward primarily because they were also politically agreeable to a President. But until yesterday students of American history would have found it difficult to refer to any Supreme Court nomination which combined lack of training on the one hand and extreme partisanship. In

this one respect the choice of Senator Black must be called out-standing. . . .

If Senator Black has given any study or thought to any aspect of constitutional law in a way which would entitle him to this preferment, his labors in that direction have been skillfully concealed. If he has ever shown himself exceptionally qualified in either the knowledge or the temperament essential for exercise of the highest judicial function, the occasion escapes recollection.[19]

Conservatives derived one consolation from the episode—the conviction that FDR had shot himself in the foot. The publisher Frank Gannett, though he called the Black appointment "another great outrage," added, "In a way, I am delighted over it because it will weaken Roosevelt. . . . He has . . . put salt on the sore and flouted the public in an amazing way. I can't understand his making such a mistake." Some weeks later, a leading Old Guard Republican rejoiced that "more of the 'plain people' as Lincoln called them are severely critical of Roosevelt. His attempt to pack the court turned a multitude against him, but his appointment of Black has made even more serious inroads into his camp."[20]

Although Black came from Alabama, no group was unhappier about his nomination than the Southern Congressmen. A sharp-tongued, unrelenting partisan who kept too much to himself, Black had never been a member of "the club." More important, he was a Southern liberal, and his selection signaled Roosevelt's determination to back those who were attempting to transform the conservative structure of Southern politics, an inclination later manifested in the 1938 purge. A Georgia Congressman called the nomination "the worst insult that has yet been given to the nation"; a Texas Congressman said, "I wouldn't appeal a case with him there." Black had particularly antagonized Southern conservatives by sponsoring the wages and hours bill, which they claimed was denying their constituencies a competitive advantage granted by God. When the veteran Virginia Senator Carter Glass heard the nomination called a triumph for the common man, he snapped, "They must be Goddam common!" Asked by reporters for a comment on Black, he replied, "Don't start me off again."[21]

Yet Roosevelt and his supporters knew very well that there was not a thing the Senate could, or would, do about it. So strong was the sense of collegiality that it was inconceivable that the Senate would fail to confirm one of its own. A Democratic official wrote gleefully: "The blow to the chin he delivered in the nomination of Senator Black to the supreme bench is a source of unending amusement to me. I can imagine the various caucuses being held by the opposition senators to find a way out and still have salve for senatorial courtesy." As the President told Democratic Chairman James A. Farley, "They'll have to take him."[22]

The Senate proved unwilling to entertain the real objections many felt to the nomination. It would not consider the assertion that Black was too liberal, because ideological differences were not regarded as proper grounds for refusing to confirm a fellow Senator; nor was Black's lack of judicial background explored, since it could not be conceded that any member of the upper house might be unqualified to sit on the Supreme Court. The little consideration given the appointment therefore focused on technical matters. William E. Borah of Idaho claimed that since Van Devanter had taken advantage of legislation enacted earlier in the session allowing retirement rather than resignation, he was still a member of the Court, and there was no vacancy for Black to fill. Ashurst retorted that if all nine Justices retired or went mad, according to Borah's reasoning, there would be no Court; even Van Devanter thought the argument was nonsense, since he had no intention of ever returning to the bench. When Cummings first aired this possible difficulty, Roosevelt, he noted, "laughed heartily about it and I added that the matter might approach the aspects of comic opera." In like vein, a lawyer who had been opposed to the Court plan wrote Ickes:

> Borah's latest attitude is amusing. I wonder how we would get along if the eight remaining members of the court were to tender their resignations? By the gospel of Borah there would still be no vacancies, but unfortunately (and probably to your great delight) we would have no Supreme Court at all.

Others speculated that Black was ineligible for another reason: since the recent legislation also guaranteed the pensions of retiring Justices, Congress had increased their emoluments, and the Constitution forbade a member of Congress to accept a post under such circumstances. Few thought much of that argument either.[23]

Two days after the nomination, a more explosive consideration arose—it was said that Black, at the outset of his career, had been associated with the Ku Klux Klan. The National Association for the Advancement of Colored People and the Socialist Party each urged the Senate to explore Black's racial attitudes. The Socialist leader Norman Thomas also asked the Judiciary Committee to investigate the nominee's opposition during the Hoover administration to proposals to equalize relief between whites and blacks, his hostility to antilynching legislation, and his silence about the "Scottsboro boys," a group of blacks convicted in Alabama in what appeared to be an outrageous miscarriage of justice. "We fully appreciate Senator Black's championship of labor legislation," Thomas said, but "no other excellence can fit a man for the Supreme Court whose record is marred by race prejudice."[24]

Despite these reservations, the nomination moved quickly through committee, though not without occasioning some animosity. Matthew Neely of West Virginia, an Administration stalwart, allotted the matter only two hours in a meeting of his subcommittee on Friday, August 13, the day after the nomination; the subcommittee then reported the recommendation by a vote of 5–1, with only a Vermont Republican dissenting on constitutional grounds. On the following Monday, as the Judiciary Committee convened behind closed doors, William Dieterich of Illinois accused certain committee members of trying to "besmirch" their colleague by linking him to the Ku Klux Klan. Dieterich's tirade nearly resulted in a fistfight with a fellow Democrat when the conservative Nebraskan Senator Edward Burke charged at him. Although "tempers flared to white heat," the committee approved the nomination, 13–4.[25]

When the full Senate took up the Black appointment on August 17, Senator Royal S. Copeland of New York opened the debate before crowded public galleries. He asserted that his Alabama colleague's first election to the Senate in 1926 had been supported by the Klan, and he read a *New York Times* report on Black's exploitation of anti-Catholic sentiment in attacking the presidential ambitions of Alfred E. Smith. Copeland asserted, "We are free because we are guarded by the Supreme Court. Catholics, Protestants, Negroes, Jews, Gentiles, all of us, are guarded by the Supreme Court. But what will happen if a half-dozen men of the mental bias of the nominee should be seated on the bench? . . . Does the leopard change his spots? Will Mr. Justice Black be any different from Candidate Black? . . . Naturally we wonder what Mr. Justice Black would do were another Scottsboro case appealed to the Supreme Court."[26]

Copeland made no headway with his charges, because they were regarded as blatantly political and because the Senate received reassurances. Many believed that Copeland, an anti-New Deal Democrat who was running for mayor of New York City, was exploiting the Klan issue to curry favor with ethnic voters. Although Black left the question unresolved when cornered by some of his supporters during the debate, the unpredictable Borah came to his aid. The GOP maverick, who eventually voted against confirmation on the technical ground of ineligibility, conceded that Senators had received thousands of telegrams about Black and the KKK, but insisted, "There has never been at any time one iota of evidence that Senator Black was a member of the Klan. . . . We know that Senator Black has said in private conversation, not since this matter came up but at other times, that he was not a member of the Klan." When Copeland asked Borah how he would vote if he knew that Black was or had been a Klansman, the Idaho Senator replied, "If I knew that a man was a member of a secret association organized to spread racial antipathies and religious intolerance through the country, I should certainly vote against him for any position."[27]

Late in the afternoon of August 17, just five days after the Black nomination was made and after only six hours of debate, the Senate confirmed the appointment by a lopsided 63–16. Of the Republicans present, all but three voted "nay," as did six Democrats, including Burke and Copeland. But some of the most reactionary Southern Democrats, who had bitterly fought the Court plan, ended up in the "yea" column. Ickes recorded, "Even 'Cotton Ed' Smith, of South Carolina, who 'God-damned' the nomination all over the place when it was first announced, didn't have the courage to stand up and vote against a fellow Senator from the Deep South." The Klan issue had fizzled, but it left some uneasiness. In Washington, a one-liner went from mouth to mouth: "Hugo won't have to buy a robe; he can dye his white one black." Despite the rumbling about the KKK, Roosevelt and the New Dealers had apparently won a stunning victory, less than a month after the opposition thought FDR was on the ropes. Ickes concluded: "So Hugo Black becomes a member of the Supreme Court of the United States, while the economic royalists fume and squirm and the President rolls his tongue around in his cheek."[28]

After Congress adjourned, Hiram Johnson wrote a confidant in California:

> This was a most unsatisfactory session. We wound up by confirming Black, who is unfit to be a Supreme Court Justice. . . . Had it not been for me, Black's nomination would have gone through with a "Hurrah!" . . . Borah and other distinguished patriots wished it so, but I had "guts" enough to stop it. I accomplished nothing—save that sixteen men in the Senate showed their feeling of his unfitness. I understand he was a member of the Ku Klux Klan when first elected to the Senate. He never dared say anything about it subsequently, and Borah and his other friends saw to it that he was not called as a witness.[29]

Once Black was confirmed, the hubbub died down. Congressmen left the capital, and Black, after getting measured for his elegant ebony robes, sailed with his wife to Europe for a vacation. His name soon disappeared from the newspapers, and the controversy appeared to be at an end.

III

On September 13, the Pittsburgh *Post-Gazette* detonated a bomb. It published the first of six articles by Ray Sprigle, an enterprising reporter who had dug up original materials, including the transcript of a Klan meeting, conclusively connecting Hugo Black to the KKK.[30] The series grabbed front page headlines in newspapers throughout the country.

Sprigle began, "Hugo Lafayette Black, Associate Justice of the United States Supreme Court, is a member of the hooded brotherhood that for ten long blood-drenched years ruled the Southland with lash and noose and torch, the Invisible Empire, Knights of the Ku Klux Klan." Since it was generally suspected that Black had once had a KKK relationship, that aspect of the allegation hardly constituted news. Sprigle developed three points in his series, however, that were very damaging. First, he demonstrated that Black had not merely run with Klan backing, but had actually been a member of the organization. He gave an account of the night of September 11, 1923, when Black pledged that he would never divulge, even under threat of death, the secrets of the Klan; surrounded by white-robed members of the Robert E. Lee Klan No. 1 in Birmingham, Black had vowed, "I swear that I will most zealously and valiantly shield and preserve by any and all justifiable means and methods . . . white supremacy."

Second, Sprigle recounted vivid examples of the views held by the Klansmen with whom Black had associated. In a meeting in Birmingham on September 2, 1926, the Imperial Wizard, Hiram Wesley Evans, said, "We find that America up to now has done all that has been worthwhile under the leadership of native-born, white, gentile, Protestant men. . . . There isn't a Negro in Alabama that dares open his mouth and say he believes in social equality of the black man. . . . I mean to tell you any time they propose to produce equality between me and a certain said Negro they are simply going to have to hold a funeral for the Negro." The Imperial Wizard added that Northern Negroes "will be murdered by the Yankees that have gotten all the sass from the Negroes that they want." On that same occasion, the KKK's Imperial Legal Adviser in Washington observed, "To come down here now and find that you have given us a man named Black who wears 'white'—do you get that boys—to occupy a seat in the Senate of the United States is like getting an inspiration before baptism." Turning to Bibb Graves, who had just won the Democratic nomination for governor, tantamount to election, he added, "I am so glad that you have a man all but elected governor who comes from a town that, prior to his advent as Exalted Cyclops of the local Klan, I am told was owned by the Jews, controlled by the Catholics and loved by Negroes [Laughter and applause]. Now he tells me that the Jews have a foreclosure sale at bankruptcy, selling out, the Catholics are on the run, and the Negroes are in hiding [Applause]."

Most of Black's own remarks that afternoon were unexceptionable. In fact, he spoke of the "principles of liberty which were written in the Constitution of this country" and the ideal of loving one's enemies. But he also assured the assembled Klansmen, "I realize that I was elected by men who believe in the principles that I have sought to advocate and which are the principles of this organization," and said to them and to the Grand Dragon, "I thank you from the bottom of a heart that is yours."

Finally, Sprigle made a third and critical contribution—he established that, on the same afternoon in 1926, Black, who had resigned from the Klan in the summer of 1925 for reasons of political expediency, had been awarded a special life membership, a gold "grand passport." Black had thanked the Klan for this honor, which only a half dozen men in the United States had received. Most important, the card was presumably still valid because there was no evidence in the Klan archives that it had been returned. In short, Sprigle was saying not merely that Black had been elected with Klan backing, not merely that Black had once been a bona fide member of the KKK, not merely that Black had thanked the Klan leaders for their aid, but that Black was *still* a member of the Ku Klux Klan.[31]

Sprigle's articles prompted denunciations of Black and Roosevelt that far exceeded, in both volume and vehemence, the protests that had greeted the nomination in August when one cartoonist depicted the members of the Supreme Court assembled in their silk, eight in black and the ninth in the white robe and hood of the KKK. In the pages of the *American Mercury*, the mordant critic Albert Jay Nock called Black "a vulgar dog" and wrote that FDR's appointment of the Alabamian "was the act of a man who conceives himself challenged to do his very filthiest."[32]

Several Senators who had voted to confirm Black hastened to declare that if they had known of his Klan connection they would have opposed his elevation to the Court. Some thought they had been duped, since Black had temporized when the KKK rumors surfaced in August and others had given assurances that there was no foundation for the allegations. Democratic Senators from New Jersey and South Dakota charged that John Bankhead of Alabama had deliberately misled them by stating that Black had not been a member of the Klan. "I feel that not only I but the rest of the Senators were deceived and imposed upon," complained Clyde Herring, and his Iowa colleague, Guy Gillette, added, "I hope something is done to keep Black from the high court bench."[33]

The issue hit directly at the core of Roosevelt's urban coalition since the main targets of the KKK had been Catholics and blacks. The revelations also embarrassed Northern Democratic Senators with large ethnic constituencies who had voted to confirm. Groups such as the Ancient Order of Hibernians demanded that Black resign or be removed, and the Catholic Club of the City of New York deemed the appointment "a direct affront to the more than 20,000,000 Catholic citizens of the United States as well as to countless numbers of other citizens." In New Hampshire, the Knights of Columbus adopted resolutions castigating their Democratic Senator for supporting confirmation, and a member of the staff of a Democratic Senator from Rhode Island noted, "At a very large meeting of the Hibernian County Convention last night a great many Democrats were denouncing Roosevelt. Very severe criticism among the Democrats."[34]

Irish-Catholic politicians played a conspicuously disproportionate role in the campaign to get rid of Black. Representative John J. O'Connor, chairman of the House Rules Committee, reported he had been canvassing Congressmen about instituting impeachment proceedings and had found no one opposed to such a move. "If Mr. Justice Black was a member of the Klan when nominated and confirmed, his silence constituted a moral fraud upon the American people," said Representative Edward L. O'Neill, a New Jersey Democrat. "Should he further refuse to explain his present relation with that order or refuse to repudiate its principles and purposes, I anticipate that the president of the United States will request his resignation. Should Justice Black refuse, I would vote to impeach him." Lieutenant Governor Francis E. Kelly of Massachusetts drafted a resolution asking the President to insist upon Black's resignation, and Senator David I. Walsh, who favored the same course, declared, "There are two counts against him, one that Black, for political advantage joined the Klan and took the oath of a Klansman and subscribed to its creeds; two, that Black obtained his nomination and confirmation by concealment and thereby deceived the President and his fellow-Senators, especially the latter."[35]

Sprigle's articles appeared just as the campaign for the mayoralty in New York City was reaching a climax, and Senator Copeland took full advantage of the opportunity. He told a Carnegie Hall audience: "I never expected to see the day when a member of that organization, sworn to bigotry and intolerance, should become a member of the court. Shame upon him that he did not have the courage and decency to tell his colleagues in the Senate that the suspicion of his affiliation was a reality." Copeland accused his rival, Jeremiah T. Mahoney, of approving Roosevelt's action in the "placing upon the court of a Klansman who wears a black robe of court by day and a white robe of the Klan by night." "Imagine a man named Mahoney being mixed up with the Klan," his opponent spluttered. "Show me a Ku Klux Klanner and I promise he won't be alive a minute after I see him!"[36]

African-American spokesmen joined in the hue and cry. The National Association for the Advancement of Colored People urged the President to call upon Black "to resign his post in the absence of repudiation and disproof of charges" that he held life membership in the KKK. Robert L. Vann, who as editor of the Pittsburgh *Courier* and a special assistant United States attorney general was credited with playing the largest role in swinging Pennsylvania African-Americans to the Democratic party, wired Roosevelt to remove Black. "Your friends are on the spot," Vann said. "You must save your friends or you must release them."[37]

Despite this widespread sentiment, even FDR's conservative critics in the Senate conceded that nothing could be done if Black decided to stick it out. A President has no authority to oust a Justice, and since Roosevelt had been lambasted month after month for trying to tamper with the Court, he and his supporters surmised that any attempt to coerce Black into resigning would not be well received. People would be led to conclude "that, if the President should request Justice Black's resignation, he might also attempt to drive the three remaining members of the Four Horsemen—Justices McReynolds, Sutherland and Butler—from the bench." Nor did there appear to be grounds for impeachment. The civil liberties attorney Osmond K. Fraenkel observed, "I don't believe a judge can be impeached for something that happened before his appointment, but even if that were so, I do not see how he could be impeached for membership in an organization. Membership in the Klan, however politically inadvisable, is not a crime."[38]

The electrifying disclosures exasperated the President and his circle. Roosevelt, who apparently never asked Senator Black whether he had Klan associations, was annoyed after the story broke that Black had never volunteered information about his connection. When he confided to Joseph P. Kennedy that he did not understand why Black had not openly admitted that he had joined the KKK, Kennedy responded, "If Marlene Dietrich invited you to make love to her, would you say you were no good at making love?" A worried Ickes saw nothing amusing in the situation. He noted in his diary: "According to the charges now being made, Black ostensibly resigned in 1925 so as to be able to deny that he was a member but subsequently he was made a life member. If this is true, it makes a pretty bad situation." (When the diaries were

prepared for publication, Ben Cohen deleted this revealing passage.)
The situation was especially irritating to the New Dealers because Roosevelt had taken a firm stand for religious liberty in 1928 while campaigning for Al Smith, a Catholic, and had been severely criticized for having too many Jews in his administration and for giving too many benefits to blacks. Despite this record, the President now bore the onus of having brought the main battle of his second term to a culmination by naming a Klansman to the Supreme Court.[39]

Critics of the New Deal relished the President's discomfiture. The sardonic literary critic H. L. Mencken wrote: "The appointment of Hugo to the Supreme Court gave me a joy of a kind that is rare in this world, and his subsequent squirmings and tergiversations damn nigh made me bust. There will probably be no better show on this earth until a volcano lets go under New York." Washington, which so recently had been the self-confident capital of the New Deal, was now jeered at as "Ku-Kluxville-on-the-Potomac," and if the President had harbored any hope of renewing the Court struggle, that possibility, unpromising at best, was gone. As a widely read national column pointed out: "All Roosevelt's opponents have to do now when he brings up reform of the judiciary is to taunt: 'What do you want to do—put another Kluxer on the court?'" FDR himself looked foolish. The Black appointment, reported the *Kiplinger Washington Letter*, had the appearance of "a prime Presidential boner. Presidents can't afford to be made ludicrous—especially by themselves."[40]

In an editorial in the Emporia *Gazette*, William Allen White wrote:

When Franklin Roosevelt is dead and buried and all his bones are rotted, the fact that he played around with Black and appointed to the highest honorable office in American life a man who was a member of the Ku Klux Klan, as Black was charged when Roosevelt named him, well, as we started to say, when Roosevelt is dead and gone he will be remembered in the history of this day and time by the fact that he was not above dishonoring the Supreme Court by putting a Klansman there.

Why could not a man as smart as Franklin Roosevelt, as brave and as benevolent, also be wise in a day of crisis?[41]

IV

While Roosevelt's reputation was impaired by the unexpected turn of events, Black's life had become all but unendurable. The clamor followed the new Justice to Europe, where he was still vacationing when the Sprigle series broke. Journalists hounded him, first in Paris, then in London. "A dreadfully worried United States judge hid himself away in

a palatial hotel suite in London yesterday while all his fellow coun-
trymen were asking for a straight answer to a straight question," reported the British *Daily Herald.* One newspaperman jumped out of a
darkened corridor scaring Black's wife, and another seized his arm as he
emerged from a London theater. "I don't see you! I don't know you! I
don't answer you!" Black told him. The columnist Dorothy Thompson
wrote:

> In London tonight a Justice of the United States Supreme Court is barri-
> caded behind locked doors. His telephone rings but he does not answer
> it. Reporters try to interview him but in vain. This man . . . sees only
> the waiters who bring him food, the maids who tidy his rooms and the
> traffic of London moving in the streets below. . . . He is front page
> news in England, where the British are taking revenge for the Simpson
> case.

After letting it be known that he would sail back to America on a large
transatlantic liner, on which one of his fellow passengers would have
been Justice McReynolds, Black escaped from his hotel by a service
entrance and drove to Southampton where he boarded a small mail
steamer, *The City of Norfolk.* He left England, said the *Sun,* "Klandes-
tinely."[42]

No longer would Black be permitted to remain silent. Senator Walsh
said that he had to speak out to be fair to the Catholic Senators, and
to those with Catholic and Jewish constituents, who had voted for his
confirmation and who might suffer the consequences in the next election. Democratic Senator Bennett Champ Clark of Missouri commented, "I do not wish to be in the position of concluding as to the
authenticity of the charges contained in the newspapers against Justice
Black, but it does seem to me that he has had ample opportunity to
answer a simple statement of fact." As Black's vessel steamed westward
across the ocean toward Norfolk, a Gallup poll revealed that 59 percent
of those interviewed believed that he should resign if he were proven to
have been a member of the Klan. At the suggestion of Felix Frankfurter
of Harvard Law School, the young *Nation* editor Max Lerner flew to
Norfolk, made his way through throngs of reporters, one of them Ray
Sprigle in a ten-gallon hat, and at breakfast with Black aboard ship argued that he should issue an explanation. That night, Lerner spent four
more hours with Black in Alexandria. Under all of this pressure, Black
finally decided to accept an invitation to speak over the radio on October 1, but he now had less than two days to draft his remarks.[43]

The address, carried over all three national networks with three hundred stations, attracted the largest American audience of the decade, save for that tuned in to the abdication of Edward VIII. (The huge audience, however, lacked one prominent listener—Franklin Roosevelt contrived to be in the Pacific Northwest in an automobile without a radio as Black spoke.) The fact of Black's speech was a sensation because of the cardinal rule that Justices do not make statements on matters pertinent to the Court, and the dramatic nature of the occasion was enhanced when fiery crosses lit the hillsides in different parts of the country.

In his talk, Black admitted having belonged to the Klan—he could hardly have done anything else—but said that he had resigned before entering the Senate and never rejoined. He minimized the grand pass-port as an "unsolicited card" that he did not view as membership in the Klan, had never used, and had not kept. He also voiced his disdain, without naming the KKK, for "any organization or group which, any-where or at any time, arrogates to itself the un-American power to inter-fere in the slightest degree with complete religious freedom."[44]

Black's speech is remembered today as a courageous denunciation of the Klan that foreshadowed his future character as a Justice, but in truth it was not. Black neither explained his past Klan membership nor offered any apology for signing up with the KKK. He neglected to account for why he had sat through the Senate discussion of his alleged Klan con-nections without a word to anyone either in the Senate or, apparently, in the Administration. He repudiated none of the atrocities perpetrated by the Klan in Alabama while he was in the secret order. In all, he used only eleven of the thirty minutes allotted to him. The most unfortunate aspect of his talk, however, was not what he failed to say but what he did say. He spent the first third of his remarks cautioning against the possibility of a revival of racial and religious hatred, but he warned that this might be brought about not by groups like the Klan but by those who questioned his right to be on the Supreme Court. He went on to affirm that some of his best friends were Jews and Catholics, told the national audience about his longtime Jewish chum in Birmingham, and mentioned that he numbered among his friends "many members of the colored race."[45]

Rarely in the twentieth century has any statement by an American public figure brought down such abuse on him as Justice Black's brief address called forth. The press, as William F. Swindler has noted, "launched upon a Saturnalia of vituperation, some with extras before the evening was over." The New York *Herald Tribune* branded him a humbug and a coward: "The effort of Senator Black to suggest that he is the real protagonist of tolerance and that his enemies are intolerant is perhaps the greatest item of effrontery in a uniquely brazen utterance. Only a man heedless of the truth and a man afraid of his official skin could fall so low." The *Boston Post,* a paper often viewed as the popular organ of the archdiocese, called on him to step down, for "one who associates with bigots, bids for their support, takes the bigots' oath and then is so craven that he allows his friends in a crisis to deny it all, can't clear himself by asserting it was all contrary to his real character." About Black's references to Catholic, Jewish, and Negro friends, the *New York Post* said, "We might reply in kind that one of our best liberal friends was a Klansman but we still don't think he ought to be on the Supreme Court." The Newark *Ledger* added that Black had "resigned from the Klan to maintain an appearance of decency. He should resign from the Supreme Court to attain the substance of decency."[46]

Catholic outrage ranged across the political spectrum from the liberal *Commonweal* to periodicals and spokesmen on the right. "Since there was no sign of his being ashamed for himself," wrote the editor of the *Catholic World,* "I was ashamed for him; ashamed too for the Supreme Court, ashamed for the President of the United States." From Louisville a Catholic woman wired the Supreme Court: "I INSIST THAT SENATOR BLACK BE NOT ALLOWED TO SIT ON THE SUPREME COURT AND THAT ROOSEVELT AND HIS CABINET BE FORCED TO RESIGN." In a subsequent letter, she added:

> Senator Black denied religious intolerance, but don't they all? Don't President Roosevelt and his secretary, but didn't they, just the same, chase the Catholic K. C.'s off the front porch of the White House . . . when they came to call on him about religious persecution in Mexico, while he was "entertaining" the Mexican representative at a dinner paid for by Catholics? Don't they almost spit on you in the U.S. Government Service, if you are a Catholic, knowing that you have no power, no protection?[47]

The Democratic national chairman, Jim Farley, found it hard to exonerate Black. He wrote the U.S. ambassador to Spain, Claude Bowers, "I know him pretty well and have an extremely high regard for him personally. . . . He has defended me many times on the floor of the Senate, when even Senators of my own Catholic faith would not rise and say a word in my behalf. A fellow who is intolerant wouldn't do that." Nonetheless, he found his radio talk disappointing. "He admitted membership but did not in any way denounce it. . . . He had nothing to lose by . . . going on to admit it was a mistake on his part and [saying] there was no place in America for such an organization." In later years, Farley was less circumspect about his feelings. "I was in a car in Iowa when Black spoke," he said. "I thought he was awful."[48]

Roosevelt, however, had no doubt that Black's performance had carried the day. When Farley telephoned him a few days later, the President asked, "What d'you think of Hugo's speech of the other night?" "He did the best he could under the circumstances, but I think he should have hit the Klan," Farley answered. "It was a grand job," Roosevelt returned. "It did the trick; you just wait and see."[49]

The President was absolutely right. The address was inevitably applauded, if not altogether convincingly, by Black's supporters in the New Deal. "If you listened to Mr. Justice Black's radio talk," said Senator Theodore Green of Rhode Island, "I am sure that you must have felt as I did that he admirably expressed the principles on which Roger Williams founded this State." Elements of Roosevelt's urban coalition also remained loyal. Labor leaders praised Black's speech, and Rabbi Herbert S. Goldstein of Yeshiva College spoke for others in saying, "As a citizen, I do not seek 'the pound of flesh' and as a Jew, I do not seek retaliation." Most important, Black's discourse won the majority of his listeners, albeit not a substantial majority. After the broadcast, 56 percent of the people polled by Gallup responded that Black should stay on the bench, which was precisely what he had intended to do all along.[50]

V

On the morning of October 4, three days after Black's radio talk, the Supreme Court opened its fall term, and huge crowds gathered to see the former Klansman take his seat. Long queues extended for hundreds of feet in the corridor, and much of the throng was unable to enter the courtroom. When the Justices filed in, "they looked unusually and unnecessarily solemn," Cummings thought. Moreover, as the proceedings continued, they did not chat with one another or nod to people they knew in the courtroom, as they often did. Black, it was noted pointedly, sat to the "extreme left" of the Chief Justice. For the first time in public, the man from Clay County wore the silk robes of a Justice, but the occasion was not the hour of triumph he might have hoped for. To the dismay of his supporters, two petitions were filed to challenge his right to be on the bench. For all Black's efforts and those of Roosevelt, the controversy continued to simmer.[51]

The President quickly remedied the situation. The next day in Chicago, he delivered his historic "quarantine" address, and by nightfall the country had turned its attention from Black to foreign affairs and the prospect of a second world war. A distinguished authority on international law, John Bassett Moore, wrote, "The President never was more adroit than in his Chicago speech. All the talk about Black, balancing the budget, the C.I.O., the 'dictatorial drift,' etc. etc. . . . suddenly ceased when the war cry was raised." Critics charged that FDR had deliberately seized the headlines in order to distract attention from the Black furor. "The speech would never have been made if there had been no Black case," the isolationist Hiram Johnson protested.[52] Actually, the situation was more complex than such conspiracy notions suggested. From Washington, His Majesty's chargé d'affaires sent the British Foreign Secretary, Anthony Eden, a more balanced report:

> I have every reason to believe that the speech had long been contemplated, but the President was prepared to await the psychological moment for its delivery. He had returned from his Western tour fully convinced that, however lukewarm the feeling regarding the Supreme Court might be in those parts, the electors as a whole had not lost confidence in his personal leadership. On the other hand the regrettable "Black and Klan" incident was still front page news and required something more important to remove it to the back page. In fact unkind Wall Street wits are talking of "a red herring drawn across the Black trail." The President's arrival at Chicago coincided with the decision at Geneva to refer the Far Eastern crisis to the signatories of the Nine-Power Treaty. Here was a good opportunity for Mr. Roosevelt to make his appeal to the nation to abandon a policy of complete isolation.[53]

Although the quarantine address was followed by reduced attention to Black in the press, lawyers and Washington correspondents continued to scrutinize him closely. Even after the Court summarily dismissed the petitions to deny the new Justice a seat, every eye seemed to be inspecting him. "I went to the Court last week and had the opportunity to see Mr. Justice Black on the bench," Newton D. Baker, Wilson's Secretary of War who had become a corporation lawyer, wrote the former Supreme Court Justice, John H. Clarke. "He is young enough to make a good judge but he has a wavering expression of the eyes which he will have great trouble in straightening out if he wants to be like the judges on that Court usually are—impervious to all considerations except their view of the public good." The veteran *New York Times* columnist Arthur Krock had a different perspective:

> Mr. Justice Black's court-room demeanor provided material for interesting study. His face had gained color. His manner had acquired content. He looked benign instead of harried. But now and then, as the Chief Justice read the orders and Mr. Justice Black looked out upon the lawyers and spectators from his impregnable fortress of life tenure, an expression touched his face which is common to certain types of martyrs. It was a mixture of forgiveness and satisfaction, of pity for unreconstructed dissenters and sympathy for himself who had borne so much in comparative

silence. Charles Dickens, who gave many passages to the description of Mr. Christopher Casby, would have recognized it at once.[54]

Black might well have nourished such sentiments in his first year on the bench, for he was permitted to forget neither his Klan past nor his limited judicial background. In his first month, Black elicited scathing criticism when the conviction of one of the Scottsboro boys came up on appeal and Black disqualified himself. He aroused even more disapprobation for staking out iconoclastic views on the exegesis of the Constitution. In September, the venerable and venerated New York attorney C. C. Burlingham had written that he had come to the conclusion that the Court could "absorb" Black, adding patronizingly, "If Black will watch his step and follow 'the Sacred Three' and quietly show one of them his opinions before he submits them, he will come thru all right." But rather than meekly accommodating himself as might be expected of a newcomer tarred by scandal, he boldly advanced his own notions. "Mr. Justice Black, dissenting" became a familiar phrase; indeed, he was said to have set a record for lone dissents. By mid-May of 1938, Black had filed no fewer than nine solitary dissents. Only the cranky McReynolds approached that figure with four. Two others had entered one, and the remaining five had never dissented alone. It appeared at times, noted one writer later, that Black sought "to wrest domination by sheer shock of insolence toward his brethren, not excepting the Chief Justice." Even Max Lerner acknowledged, "Black has become a judicial crusader before he has come to maturity as a judge." Early in 1938, at a time when Justice Cardozo was very ill, Burlingham wrote Frankfurter, "The bench was a sad sight with a vacant chair at one end and a *filled* one at the other."[55]

In the month of May 1938, in Black's first spring on the Court, the painful situation came to a head. When Chief Justice Charles Evans Hughes addressed the American Law Institute, the press leaped on one sentence: "The prime necessity in making the judicial machinery work to the best advantage is the able and industrious judge, qualified by training, experience and temperament for his office." These words, seemingly unassailable save that they might be regarded as sententious, were read as a covert attack on Black. The New York *Daily News*'s Washington correspondents, John O'Donnell and Doris Fleeson, reported that "some of the lawgivers of the United States Supreme Court had hitched up their judicial robes and in dignified fashion were in the process of putting the slug on their colleague, Associate Justice Hugo L. Black."[56]

That conclusion derived in good part from awareness of the indiscretion of Harlan Fiske Stone. Once or twice a week, the journalist

Marquis Childs would call upon Stone at his Wyoming Avenue home, and they would go off for a stroll. Childs later recalled, "We would customarily trudge up the Massachusetts Avenue hill in the early winter dusk," and there Stone unburdened himself of his worries about Black, particularly about how difficult it was for the Court, with its heavy docket, to cope with the delay caused by an inexperienced judge. Childs later said that Stone was "like an old New England wood-carver, and here they suddenly brought someone in the shop who doesn't know a knife from a hoe. This really upset him very greatly."[57]

When Childs wrote a long piece for the St. Louis *Post-Dispatch* based on these conversations, Stone, far from disapproving, advised him to develop the story in a national magazine so that his views, still unattributed, would have larger circulation. Since Roosevelt had stressed the need to expedite litigation as a rationale for the Court-packing plan, he might be open to a warning about choosing untutored judges, Stone reasoned. Afterwards, Childs reflected, "In retrospect, I believe that Stone, without animus toward Black, was trying to telegraph a message to FDR so that he would be influenced in his subsequent appointments." The article, which appeared in the May issue of *Harper's*, created a hullabaloo by stating that Black's opinions frequently had to be rewritten by his colleagues in order to bring them up to the standards of the Court and that Black's incompetence had caused the other Justices "acute discomfort and embarrassment." Childs cited no Justice as his authority, but Paul Y. Anderson, a well-connected investigative reporter who had been fired by the *Post-Dispatch* for hitting the bottle once too often, told everyone whose attention he could grab at the National Press Club that Stone was the source and inspiration for the article.[58]

Yet even in these early days Black won admirers for his courage and skill. In 1938, Walton Hamilton, one of the country's most respected authorities on the Constitution, expressed his esteem for Black's cleanly written opinions and, in contrast to those who deplored Black's iconoclasm, stated his approbation for the independence of a man who "regards the sacred cows as ordinary heifers." By 1939, the Washington correspondent Erwin D. Canham was observing that "Mr. Justice Black . . . has climbed out of the pit into which the circumstances of his appointment had hurled him, and is on the way to being regarded as another Brandeis."[59]

The allusion to Brandeis suggested both a craftsmanship that demeaning references to the police court magistracy had not prepared critics for and a solicitude for civil liberties that many people had not expected of an ex-Klansman. In 1940, Black was spokesman for the Court in two notable decisions. In *Chambers v. Florida*, generally thought to be his ablest opinion, he represented a unanimous Court in holding that the convictions of four African-Americans for murder, obtained by using coerced confessions, violated the due process clause of the Fourteenth Amendment. "Under our constitutional system, courts stand against any winds that blow as havens of refuge for those who might otherwise suffer because they are helpless, weak, outnumbered, or because they are non-conforming victims of prejudice and public excitement," Black declared. "No higher duty, no more solemn responsibility, rests upon this Court, than that of translating into living law and maintaining this constitutional shield . . . for the benefit of every human being . . . — of whatever race, creed or persuasion."[60] In *Smith v. Texas*,[61] he again spoke for all nine Justices in setting aside the rape conviction of an African-American based on an indictment handed down by a grand jury from which African-Americans were excluded.

Black became best known, however, not as the eloquent voice of a unanimous Court, but as a dissenter urging the Court to break new ground on civil liberties, particularly as an advocate of uninhibited application of First Amendment rights. He also vigorously insisted upon a literal reading of the constitutional protections of the accused and persevered in urging the doctrine of "one man, one vote." Justice William O. Douglas observed in 1956, "I dare say that when the critical account is written, none will be rated higher than Justice Black for consistency in construing the laws and the Constitution so as to protect the civil rights of citizens and aliens, whatever the form of repression may be." By the 1960s, Alexander Bickel was writing of "a Hugo Black majority" on the Court, "for in this second half of Justice Black's third decade of service, the Court was overturning many a precedent that had entered the books over his dissent."[62]

Commentators who had once raised a cry about putting a Klansman on the bench ate their words. In March 1959 the Pittsburgh *Post-Gazette,* which had once boasted of the Sprigle revelations, ran a series of four articles praising Black. "He entered the court under a cloud of alleged bigotry," it stated, "and 22 years later he is a symbol for brotherhood." On Black's seventy-fifth birthday, Marquis Childs, calling him "the most eloquent champion of the rights of the individual," stated that "few men within the span of a lifetime have vindicated themselves so completely as has Justice Black. . . . It is hard to realize the storm of protest his appointment stirred." Childs continued:

> Those who knew Hugo Black had no doubt of where his convictions would lie, but they doubted his capacity to justify those convictions in the law.

This writer was one of those who at the time helped to give widespread currency to these doubts. That was a disservice to Justice Black.[63]

On the other hand, those who still clung to the KKK creed viewed Black as their implacable and contemptible enemy. Nearly a third of a century after he was appointed, a Kentuckian, outraged by one of Black's opinions, wrote his Congressman, "I am aware that Black never was anything but a police judge before FDR elevated him." On one of the many milestones of his long career, the Montgomery *Advertiser*, in an editorial, "Hugo Black at 79," observed, "He is probably a personal devil to more Alabamians than any figure other than Doctor King."[64]

Black's high reputation in his advanced years owed not a little, though, precisely to the disappointment of those who recalled his origins. The *Advertiser* reflected:

Black is seen as a redeemed Alabama Kluxer. He is viewed as a wayward son who reached the U.S. Senate with bigot ballots and then was reborn on the court as an exalted libertarian. He is more appreciated because of his dark political past. It is writ in Luke: "Joy shall be in heaven over one sinner that repenteth, more than over ninety and nine just persons, which need no repentance."[65]

When he finally stepped down in 1971, Justice Black, who had once been jeered at for his alleged lack of expertise, was praised for his "extraordinary capacity to clarify and make vivid the issues in a case" through "seemingly impregnable logic" and as one of "the court's intellectual pillars" with a reputation for "judicial integrity, dignity and tight reasoning."[66] "In his 34 years on the bench," wrote *Newsweek*, "Black's personal imprint on the law was larger than any other contemporary jurist's, an achievement that placed him among the greatest of Supreme Court Justices—Marshall, Holmes, Brandeis."[67]

Black's subsequent career made the widespread alarm expressed at his appointment seem badly misdirected and gave Roosevelt a sense of vindication. The President had remained rather touchy about the Black affair. He had especially taken umbrage at an episode at the annual banquet of the Gridiron Club, the organization of Washington correspondents, in December 1938, where one of the skits featured Black, though not by name. "At this time we transport our guests to the center of the Southern nightshirt trade," a master of ceremonies announces. "A famous fraternal organization is having a special meeting. One of its most distinguished members is returning from the North to report on what's going on there. So all aboard for Birmingham, Alabama!"

That station cry leads to a familiar tune set to new lyrics:

> When the midnight choo-choo leaves for Alabam',
> I'll be right there,
> I've got my fare.
> When I see those hooded Heroes of the Klan,
> I'll grab them by the collar,
> And I'll holler:
> "Alabam'! Alabam!" . . .
> I will be right there with bells,
> When that old Klanductor yells,
> "All aboard! All aboard! All aboard for Alabam!"

At an ensuing gathering of hooded and robed Klansmen, the Wizard explains that "since becoming famous our friend dropped the Klan," "abandoned it," and "discontinued any association with the organization," only to be interrupted by the cry, "Here he comes now!" The new arrival, greeted with calls of "Oyez, oyez, oyez!" (the traditional opening chant at sessions of the Supreme Court), declares:

> I never have considered and I do not now consider the unsolicited card given me as a membership of any kind in the Ku Klux Klan. . . . If I ever had it, I don't know where it is. If I know where it is, I won't tell. The fact is I buried it—down near the Lincoln Memorial. My passport's in the cold, cold ground.

The dinner guests, having been regaled by this parody of Black's radio address, then hear a finale set to the melody, "K-K-K-Katy":

> K-K-K-Klansman,
> Beautiful Klansman,
> You're the same old K-K-K-Klux I knew before,
> When the m-m-m-moon shines,
> Over the White House,
> We'll be watching at the K-K-K-Kourthouse door![68]

That affair continued to rankle. In February 1938, Raymond Clapper recorded in his diary an account he had received from George Holmes, the president of the Gridiron Club, about a visit Holmes had paid to Roosevelt shortly after the dinner:

> Rvt said like[d] dinner except thought one skit in bad taste. Said that was Klan skit on Black. . . . Said Harding had an illegitimate child but Grid-

iron club never use[d] anything on that. . . . Said matter was dying out skit by being printed in newspapers tended to reopen whole thing keep it agitated. Holmes told us he couldn't see analogy of Rvt's unless he meant that Black was like Nan Britton.

When *Chambers* was handed down, the President seized the opportunity at his press conference the next day to tell reporters, "I would put in a general dig that some of the Press should not only give a little praise but also a modicum of apology for things they have said in the last two years. Is that fair?"[69]

VI

Black's emergence as a champion of civil liberties has been offered as proof that Roosevelt knew what he was doing all along because he realized that the Alabamian had been an advocate of human rights throughout his life. According to this view, Black's post-1937 conduct was not a surprising new development but accorded with his pre-1937 career, for he had come out of a populist tradition in Alabama and had long been an exponent of civil liberties and a friend of labor and African-Americans. Those who advance this claim acknowledge that he had been a Klansman, but contend that the KKK was a populist, pro-labor movement that sponsored liberal, humanitarian measures, such as aid for underprivileged children.[70]

One of his defenders, the historian Bertram Wyatt-Brown, has concluded that "Black was a man of honor in its Ciceronian sense and also in the most objective meaning of the term." His membership in the Klan should be perceived as a quest for "communal bonding" by a typical "gregarious southerner searching for fellowship and power in the company of other men." Nor was there anything aberrant or pathological about the KKK, Wyatt-Brown continued. He even quoted, with no indication of disapproval, the outrageous contemporary observation of H. L. Mencken, "If the Klan lynches a Moor for raping someone's daughter, so would you or I." Though Black, for his part, "never condoned lynching and lawlessness in the turbulent 1920's, he never condemned them either," Wyatt-Brown acknowledged. But he added defensively, "The latter course would have been political suicide."[71]

The evidence for these familiar arguments is, at best, inadequate. True, Black was never associated with Klan violence,[72] he had been an attorney for unions, and he was responsible for reforms in court procedure in Alabama. Nevertheless, the link of Black to populism has been too easily assumed, quite apart from the difficulty of showing the con-

nection between populism and modern civil libertarianism. Black did
have African-American clients, but he was also reproached for making a
blatant appeal to race prejudice while defending the accused murderer
of a priest. The strongest statement that Daniel M. Berman could make
in his informative article in the *Catholic University of America Law Review*
was that "there is no evidence that Judge Black treated Negroes any
more harshly than whites." In 1928, Black had questioned permitting
African-Americans to vote, and as late as 1932, he had opposed a government relief bill because it would, in code language, interfere with
"social habits and social customs." The Washington correspondent Paul
Y. Anderson reported that Black "became hysterical over the prospect
of a federal relief plan which might feed Negroes as well as whites, and
gave an exhibition which brought a blush to the face of [the racist] Tom
Heflin, lurking in the rear of the chamber."[73]

The one thing the country knew for certain about his attitude on race
in 1937 was that, in the very month he was appointed to the Supreme
Court, Black was planning to speak in the Senate against an antilynching bill. Black, indeed, had talked at such length against the previous antilynching measure (some seven hours) that it required the rest of
the afternoon and part of the next day for the clerk to read his address
into the *Congressional Record*. That fall, when Black was in his second
month on the bench, Senator Tom Connally of Texas, in the midst of
a Southern filibuster, had the clerk once again read aloud those 1935
remarks by Black denouncing antilynching legislation as a monstrous
effort by venal African-Americans in the North "who have gone over
this land holding aloft the ancient torch of prejudice and passion and
hate, thereby contributing no benefit to the people of their race; simply
attempting to stir up an antagonism which does not exist between the
white people of the south and the colored people of the south."[74]

Throughout his years on the Court, Black showed an unbecoming
insensitivity toward what troubled people about his association with the
Klan. When in a 1968 television interview Eric Sevareid asked him if
the controversy over the Sprigle series was the great crisis of his career,
Black answered that it had not been a crisis at all. There was nothing
new about the revelations, he insisted, and the KKK in Alabama had
only been one of a number of lodges he had joined—like the Knights
of Pythias and the Odd Fellows. No doubt some of the Klansmen had
been racist, but that would have been true of any lodge. "Nearly all the
preachers belonged to it," he remarked. Nonetheless, he had resisted
signing up for a long while. He had joined only on the insistence of a
Jewish friend, he told his wife. On another occasion, she noted in her
diary, Hugo woke up during the night and, unable to get back to sleep,

told her that his biggest mistake was becoming a member of the Klan. It was an error, though, not because in retrospect he felt remorse about having been a member of an assembly of bigots but because it cost him the 1944 vice-presidential nomination on the ticket with FDR and hence, presumably, the White House.[75]

There is every reason to assume that when he made the appointment, Roosevelt had knowledge of Black's KKK past. At a press conference in September, when asked, "Prior to the appointment of former Senator Black, had you received any information from any source as to his Klan membership?" he responded, "No." The President may not have known about "membership," though Black many years later claimed that he did, but it is inconceivable that he had no awareness of a Klan connection. It was widely recognized, at the very least, that the Alabama Senator had Klan backing when he was first elected to the U.S. Senate. In fact, as a writer in the *Washington Post* noted, "It is difficult to find a sketch of Senator Black which does not contain some reference to the Ku Klux Klan." For Roosevelt to have ascertained that Black had KKK connections, Turner Catledge of the *New York Times* pointed out, "all he would have had to do was to turn around at any of his closed circle meetings and ask Charlie Michelson, who wrote just that when he was a correspondent of the New York *World* back in 1926 when Black was nominated and elected." In addition, because of his annual sojourns in Georgia, at his second home in Warm Springs, the President would have been likely to have acquired good intelligence about the politics of neighboring Alabama.[76]

There is no evidence, however, that awareness of this past caused Roosevelt to think twice about appointing Black, and it is improbable, given the temper of the times, that civil liberties considerations loomed large in his mind in deciding upon a nominee. The central issue in the Court crisis had been the fate of New Deal economic legislation, and the President was looking for someone to legitimate the growth of the State. Concentration on such matters, rather than civil liberties and civil rights, reflected the basic attitudes of 1930s liberalism. It is true that interest in civil liberties and civil rights grew during the Depression, partly as a consequence of government activities: initiatives, in the Justice Department, the inclinations of administrators such as Harold Ickes, the example set by Eleanor Roosevelt, and the spirit of concern that the New Deal conveyed. Not until the 1940s, however, did civil liberties and civil rights come to have a truly prominent place on the agenda of American liberalism.[77]

For many New Deal supporters, Black's KKK affiliation was distressing, but it was not thought to be central, as it would be today.

Klan membership was regarded as the entry fee Black had to pay for political advancement in Alabama, nothing more. Senator George Norris, the most respected of all the progressives and father of the TVA, who had fought the Klan and been fought by it, called the naming of Black "a wonderfully good appointment." He added, "Even if he was a member of the Klan, there's no legal objection to that. I've an idea many members of the House and the Senate belong to the Klan also but that is their privilege."[78]

Progressives characterized the outcry against Black as a conservative plot to discredit the Roosevelt administration and thereby scuttle the New Deal and prospects for reform. They did not attack what was said about Black, but rather who said it; when Sprigle's series appeared, Black's supporters concentrated their fire on his publisher, Paul Block, and other hostile newspaper titans such as William Randolph Hearst. They offered the defense, in the liberal columnist Heywood Broun's words, that "few justices of the Supreme Court swim up to the high bench as immaculate as Little Eva on the way to Heaven." Moreover, they contended that the elements opposed to Black would not have shown the same intense concern about the past of a reactionary nominee. Another liberal columnist, Jay Franklin, wrote:

> One point only should be made in relation to these charges: If Hugo L. Black had been a labor-baiter, a trust corporation attorney, a man who had amassed a fortune and achieved political prominence as a result of helping the banks, utilities and corporations to loot the State of Alabama and stifle competition by strongarm monopolies, he could have engaged in devil-worship, he could have practiced polygamy, he could have hunted down run-away sharecroppers with blood-hounds, and eaten babies for breakfast, for all that his conservative Northern critics would care.[79]

When Copeland raised the issue of Black's Klan connections in the New York City campaign, the liberal press responded not by examining the issue but by denouncing Copeland as a "stooge" of William Randolph Hearst. The New Yorker, said the Philadelphia *Record*, "staged the most obscene one-man medicine show the Senate chamber has seen since the days of Thad Stevens." He "made a grand-stand play for the Jewish vote, the Irish vote, the Negro vote and the 'Gentile' vote. It is a mystery that he overlooked the Arabian vote." By the *Record*'s calculation, it was not Black but Copeland who was guilty of bias, for "Dr. Copeland tried to smear with slimy race prejudice one of America's outstanding progressives."[80]

The New Dealers insisted that Black should be measured by the yardstick of twentieth-century social reform and by the imperatives of the Great Depression. *The Progressive,* the organ of the La Follette dynasty in Wisconsin, noting Black's "excellent and long standing record of liberalism," pointed out that Black had fought the big-navy lobby and the power trust. Congressman David Lewis, a Maryland Democrat who had co-sponsored the Social Security bill, asserted, "The real issue is not Black's qualifications, but whether the court is going to keep out of the 'nullification business'—that is quit vetoing acts of Congress." A Providence newspaper observed, "We don't like the idea of a Supreme Court Judge having been at any time or for whatever purpose associated with the Ku Klux Klan, but the issue is not religion, it is not race or creed; the issue is economics."[81]

In its "Topics of The Times" column, the *New York Times* satirized this sentiment in *Alice in Wonderland* style:

> After a while the White Rabbit summed up the debate, nobody dissenting.
>
> "You see, Alice," he said, "it's all because we have recently discovered that all life is functional. Once upon a time people thought there were definite things like truth, justice, honor, mercy, courage, and so forth. But now we know these things are only functions of the economic system.
> . . . That is why Liberals in the United States feel it does not matter if a member of the Supreme Court used to belong to the KKK. The only important thing is how does he stand on the question of 1 1/2 cents per kilowatt hour f.o.b. Norris Dam."[82]

This preoccupation with economic policy had been a critical determinant of the President's selection of Black. Roosevelt would have wanted a liberal under any circumstances, and at this particular moment such a choice seemed imperative to hold Hughes and Roberts. If a committed New Dealer were to join Brandeis, Cardozo, and Stone, he would create a critical mass of four who would be a strong inducement to the other two to abandon the three remaining conservatives. The President had no enthusiasm at all for Judge Bratton, the favorite of the Senate. "Bratton belongs to a judicial school of thought that ought not to be represented on the bench," he later told Farley. Black, on the other hand, was a true believer in expanding governmental power.[83]

Far from seeking to placate Congress by picking a moderate like Bratton, Roosevelt wanted to make clear that he was as committed to the New Deal as ever, and his selection of Black was a symbolic and defiant act. FDR's original plan seems to have been motivated by a desire not only to reform the Court but also to punish the Justices for wronging him in the past. The Black nomination afforded the President another opportunity to express his contempt for the illusion that the Court was a body that lived on Mount Olympus and his conviction that it was essentially a political agency. The Senate was even more of a target for revenge, for it had just humiliated him in the Court-packing battle. Donald Richberg, a prominent New Dealer, confided, Clapper noted, that "Roosevelt was mad and was determined to give Senate the name which would be most disagreeable to it yet which it could not reject."[84]

On the final morning, when Cummings returned to the White House, the President told him that he had written on a piece of paper the names of Black and Reed with the advantages and disadvantages of choosing one or the other. That was like the method employed in some detective stories, Cummings interjected. Yes, he often used it, Roosevelt responded, and this time it had led him to a decision: Black, even though "if you decided the matter purely on the matter of experience as a lawyer and in the court, especially the Supreme Court, . . . Stanley was far ahead." "Other things," however, "over-balanced" that consideration, especially the fact that Black came from an unrepresented circuit with a lot of states in it. Cummings had no doubt of what the consequences would be. "The appointment of Black," the Attorney General commented in his diary, "will certainly stir up the dry bones."[85]

Black's lack of a substantial judicial background did not deter Roosevelt, largely because that was not a matter of much concern to him but also because it was not so unusual. Of the members of the Court at the time, only Cardozo had served as a judge before being named.[86] During the furor over the Black appointment, Felix Frankfurter wrote:

> I wish some of my patriotic friends would know a little American history. It would do most lawyers and editors good to read the sewage that was poured out on Taney's head when Jackson appointed him. . . . From this talk about great legal experience and fine judicial qualities one would suppose that McReynolds and Sanford and Sutherland and Butler and Roberts were men of wide culture and juristic detachment when they got on the Supreme Court.[87]

The President's trust in Black's liberal proclivities proved well founded. So faithful was Justice Black to the tenets of the New Deal that it was even rumored that Tommy Corcoran wrote his opinions. "Although Black's appointment did not mark the precise chronological point from which the Court's philosophy began its deviation from its previous path," one of his biographers, Charlotte Williams, later remarked, "it was this event which made it plain beyond all doubt that the Court was about to be reconstituted in the image of the New Deal."

Black immediately gave the Administration a 6–3 majority on the Court, and his lone dissents indicated that he favored even more advanced stands than the "liberal" Justices: Brandeis, Cardozo, and Stone. One commentator has calculated that in sixty cases from 1938 through 1958, Black sustained workingmen's claims in every case but one, and that in the decade beginning 1949, in nineteen Sherman Act conflicts between business and consumer interests, "only Mr. Justice Black found a violation of the law in every instance."[88]

Black's appointment turned out to be only the first of many for the President, and, in nominating this outspoken liberal, he set the pattern that most of the other selections for "the Roosevelt Court" would follow. To the Supreme Court would go progressives such as Frank Murphy and William O. Douglas who shared Black's enthusiasm for the New Deal. The typical appointee would, like Black, be several years younger than President William Howard Taft's representative choice. Only once would FDR pick a man with prior experience in the federal judiciary; indeed, Black was exceptional in that, save for Wiley Rutledge, the former police court magistrate was the only Roosevelt appointee who had ever served as a judge prior to joining the Court.[89]

So rapidly did the composition of the Court change under Roosevelt and Truman that by the late 1940s Black, whose tenure seemed so precarious in 1937, was the senior member. Black was to remain on the bench through the thirties, forties, fifties, sixties, and into the seventies. When he was eighty-one, the *Washington Post* noted, "Only 96 men have sat on the Supreme Court in our history and Hugo Black has sat there with 27 of them."[90] When he completed his thirty-third term in 1971, only four Justices in the history of the Court had served so long, and only two—Roger Taney and Oliver Wendell Holmes, Jr.—were still on the bench at his age. He would fall only months short of establishing a new record for length of service as a Justice.

The Black controversy is rich in paradox and irony—a former Klansman becoming one of the century's leading exponents of civil liberties, a Justice chosen for one set of reasons winning fame for accomplishments that had hardly been anticipated, an Alabamian who created alarm among African-Americans when he was nominated but who lived to be denounced as a foe of the white South—but not least of the many ironies is the fact that the President's bitterly fought campaign to rejuvenate the Court by terminating tenure at the age of seventy would end in his naming, as his first appointee, a man who would still be on the bench on his eighty-fifth birthday and whose lengthy and brilliant career would be seen as a testament to FDR's perspicacity.

The Constitutional Revolution
of 1937

[I first explored the subject of the Constitutional Revolution of 1937 in a lecture at the Fourth Annual Conference of the Canadian Association for American Studies at McGill University, "Canada and the United States in the Great Depression," on November 15, 1968. Save in a poorly transcribed typescript edition of the conference proceedings, the essay has not been published before and has been substantially revised since its original presentation in Montreal.]

I

In common with many other nations during the Great Depression, the United States undertook a vast increase in the power of the State. Before Franklin D. Roosevelt's inauguration in March 1933, the national government, the political scientist V. O. Key later noted, "had been a remote authority with a limited range of activity. It operated the postal system, improved rivers and harbors, maintained armed forces on a scale fearsome only to banana republics, and performed other functions of which the average citizen was hardly aware."[1] But in FDR's First Hundred Days, the New Deal Congress enacted fifteen laws, including such precedent-shattering statutes as the National Industrial Recovery Act, which sanctioned the cartelization of industry; the Agricultural Adjustment Act, which subsidized staple farmers; the Tennessee Valley Authority law, which launched an ambitious experiment in public power development and regional planning; and a series of measures establishing federal responsibility for relief of the unemployed. In the Second Hundred Days of the summer of 1935, Congress approved another cornucopia of laws, among them the National Labor Relations Act (the

Wagner Act), guaranteeing the right of collective bargaining; the Guffey Coal Act, imposing wage and price constraints on the coal industry; the Public Utility Holding Company Act, including a "death sentence" on gargantuan power combines; and the Social Security Act, which, by setting up old age pension, unemployment insurance, and other systems of benefits, put the United States on the road toward the Welfare State. At the same time the activities of state governments burgeoned. These abrupt changes raised a formidable challenge to the traditional doctrines of the Supreme Court, precipitated a constitutional crisis, and, in the end, resulted in nothing less than a "Constitutional Revolution."[2]

II

From the outset many of the New Dealers feared that the Supreme Court would refuse to validate this unorthodox enlargement of authority. Four of the nine Justices—James McReynolds, Willis Van Devanter, George Sutherland, and Pierce Butler—could be expected to draw on a laissez-faire tradition of constitutional interpretation that they had helped to make. Van Devanter and McReynolds had taken part in the notorious 5–4 decision of *Hammer v. Dagenhart*[3] (1918) striking down the Child Labor Act of 1916 by presuming to pass judgment on the motives of Congress. The Court ruled that Congress could not ban the shipment in interstate commerce of goods produced by children because Congress was seeking to control intrastate activities and because the products were harmless.

To balk the expansion of governmental power under the New Deal, the "Four Horsemen" needed to win over only one of the other five Justices. Three of them—Louis Brandeis, Benjamin Cardozo, and Harlan Fiske Stone—were viewed as sympathetic to the new departure, although it was not clear that they would approve anything so unfettered as the National Industrial Recovery Act. But the two remaining judges—Chief Justice Charles Evans Hughes and Owen Roberts—were thought to be doubtful. That perception, especially with respect to Roberts, soon proved well-founded. In the first tests, the Court, by 5–4 decisions, upheld state and national laws, notably in the 1934 *Nebbia* case where Roberts gave a very broad reading to the regulatory authority of a state government.[4] But in the spring of 1935 Roberts joined the Conservative Four in asserting judicial supremacy. His opinion for a new 5–4 majority in the *Rail Pension* case not merely held that the Railroad Retirement Act of 1934 was invalid, but also strongly implied that any other pension law for railroad workers that Congress might see fit to enact would also be unconstitutional.[5]

In 1935 and 1936, over an unwontedly destructive sixteen-month period, the Court demolished a number of acts of Congress, as well as
important state legislation. Such landmarks as the National Industrial
Recovery Act and the Agricultural Adjustment Act fell to the judicial
axe. Some of the decisions were unanimous, notably the *Schechter* ruling
invalidating the NIRA; all the judges agreed that the government had
exceeded its power in attempting to regulate the kosher poultry business.[6] But in most of the cases, a minority of Stone, Brandeis, and Cardozo, sometimes joined by Hughes, dissented, with Stone, especially,
biting in his disapproval of the reasoning of his brethren.

The Supreme Court during these months frequently went out of its
way to frustrate the Roosevelt administration. It revived doctrines that
had languished for decades or employed rubrics that had never before
been used to invalidate an act of Congress. Until the age of Roosevelt,
the Court had never found an act of Congress unconstitutional for dele-
gating legislative power to the Executive, but starting in 1935 it did so
three times in little more than a year. The Court even disregarded the
specifically stated intent of Congress as expressed in the statutes. In the
Carter case, it struck down both the labor and price-fixing provisions of
the Guffey Coal Act, although Congress had stipulated that the two
sections were separable.[7] In *Ashton*, it ruled that the Municipal Bankruptcy Act invaded the rights of the states, despite the fact that the law
required the consent of the states and that the consent had been given.[8]

The prevailing majority on the High Court displayed the same arro-
gance toward state legislatures. In 1935, in *Colgate v. Harvey*, it invalidated a Vermont law by resuscitating the privileges or immunities clause
of the Fourteenth Amendment, which had lain dormant since the *Slaughterhouse Cases* of 1873 had established that the clause applied only to the
rights of national citizenship. Stone's dissent attacked Sutherland's "feeble" attempt to justify applying an "almost forgotten" clause which in
forty-four earlier cases the Court had refused to use.[9] The Court created
a much greater furor the following year when it struck down a New
York minimum wage law for women in *Tipaldo*, a ruling that indicated
that the majority of the bench was hostile to social legislation, irrespective of whether it emanated from Washington or a state legislature.[10]

The Court employed several different doctrines to circumscribe Big
Government. By making rigid distinctions between production and commerce, it narrowed the scope of Congressional authority over industry.
The Court followed in the footsteps of Chief Justice Melville Fuller's
pronouncement in 1895 that Congress had no power over enterprises
whose effect on commerce was indirect, no matter how extensive, because the difference between "direct" and "indirect" was one of kind

rather than degree.[11] Justice Sutherland stated unreservedly in *Carter*: "The local character of mining, or manufacturing and of crop growing is a fact, and remains a fact, whatever may be done with the products."[12] In his *Butler* opinion, Roberts sharply restricted the power of Congress to tax and spend to promote the general welfare. He reasoned that the AAA's processing levy was not really a tax but a stratagem for controlling agricultural production, an activity which, since it encroached on the reserved powers of the states, was forbidden to Congress.[13] This mischievous opinion had recourse to the conception of "dual federalism,"[14] which wielded the Tenth Amendment as a weapon to deny the powers of the national government. To forestall government transgressions of property rights, especially through labor legislation, the Court perpetuated the fiction of freedom of contract in the due process clauses of the Fifth and Fourteenth Amendments, which were held to place substantive as well as procedural restraints on government action.[15]

III

In the spring of 1937, though, in the midst of the controversy over President Roosevelt's Court-packing message, the Court began to execute an astonishing about-face. On March 29, 1937, it dramatically altered American jurisprudence by ruling, 5–4, that a minimum wage law of the state of Washington was constitutional.[16] Although the statute was essentially the same as the New York act the Court had struck down in *Tipaldo* ten months earlier, Roberts aligned himself with the majority that sustained the Washington law.[17] Chief Justice Hughes, speaking for the Court, pointed out that the Constitution neither spoke of freedom of contract nor recognized an absolute liberty. The opinion, which dealt a heavy blow to substantive due process, also jettisoned the *Adkins* precedent. That same afternoon, the Court approved three acts of Congress extending federal power.[18] "What a day!" Robert H. Jackson later wrote. "To labor, minimum-wage laws and collective bargaining; to farmers, relief in bankruptcy; to law enforcement, the firearms control. The Court was on the march!"[19]

Despite the "conversion" of Roberts in the Washington minimum wage case, almost no one expected the Court to sustain the Administration in all five of the National Labor Relations Act cases decided two weeks later.[20] The government seemed virtually certain to win an interstate bus company case that lay midstream in the "current of commerce." But challenges by the Jones and Laughlin steel firm and the Fruehauf trailer company raised serious questions about federal authority over manufacturing, while an Associated Press case ran the added hazard of a freedom of press issue. At the beginning of April, New York's most prominent attorney wrote of the Wagner Act, "Some of the wise men of the east think it will be sustained so far as buses and the Associated Press are concerned, but not otherwise," and that same week a nationally syndicated columnist reported that "outside opinion" was "virtually unanimous" that the government would lose the three manufacturing cases, which were "clearly not interstate commerce." Even the government's attorneys thought the Administration would meet defeat on a case involving a small Richmond, Virginia, clothing company. In 1935, Cummings had remarked in his diary on "the Wagner Bill, which I regard as of rather doubtful constitutionality," a sentiment he relayed to Roosevelt, and on April 12, the chairman of the NLRB went to the Supreme Court building to hear the decision in the expectation that he would learn that he was out of a job.[21]

That day, however, the Court surprised friend and foe by sustaining the Administration in all five cases, the bus case unanimously, the rest by 5–4 decisions in which Roberts once more helped compose the majority.[22] In the central opinion in *Jones and Laughlin*, Hughes asserted: "Although activities may be intrastate in character when separately considered, if they have such a close and substantial relation to interstate commerce that their control is essential or appropriate to protect that commerce from burdens and obstructions, Congress cannot be denied the power to exercise that control."[23]

The Chief Justice admitted to no change in the doctrines of the Court, and even cited the *Schechter* opinion in support of his argument at one point, but commentators found it difficult to square the Wagner Act decisions with recent rulings.[24] Less than a year earlier, the majority had stated that "the relation of employer and employee . . . in all producing occupations is purely local in character."[25] It could be claimed that the difference in size between the Jones and Laughlin steel empire and the Schechters' chicken coop was decisive. But in the Richmond clothing company case the majority sustained the application of the Wagner Act to a firm whose production had a minimal effect on interstate commerce. It was clear that, for all of Hughes's efforts to maintain continuity, he was no longer following the distinction between "direct" and "indirect" effects which had prevailed as recently as 1936.

In the light of the recent rulings of the Court, McReynolds's dissent seemed comprehensible. If Congress could intervene in the affairs of a business which employed only eight hundred of the 150,000 workers in the men's clothing business, it could regulate "almost every field of human industry," McReynolds protested. "A more remote and indirect interference with interstate commerce or a more definite invasion of the powers reserved to the states is difficult, if not impossible, to imagine," he fulminated. As to the claim that such activities affected commerce, McReynolds countered: "Almost anything—marriage, birth, death—may in some fashion affect commerce."[26]

The country had no doubt that the Wagner Act decisions sanctioned a formidable augmentation of government power. The Detroit *News* ran the story under the headline:

WAGNER RULING OPENS NEW LABOR ERA
U.S. Grip
in Industry
Validated

Its Washington correspondent, Jay Hayden, wrote that the opinions approved "almost complete nationalization of American industry—entailing an increase in Federal authority over the work-a-day lives of the people so complete as to constitute a revolutionary change in the American form of government." One periodical stated the consequences of the decisions flatly: "The constitutionality of the Wagner law means that the nation's business can be nationally controlled." The Court, it noted, "so broadened the legal interpretation of what forms or affects interstate commerce that the main doubt in industrial cases to be argued in the courts henceforth will not be what is included under the controlling powers of the national government, but what is not."[27]

Yet even after the Court had handed down the path-breaking Wagner Act decisions, the Administration fretted about how it would fare in three pending Social Security Act cases. If the Court upheld the law, it would be validating a statute which more than any other symbolized the permanency of the Welfare State. Opponents of the New Deal protested that the Act trenched upon the reserved power of the states and employed the taxing power for social ends, the very behavior to which Justice Roberts had objected in *Butler*. Assistant Attorney General Robert Jackson told a newspaper columnist afterwards that the Administration's "whole argument was pointed at Roberts. I was arguing to a one-man court."[28]

The government's anxiety turned out to be baseless when on May 24 the Chief Justice nodded to Cardozo to read the opinion in the first of the Social Security cases. As the Court's spokesman in a 5–4 decision, Cardozo denied that credits to induce the states to enact unemployment compensation statutes were coercive, even though state laws had to conform to federal standards before the credits would be granted.[29] Speaking for six of his brethren, Cardozo also delivered a second opinion sustaining the old-age pension system.[30] In validating the benefit provisions with the observation that "Congress may spend money in aid of the 'general welfare,' " he rested his conclusion, somewhat ironically, on Roberts's opinion in *Butler*.[31] By 5–4, the Court in a third case sustained an Alabama unemployment compensation law. Stone dismissed the claim that a tax on employers and employees had not been imposed for a public purpose and noted that the Constitution did not prohibit cooperation between state and national governments.[32]

Together with the decisions in the Wagner Act cases, the Social Security rulings took a long stride away from the doctrine of dual federalism. Moreover, the Court gave its approval to the cooperation of the federal and state governments in carrying out the law, despite the fact that the Court had disapproved such an arrangement in the municipal bankruptcy decision a year earlier. Though the Social Security decisions "did not overrule the *Butler* doctrine," one historian has pointed out, "they were . . . based upon views of federal power fundamentally different from those expressed in the earlier case. For nowhere in the *Steward* and *Helvering* cases is there an intimation that a valid exercise of federal power is limited by the existence of any of the reserved powers of the states."[33] Indeed, Cardozo's reasoning bore a marked resemblance to Stone's dissent in *Butler*. The Court validated the power of Congress to tax and spend for the general welfare, and it repudiated by implication Roberts's contention in *Butler* that conditional federal grants were coercive. Since Roberts associated himself with Cardozo's opinion, he apparently no longer held to the view he had advanced just sixteen months before.

From 1937 on, the relationship among the branches of government shifted dramatically, as an era of "judicial supremacy" gave way to deference by the Supreme Court to Congress. The New Court committed itself, at least in the realm of social welfare legislation, to the doctrine of judicial self-restraint that Stone had called for in his dissent in *Butler* and that had earlier been advanced by Justice Holmes. Speaking for the Court in 1939, Chief Justice Hughes said bluntly: "It is of the essence of the plenary power conferred that Congress may exercise its discretion in the use of the power. Congress may choose the commodities and places to which its regulation shall apply. Congress may consider and weigh relative situations and needs. Congress is not restricted by any technical requirements."[34] As the legal historian Bernard Schwartz has written:

To the post-1937 Supreme Court, the Congress, charged with all of the legislative powers granted by the Constitution, is entitled to its own choice among all rationally permissible opinions as to what the Constitu-

tion allows. To set aside the enactments of such a body, representing in
the legislative field the ultimate sovereign, should be a solemn, unusual,
and painful act.[35]

Furthermore, in an astonishingly brief period Roosevelt gained the
opportunity to remake the Court. By February 1941, all of the Four
Horsemen had left the bench (as had Cardozo and Brandeis). To succeed them, the President picked such faithful lieutenants as Solicitor
General Stanley Reed, Attorney General Robert H. Jackson, and William O. Douglas of the Securities and Exchange Commission, as well as
the loyal New Deal Senator, Hugo Black; his close adviser, Felix Frankfurter of the Harvard Law School; and Frank Murphy, who as governor
of Michigan had enraged business elements by refusing to use force
against sitdown strikers. When Hughes stepped down in June 1941, the
President elevated Stone, the author of blistering dissents against the
Conservative Four, to the Chief Justiceship. To the vacancy created by
Stone's promotion, Roosevelt appointed Senator James F. Byrnes, and
when Byrnes left the bench to supervise wartime mobilization, he
named the much more liberal Wiley B. Rutledge of Iowa. Although the
Court had altered some of its views decisively before any new Justice
had been named, the personnel of the "Roosevelt Court" selected by the
President not only guaranteed the permanence of the change but moved
the Court to positions that went far beyond what Roberts was willing
to sanction.[36]

IV

Beginning in 1937, the Supreme Court upheld every New Deal statute
that came before it. In 1938, a new Agricultural Adjustment Act authorized the Secretary of Agriculture, subject to a two-thirds vote of staple
farmers, to fix quotas on crops and impose stiff penalties on any grower
who marketed in excess of the quota assigned to his farm. Tobacco
farmers challenged the constitutionality of the law on the grounds that
it denied due process, delegated legislative authority to the executive,
and, by seeking to regulate production, infringed the powers reserved
to the states by the Tenth Amendment—arguments that only a short
time before would have carried the day. But in *Mulford v. Smith* (1939),
the Court sustained the law, 7–2 (Butler and McReynolds dissenting),
and Hughes assigned the opinion of the Court to none other than Justice Roberts, who less than three years earlier had spoken for the Court
in overturning the first AAA. Years later, Stanley Reed suggested, as
"purely" a matter of "speculation," that Hughes may have chosen Roberts

to give him a chance to say something positive about government regulation of farming by approaching it from the angle of the commerce, rather than the taxing and spending, power "and not be left with the idea that he was so oblivious to the difficulties of the national welfare and national encouragement of agriculture that nobody could get at him."[37]

Roberts denied that the statute regulated production and insisted it merely imposed stipulations at the "throat where tobacco enters the stream of commerce." Congress, he asserted, could not only limit the amount of a commodity shipped in interstate commerce but could prohibit transportation of a commodity altogether if it so desired. Nor, he said, without even a backward glance at *Hammer*, did it matter whether these products were harmful or "ordinary." To the charge that Congress had enacted the law with the deliberate intent of controlling output, Roberts responded that "the motive of Congress in exerting the power is irrelevant to the validity of the legislation."[38] In short, the Court was now saying that Congress could, by indirection, do what Roberts and his colleagues had said in *Butler* Congress could not do: regulate agricultural production.[39]

In sanctioning federal control of farming, the Roosevelt Court interpreted the commerce power to allow a multitude of governmental activities in spheres that once would have been regarded as local. Three months before the *Mulford* opinion, the Court, in validating a tobacco inspection act, had upheld federal regulation of tobacco auctions despite the fact that the product had not yet started to move, a distinction it had found vital in *Carter*. "Where goods are purchased in one State for transportation to another," Hughes declared, "the commerce includes the purchase quite as much as it does the transportation."[40] Other decisions established national control of the price of milk, even when the entire transaction from dairy barn to kitchen took place wholly within the borders of a state, and sustained the Secretary of Agriculture's authority over the dairy industry, though one of these rulings went too far not only for Roberts but also for Hughes, who joined Butler and McReynolds in dissent.[41]

None of these agricultural decisions, however, so electrified legal circles as did *Wickard v. Filburn* (1942).[42] In this case, the Court held that an Ohio chicken farmer growing twenty-three acres of wheat, all of which would be consumed by fowl in Roscoe Filburn's yard, so affected interstate commerce that the Secretary of Agriculture could impose marketing penalties on him. By so ruling, the Court assigned to the dustbin of history not only the criterion of direct and indirect effects but almost any distinction between commerce and production as a relevant standard for determining constitutionality. "It was now evident," the political scientist Robert McCloskey later wrote, "that Congress could reach just about any commercial subject it might want to reach and could do to that subject just about anything it was likely to want to do, whether for economic, humanitarian, or other purposes."[43] Noting the way in which the line between national and local authority over commerce had been erased, a federal judge observed sardonically that maybe "the cackle of the farmer's hen as she announces completion of her daily chore, or the squeal of the pig in its struggle to become a porker, are not beyond this boundary line, but in this we can give no assurance."[44]

The Court took the same generous view of the applicability of the commerce power to the government's activities in the field of hydroelectric power. In 1938, the hotly contested Public Utility Holding Company Act survived its first challenge when the Court found that a section of the statute requiring utility companies to register with the SEC was a legitimate exercise of Congressional authority over businesses engaged in interstate commerce.[45] Not until 1946 did the Court rule on the most controversial feature of the law, the "death sentence" provision. In two decisions that year, the Court validated the section of the act authorizing the SEC to break up holding companies and order such concerns to divest themselves of parts of their empires.[46] "This broad commerce clause," Justice Murphy stated, "does not operate so as to render the nation powerless to defend itself against economic forces that Congress decrees inimical or destructive of the national economy. Rather it is an affirmative power commensurate with the national needs. . . . And in using this great power, Congress is not bound by technical legal conceptions."[47]

Two Supreme Court decisions permitted the directors of the Tennessee Valley Authority, who had been under legal fire from the inception of the agency, to breathe more easily. The Court in 1938 rejected a plea from private utilities to enjoin federal loans to municipalities for electric power projects, and the following year it turned down a similar request from eighteen utility firms who wanted to prohibit the TVA from distributing and selling electric power. "Had this injunction been sustained," one writer commented, "what was left of TVA could easily have been swept up with a whisk-broom." In both cases, the Court held that the plaintiffs had no right to be exempt from competition and, having failed to show a material interest, did not have standing. The defeat of the power companies was made all the more compelling by the fact that the first opinion was delivered by Justice Sutherland and the second by Justice Roberts. With all hope of salvation in the courts gone, the Tennessee Electric Power Company liquidated itself by selling out to the TVA.[48]

The Roosevelt Court also extended the scope of federal authority over waterways, a matter of importance both for regional planning and for hydroelectric power development. In the past, the commerce power had extended only to navigable streams, but in 1940 the Court upheld Federal Power Commission control of the non-navigable upper reaches of the New River in West Virginia because the stream could conceivably be made navigable.[49] "Now," the holding company lawyer, Wendell Willkie, grumbled, "the water in the toilet in the men's room is navigable."[50] Navigability, the Court added, was not the only basis for the exercise of national authority. "Flood protection, watershed development, recovery of the cost of improvements through utilization of power are likewise parts of commerce control," it declared.[51] In the following year, the Court sustained an act of Congress authorizing a flood control dam on a non-navigable section of the Red River in Oklahoma, despite the state's contention that the federal government was primarily interested in generating electricity at the site.[52] These decisions not only enhanced national authority at the expense of the states but also affected business-government relationships by sanctioning New Deal experiments that trespassed on the domain of the private utilities.

In FDR's second term, the Court twice validated legislation that had been struck down in his first term but had been revised and re-enacted. In 1938 in *Bekins* the Court sustained the Municipal Bankruptcy Act of 1937, although the law differed little from the 1934 statute that had been struck down in *Ashton*.[53] Hughes made a lame effort to distinguish the two cases, but in 1946 Justice Rutledge commented that *Ashton* "may be said in effect to have been overruled" by *Bekins*.[54] Two years later, the Court sanctioned the Bituminous Coal Act of 1937, a law resembling the one that had been held unconstitutional in *Carter*.[55] Indeed, in upholding the power of Congress to fix coal prices and establish market rules, Douglas's opinion cited dissents in *Carter* by Hughes and especially by Cardozo. "Congress under the commerce clause is not impotent to deal with what it may consider to be dire consequences of *laissez-faire*," Douglas asserted, in what one historian has suggested "seemed a belated slap at the majority" in *Carter*. Douglas conceded that the 19 1/2 percent penalty tax levied upon noncomplying producers was "primarily a sanction" rather than a revenue measure, but emphasized that Congress could lawfully "impose penalties in aid of the exercise of any of its enumerated powers." No longer, he added, was there "a no man's land between the state and federal domains."[56] So substantially had the balance of the Court shifted in three years that only one Justice, McReynolds, dissented.

When the Court was asked to rule on the constitutionality of the Fair Labor Standards Act of 1938, it confronted a direct challenge to prior judicial pronouncements. The law, in addition to regulating wages and hours, prohibited the shipment in interstate commerce of products from companies employing child labor, a provision that essentially re-enacted the child labor law of 1916 struck down in *Hammer v. Dagenhart*. But in 1941, with all of the Four Horsemen gone, a unanimous Court found the Fair Labor Standards Act constitutional.[57] "The conclusion is inescapable," Justice Stone stated, "that *Hammer v. Dagenhart* was a departure from the principles which have prevailed in the interpretation of the Commerce Clause both before and since the decision and that such vitality, as a precedent, as it then had has long since been exhausted. It should be and now is overruled." In extinguishing *Hammer v. Dagenhart*, which had plagued reformers for a generation, the Court commented that the distinction in that case between Congressional authority over harmful and harmless objects was "novel when made and unsupported by any provision of the Constitution" and had "long since been abandoned." Stone's opinion, in validating federal authority over wages and hours, asserted, too, that Congress could "regulate intrastate activities where they have a substantial effect on interstate commerce."[58] In reaching this conclusion, he ignored *Schechter* and brushed aside *Carter*. "It is not too much to say," one historian has written, "that *United States v. Darby* is one of the half-dozen most important cases in the whole 180-year history of American constitutional law."[59]

A series of decisions amplified the interpretation of the commerce clause in the Wagner Act opinions. The Court in 1938 upheld the application of the National Labor Relations Act to a cannery that obtained its fruit from within the state and shipped little more than one-third of its finished products across state lines. Hughes stressed that the distinction between direct and indirect effects, "necessarily one of degree," could not be reduced to "mathematical or rigid formulas."[60] Even wholly intrastate operations came within the orbit of Congressional power when the Court upheld the jurisdiction of the National Labor Relations Board over a utility that sold none of its electric power outside the state and of a small garment company that delivered its output wholly within one state.[61] These decisions indicated that to justify the exercise of national authority the government did not have to demonstrate either that a firm was directly involved in interstate commerce or that it did a large volume of business.

In the next few years, the Court showed how far it was willing to stretch the commerce clause. In *A. B. Kirschbaum v. Walling*, it upheld the application of the Fair Labor Standards Act to employees who were not engaged in production for interstate commerce at all but operated a loft whose tenants produced garments for sale in interstate commerce. [62] Justice Felix Frankfurter implied that the scope of federal authority might be even more extensive than either the provisions of the statute or this particular ruling. In subsequent decisions, the Court ruled that the law applied to a night watchman in a veneer plant; to porters, elevator operators, and other employees of a New York office building; and to window cleaners. [63]

So readily did the New Court validate the aggrandizement of the national government that many feared the United States was rapidly becoming a unitary state. When conflicts arose between the authority of the federal government and that of the states, the Court made clear that the national will would prevail. It recognized the full implications of the supremacy clause by requiring states to submit to federal regulatory statutes. Thus it held that the Emergency Price Control Act of 1942 applied to a state that sold timber from school lands. [64] While the Court lowered barriers against the exercise of national authority in local affairs, it struck down state laws that impeded the flow of commerce. [65] Although the Court all but abdicated its function of invalidating acts of Congress, it found twenty-six state laws unconstitutional in little more than four years after the President's message of February 5, 1937. [66] This series of events led commentators to ask "whether the states are not doomed to become mere vestigial survivals of a formerly flourishing federal system." [67]

Yet, in fact, expansion of the power of the states accompanied this augmented national authority. The federal and state governments frequently extended their activities not at each other's expense but by moving into the no-man's-land in which neither had been able to function before. As a consequence of the wider use of instrumentalities such as federal grants-in-aid by the New Deal, "the decade of the Great Depression," one scholar has concluded, "witnessed a revitalization of American federalism." In the same years that it legitimized the enhanced power of the national government, the Court also sanctioned a wide range of social legislation by the states. Though the Fourteenth Amendment had been employed fourteen times in the four years before February 5, 1937, to safeguard property rights, it was used only twice for that purpose in the next four-year period. [68]

The Roosevelt Court showed a deference toward state legislatures that contrasted sharply with the attitude of the Court in the *Tipaldo* era. For the most part, the Court restrained itself from passing judgment on the desirability of the legislation that came before it. In 1934, Justice McReynolds had said audaciously that "this Court must have regard to the wisdom of the enactment."[69] But in 1940 Justice Frankfurter insisted that it was not relevant that "state action may run counter to the economic wisdom either of Adam Smith or of J. Maynard Keynes, or may be ultimately mischievous even from the point of view of avowed state policy. Our inquiry must be much narrower."[70] At the end of the decade, the Court made another disavowal when, in validating a state law, it declared, "We cannot undertake a search for motive in testing constitutionality."[71] Two years later, the Court summarized its experience: "Our recent decisions make plain that we do not sit as a superlegislature to weigh the wisdom of legislation nor to decide whether the policy which it expresses offends the public welfare."[72] This attitude gave the legislatures an advantage in facing legal challenges that they had rarely had before. The Court's test of constitutionality, noted one writer, "places an impossible burden upon the party attacking the law: he must show not only that no basis for the law exists in fact, but also that the legislature could not in good faith believe such a need to exist."[73]

The High Court revealed its sunnier disposition toward state activities in a variety of ways. It displayed a willingness to approve regulations of the economy so long as they were not flagrantly discriminatory and did not intrude upon the authority of Congress.[74] The Court also showed a good deal of tolerance for the attempts of state and municipal governments to find novel sources of revenue at a time when the burdens of government were heavy and conventional sources were drying up.[75] In reaching such judgments, the Justices did not hesitate to overturn precedents of "the Old Court," the Supreme Court of the pre-1937 era. When in 1940 the Court validated a Kentucky law taxing out-of-state deposits of its citizens at five times the rate of accounts within the state, it discarded *Colgate v. Harvey*[76] after a shelf life of only five years.

The Roosevelt Court also manifested respect for the sensibilities of state courts. In 1938, in overruling the century-old precedent of *Swift v. Tyson*, the Court enhanced the position of states in the federal system by obliging federal courts to apply the local common law, as interpreted by state judges, in diversity-of-citizenship cases, though it had a hard time articulating why it had resolved on this departure. Felix Frankfurter, who worshipped Brandeis, regretted that the Justice, in his opinion for the Court, showed a "disregard of the history of juristic philosophy"; and Stanley Reed, though it made him uncomfortable to do so in his very first case, felt obliged to file a concurrence. "Working out its implication," one scholar later remarked, "has ever since provided a livelihood for many lawyers and headaches for all federal judges."[77]

In scrutinizing state laws, the Court all but abandoned "substantive due process," save as a shield for civil liberties. Justice Black even wanted to deny that the word "person" in the Fourteenth Amendment included protection for a corporation.[78] No other judge would follow him that far, and he did not persist in this argument, but neither did the Court seek, as it had so often in the past, to substitute its judgment for that of a legislature. In 1955, in a unanimous ruling, Justice William O. Douglas announced, "The day is gone when this Court uses the Due Process Clause of the Fourteenth Amendment to strike down state laws, regulatory of business and industrial conditions, because they may be unwise, improvident, or out of harmony with a particular school of thought."[79]

In the same years that the New Court was validating state and federal laws, it showed a much more charitable attitude toward independent regulatory commissions, which the Old Court had bristled at as upstart rivals with *nouveaux riches* manners. It was much less likely to question the fact-finding of government agencies or to insist on circumscribing their powers. From 1941 to 1946, the eight most important regulatory agencies received favorable rulings in nearly three-quarters of the 143 cases.[80] The Court even insisted that commissions had greater powers than the agencies themselves claimed to possess.[81]

The metamorphosis of the Supreme Court in this field can best be seen in the *Morgan* litigation, which it confronted four times in five years. In 1936, the Old Court had ruled against the government, and as late as the spring of 1938 the Court had held, 6–1, that the Secretary of Agriculture had denied "the rudimentary requirements of fair play" in fixing maximum rates that the Fred O. Morgan Sheep Commission Company could charge at the Kansas City stockyards. But in 1939 the Supreme Court found for the government, and in 1941 it admitted that the Court had erred earlier in requiring the Secretary of Agriculture to submit to interrogation. "Just as a judge cannot be subjected to such a scrutiny, . . . so the integrity of the administrative process must be equally respected," it affirmed.[82]

Some believed that having virtually relinquished its function of "Supreme Censor" of economic legislation, the Court would have almost nothing of any importance left to do, but instead the Justices carved out an expanded sphere of authority in civil liberties, civil rights, and the democratization of the political system. In 1937, the very year that the Court changed course on regulatory legislation, it handed down a 5–4 decision that breathed new life into the "clear and present danger" test for free speech.[83] Within a year, the Court had moved toward establishing a "preferred position" for the constitutional guarantees of liberty of expression and had placed new handicaps on the "separate but equal" doctrine of racial segregation.[84]

The Court declined to defer to legislative judgment on questions involving personal rights as it did on economic matters. During the four years before FDR's Court-packing message, the Court had invalidated state legislation involving civil liberties only twice; in the next four years, it did so twelve times.[85] The Court threw its protective cloak around black prisoners and migrant workers, union organizers and newspaper editors, pickets and religious pamphlet peddlers.[86] The civil libertarian bent of the Roosevelt Court appears to have been a largely unanticipated consequence of the President's endeavor in 1937. Despite some backsliding during World War II and the McCarthy era, however, the new emphasis of the Court persisted for most of the next half-century.

V

This remarkable turnabout has led commentators to speak of "the Constitutional Revolution of 1937," distinguished by the virtual abandonment by the Court of its most important activity in FDR's first term and, indeed, for decades before. "Since 1936 the Supreme Court has not invalidated a single economic control on substantive due process grounds, and the rationale of the one case striking down an economic regulation on equal protection grounds was later overruled," one commentator has pointed out. "In 1937, the constitutional foundation of common-law thought collapsed," the legal historian Donald Gjerdingen has written. "On March 29, 1937, the mosaic shattered. . . . The Court, judicial review, and constitutional law have not been the same since."[87]

To be sure, the Constitutional Revolution did not destroy all the features of the pre-1937 landscape. In particular, the institution of the Supreme Court escaped the tumult of the 1937 struggle with its prerogative of judicial review intact, if not unscathed. Although the powers of the President were enlarged, the Court, in the *Steel Seizure* case, made clear that they were not limitless.[88] If Congress received judicial sanction for extending its authority over enterprises formerly thought to be intrastate in character, the Court still regarded some areas of activity as local.[89] Though the Roosevelt Court took a more accepting view of the actions of administrative agencies, it did not hesitate to slap the Federal Communications Commission for failing to grant fair hearings, and it frequently showed its displeasure with the behavior of the Interstate Commerce Commission. Even in the post-1937 era, the Court continued to oversee the operation of the federal system—to referee collisions between and among the states and to prevent the states from infringing on national power. Some two decades after the 1937 divide, Thomas Reed Powell of Harvard Law School wrote that, despite the broad reach of *Darby*, a new child labor law "could not in my judgment go so far as to forbid transportation of persons or property from a state where there is a poll tax requirement for voting, where the expenditure for schools is less than at a prescribed rate, where the age of consent is less than eighteen, [or] where divorces are granted on a residence or pretended domicile of so short a period as six weeks."[90]

Moreover, despite the fact that the Court has overturned no important economic regulation by Congress in more than half a century, no one can say with certainty what would happen if an administration sought to embark on a program of nationalization. The "revolution" that has occurred has taken place within the confines of the capitalist system. Less than two years after the *Jones and Laughlin* "revolution," the Court revealed an ongoing concern for property rights when it invalidated an NLRB order requiring the Fansteel Metallurgical firm to rehire discharged sitdown strikers. The sitdown, the Court said, was "a high-handed proceeding without shadow of legal right."[91]

At no time since 1937 has the Court faced any peacetime operation as ambitious as the National Recovery Administration, and the warning against unconstitutional delegation of powers may still hang over the heads of social planners.[92] In 1946, Carl Swisher concluded, "Ultimately, perhaps, when the extension of governmental action reaches the approximate limits of the area to which the dominant sentiments of the people would have it go, the Court may again resume the function of limiting the scope of governmental power by constitutional interpretation."[93] In 1974, the Court actually cited *Schechter*, though in dissent Justice Thurgood Marshall called the improper delegation doctrine in that case "as moribund as the substantive due process approach of the same era . . . if not more so." Only six years later, Justice William Rehnquist declared:

> We ought not to shy away from our judicial duty to invalidate unconstitutional delegations of legislative authority solely out of concern that we should thereby reinvigorate constitutional doctrines of the pre-New Deal era. . . . Indeed, a number of observers have suggested that this Court should once more take up its burden of ensuring that Congress does not unnecessarily delegate important choices of social policy to politically unresponsive administrators.[94]

Such considerations have led some commentators to deny that there was a Constitutional Revolution in 1937 or to insist that the conception be severely qualified. Alfred H. Kelly and Winfred A. Harbison wrote: "The 'revolution' of 1937 did not break the continuity of American constitutional development in any decisive respect. In that sense it was not a revolution at all."[95] Some writers argue either that 1937 represented no shift in the postulates of the Court or that whatever change did occur was the logical consequence of decisions already handed down by the Old Court. They point out that the demise of the due process clause began with the *Nebbia* opinion in 1934, and that a significant step toward overturning *Hammer v. Dagenhart* had been taken with the unanimous decision validating the Ashurst-Sumners Act a month before the President announced his Court-packing plan.[96] The Hughes Court had at about the same time made an important concession toward the exercise by states of the taxing power.[97] In the realm of civil liberties, the Court had, in the six years before the 1937 crisis, struck down California's "red-flag" law; twice upheld the legal rights of the "Scottsboro boys," young black men who had been wrongfully prosecuted and convicted in Alabama; shielded newspaper publishers and editors in Minnesota and Louisiana from legislative reprisals; and ruled that a conviction resulting from a coerced confession denied due process.[98]

Critics of the "Constitutional Revolution" concept have no trouble explaining away the fact that the Court invalidated so many New Deal statutes before 1937 and upheld every one thereafter. They claim that Congress, having been chastened by the *Schechter* and *Butler* opinions, drafted legislation more carefully thereafter.[99] Furthermore, they do not acknowledge that the Wagner Act decisions marked a great departure.[100] Merlo J. Pusey noted that Hughes's opinion in *Jones and Laughlin* was "superficially said to be a reversal of what he had written in the NRA and Carter Coal cases," but, Hughes's biographer insisted, "the same basic principle underlies all three of these opinions."[101]

Other commentators concede that 1937 marked a transformation, but they assert that the Roosevelt Court, far from generating new doctrine, was simply restoring continuity with earlier decisions. Some, especially Chief Justice Hughes's champions, point to the use the Roosevelt Court made of Hughes's opinion in the 1914 *Shreveport* case, which sustained the authority of the ICC over intrastate rates despite the fact that the statute had exempted such rates.[102] In this view, it is not the New Court which behaved aberrantly but its immediate predecessors in the two decades before 1937. The Roosevelt Court did reject precedents, it is noted, but often by returning to prior doctrines that had been abandoned. Thus *Madden v. Kentucky* overruled a five-year-old precedent which had scuttled a sixty-two-year-old precedent.[103] Finally, some who agree that the Court beginning in 1937 reversed a century-old tradition of hostility to a strong national government believe that the New Court was only returning to the doctrines of Chief Justice John Marshall. On the day the Court handed down the Wagner Act rulings, the columnist Raymond Clapper noted in his diary: "Robert Jackson (asst. atty. gen.) in court lunch room. He said off the record, 'These decisions go back to John Marshall's conception of nationalism. They [are] not in line with recent decision but are in line with earlier decisions.'"[104]

VI

These objections are not all without merit, but they fall short of raising a formidable challenge to the conception of a Constitutional Revolution. If Roberts showed a responsiveness to government experimentation in *Nebbia*, he surely did not do so in several ensuing cases in which he joined the Conservative Four. Moreover, the controversy about whether Roberts switched in the two minimum wage cases has distracted attention from a matter that should be beyond dispute: the change in his views from the *Rail Pension* and *Butler* opinions of 1935-36 to the post-1936 decisions, a shift that is unmistakable. Furthermore, Roberts was not the only Justice to retreat. As the historian Michael Parrish has written, the notion that the Court did not shift "glosses over much of the Chief Justice's language in *Schechter* and *Carter Coal*, dismisses the contrary estimate of several contemporaries, and overlooks Hughes' anti-New Deal posture in cases such as *Butler* and *Jones*."[105]

Although the Hughes Court lit beacon lights in civil liberties and civil rights, one must remember that as late as 1935 a Court that included Hughes, Brandeis, Cardozo, and Stone upheld the white primary unanimously. It is often said that the Four Horsemen were ardent civil libertarians, but, though on a number of occasions one or more of them opposed denial of rights, they were a solid bloc dissenting in the *Near* freedom of press case and once again in the pivotal year of 1937 in the case of Angelo Herndon, a black Communist defendant. Later that year, when the Court validated a provision of a statute making inadmissible in federal courts evidence obtained by wiretapping, Sutherland and McReynolds were in the minority. For the future of civil liberties in America, Roosevelt's appointees would make a difference.[106]

In view of the Court's own confessions of error, one cannot seriously believe that more expert draftsmanship explains the new dispensation. Furthermore, the argument is anachronistic; the Old Court invalidated statutes such as the Guffey Coal Act that were enacted after *Schechter*, while the New Court validated such 1933 laws as the Tennessee Valley Authority Act. Nor, once Stanley Reed took over in 1935 from FDR's unfortunate first choice as Solicitor General, could the presentation of cases be faulted. "You will want to see . . . the altogether admirable brief which Stanley Reed and his assistants are preparing for the appeal in the Butler—the AAA—case," Felix Frankfurter wrote Roosevelt in the fall of 1935. "You will relish it for its own sake." As Michael Parrish has noted, the contention that the Court crisis was brought about by inept New Dealers "is a curious argument in view of the fact that those who prepared briefs and argued before the Court in 1935 and 1936 included, among others, Stanley Reed, Dean Acheson, John Lord O'Brian, Paul Freund, John Dickinson, Alger Hiss, and Benjamin V. Cohen—a rather formidable group of lawyers. Poorly drafted laws, weak briefs, and careless arguments may explain the demise of the NRA, but it is difficult to extend this theory to include the judicial veto of the Triple A or the Guffey Coal Act."[107]

Nor should one take too seriously the fact that the Roosevelt Court made use of earlier precedents or that the government minimized the differences between decisions such as *Carter* and *Jones and Laughlin*. Both the New Court and the Administration had a stake in claiming respectable ancestry and obeisance to *stare decisis*. If the revolution was not total, no revolution is; the France of Robespierre did not differ in all respects from the *ancien régime*. Although Hughes anticipated some of the doctrines of the New Court in the *Shreveport* case, the opinions he wrote in *Schechter* and *Carter* had quite different implications.[108] The Roosevelt Court undoubtedly was indebted to the liberal nationalism of Associate Justice Hughes, but the reach of the national government approved in *Wickard v. Filburn* went well beyond any of Hughes's earlier opinions.

The world of twentieth-century America differs too much from the simpler society of Marshall's day to make comparisons profitable. As a leading authority on the Chief Justice has pointed out, "In evaluating Marshall's jurisprudence, it must be remembered that the federal regulatory state was a century away."[109] Besides, Marshall's reasoning served to foster the expansion of a market economy, while the New Court sanctioned government curbs on entrepreneurs. Scholars of the most widely differing views have scoffed at the Marshall derivation. "In any other field but law," Bruce Ackerman has remarked, "it would be laughable to assert that Alexander Hamilton and John Marshall did all the really tough work in elaborating the constitution of the modern welfare state, and that Franklin Roosevelt and the New Deal Congress were basically acting out a vision of active national government *already* fully established by the People in the aftermath of the American Revolution."

Writing from a very different perspective, Richard Epstein has observed: "Nowhere does Marshall even mention any possible power of Congress to regulate local manufacture or agriculture at all. . . . Marshall's interpretation was decisively rejected only in 1937."[110]

To demonstrate the extent to which a shift occurred, one need only compare the opinions of the Court before and after Roosevelt's message. "No event, or series of events, has ever before produced so many changes in constitutional doctrine within so short a time," noted Benjamin F. Wright in 1942. "In the four subsequent terms of Court the reversals and distinctions have been so numerous and so sweeping that today much of the constitutional law of 1936 appears to belong to a different constitution."[111] The Court had come a long way since Justice Butler asserted in *Tipaldo* "that the State is without power by any form of legislation to prohibit, change or nullify contracts between employers and adult women workers as to the amount of wages to be paid."[112] Milch cow and garment worker, mountain stream and factory loft, all now came within the domain of the federal government.

"The year 1937 marks a major divide in the constitutional jurisprudence of the American nation and in the decisional philosophy of the Supreme Court," a recent survey concluded. "This is so much the fact that future histories of the Supreme Court may well divide the Court's development since 1790 into two fundamental periods, pre- and post-1937." In a similar manner, Bruce Ackerman has asserted that for some four decades "judges and lawyers have been constantly treating the 'switch-in-time' in 1937 as *the* event separating the modern republic from earlier eras of constitutional law."[113]

In the ten terms from 1937 through 1946, the Court reversed thirty-two of its earlier decisions. Eight of the precedents had been adopted unanimously. At the outset, the Court moved circumspectly, because Chief Justice Hughes believed in maintaining continuity. Although some thought that the Wagner Act decisions required a repudiation of *Schechter* and *Carter*, Hughes, as the political scientist C. Herman Pritchett observed, "apparently decided that these two decisions were too young to die, like the princes in the Tower, and that it would be preferable to distinguish rather than extinguish them."[114] But as the composition of the Court changed, the death rate for precedents soared. Some were venerable. The Court in 1939 overturned *Collector v. Day*, an 1870 decision that had given federal employees immunity from state taxation,[115] and in 1944 it exterminated *Paul v. Virginia* (1869), which had established that the insurance business was not commerce.[116] On the other hand, in addition to putting *Colgate v. Harvey* out of its misery after only five years, the Court, in invalidating Texas's white primary law, disowned an opinion Justice Roberts had delivered less than a decade before.[117] In his lone dissent in the new case, Roberts protested "that the instant decision, overruling that announced about nine years ago, tends to bring adjudications of this tribunal into the same class as a restricted railroad ticket, good for this day and train only."[118]

Constitutional lawyers found a world remade. In 1939, Thomas Reed Powell commented, "In one of my sections I am now teaching intergovernmental relations between 11 and 12, and before I make any statement on Monday, I always take out my watch to see what time it is in order to know whether I am safe in making the remark." Two years later, in like spirit, a former Yale Law School dean, who had been named by Roosevelt to the Second Circuit, told a noted Princeton scholar:

> I have been meaning to write you for some time to commiserate for the way in which the Supreme Court is now taking away all the capital and business of constitutional law teachers. I had better write now because by the time the decisions are announced this noon there may be nothing left. When I remember the amount of time I used to spend in demonstrating how awful *Hammer v. Dagenhart* was, I am wondering what you who remained in the business are finding to do.[119]

Ever since 1937, jurisprudence has been haunted by the memory of that year, though not everyone has drawn the same lessons from it. In reflecting on having lived through the controversy over FDR's Court-packing plan and the Constitutional Revolution of 1937, Herbert Wechsler observed:

> The problems for all of us became: How can we defend a judicial veto in areas where we thought it helpful in American life—civil liberties area, personal freedom, First Amendment—and at the same time condemn it in the areas where we considered it unhelpful? . . . Having learned through that experience of the consequences of judicial excess, we became highly sensitive to it, and on the whole, I should say, eager to develop the type of critique that would contribute to avoiding it.

A younger scholar such as Laurence Tribe, he added, understandably had a different outlook. "Here's somebody who wasn't born when the problems that I'm talking about arose, and came to this field at a much later time, and whose approach to activism is accordingly more tolerant." Even younger scholars, though, have shown sensitivity to the 1937 legacy. "The conservative critics of the Warren Court," Duncan Kennedy has written, "have taught us to see the strong parallel between the right-wing interventionism of the period 1890-1937 (the rights of property and contract) and the left-wing interventionism of 1955-1970 (equality)."[120]

In recent years, especially, the fear of repeating the mistakes of the pre-1937 era has served as a deterrent on judicial activism, or at least as a rationale for hesitancy. In 1986, in explaining why the Court refused to strike down a Georgia law criminalizing sodomy, Justice Byron White said:

> The Court is most vulnerable and comes nearest to illegitimacy when it deals with judge-made constitutional law having little or no cognizable roots in the language or design of the Constitution. That this is so was painfully demonstrated by the face-off between the Executive and the Court in the 1930's, which resulted in the repudiation of much of the substantive gloss that the Court had placed on the Due Process Clauses of the Fifth and Fourteenth Amendments.[121]

For the most part, though, these misgivings came only after a long era of judicial activism of a markedly different kind from that of the Old Court.

The Constitutional Revolution of 1937 altered fundamentally the character of the Court's business, the nature of its decisions, and the alignment of its friends and foes. From the Marshall Court to the Hughes Court, the judiciary had been largely concerned with questions of property rights. After 1937, the most significant matters on the docket were civil liberties and other personal rights. In its 1935 term, the Court took up issues of civil liberties and civil rights in only two of its 160 written opinions; in its 1989 term, it did so on sixty-six occasions out of 132.[122] For more than a century before 1937, the Court had been inclined to safeguard entrenched interests from reform-minded legislatures. But after the Constitutional Revolution, McCloskey observed drily, "The businessman, so long the Court's darling, was shorn of his constitutional fleece and now faced popular sovereignty protected by nothing save his own ample private resources." While from 1800 to 1937 the principal critics of the Supreme Court were social reformers and the main supporters people of means who were the principal beneficiaries of the Court's decisions, after 1937 roles were reversed, with liberals commending and conservatives censuring the Court.[123]

Like the Calvinism of Dr. Holmes's one-hoss shay, the doctrines of the Old Court collapsed in a day—but only after a long period of disintegration. As E. S. Corwin pointed out, "The Court was always a house more or less divided against itself as to the soundness of *Laissez Faire's* intellectual pretensions. What is more, it came to be increasingly exposed to the play of ideas and of events which challenged those pretensions with growing insistence."[124] Occasional decisions—and, even more, dissents—had suggested recognition of the fact that a national economy required an expanded role for the State. Yet through much of the two decades prior to the First Hundred Days, the Court had set itself against any magnification of authority in Washington or in state capitals.

The Great Depression presented the necessity for government action with a special urgency, and when even then the Justices resisted, their fate was sealed. "The depression, and the New Deal which was its reflex, were forces too cosmic for those Canutes to withstand," McCloskey concluded. "Finally, the waves dislodged even the partial and contingent grip on economic affairs that the judiciary had once enjoyed. . . . When the extreme negativist position of 1935-36 was forsaken, as it had to be, the Court could find no stopping place short of abdication."[125] In 1937 the Supreme Court began a revolution in jurisprudence that ended, apparently forever, the reign of laissez-faire and legitimated the arrival of the Leviathan State.

The Birth of America's Second Bill of Rights

[This essay first took the form of a paper delivered in the French Senate in Paris in October 1986 on the occasion of the centennial of France's gift of the Statue of Liberty to the United States. The conference, entitled "The Concept of Liberty: Its Development and Meaning in France and the United States," was jointly sponsored by the West European Program of the Woodrow Wilson International Center for Scholars at the Smithsonian Institution in Washington, D. C., and by the Comité Officiel Franco-Américain pour la Célébration du Centenaire de la Statue de la Liberté. The paper was subsequently published in Joseph Klaits and Michael H. Haltzel, eds., *Liberty/Liberté: The American and French Experiences* (Baltimore: The Johns Hopkins University Press, 1991). I have expanded the essay very considerably since then.]

When, as a consequence of the genius of Edouard Laboulaye and the generosity of the French nation, the majestic Statue of Liberty was unveiled in New York harbor in the autumn of 1886, the American people were properly appreciative—but nonetheless regarded the gift as only their due. Had not the citizenry of "the land of the free," they asked, enshrined in their Constitution a Bill of Rights that made their country's charter the model for those who treasured liberty throughout the civilized world? In truth, however exaggerated their view of the uniqueness of their situation, they did have more than a little reason for pride. Yet not only were there a great many Americans in 1886 who did not enjoy all the blessings of liberty, but the constitutional order was, far more than was recognized then or is fully recognized even today, in one critical respect seriously deficient.

To illustrate that reality, I begin my course on the U.S. Supreme

Court at the University of North Carolina at Chapel Hill with a ficti-
tious scenario. The year, I tell my students, is 1859. The North Carolina state legislature, they are to imagine, has enacted a law stipulating
that any criticism of the state government, no matter how gentle, is
punishable by death. A local newspaper publishes an editorial mildly
critical of the governor. The editor is arrested and hauled off to prison
to await prosecution for an offense that could cost him his life.
What protection, I ask, does he have under the United States Constitution?

Because it is the first day of class, students might be expected to be a
bit shy about speaking out, but this question seems so easy that they
are not at all hesitant, and from every spot around the seminar table
answers are called out. "Freedom of the press." I shake my head, no.
"Freedom of speech." No. "Right to a fair trial." No. "Habeas corpus."
No. "The Bill of Rights." No. "The First Amendment." No. "The first
eight amendments." No. Finally, they subside in puzzlement and await
the answer. And it comes as a shock to them to learn that the answer is
that the editor has *no* protection under the U.S. Constitution, none
at all.[1]

The students are baffled. But does the Constitution not provide, they
ask, for freedom of press and freedom of speech? What about the Bill
of Rights? What about the First Amendment? Well, I answer, what does
the Constitution actually say? They think about that, and some of them
scurry to their books, and before long, one of the quicker students
grasps what the problem is. The Constitution says in the First Amendment of the Bill of Rights:

> Congress shall make no law respecting an establishment of religion, or
> prohibiting the free exercise thereof; or abridging the freedom of speech,
> or of press; or the right of the people peaceably to assemble, and to
> petition the Government for a redress of grievances.

To repeat, "*Congress* shall make no law. . . ." The restrictions apply
wholly to the *national* government. The First Amendment says nothing
at all about the states, which are free to act as they will.[2]

The U.S. Supreme Court had affirmed this reality—that the Bill of
Rights does not apply to the states—in 1833 in a case involving not
civil liberties but property rights. When the seaport town of Baltimore
began to pave its streets, it diverted some of its streams, with the consequence that the channel to Barron's Wharf, a splendid deep-water facility, became so heavily silted that it was rendered virtually worthless.
Barron sued the city on the grounds that it had violated his rights under

the Fifth Amendment by taking property "for public use without just compensation." But in his very last opinion, Chief Justice John Marshall declared that the Bill of Rights, including the Fifth Amendment, contained "no expression indicating an intention to apply them to the state governments. This court cannot so apply them."[3]

The Court restated that principle in 1845 in a case that grew out of a dreadful yellow fever epidemic. To curb the spread of the disease, the city of New Orleans confined funerals to one chapel. When a priest carried out funeral rites not in that chapel but in another Catholic church, he was arrested and fined. He appealed to the U.S. Supreme Court on the ground that his conviction violated the free exercise of religion clause of the First Amendment. But the Court denied his claim. "The Constitution" it explained, "makes no provision for protecting the citizens of the respective States in their religious liberties."[4]

That omission left a considerable gap in the guarantees of liberty in America, for, though when we consider the need for safeguarding freedom we think first of the threat from the national state, liberty has, in fact, been more menaced in localities. To be sure, there have been serious transgressions by the national government: episodes such as the Alien and Sedition Acts in the early republic, the persecution of dissenters in World War I and its aftermath, and the frenzy of McCarthyism in the 1950s. But the Bill of Rights, as interpreted by the U.S. Supreme Court, has provided little shield against federal action. As the historian Henry Steele Commager pointed out in 1943, the record of the highest tribunal "discloses not a single case, in a century and a half, where the Supreme Court has protected freedom of speech, press, assembly, or petition against Congressional attack."[5] Furthermore, the incursions by the national government have usually turned out to be short-lived, limited to a brief war crisis, whereas the denial of rights by state and local governments has not infrequently been endemic. Throughout our history, a black in Mississippi had far more to fear from state than federal authority, and the absence of any provision in the U.S. Constitution to protect his or her rights against abuse by local sovereigns was a grievous shortcoming.

The year 1859 in the scenario, however, was chosen advisedly, for something was soon to happen that had the potential for radically changing that situation by revolutionizing the relationship of the national government to the states. Out of the Civil War and Reconstruction came three constitutional amendments, one of which was eventually to prove of enormous significance for civil liberties. Especially encouraging was the first section of the Fourteenth Amendment, ratified in 1868, which reads:

No State shall make or enforce any law which shall abridge the privileges or immunities of citizens of the United States; nor shall any State deprive any person of life, liberty, or property, without due process of law; nor deny to any person within its jurisdiction the equal protection of the laws.

It was far from clear, though, what Congress had in mind when it approved those words. Did it intend to have all the Bill of Rights, which had bound only the national government before, henceforth be just as binding on the states, so that the New Orleans priest and the hypothetical North Carolina editor would have the same protection of fundamental rights from action by the states that they had hitherto enjoyed, at least in theory, from transgression by the federal government? That is a question scholars and statesmen have been debating for more than a century, and the question is still unresolved. In actuality, the issue would be decided by neither historians nor legislators, although both would be influential, but by the U.S. Supreme Court, for, as Charles Evans Hughes once observed, "the Constitution is what the judges say it is."[6]

And when the Court began to interpret the Fourteenth Amendment, it indicated that the amendment had changed virtually nothing. The New Orleans priest and the hypothetical North Carolina editor appeared to be no better off than they had been before the Fourteenth Amendment was ratified. When the Court first explored the meaning of the Fourteenth Amendment, in a major pronouncement in 1873,[7] it construed "privileges or immunities" so narrowly that virtually nothing has been heard of that clause from that day to this.[8]

Much more important has been the due process clause of the Fourteenth Amendment, but it, too, got off to an unpropitious start. The Court first took a serious look at the meaning of that passage for civil liberties in a case arising out of marital infidelity in the capital city of California.[9] In February 1882, Joseph Hurtado, who had already killed one man in a barroom brawl and gotten away with it, shot and bludgeoned to death on a Sacramento street a Chilean immigrant who had been carrying on an affair with Hurtado's wife, Susie. He was tried, convicted, and sentenced to hang. Hurtado's lawyers claimed that his rights had been violated because he had not been indicted by a grand jury, as stipulated by the Fifth Amendment of the U.S. Constitution, which, they said, had been absorbed in the due process clause of the Fourteenth Amendment, restricting state governments in the same way that the national government was bound.[10]

In 1884, however, the Supreme Court, in *Hurtado v. California*, ruled against the murderer. It accepted the contention of counsel for the state that the due process clause of the Fourteenth Amendment was identical with the due process clause of the Fifth Amendment and that, since the grand jury provision was listed alongside the due process clause of the Fifth Amendment, it was not embraced by the phrase "due process." Otherwise, counsel had pointed out, the Framers would have been guilty of "surplusage and mere verbiage," and there was no reason to make that assumption. This reasoning, if fully accepted, implied that none of the Bill of Rights was absorbed in the due process clause of the Fourteenth Amendment, since the first eight amendments included both a due process clause and separate listings of freedoms such as those of speech and the press. The Court did acknowledge that the due process clause of the Fourteenth Amendment safeguarded those "fundamental principles of liberty and justice which lie at the base of all our civil and political institutions," but it declared that the states should not have rigid procedures imposed on them, for to do so "would be to stamp upon our jurisprudence the unchangeableness attributed to the laws of the Medes and Persians." Despite the Fourteenth Amendment, Hurtado was to hang.[11]

That decision, coming in the very year that Bartholdi and Eiffel were putting the finishing touches on the Statue of Liberty in Paris, defined the constitutional situation in late nineteenth-century America. The Fourteenth Amendment had promised a new beginning; the Court in some of its language had indicated it might at some point recognize a departure; but no one had yet derived any palpable benefit. Not until 1897, a generation after the Fourteenth Amendment was ratified, did the Court first intimate that the Amendment might incorporate any of the Bill of Rights, and that observation came in a railroad property case that had no immediate consequence for individual liberties. Moreover, despite that observation, the plaintiff lost.[12]

Even at the end of the century, the Court was still unwilling to incorporate the Bill of Rights in the Fourteenth Amendment, as an outlaw named "Gunplay" Maxwell found out. In 1898, Maxwell and a partner robbed a bank in Springville, Utah, of more than three thousand dollars in gold coins and took off in a horse and buggy for a canyon hideaway. A posse went after them, killed Maxwell's sidekick in a shootout, and arrested Maxwell, who was tried, found guilty, and sentenced to a long prison term. He had been convicted, though, by an eight-person jury, not by the twelve required in federal courts, and his attorney argued that he had been denied the right to a proper trial since, he maintained, the Fourteenth Amendment imposed national standards on the states. The Supreme Court, however, in a decision in 1900, turned down that contention. In fact, it went out of its way to say that the Fourteenth

Amendment had effected no new curbs on the behavior of the states. As a result, "Gunplay" Maxwell had to go to jail, though after a brief time his sentence was commuted, with the consequence that "Gunplay" soon lost his life in a gunfight with a desperado named "Shoot-em-up Bill." So at the start of the new century plaintiffs were still no better off than they had been at the time of the hypothetical scenario in 1859.[13]

Defense lawyers, however, are a persistent lot, and the avenue of the Fourteenth Amendment seemed too promising to give up on, especially since counsel in civil liberties cases had been receiving help from an unexpected quarter. Not only had railroad attorneys been prodding the Court to absorb certain features of the Bill of Rights in the Fourteenth Amendment as a shield for business interests, but also conservative theorists, notably William D. Guthrie, had advanced powerful arguments for the nationalization of the Bill of Rights. Furthermore, the reasoning of the Court in the late nineteenth-century cases revealed that it had yet to work out a consistent rationale for coping with such pleas, and one Justice, John Marshall Harlan, was firmly convinced that the Fourteenth Amendment did incorporate all of the Bill of Rights.[14]

Not long after "Gunplay" went to perdition, the Supreme Court got yet another opportunity to change its mind. This case arose out of the shocking collapse early in 1903 of two financial institutions in Asbury Park, New Jersey. An investigation revealed fraud and deception, especially by the president of the Monmouth Trust, one Albert Twining, who was sentenced to six years in prison at hard labor after a trial in which both the prosecutor and the judge called attention to the fact that he had not taken the stand to prove his innocence. Twining's attorney appealed to the U. S. Supreme Court on the grounds that his client's rights had been violated, because, he said, the Fourteenth Amendment embraced the clause against self-incrimination of the Fifth Amendment. The unusual procedures of the New Jersey courts, his lawyer noted, left Twining in an impossible position, for, if he had taken the stand, the state could have brought out the fact that he had been convicted, in a previous prosecution, of falsifying bank records. On the other hand, by not testifying, he was said to be admitting guilt.

In 1908, in the seminal case of *Twining v. New Jersey*, the Court denied Twining's claim. Justice William H. Moody declared brusquely that the question whether the Bill of Rights applied to the states via the privileges or immunities clause "is no longer open in this Court." He did acknowledge that it was "possible that some of the personal rights safeguarded by the first eight Amendments against National action may also be safeguarded against state action, because a denial of them would be a denial of due process of law." But he then went on to emphasize, "If this is so, it is not because those rights are enumerated in the first eight Amendments, but because they are of such a nature that they are included in the conception of due process of law." The due process clause, he maintained, did not afford a right against self-incrimination, for that right, which had evolved only recently, was not fundamental.[15] This ruling—that the U.S. Constitution established no right against self-incrimination in state prosecutions—was to last all the way until 1964.[16]

The country had now gone through the 1870s, 1880s, 1890s, and would go through the first two decades of this century and more, with the situation regarding the nationalization of civil liberties essentially unchanged from what it had been before the Civil War. Some liberties, the Court suggested in *Twining*, might be regarded as aspects of due process of law, but not because they had been set down in the Bill of Rights. Hence, the barrier created by the reasoning in *Hurtado* was not dismantled. During these years, the Court evolved the conception of "liberty of contract," but it did not perceive freedom of expression to be an aspect of "liberty." As one scholar has observed, "the Court was in the habit of using the due process clause as a big stick in areas in which the textual justification for so wielding the Constitution was nonexistent. Therefore, one might have thought it would not have had much trouble including freedom of speech in fourteenth amendment 'liberty.' " But in the years before World War I, another scholar has concluded, there was "pervasive judicial hostility to the value of free speech."[17]

On the Supreme Court, Justice Harlan continued to speak out, but no one heeded. When in 1907 the Court sustained the contempt conviction of a feisty Denver editor for criticizing Colorado's conservative judiciary, Harlan, in dissent, declared that it was "impossible to conceive of liberty as secured by the constitution against hostile action, whether by the nation or by the states, which does not embrace the right to enjoy free speech and the right to have a free press." The farthest that Justice Oliver Wendell Holmes, Jr., later thought of as a champion of freedom, could be persuaded to go, though, in his opinion for the Court in this case was to leave "undecided the question whether there is to be found in the Fourteenth Amendment a prohibition similar to the first." A decade later, six years after Harlan's death, the Court announced that the Fourteenth Amendment did not incorporate the right to trial by jury.[18]

World War I and its immediate aftermath brought no significant change. In the wartime cases, Holmes and Louis D. Brandeis articulated civil libertarian doctrines, but neither embraced incorporation. In 1920 Brandeis appeared to break new ground in saying, "I cannot believe that the liberty guaranteed by the Fourteenth Amendment includes only liberty to acquire and to enjoy property," but Brandeis made these remarks only after saying that the Fourteenth Amendment was not relevant to the case. [19] As late as 1922 the Supreme Court asserted that "neither the Fourteenth Amendment nor any other provision of the Constitution of the United States imposes upon the states any restrictions about 'freedom of speech.' "[20] It was not, indeed, until 1925, just two generations ago, that the Court first said clearly that some, at least, of the Bill of Rights applied to the states, and even then, the plaintiff lost.

The milestone case of 1925, which took a long time to make its way to the Supreme Court, arose out of the Red Scare following World War I. Early in November 1919, the Lusk Committee of the New York state legislature dispatched seven hundred policemen on a dragnet raid of radical headquarters. Of the more than five hundred people they arrested, the biggest catch was twenty-eight-year-old Benjamin Gitlow, a former member of the New York state legislature who was leader of the left-wing faction of the Socialist Party that would soon help found the Communist Party. Though the raids caught a number of innocent people, Gitlow was a genuine Bolshevik. He was charged under New York's Criminal Anarchy Act of 1902, adopted after the assassination of President McKinley in Buffalo, because he had several months earlier taken part in writing and disseminating a thirty-four-page "Manifesto" in *The Revolutionary Age* denying that change could come through the democratic legislative process and saying that it was imperative "to destroy the parliamentary state." Gitlow did not dispute this accusation. Indeed, to the despair of his well-known attorney Clarence Darrow, he insisted on telling the jury "no jails" would stop him from promoting the principles of the Left Wing Manifesto and saying, "I ask no clemency." Under these circumstances, and in a trial, as Paul Murphy has said, "before a silk-stocking jury and a highly property-conscious judge," it is hardly surprising that the jury took less than an hour to convict him. In February 1920, Gitlow was given the maximum sentence of five to ten years, and as he sat on his cot "in a daze," after the doors of his jail cell closed behind him, he had no doubt that he would spend a full ten years in the penitentiary at Sing Sing. [21]

To Gitlow's side, though, came a new organization that had emerged from the travail of pacifists and conscientious objectors in World War I: the American Civil Liberties Union. The ACLU's attorney sought to persuade the Supreme Court that the Fourteenth Amendment embraced one of the vital clauses of the First Amendment: the right of free speech. Furthermore, he maintained that Gitlow's activities did not constitute a clear and present danger to the community, for as the political scientist Richard Cortner has observed:

There had been no showing by the state of New York that the Left Wing Manifesto had induced anything other than massive yawning among the public of New York, and as Zechariah Chafee has said, any "agitator who read these thirty-four pages . . . to a mob would not stir them to violence, except possibly against himself."[22]

When the Court finally handed down its decision in *Gitlow* in 1925, some six years after the issuance of the Left Wing Manifesto, it made a historic statement. "For present purposes we may and do assume," it said, "that freedom of speech and of the press—which are protected by the First Amendment from abridgment by Congress—are among the fundamental personal rights and 'liberties' protected by the due process clause of the Fourteenth Amendment from impairment by the States." In a seminal article in the *Harvard Law Review*, the legal historian Charles Warren commented:

No one who read Judge Sanford's opinion would imagine that, for over fifty years, counsel had, time and again, attempted to get the Court to hold that rights similar to the right of freedom of speech were protected by the Fourteenth Amendment against infringement by State legislation, and that in every instance the Court had declined so to hold. Yet, in this *Gitlow* case, without even mentioning these previous cases, the Court assumes, without argument, that this right of free speech is so protected by the Fourteenth Amendment. Thus, by one short sentence, rights, the protection of which have hitherto been supposed to be within the scope of the State Courts alone, are now brought within the scope of Federal protection and of the United States Supreme Court.[23]

For the first time since ratification of the post-Civil War amendments, the Court was at last willing to say unequivocally: Yes, the Fourteenth Amendment does include some of the original Bill of Rights, now applied to the states. This acknowledgment, though, did Ben Gitlow no good because, characteristically, the Court went on, despite these words, to uphold his conviction.[24] Nearly six decades after the adoption of the Fourteenth Amendment, the Court had yet to reverse any conviction or to strike down any state law for violating civil liberties.

That situation changed dramatically, however, in the fertile year of 1931 when, on two occasions, the Court entered new territory. The first of the cases grew out of a raid launched on a Communist Party youth camp in the San Bernardino range in California. Arrested were one man and six women, including "the girl Red," as newspapers called her, nineteen-year-old Yetta Stromberg. Like Gitlow, these were no liberal innocents, but bona fide Communists. Each morning at seven the children at the camp, under Yetta's tutelage, participated in raising the flag of the Soviet Union with its hammer and sickle to the top of a pole; the children then pledged allegiance to "the workers' red flag, and to the cause for which it stands." Yet having arrested these people, what was the state to charge them with? Nobody could figure that out until someone remembered that in 1919 the California legislature had enacted a law forbidding flying a red flag for seditious purposes. The seven were indicted and convicted of violating that statute. The lone man escaped a prison term by committing suicide. The women, though, received stiff sentences with the heaviest meted out to Yetta Stromberg, one to ten years in San Quentin—for displaying a red flag. [25]

With the help both of the ACLU and a Communist front legal association, the International Labor Defense, Yetta carried her case to the United States Supreme Court, and on May 18, 1931, in *Stromberg v. California*, the Court, in an opinion delivered by the new Chief Justice, Charles Evans Hughes, reversed her conviction because a portion of the red flag law denied the freedom of speech guaranteed by the Fourteenth Amendment. "It has been determined," the Chief Justice said, "that the conception of liberty under the due process clause of the Fourteenth Amendment embraces the right of free speech [in the First Amendment]." [26]

Two weeks later came another significant decision, this one involving a scoundrel named J. M. Near. Together with an equally unsavory character, Howard Guilford, who, Fred Friendly has declared, "always had one foot in jail," Near ran a scandal sheet, the *Saturday Press*, that accused public officials in Minneapolis of being in league with a gambling syndicate, and first citizens of licentious misconduct. A representative headline read: "Smooth Minneapolis Doctor With Woman in St. Paul Hotel." The Twin Cities were notorious for venality—Lincoln Steffens had once written of "The Shame of Minneapolis"—and a Minneapolis cop recalled, "You could get anyone killed in the Twin Cities for five hundred dollars," maybe less. But the weekly went beyond legitimate exposure to engage in character assassination: it denigrated blacks, Catholics, and labor leaders; and it was viciously anti-Semitic. It called on "the decent citizens of Minneapolis" to "rid the city of these criminal Jews," and resorted to racial stereotyping. "Practically every vendor of vile hooch, every owner of a moonshine still, every snake-faced gangster and embryonic egg in the Twin Cities is a JEW," the *Saturday Press* asserted. "It is Jew, Jew, Jew, as long as one cares to comb over the records." Moreover, the two men may well have been involved in an extortion racket, threatening to publish defamatory stories unless they were paid off. Guilford had at various times been convicted of criminal libel, arrested for carrying concealed weapons, and charged with extortion. (In 1934, gangsters would overtake him in a posh section of town, and shoot off his head.) In short, though the name of Jay Near has a secure place in the annals of freedom of the press, he was no heroic crusading editor.[27] (In that regard, Near was typical, for as Cortner has noted, the litigants who brought about a Second Bill of Rights were "murderers, thieves, bookies . . . , university professors, narcotics addicts."[28])

The case of *Near v. Minnesota* had been precipitated in 1927 by a county attorney and future Farmer-Labor governor who was an advanced progressive but was rumored to have ties to the underworld. Floyd Olson had been personally attacked by the weekly, and, having been reared in a Jewish neighborhood, resented the anti-Semitic slurs. One historian has noted that "young Floyd acted as the Shabbos Goy for many of his Jewish neighbors. Throughout his political career, Olson was better able to campaign in Yiddish than in either Swedish or Norwegian. It is not surprising, then, that he should surround himself with his Jewish friends when he became Hennepin County Attorney late in 1920 and Governor a little over ten years later." Olson obtained an injunction to restrain Near and Guilford from further publication under a statute authorizing abatement as a public nuisance of any "malicious, scandalous and defamatory" publication, and the *Saturday Press* was unquestionably all three. The law, which had been enacted in response to the anger aroused by scandal sheets' plaguing the state, had considerable support from the daily press, and it was validated by the Minnesota Supreme Court.[29] Nonetheless, Near's case was carried to the U.S. Supreme Court—not by liberals or radicals but by the publisher of the arch-conservative Chicago *Tribune*, Colonel Robert R. McCormick, who saw in Minnesota's "gag law" a threat to the press everywhere.[30]

Early in June 1931, the Supreme Court, by 5–4, with yet another opinion by Charles Evans Hughes, struck down the Minnesota act. "The fact that the liberty of the press may be abused by miscreant purveyors of scandal does not make any the less necessary the immunity of the press from previous restraint in dealing with official misconduct," the Chief Justice said. "It is no longer open to doubt," he declared in the most important sentence of his opinion, "that the liberty of the press and of speech is within the liberty safeguarded by the due process clause of the 14th Amendment."[31]

So after three-quarters of a century of silence or denial, the Supreme Court had at long last announced in a two-week interval in 1931 that two aspects of the eighteenth-century Bill of Rights that restrained the national government—freedom of speech and freedom of press—now applied to state governments as well. How did that happen? Why did the Supreme Court so abruptly change its mind? It is not at all clear. All we know is that the Court first enunciated this principle almost off-handedly in 1925 in *Gitlow*, and by 1931, a majority of five Justices, two of them newly appointed, took the *Gitlow* principle for granted and saw no need to offer a well-wrought justification for what it was doing. The whole transition has been designated by the political scientist Klaus Heberle as "absent-minded incrementalism." He concluded: "The Court as a whole did not at any point in the process address itself to the problem of the relation between the federal courts and state governments, did not discuss it, and did not evince any particular awareness that the problem was involved. . . . It appears then that a major constitutional shift was effected without a coherent discussion of the merits."[32]

Once the Court, for whatever reason, accepted the principle, it managed to absorb more and more of the Bill of Rights into the Fourteenth Amendment, but commentators differ about when that course of events resumed. Some trace the incorporation of religious guarantees of the First Amendment to *Hamilton v. Regents*, a 1934 case arising from the claim of two UCLA students who were the sons of Methodist ministers that they had been wrongfully suspended for not attending ROTC classes since they were conscientious objectors. In a concurrence joined in by Brandeis and Harlan Fiske Stone, Benjamin Cardozo said, "I assume for the present purpose that the religious liberty protected by the First Amendment against invasion by the nation is protected by the Fourteenth Amendment against invasion by the states." But since the Court ruled against the students, *Hamilton* can only be regarded as dictum.[33]

In like manner, *Powell v. Alabama* (1932) has often been misconstrued as incorporating the Sixth Amendment's provision for right to counsel into the Fourteenth Amendment. Some of the Supreme Court's language about the shocking trial of the "Scottsboro boys" lent itself to this misconception. Justice George Sutherland said that defendants—impoverished young blacks sentenced to death in Alabama after being falsely charged with raping two white women on a freight train—had a right to effective counsel, and to deny them that right "would be little short of judicial murder." But Sutherland did not draw upon the Sixth Amendment, and the reach of his opinion was sharply circumscribed.[34]

Yet though *Powell* did not turn on absorption of the Sixth Amendment, the Court subsequently behaved, for a time, as though it did. In a series of cases, the Court indicated, as it said in 1936 in striking down a law aimed at the press in Huey Long's Louisiana, that "certain fundamental rights, safeguarded by the first eight amendments against federal action, were also safeguarded against state action by the due process of law clause of the Fourteenth Amendment, and among them the fundamental right of the accused to the aid of counsel in a criminal prosecution." In fact, contrary to what the Court assumed, the Sixth Amendment had long been understood to imply only the right to *engage* counsel, not until 1938 did the Court say that in *federal* trials there was an affirmative right to have counsel *supplied.* Four years later, in the case of a poor, ill-educated Maryland farmhand forced to defend himself when his request for appointed counsel was denied, the Court, in *Betts v. Brady,* made clear that *Powell* and the subsequent rulings had not established a right to have counsel furnished in state prosecutions, and it found no relevance in the Sixth Amendment.[35]

The first indisputable advance after the great divide of 1931 came in a case that, like *Gitlow* and *Stromberg,* arose out of a red scare. In 1934, a maritime strike led by an Australian-born radical sent a shudder through the middle class when it tied up the entire Pacific coast from San Diego to Vancouver and in San Francisco even resulted, however briefly, in resort to the most feared of labor's weapons: a general strike. On July 11, in an effort to break the strike in Portland, Oregon, the police shot four pickets and raided Communist headquarters. When, two weeks later, the Communists staged a protest rally, the Portland police arrested four Communists, one of them Dirk De Jonge, who had been the Communist candidate for mayor of the city. He was convicted of violating the state's criminal syndicalism law of 1919 by organizing the rally, even though nothing unlawful was said or done at the meeting, and sentenced to seven years in prison.

But in January 1937, the U.S. Supreme Court in *De Jonge v. Oregon,* with Hughes once more writing the opinion, reversed the conviction and struck down the syndicalism law. The "right of peaceable assembly," said the Chief Justice, "is a right cognate to those of free speech and free press and is equally fundamental."[36] So still another provision of the Bill of Rights had been absorbed into the due process clause of the Fourteenth Amendment. What before had constrained only the national government now restricted the states too.

Having gone this far, was there any stopping place? All of the rights of freedom of expression in the First Amendment were now part of the Fourteenth Amendment. Was all of the rest of the Bill of Rights—in particular the provisions respecting the rights of the accused in criminal cases—to be incorporated too?

In a ruling later in the same year as *De Jonge,* the Court indicated how far it was prepared to go. In 1935, Frank Palko and an accomplice had smashed the window of a store in Bridgeport, Connecticut, and when two policemen sought to apprehend them, Palko had shot and killed both officers. He was charged with first-degree murder but convicted of murder in the second degree, which spared his life. The prosecution, believing that the judge had made errors that had led to the lighter sentence, appealed the verdict, and Connecticut's highest court agreed that Palko would have to stand trial again. In this second trial, he was found guilty once more, but this time of murder in the first degree, and was sentenced to die in the electric chair.

Palko's attorneys carried his case to the U.S. Supreme Court with the contention that Palko's second trial constituted double jeopardy and that the Fourteenth Amendment embraced the provision against double jeopardy of the Fifth Amendment. Indeed, they mounted an argument for total incorporation: "Whatever would be a violation of the original bill of rights (Amendments 1 to 8) if done by the federal government is now equally unlawful by force of the Fourteenth Amendment." The state of Connecticut, on the other hand, pointed out that the Court had twice denied that the Fourteenth Amendment embraced the Fifth Amendment—in the cases of the vengeful husband Hurtado and of the Asbury Park banker Twining. It was up to the U.S. Supreme Court to resolve these conflicting claims.

In the very important case of *Palko v. Connecticut*, decided in December 1937, the U.S. Supreme Court ruled in favor of the state. There was a hierarchy of rights, Justice Cardozo explained. "Freedom of thought and speech," he declared, was "the matrix, the indispensable condition, of nearly every other form of freedom," and hence on a higher "plane of social and moral values" than less salient liberties. In saying that, he brought together and elevated in significance the corpus of First Amendment opinions since *Gitlow* that had never been so well articulated. But all of the Bill of Rights did not apply to the states through the Fourteenth Amendment, he declared. "There is no such general rule." Only those rights were absorbed that were "of the very essence of a scheme of ordered liberty." The right against double jeopardy was not of the very essence, he said; nor were a number of other rights he listed that could be found in the first eight amendments.[37] Frank Palko would die in the chair.

Cardozo's opinion in *Palko*, however useful in legitimating First Amendment rights, drew criticism for its confused reasoning and for bringing to an abrupt halt efforts to absorb other parts of the Bill of Rights into the Fourteenth Amendment. Robert Cushman wrote of Cardozo's opinion: "Having built up the strongest and most lucid argument to date that the sixth amendment right to counsel had been incorporated into due process, the Court, like the cow that gives a good pail of milk and then kicks it over, proceeded to destroy its former argument completely with a different, and wholly incompatible, explanation." Another commentator, John Raeburn Green, has written:

> If he had been determined to turn back the rising tide of liberty in respect to the rights of the accused in criminal prosecutions, he could hardly have done it more effectively than by this opinion. . . . The essence of this belletristic essay, which gave the scantiest consideration to profoundly important matters, was that the rights of the accused guaranteed by the Bill of Rights were nice things to have, no doubt, but luxuries, not necessities. . . . In this deliberate fashion Mr. Justice Cardozo went out of his way to crush to earth all libertarian heresy. [38]

The Court, though, soon demonstrated that it was prepared to carry the rest of the *First* Amendment—the religious liberties—into the Fourteenth Amendment, in no small part because of challenges raised by one obstreperous religious sect. It is doubtful that any organization in our history has brought about more Supreme Court rulings on its behalf or more affected the course of civil liberties than the Jehovah's Witnesses, despite the reality that they were unalterably opposed to government and all of its works. Some of their difficulty with the law stemmed from the fact that they were no less hostile to the Catholic Church. Many Catholics were understandably offended by a sect that aggressively promoted pamphlets and records likening their church to a "harlot" or calling it "the representative of the devil." On a spring day in 1938, a Jehovah's Witness named Cantwell and his two teen-aged sons, armed with anti-Catholic tracts and recordings, started their rounds in a neighborhood of New Haven that could not have been more ill-chosen (it was 90 percent Catholic). A Catholic woman to whom they spoke phoned the police. They were arrested and subsequently convicted. The main counts against them were breach of the peace, though they had not behaved coercively, and, much more important, violation of a state law requiring a permit to solicit for a religious purpose. In May 1940, the U.S. Supreme Court reversed their convictions and struck down the Connecticut law authorizing an official to determine "what is a religious cause" as a denial of the free exercise of religion. The Fourteenth Amendment, the Court said, "embraces the liberties guaranteed by the First Amendment. The First Amendment declares that Congress shall make no law respecting an establishment of religion or prohibiting the free exercise thereof. The Fourteenth Amendment has rendered the legislatures of the states as incompetent as Congress to enact such laws." [39]

With the *Cantwell* decision, later amplified by dictum in an opinion on a case involving busing to parochial schools in New Jersey, [40] the

Court had absorbed all of the First Amendment into the Fourteenth Amendment.[41] Having done that, the Court might be expected to incorporate all of the rest of the Bill of Rights, which was precisely what Hugo Black and some other Justices sought to do. But the majority of the Court, led by Felix Frankfurter, strongly opposed that course, both as a misreading of the meaning of the Fourteenth Amendment and as an inappropriate effort to impose a single national standard on the states. For more than twenty years after *Cantwell*, the movement toward creation of a Second Bill of Rights was at a standstill, though not without passionate exchanges between Frankfurter and Black and their partisans.

In 1949, the controversy came to a head in a case deriving from the burglary of a Los Angeles apartment during which a sixty-four-year-old widow was badly beaten and strangled. A black man, Dewey Adamson, was convicted of her murder after a trial in which the prosecutor made full use of the accused's failure to take the witness stand in his defense. Adamson had faced a dilemma. If he testified, the jury would learn that he had previous felony convictions and be disposed against him. If he did not, his refusal could be depicted as a confession of guilt. In carrying the case to the Supreme Court, Adamson's lawyer claimed not only that the prosecution had inflamed racial animosity but that his client had been denied the right against self-incrimination, which he maintained had been absorbed into the Fourteenth Amendment from the Fifth Amendment.

In short, the Court confronted the very issue that had been raised more than four decades earlier in the case of the Asbury Park banker, Twining, and, once more, despite all that had happened since, the outcome was the same. The Court was not willing in 1949 to do for criminal procedure what it was pleased to do for freedom of expression. In a 5–4 decision in *Adamson v. California*, Justice Stanley Reed, for the Court, denied that the privilege against self-incrimination had been incorporated into either the privileges or immunities clause or the due process clause.[42] Hugo Black and three other Justices dissented, but to no avail. Dewey Adamson would die in the San Quentin gas chamber.

Adamson gave Frankfurter, the leader of one of two opposing blocs on the Court, an opportunity to set out his ideas. In an elaborate concurrence, he underscored his belief that some particulars of the first eight amendments "express the restricted views of Eighteenth-Century England." He declared that "as judges charged with the delicate task of subjecting the government of a continent to the Rule of Law we must be particularly mindful that it is 'a *constitution* we are expounding,' so that it should not be imprisoned in what are merely legal forms even though they have the sanction of the Eighteenth Century." In the seventy years since the Fourteenth Amendment was ratified, Frankfurter said, forty-three Justices had commented on it and only one, "who may respectfully be called an eccentric exception," an allusion presumably either to Black or to the first Justice Harlan, believed that the due process clause was "a shorthand summary of the first eight Amendments."[43]

Frankfurter's concurrence drew not just one but two rejoinders. "With full knowledge of the import of the *Barron* decision, the framers and backers of the Fourteenth Amendment proclaimed its purpose to be to overturn the constitutional rule that case had announced," Black asserted, and he offered a thirty-three-page appendix to document that contention. "I cannot consider the Bill of Rights to be an outworn Eighteenth Century 'strait jacket' as the *Twining* opinion did," he added. Justice Frank Murphy, in a separate dissent in which Wiley Rutledge joined, accepted Black's view that the Bill of Rights should be "carried over intact into the first section of the Fourteenth Amendment," but wanted to go still further. There might be violations, he maintained, that would "warrant constitutional condemnation . . . despite the absence of a specific provision in the Bill of Rights."[44]

The *Adamson* ruling typified the period of two decades following *Cantwell* when every attempt to extend the Bill of Rights protections to the states met defeat. In 1949, in *Wolf v. Colorado*, the Court sustained the conviction of a Denver obstetrician for performing abortions, though it was based on evidence found in the doctor's office that was seized without a warrant. The Court declared, in an opinion by Frankfurter, that for police to behave so arbitrarily violated the security that was at "the core" of the Fourth Amendment, and hence transgressed the due process clause of the Fourteenth Amendment. It refused, though, to apply to the states the exclusionary rule of federal court procedure. In essence, then, state officers were being told that they could no longer engage in illegal search and seizures, but, if they did, the tainted evidence they discovered would be admissible if state courts accepted it. Fred Graham, a commentator on the Supreme Court, later wrote of the "checkerboard of human rights" that resulted from this reasoning:

> If a person had driven across the country at that time from New York to San Francisco, he would have passed through four states . . . in which the police would have been unlikely to search him or his car without probable cause, since their courts would not have permitted the fruits of the search to be used in evidence. In eight others . . . officers could have made a search which did not measure up to Fourth Amendment standards and could have used the findings against the traveler in court.[45]

Subsequent decisions revealed a similar reluctance to expanding the domain of the Fourteenth Amendment. After a man accused of killing his wife and his three children received a long sentence, he was tried again and got a longer sentence, then tried a third time and sentenced to death. Divided 5–4, the Court in 1958 upheld the conviction that resulted in the death penalty, though Black argued that three trials violated the protection against double jeopardy that he said was incorporated in the Fourteenth Amendment.[46] As late as 1959, in the wake of these opinions, the political scientist David Fellman could write, "The Supreme Court has consistently ruled that not all of the provisions of the federal Bill of Rights, but only those which are essential to justice, fall within the scope of the federal remedy. . . . In other words, it is clear that in the jurisprudence of the Supreme Court, some rights are more important than others."[47]

The breakthrough did not come until 1961, in a case with another improbable hero, or in this instance, heroine. Four years earlier, acting on a tip, Cleveland police, apparently without a search warrant, had broken into the home of Dollree Mapp, a twenty-nine-year-old African-American woman who had been married to the boxer Jimmy Bivins; had later been the great good friend of another fighter, the champion Archie Moore; and was rumored to be hiding a bombing suspect and involved in the numbers racket. Sure enough, the police found paraphernalia in her basement, though no fugitive, and as a result the state prosecuted her on a numbers charge, only to have a jury acquit her. The state, though, was not content to let the raid go to waste. In carrying out the raid, the police had stumbled on a few items of pornography in her home, so the state arraigned her a second time, and in this trial got a conviction. For possessing obscene materials serendipitously discovered in an invasion of her home conducted without a visible warrant, Dolly Mapp was sentenced to not less than one year in the state women's reformatory.

When the case was appealed to the U.S. Supreme Court, the state of Ohio maintained that whether there was a search warrant was irrelevant, for as recently as *Wolf* in 1949 the Court had said that states did not have to follow the procedures required of the federal government. But in June 1961, in *Mapp v. Ohio*, the Court ruled that the Fourteenth Amendment absorbed the Fourth Amendment's prohibition of unreasonable searches and seizures and just as the federal government might not use evidence obtained illegally, neither might the states. "Our decision, founded on reason and truth," Justice Clark declared, "gives to the individual no more than that which the Constitution guarantees him, to the police officer, no less than that to which honest law enforcement is entitled, and, to the courts, that judicial integrity so necessary in the true administration of justice."[48]

Mapp proved to be only the beginning of a decade of holdings by the Warren Court in this field. In the very next year, another segment of the eighteenth-century Bill of Rights was brought into the scope of the Fourteenth Amendment as the consequence of an episode on a Los Angeles street in 1960. A policeman halted a car and on noticing what he said were "numerous fresh needle marks" on the arm of one of the passengers, Walter Robinson, arrested him for addiction to narcotics. Robinson stoutly denied that he was a junkie and explained that the marks came from an allergic reaction to vaccinations he had been given in the army. Nonetheless, he was convicted and sentenced to ninety days in jail. Two years later, in *Robinson v. California*, the U.S. Supreme Court reversed his conviction on the grounds that to imprison a man not for any particular act but merely for a condition was cruel and unusual punishment. Though ninety days did not appear to be an excessive sentence, Justice Potter Stewart acknowledged, even "one day in prison would be cruel and unusual punishment for the 'crime' of having a common cold." The decision, however, came too late for the appellant. A year before the Court handed down its ruling, Walter Robinson had died—of a drug overdose. There were needle marks on his body. He was only twenty-six years old. But in his short lifetime, he had been unwittingly responsible for the absorption of the Eighth Amendment's ban on cruel and unusual punishment into the Fourteenth Amendment.[49]

By now, the Warren Court was breaching the wall separating the Fourteenth Amendment from the first eight amendments at a breakneck pace: 1961, *Mapp*; 1962, *Robinson*; then in 1963 came *Gideon v. Wainwright*. Many who hear about the *Gideon* case for the first time—about a man in a Southern prison claiming that he has been denied justice—assume that Gideon was black. In fact, as the movie in which he was portrayed by Henry Fonda made clear, he was white and another improbable hero—a ne'er-do-well who had spent seventeen of his fifty years in prison on four felony convictions. When in 1961 Gideon was arrested yet again—this time on the charge of breaking and entering a poolroom—, he demanded that the state appoint a lawyer to represent him. The judge patiently explained to him that under Florida law an indigent defendant was entitled to be provided with counsel only when on trial for a capital offense. With no attorney to represent him, Gideon was convicted and sentenced to five more years in jail.

Certain that the Constitution required the state of Florida to furnish him with counsel, Gideon from his prison cell scribbled a petition to the U.S. Supreme Court. If he had understood the law better, he would not have bothered, for, contrary to what he assumed, the Court had said that the Fourteenth Amendment did not require the states to do what the national government must under the Sixth Amendment—supply counsel not only in capital cases but also in serious non-capital cases. Nevertheless, of the many paupers' petitions that reached the Court that year, this one struck a spark, not by chance for Chief Justice Warren had instructed his clerks to keep their eyes out for a case that would allow the Court to take another look at *Betts v. Brady*. The Court not only accepted Gideon's petition, but appointed perhaps the most skillful member of the D.C. bar to represent him—Abe Fortas. Asked afterwards if he had ever desired to meet Gideon, Fortas answered, "Why the hell would I want to meet a son of a bitch like that? He's no good." But that sentiment did not deter him from representing his client with his characteristic vigor and acuity. [50]

In March 1963 the Court, in a unanimous decision, reversed Gideon's conviction. Henceforth, states as well as the national government would have to provide counsel for impoverished defendants who were accused of serious offenses, a principle that within a decade was extended to misdemeanors punishable by jail terms of as little as a day. Though not all of the judges operated from the same premise, the Court had absorbed into the Fourteenth Amendment the provision for right to counsel of the Sixth Amendment.

Gideon stood trial a second time for the poolroom charge, but this time, represented by counsel, he was acquitted. Neither his victories in the courts, nor the fame engendered by Anthony Lewis's book about him, however, notably improved his position in society. Only two years after the Supreme Court's decision, Clarence Gideon, always a drifter, was arrested in Kentucky—for vagrancy. Not long after, he would be buried in a pauper's grave. [51]

Almost every year in the 1960s brought a new victory for the incorporationists. In 1964, in *Malloy v. Hogan*, a case involving a Hartford bookie, the Court absorbed the clause against self-incrimination of the Fifth Amendment into the Fourteenth Amendment, thereby reversing the holdings in *Twining* and *Adamson*. [52] (*Malloy*, in turn, led to that standby of every TV cops-and-robbers show, *Miranda*, requiring that police read suspects their rights to silence and to counsel before interrogating them. [53]) One year later, in 1965, in a case stemming from the holdup of a 7–11 store in Houston, Hugo Black declared, "We hold today that the Sixth Amendment's right of an accused to confront the witness against him is a fundamental right and is made obligatory on the States by the Fourteenth Amendment." [54] Two years later, in 1967, in another Texas case, this one, like *Hurtado*, involving jealousy and murder, the Court incorporated into the Fourteenth Amendment the Sixth Amendment right to compel testimony on behalf of a defendant. Fred Graham has written:

> Never before had a country's judiciary undertaken to change the law as drastically as the United States did during this period. As Erwin N. Griswold, then one of the Court's most effective defenders, wryly put it in 1965, "Some things have recently been found in the Federal Constitution that were not previously known to be there."[55]

These decisions came at the height of the civil rights revolution in the South, and it was inevitable that the movement for racial equality would leave its mark. When five Duke University and two University of North Carolina professors joined in an attempt to desegregate a Jim Crow restaurant in Chapel Hill, they were beaten and prodded with a broomstick, hosed down with water as they sat outside the eating place on a frigid January night, taunted with the cry, "Kill them, get the professors," and then arrested for criminal trespass. One of the members of the Duke faculty, a young assistant professor of zoology, Peter H. Klopfer, was put in an awful limbo when the state would neither prosecute him, after its first effort had ended in a mistrial, nor drop charges, but kept open the possibility that at any time in the future it might haul him into court. In 1967, the Supreme Court, in *Klopfer v. North Carolina*, made the Duke professor's case the occasion for holding for the first time that the Fourteenth Amendment absorbed the Sixth Amendment's guarantee of a speedy trial.[56]

After that ruling, there was just one part of the Sixth Amendment that had never been incorporated into the Fourteenth Amendment: the clause on trial by jury. But only a year after the Duke professor's case, the Court handed down a decision in litigation that arose in one of the last strongholds of Jim Crow, a parish in Louisiana dominated by Leander Perez. So bitter was Perez's resistance to the civil rights movement, which he called a "Zionist-Communist" conspiracy, that he was excommunicated from the Catholic Church. But he and his henchmen went too far in persecuting a young black man, who, on questionable testimony, was fined and sentenced to jail for striking a white boy, after a trial without a jury. Gary Duncan, though, had the good fortune to be defended by an able young attorney who had edited the law review at Columbia and who had given up a job with a prestigious Washington firm to take on the difficult and dangerous work of a volunteer civil rights attorney. When he presented his client's case to the U.S. Supreme Court, Justice Brennan was heard to murmur, "He did a nice job, didn't he?" In 1968 the Court approached the end of its task of absorbing the Sixth Amendment into the Fourteenth Amendment when it held that the states were required to abide by the jury trial clause, thereby giving "Gunplay" Maxwell, in a case far removed from the Utah frontier of the turn of the century, a posthumous victory.[57]

Only one matter generally agreed to be of significance remained. Early in the summer of 1969, in *Benton v. Maryland*, the Court ruled that the double jeopardy clause of the Fifth Amendment represented "a fundamental ideal in our constitutional heritage . . . that . . . should apply to the States through the Fourteenth Amendment." In so holding, the Court overturned its decision in the matter of Palko, the Connecticut cop killer. "Our recent cases have thoroughly rejected the *Palko* notion that basic constitutional rights can be denied by the States," Justice Thurgood Marshall declared. "*Palko*'s roots had . . . been cut away years ago. We today only recognize the inevitable."[58]

Benton essentially completed the process of incorporating the Bill of Rights into the Fourteenth Amendment.[59] Save for the Second Amendment, which most commentators have chosen to ignore, those few segments still not absorbed are unimportant.[60] And with a nice sense of fitness, this final accomplishment of the Warren Court, which had hardly let a year go by in the 1960s without expanding further the meaning of the Fourteenth Amendment, came on June 23, 1969, Earl Warren's final day as Chief Justice of the United States. The consequence of these decades of developments has been nothing less than what Richard Cortner has called "our second bill of rights, a bill more salient to the liberty of the average American than the original document."[61]

Notes

1. Mr. Justice Holmes and Three Generations of Imbeciles

1. Catherine Drinker Bowen, *Yankee from Olympus* (Boston, 1944). For another admiring work, see Francis B. Biddle, *Justice Holmes, Natural Law, and the Supreme Court* (New York, 1961).

2. Alexander M. Bickel, *The Unpublished Opinions of Mr. Justice Brandeis* (Cambridge, Mass., 1957), p. 241; Charles Wyzanski, "The Democracy of Justice Oliver Wendell Holmes," *Vanderbilt Law Review*, 7 (April 1954), 311. For other tributes to Holmes, see the citations in Yosal Rogat, "Mr. Justice Holmes: A Dissenting Opinion," *Stanford Law Review*, 15 (December 1962), 3–5n.

3. *Schenck v. United States*, 249 U.S. 47 (1919) at 52.

4. Mark de Wolfe Howe, ed., *Holmes-Laski Letters* (2 vols., Cambridge, Mass., 1953), 1: 249; Felix Frankfurter, *Mr. Justice Holmes and the Supreme Court* (Cambridge, Mass., 1961).

5. *Lochner v. New York*, 198 U.S. 45 (1905) at 75; *Schenck v. United States*, 249 U.S. 47 (1919) at 52.

6. E. S. Corwin, "Bowing Out 'Clear and Present Danger,' " *Notre Dame Lawyer*, 27 (Spring 1952), 325–26.

7. *Buck v. Bell*, 274 U.S. 200 (1927).

8. Ellen Chesler, *Woman of Valor: Margaret Sanger and the Birth Control Movement in America* (New York, 1993), pp. 195, 215; Walter Berns, "Buck v. Bell: Due Process of Law?," *Western Political Quarterly*, 6 (December 1953), 772; Mark H. Haller, *Eugenics: Hereditarian Attitudes in American Thought* (New Brunswick, N. J., 1963), p. 76; Robert J. Cynkar, "*Buck v. Bell*: 'Felt Necessities' v. Fundamental Values?," *Columbia Law Review*, 81 (October 1981), 425. For the British experience, see Richard Soloway, *Demography and Degeneration: Eugenics and the Declining Birthrate in Twentieth-Century Britain* (Chapel Hill, N. C., 1990).

9. Harry Laughlin, *Eugenical Sterilization in the United States* (Chicago, 1922),

pp. 446–51; Daniel J. Kevles, *In the Name of Eugenics: Genetics and the Uses of Human Heredity* (New York, 1985), p. 102.

10. J. David Smith and K. Ray Nelson, *The Sterilization of Carrie Buck* (Far Hills, N. J., 1989), p. 33.

11. Paul A. Lombardo, "Three Generations, No Imbeciles: New Light on *Buck v. Bell,*" *New York University Law Review,* 60 (April 1985), 30–62.

12. *Williams v. Smith,* 190 Ind. 526, 121 N. E. 2 (1921).

13. Stephen Trombley, *The Right to Reproduce: A History of Coercive Sterilization* (London, 1988), p. 89; Smith and Nelson, *Sterilization of Carrie Buck,* p. 108; *Record* in *Buck v. Bell,* p. 34; Lombardo, "Three Generations," p. 61. Stephen Jay Gould found Vivian to be "a perfectly normal, quite average student, neither particularly outstanding nor much troubled." Stephen Jay Gould, "Carrie Buck's Daughter," *Natural History,* 93 (July 1984), 18.

14. Clement Vose, *Constitutional Change: Amendment Politics and Supreme Court Litigation Since 1900* (Lexington, Mass., 1972), pp. 14–15; Allan Chase, *The Legacy of Malthus: The Social Costs of the New Scientific Racism* (New York, 1977), p. 314; *Record,* pp. 33–34.

15. *Record,* p. 9; *Briefs,* p. 27; *Buck v. Bell,* 143 Va. 310 (1925).

16. *Buck v. Bell,* 143 Va. 310, 130 S. E. 516 at 517.

17. Vose, *Constitutional Change,* p. 16; Lombardo, "Three Generations," p. 56.

18. *Munn v. Illinois,* 94 U.S. 113 (1877) at 143.

19. *Buck v. Bell,* 274 U.S. 200 (1927) at 201–2.

20. Ibid., at 203–4.

21. Ibid., at 205–8.

22. *Jacobson v. Massachusetts,* 97 U.S. 11 (1905).

23. Vose, *Constitutional Change,* p. 18; J. E. Coogan, S. J., "Eugenic Sterilization Holds Jubilee," *Catholic World,* 177 (April 1953), 44.

24. Berns, "Buck v. Bell," p. 762. In Oregon in the Great Depression, Anthony J. Badger has noted, "Governor Martin . . . wished that the needy aged and feeble-minded could be chloroformed." Anthony J. Badger, *The New Deal: The Depression Years, 1933–40* (New York, 1989), p. 194.

25. *New York Times,* February 23, 1980.

26. *Washington Post,* December 30, 1980; February 23, 1980.

27. Trombley, *Right to Reproduce,* pp. 245–48.

28. *Washington Post,* December 13, 1980; Vose, *Constitutional Change,* p. 113; Berns, "Buck v. Bell," p. 773.

29. J. H. Landman, quoted in Coogan, "Eugenic Sterilization," p. 47. See, too, Richard A. Estacio, "Sterilization of the Mentally Disabled in Pennsylvania: Three Generations Without Legislative Guidance Are Enough," *Dickinson Law Review,* 92 (Winter 1988), 409–36.

30. Quoted in Elliott A. Brown, "Case Histories, Interest Group Litigation, and Mr. Justice Holmes: Some Unexplored Questions on Psycho-Political Behavior," *Emory Law Journal,* 24 (1975), 1070–71n. Indicative of the large critical literature challenging Holmes's philosophical assumptions are Francis E. Lucey, "Holmes: Liberal—Humanitarian—Believer in Democracy?," *Georgetown Law*

Journal, 39 (May 1951), 523–62; and Ben W. Palmer, "Hobbes, Holmes, Hitler," *American Bar Association Journal,* 31 (November 1945), 569–73. Charles E. Wyzanski offers a spirited defense in "The Democracy of Justice Holmes," *Vanderbilt Law Review,* 7 (April 1954), 311–24. "The damned trouble with Holmes," Henry Luce once remarked, "is that his devotees are always saying he didn't really mean what he said—and I guess he didn't." Luce to John M. Vorys, March 12, 1957, Vorys MSS, Ohio Historical Society, Columbus, Ohio, Box 85. For the changes in Holmes's reputation over time, see Samuel Krislov, "O. W. Holmes: The Ebb and Flow of Judicial Legendry," *Northwestern University Law Review,* 52 (September-October 1957), 514–25.

31. Berns, "Buck v. Bell," pp. 763–66. Berns's allusions are to three cases that are regarded as landmarks in the expansion of civil liberties. In *Gitlow v. New York* (268 U.S. 653 (1925)), the Court first acknowledged that a First Amendment guarantee was incorporated in the Fourteenth Amendment. In *Hague v. CIO* (397 U.S. 496 (1939)), the Court struck down an ordinance put through by the autocratic mayor of Jersey City, Frank Hague, as a violation of the right of assembly. And in *West Virginia State Board of Education v. Barnette* (319 U.S. 628 (1943)), the Court, discarding a recent precedent, invalidated a law requiring school pupils to salute the flag, a ritual that conflicted with the religious precepts of the Jehovah's Witnesses.

32. Oliver Wendell Holmes, Jr., "Law and Social Reform," in Max Lerner, ed., *The Mind and Faith of Justice Holmes* (Boston, 1943), p. 400; Irving Bernstein, "The Conservative Mr. Justice Holmes," *New England Quarterly,* 23 (December 1950), 435; Holmes, "Montesquieu," in Lerner, *Mind and Faith,* p. 378.

33. Holmes, "Ideals and Doubts," *Illinois Law Review,* 10 (May 1915), 3; Holmes, "Law and Social Reform," in Lerner, ed., *Mind and Faith,* pp. 28, 401; Holmes to Dr. Wu, July 21, 1925, quoted in David H. Burton, *Oliver Wendell Holmes, Jr.* (Boston, 1980), p. 141.

34. James Bishop Peabody, ed., *Holmes-Einstein Letters* (New York, 1964), p. 267; Howe, ed., *Holmes-Laski Letters,* 2: 942, 939.

35. Coogan, "Eugenic Sterilization," p. 46; Samuel Joseph Konefsky, *The Legacy of Holmes and Brandeis* (New York, 1956), p. 183; Larry Martin Roth, "Touched with Fire, Forged in Flame: Holmes and a Different Perspective: Symposium—Mr. Justice Holmes: The Man and His Legacy," *University of Florida Law Review,* 28 (Winter 1976), 368. In 1922, Brandeis said, according to Felix Frankfurter's notes, "Holmes has no realization of what moves men—he is as innocent as a girl of sixteen is supposed to have been. And most of the time it doesn't matter in his position. Goes off sometimes in construing statutes because he doesn't understand or appreciate facts." Melvin I. Urofsky, ed., " The Brandeis-Frankfurter Conversations," *Supreme Court Review 1985,* p. 307.

36. Cynkar, *"Buck v. Bell,"* p. 1458; *Commonwealth v. Pear,* 183 Mass. 242, 248, 66 N. E. 719, 72 (1903), cited in Cynkar, *"Buck v. Bell,"* pp. 1458–59; John B. Gest, "Eugenic Sterilization: Justice Holmes vs. Natural Law," *Temple Law Quarterly,* 23 (April 1950), 307; Charles P. Kindregan, "Sixty Years of Compulsory Eugenic Sterilization: 'Three Generations of Imbeciles' and the Constitution of

the United States," *Chicago-Kent Law Review*, 43 (Fall 1966), 143; Martin B. Hickman, "Mr. Justice Holmes: A Reappraisal," *Western Political Quarterly*, 5 (March 1952), 71. Holmes did not even get the nomenclature right. Carrie Buck graded out not as an "imbecile" but as a moron. For another devastating attack on Holmes's opinion, see Rogat, "Mr. Justice Holmes," 282–91.

37. Sheldon M. Novick, *Honorable Justice: The Life of Oliver Wendell Holmes* (Boston, 1989), pp. 351–52. It appears likely that most, perhaps all, of the Justices shared Holmes's hereditarian outlook.

38. Kevles, *In the Name of Eugenics*, p. 109; Trombley, *Right to Reproduce*, p. 99; Walter Lippmann, "The Mystery of the 'A' Men," *New Republic*, November 1, 1922, p. 246.

39. Chase, *Legacy of Malthus*, pp. 315, 317. Dysgenics is the study of what causes degeneration in offspring. The claim that "universal agreement was reached during the 1920s on the propriety of passing compulsory sterilization statutes" (Chesler, *Woman of Valor*, p. 215) is a gross overstatement.

40. John M. Conley, " 'The First Principle of Real Reform': The Role of Science in Constitutional Jurisprudence," *North Carolina Law Review*, 65 (June 1987), 939.

41. Chase, *Legacy of Malthus*, p. 315.

42. Jules B. Gerard, "Capacity to Govern," *Harvard Journal of Law and Social Policy*, 12 (Winter 1989), 107–10.

43. *Holmes-Laski Letters*, 1: 249; Mary L. Dudziak, "Oliver Wendell Holmes as a Eugenic Reformer: Rhetoric in the Writing of Constitutional Law," *Iowa Law Review*, 71 (March 1986), 856.

44. *Meyer v. Nebraska*, 262 U.S. 390 (1923).

45. Smith and Nelson, *Sterilization of Carrie Buck*, pp. 213–21; Lombardo, "Three Generations," pp. 60–61; Gould, "Carrie Buck's Daughter," p. 18.

46. The Court has twice, though, come close. In 1942, it took under consideration the case of Arthur Skinner, a convicted chicken thief and armed robber, who had fallen under the provisions of Oklahoma's Habitual Criminal Sterilization Act which applied to those who had committed three felonies but exempted criminals such as embezzlers. The Court struck down the law because it took seriously the equal protection claim that Holmes had scoffed at as an argument of "last resort." Justice Jackson also suggested a willingness to deal with the substantive issue. He declared, "There are limits to the extent to which a legislatively represented majority may conduct biological experiments at the expense of the dignity and personality and natural powers of a minority—even those who have been guilty of what the majority define as crime." *Skinner v. Oklahoma*, 316 U.S. 535 (1942) at 546. See, too, Stone's concurrence at 544.

In 1969 the Court appeared ready to rule on the vitality of *Buck v. Bell*. A Nebraska law required patients at the Beatrice State Home (for the mentally defective) to agree to sterilization as a condition for release, and when one Gloria Cavitt refused to be operated on, the state board of examiners ordered the operation anyway, despite the objections of her appointed guardian. The guardian, an attorney, brought suit, but the Nebraska Supreme Court sustained the board's action. The U.S. Supreme Court then noted probable jurisdiction. The Nebraska legislature, however, not only repealed the law, but added a stipulation that "no sterilization could be done even though a pending Court order indicated otherwise," words specifically designed to spare Gloria Cavitt. No operation was performed, and Cavitt was released, thus rendering the case moot. Vose, *Constitutional Change*, p. 19.

47. Raleigh *News and Observer*, January 20, 1983. For developments over the past two decades, see Edward J. Spriggs, Jr., "Involuntary Sterilization: An Unconstitutional Menace to Minorities and the Poor." *New York University Review of Law and Social Change*, 4 (Spring 1974), 127–51; Richard K. Sherlock and Robert D. Sherlock, "Sterilizing the Retarded: Constitutional, Statutory and Policy Alternatives," *North Carolina Law Review*, 60 (1982), 943–83; and Elizabeth S. Scott, "Sterilization of Mentally Retarded Persons: Reproductive Rights and Family Privacy," *Duke Law Journal*, (November 1986), 806–65.

48. Even under the 1981 law, however, Virginia remained one of ten states permitting coercive sterilization of the mentally retarded under certain circumstances. For understanding subsequent developments in Virginia, I have greatly benefited from reading an excellent paper written for my graduate seminar at the University of North Carolina at Chapel Hill: Brian Matney, "One Day Before Spring: Practical Eugenics and the History of Virginia's Sterilization Law."

49. *Washington Post*, February 23, 1980.

2. Mr. Justice Roberts and the Railroaders

1. W. Fred Cottrell, *The Railroader* (Stanford, Cal., 1940), p. 17; G. H. Burck, "Another Golden Age Goes Haywire," *American Mercury*, 26 (July 1932), 315; "Accident Experience of American Steam Railroads in 1934," *Monthly Labor Review*, 42 (February 1936), 373.

2. Cottrell, *Railroader*, p. 83.

3. Ibid., pp. 83, 96.

4. Herbert Harris, *American Labor* (New Haven, 1938), p. 250. The brotherhoods gained added strength when amendments to the Railway Labor Act in 1934 spurred the displacement of company unions; from 1933 to 1935, a total of 550 company unions gave way to national unions.

5. Burck, "Another Golden Age," p. 318.

6. John F. Stover, *The Life and Decline of the American Railroad* (New York, 1970), pp. 156, 178.

7. Carlton J. Corliss, *Main Line of Mid-America: The Story of the Illinois Central* (New York, 1950), p. 428.

8. Earl Latham, *The Politics of Railroad Coordination, 1933–1936* (Cambridge, Mass., 1959), p. 8; H. M. Douty, "Ferment in the Railroad Unions," *Nation*, November 30, 1932, p. 526.

9. Anthony J. Badger, *The New Deal: The Depression Years, 1933–40* (New York, 1989), p. 13.

10. U.S. Department of Labor, *Earnings and Standard of Living of 1,000 Railway Employees During the Depression* (Washington, 1934); *New Republic*, October 17, 1934, pp. 257–58; "Earnings and Living Standards of Railway Employees During the Depression," *Monthly Labor Review*, 39 (October 1934), 855–56.

11. Cottrell, *Railroader*, pp. 85–86.

12. Herman L. Ekern, "Railroad Pensions," *American Labor Legislation Review*, 24 (September 1934), 124–25.

13. Reed C. Richardson, *The Locomotive Engineer, 1863–1963* (Ann Arbor, 1963), pp. 395–96; *New York Times*, June 27, 1934.

14. Domenico Gagliardo, *American Social Insurance* (New York, 1949), p. 139.

15. *New York Times*, July 2, 1934.

16. Samuel I. Rosenman, ed., *The Public Papers and Addresses of Franklin D. Roosevelt* (13 vols., New York, 1938–50), 3: 329–30. Even the sponsor of the rail pension bill acknowledged "that the President hesitated about signing the bill on account of the financial question involved." Robert Crosser to J. L. Milligan, July 20, 1934, Crosser MSS, Ohio Historical Society, Columbus, Ohio, Box 5. See, too, Claude Moore Fuess, *Joseph B. Eastman* (New York, 1952), p. 225.

17. *Alton R. R. Co. v. R. R. Retirement Board*, 62 Wash. L. Rep. 833 (Sup. Ct. D. C. 1934).

18. *Nation*, August 22, 1934, p. 218.

19. Harold M. Stephens to Felix Frankfurter, February 19, 1935, Frankfurter to Stephens, April 24, 1935, Stephens MSS, Library of Congress (LC), Box 14.

20. *Railroad Retirement Board et al. v. Alton Railroad Co. et al.*, 295 U.S. 330 (1935). All subsequent quotations from the opinions are located here. Alton Railroad figured so prominently in the case merely because it was alphabetically first on the list of the Class I carriers challenging the Act.

21. "The Court Rules Out Security," *Nation*, May 22, 1935, p. 588. The author of the anonymous piece is identified in H. M. S., "Memorandum for the Attorney General," May 21, 1935, Stephens MSS, Box 124.

22. Charles A. Beard, "Social Change v. the Constitution," *Current History*, 42 (July 1935), 345.

23. Benjamin Cardozo to Charles Evans Hughes, April 19, 1935, Stone MSS, LC, Box 61. Cardozo, in the final sentence quoted, misconstrues Roberts's argument for Roberts never went so far as to say that the government should instruct the railroads to discharge workers.

24. Hughes also dealt with an issue that the majority never reached—the fact that the law applied to railroad employees such as bookkeepers who were not actively engaged in interstate commerce. The Chief Justice noted that a generation earlier the Court had validated such coverage for interstate carriers.

25. *Washington Post*, May 7, 1935; *News-Week*, May 11, 1935, p. 18; James M. Beck to John A. Garver, May 23, 1935, Beck MSS, Princeton University, Princeton, N. J., Box 4.

26. "Roberts," Drew Pearson MSS, Lyndon B. Johnson Library, Austin, Tex., F 168.

27. Leonard Baker, *Back to Back* (New York, 1967), pp. 123–24.

28. Walter Lippmann, *Interpretations, 1933–1935* (New York, 1936), p. 278.

29. U.S. Congress, *Hearings Before a Subcommittee of the Committee on the Judiciary, U.S. Senate,* 83d Cong., 2d sess., on S. J. Res. 44 (Washington, 1954), pp. 8–9.

30. Felix Frankfurter to Louis Brandeis, May 7, 1935, Brandeis MSS, University of Louisville Law Library, Louisville, Ky., G 9; P. J. Hasey to FDR, May 6, 1935, NA Department of Justice 235460; Fred Rodell, *Nine Men* (New York, 1955), pp. 232–33; Robert H. Jackson, *The Struggle for Judicial Supremacy* (New York, 1941), pp. 104–5. See, too, George Read Nutter MS. Diary, Nutter MSS, Massachusetts Historical Society, Boston, Mass., May 7, 1935.

31. "A Dred Scott Decision," *New Republic,* May 22, 1935, pp. 34–35. "God knows there ought to be more brimstone and vitriol in the composition," Frankfurter wrote the editor of the *New Republic.* Felix Frankfurter to Bruce Bliven, May 9, 1935, Frankfurter MSS, LC, Box 25.

32. "The Court Rules Out Security," *Nation,* p. 588.

33. Charles E. Clark to Thomas Corcoran, April 26, 1937, Corcoran MSS, LC, Box 192. In addition, he found one favorable and one adverse prior to the Supreme Court decision, a curious category.

34. *Columbia Law Review,* 35 (June 1935), 933–34; *St. John's Law Review,* 10 (December 1935), 57; *Minnesota Law Review,* 20 (December 1935), 55.

35. Samuel Hendel, *Charles Evans Hughes and the Supreme Court* (New York, 1951), pp. 231–32; Thomas Reed Powell, "Commerce, Pensions and Codes, II," *Harvard Law Review,* 49 (November 1935), 15.

36. *Fordham Law Review,* 4 (November 1935), 500–501; *American Labor Legislation Review,* 25 (June 1935), 87.

37. *New York Times,* May 7, 1935; *Washington Post,* May 7, 1935; New York *Herald Tribune,* May 7, 1935.

38. Harlan Fiske Stone to Felix Frankfurter, May 9, 1935; Stone to Frankfurter, August 10, 1935, Frankfurter MSS, LC, Box 105; Stone to Thomas Reed Powell, May 31, 1935, Stone MSS, Box 24; Stone to Marshall and Lauson Stone, May 9, 1935, Stone MSS, Box 3; *Lochner v. New York,* 198 U.S. 45 (1905). "Your article in the *New Republic* on the *Railroad Retirement* case is great," Stone wrote Frankfurter. "It gets at the kernel of the matter." Harlan Fiske Stone to Felix Frankfurter, May 21, 1935, Stone MSS, Box 13.

39. *New York Times,* May 7, 1935; Edward Keating MS. Diary, May 6, 1935, Keating MSS, Western Historical Collections, University of Colorado, Boulder, Col. See, too, D. B. Robertson to FDR, January 22, 1936, National Archives (NA) Department of Justice 235460; *Business Week,* May 11, 1935, p. 8.

40. Edward Keating MS. Diary, May 7, 11, 1935.

41. Ibid., May 13, 15, 1935. See, too, copy of H. R. 8100, Robert Crosser MSS, Box 6.

42. James C. Duram, "The Labor Union Journals and the Constitutional Issues of the New Deal: The Case for Court Restriction," *Labor History,* 15 (Spring 1974), 219–20.

43. Rexford G. Tugwell MS. Diary, May 9, 1935, Tugwell MSS, Franklin

D. Roosevelt Library (FDRL), Hyde Park, N. Y.; Harry Hopkins MS. Diary, May 12, 1935, Hopkins MSS, FDRL, Box 6; Harold M. Stephens, Memorandum for the Attorney General, May 6, 1935, Stephens MSS, Box 136; Edward Keating MS. Diary, May 21, 1935, Keating MSS. Andrew Mellon, Secretary of the Treasury in the Republican administrations of the 1920s, was regarded as the personification of government on behalf of the rich.

44. *Literary Digest*, May 18, 1935, p. 12; Thomas Creigh to Paul Shoup, May 7, 1935, Shoup MSS, Stanford University, Stanford, Cal., Box 1. See, too, *New York Times*, May 12, 1935; Baltimore *Sun*, May 6, 1935; St. Louis *Post-Dispatch*, May 6, 1935.

45. *Business Week*, May 11, 1935, pp. 7, 36.

46. H. S. C., Memorandum for Mr. MacLean, May 11, 1935, NA Department of Justice 235773.

3. The Case of the Contentious Commissioner

1. *Schechter v. U.S.*, 295 U.S. 553; *Dred Scott v. Sandford*, 19 How. 393 (1857). I am happy to acknowledge my indebtedness to an exemplary paper on the *Humphrey* and *Myers* cases, "Two Against the President," prepared for a graduate colloquium on the American political process at Columbia University by John W. Chambers.

2. See, for example, C. Perry Patterson, *Presidential Government in the United States* (Chapel Hill, 1947), p. 153.

3. Edward Keating MS. Diary, May 27, 1935, Keating MSS, Western Historical Collections, University of Colorado, Boulder, Col.

4. W. E. Humphrey to C. B. Bagley, February 3, 1912, Bagley MSS, University of Washington, Seattle, Wash. The letters in these and other collections at the University of Washington were kindly made available to me on microfilm by Richard C. Berner and Robert E. Burke.

5. Humphrey to E. G. Eames [sic], October 29, 1906, Edwin G. Ames MSS, University of Washington.

6. Jones to Joshua Green, April 10, 1917; Dollar to Jones, April 12, 1917; Tacoma *Times*, May 4, 1917, clipping, Wesley Jones MSS, University of Washington.

7. G. Cullom Davis, "The Transformation of the Federal Trade Commission, 1914–1929," *Mississippi Valley Historical Review*, 49 (December 1962), 447. See, too, Humphrey to E. G. Ames, October 27, 1919, Ames MSS.

8. Claudius O. Johnson, "George William Norris," in J. T. Salter, ed., *The American Politician* (Chapel Hill, 1938), p. 90. See, too, Robert W. Bingham to Ulric Bell, August 2, 1937, Bingham MSS, Library of Congress (LC), Box 24.

9. Thomas C. Blaisdell, Jr., *The Federal Trade Commission* (New York, 1932), p. 82.

10. G. Cullom Davis, "Transformation of FTC," pp. 448–51.

11. Pinchot to Humphrey, February 22, 1928; Humphrey to Pinchot, n.

d., Humphrey MSS, LC, Box 1. See, too, mimeographed statements, William E. Humphrey MSS, Box 2; Humphrey to Coolidge, October 10, 1927, Humphrey MSS, Box 1.

12. For the role of the courts, see Myron W. Watkins, "An Appraisal of the Work of the Federal Trade Commission," *Columbia Law Review*, 32 (February 1932), 278.

13. Humphrey to Arthur Robinson, January 27, 1928, Humphrey MSS, Box 1; Robert E. Cushman, *The Independent Regulatory Commissions* (New York, 1941), p. 226.

14. James M. Landis, "The Legislative History of the Securities Act of 1933," *George Washington Law Review*, 28 (October 1959), 34.

15. Memorandum, Franklin D. Roosevelt Library (FDRL), Hyde Park, N. Y., OF 100, Box 1. Roosevelt misspelled Ferguson's name. The entry "Perk" is bewildering. It could conceivably be shorthand for "perquisites," but that seems improbable; it appears to refer to a person and someone Roosevelt knew well enough to use an abbreviation. The obvious name is that of Frances Perkins, but if he thought, at this early stage, of moving her from her post as Secretary of Labor (and that seems highly unlikely), it could only have been a passing thought.

16. Humphrey to FDR, July 19, 1933, FDRL OF 100, Box 2. See, too, E. D. Smith to FDR, July 13, 1933.

17. Humphrey to Dill, July 25, 1933; Dill to FDR, July 28, 1933, Humphrey MSS, Box 1. For Humphrey's conception of loyalty, see Pendleton Herring, "The Federal Trade Commissioners," *George Washington Law Review*, 8 (January-February 1940), 353. As early as 1912 he had telegraphed: "In view of attitude of Star and the rest of outfit of Anarchists can you not persuade Dovall to stop fighting me for judgeship. I feel that I have a right to ask my friends to protect my reputation." Humphrey to E. G. Ames, January 15, 1912, Ames MSS.

18. FDR to Humphrey, July 25, 1933, FDRL OF 100, Box 2.

19. Humphrey to FDR, August 1, 1933; FDR to Humphrey, August 4, 1933, Humphrey MSS, Box 1.

20. Humphrey to C. C. Dill, August 29, 1933, Humphrey MSS, Box 1.

21. Humphrey to FDR, August 11, 1933, Humphrey MSS, Box 1.

22. Humphrey to Dill, August 18, 1933, Humphrey MSS, Box 1.

23. Dill to Humphrey, August 21, 22, 1933; Humphrey to C. C. Dill, August 28, 1933, Humphrey MSS, Box 1. Dill's second note addressed him as "Dear Humphreys." Humphrey's hometown newspaper, the Seattle *Times*, which may have had access to confidential information, stated: "In the present instance he is acting under the advice of Republican Senate leaders." *Congressional Record*, 73d Cong., 2d sess., p. 1682.

24. Moreover, by now, Dill, understandably, was miffed. He replied to Humphrey: "I assure you I never for one moment thought our friendship was strained. I have done more for you than I ever did for any Republican in this country." C. C. Dill to Humphrey, September 1, 1933, Humphrey MSS, Box 1.

25. FDR to Marvin H. McIntyre, August 18, 1933; Stephen T. Early to FDR, August 17, 1933, FDRL OF 100, Box 1.

26. William Stanley to Stephen T. Early, August 19, 1933; R. F. to Early, August 22, 1933; Raymond Stevens to FDR, August 26, 1933; Stevens to Cummings, August 26, 1933; Memorandum, probably from Stevens, n. d., FDRL OF 100, Box 2.

27. FDR to Humphrey, August 31, 1933, Humphrey MSS, Box 1.

28. Harold L. Ickes MS. Diary, LC, June 4, 1935; A. A. Berle, Jr. MS. Diary, Berle MSS (privately held), September 14, 1937. Mr. Berle permitted me to read his diaries in his office in Manhattan.

29. Humphrey to C. C. Dill, September 2, 1933; Humphrey to FDR, September 11, 1933, Humphrey MSS, Box 1.

30. Humphrey to McCarthy, September 17, 1933; McCarthy to FDR, September 18, 1933, FDRL OF 100, Box 2; Omaha *World Herald*, n. d., clipping; Humphrey to FDR, September 27, 1933, Humphrey MSS, Box 1.

31. Mathews to M. J. McIntyre, October 3, 1933, and McIntyre's notations, FDRL OF 100, Box 2; FDR to Mathews, October 7, 1933, FDRL OF 100, Box 1; FDR to Humphrey, October 7, 1933, Humphrey MSS, Box 1.

32. Humphrey to FDR, October 10, 1933, Humphrey MSS, Box 1. Humphrey added: "This letter will probably be withheld from you. If not, one of your secretaries will probably disclose to you the facts which have influenced him to join so persistently in the demand for my removal. He knows that he arranged over the White House telephone for a certain attorney to have a personal interview with me. In that interview, the attorney demanded that I in my official capacity, as a Member of the Federal Trade Commission, take certain action favorable to his clients in a private litigation which was then being prosecuted. I refused to accede to his demands, and I was sustained in this action by the unanimous vote of the Commission."

33. A memorandum from "M. B. H.," undated but penciled "September," stated: "I hope Mr. H. will preserve his inchoate right to accruing salary by appearing regularly at each regular session, even though it be but to acquiesce in the action of the Commission in excluding him and bowing himself out." Humphrey MSS, Box 1.

34. Humphrey to Mathews, October 9, 1933; Humphrey to FTC, FTC to Humphrey, October 9, 1933; Press release, FTC, October 9, 1933; Humphrey to Rudolph Schwickardi, October 9, October 17, 1933; Humphrey to Otis Johnson, *et al.*, November 2, 1933; R. L. Golze to R. B. Schwickardi, November 11, 1933, Humphrey MSS, Box 1; *New York Times*, October 10, 1933.

35. Humphrey to Donovan, October 20, 1933, Humphrey MSS, Box 1.

36. Humphrey to Donovan, January 19, 1934, Humphrey MSS, Box 1.

37. *Congressional Record*, 73d Cong., 2d sess., pp. 1679–84; 1289–91. Norman Thomas was the leader of the Socialists. Cushman overstated the matter in writing that Roosevelt's action "evoked no protest in either house of Congress and practically no comment." Cushman, *Independent Regulatory Commissions*,

p. 226. In addition to these few protests in Congress, widespread objections in newspaper editorials greeted news of the ouster.

38. The actual docket title of the case was *Rathbun, Executor v. United States*, and, consequently, some commentators refer to it as the *Rathbun* case. But it is more generally known as *Humphrey's Executor v. U.S.*

39. Lewis Wood, "A Hard-Working Lawyer Joins the High Court," *New York Times Magazine*, January 30, 1938, p. 9; Leonard Baker, *Back to Back* (New York, 1967), p. 115; Stanley Reed, Columbia Oral History Collection (COHC), Columbia University, New York, N.Y., p. 173. The unedited transcript of that interview is in the Reed MSS, University of Kentucky, Lexington, Ky., Box 282.

40. 19 Stat. 80, 81 (1876), U.S. Comp. Stat. (1916) 7190.

41. *Shurtleff v. United States*, 189 U.S. 311, 316–17 (1902). See, too, *Ex parte Hennen*, 13 Pet. 230, 258 (1839); *Parsons v. U.S.*, 167 U.S. 324, 339 (1897); Carl Russell Fish, "Removal of Officials by the Presidents of the United States," *Annual Report of the American Historical Association: The Year 1899* (2 vols., Washington, 1900), 1: 67–86.

42. Alpheus Thomas Mason, *Harlan Fiske Stone* (New York, 1956), p. 231n.

43. Mason, *Stone*, pp. 222–31; Mason, *William Howard Taft: Chief Justice* (New York, 1965), pp. 225–55; Henry F. Pringle, *The Life and Times of William Howard Taft* (2 vols., Hamden, Ct., 1964), 2: 1023–27; Taft to Stone, n. d.; Taft to Stone, December 26, 1925, Stone MSS, LC, Box 54.

44. 272 U.S. 52 (1926) at 135. James M. Landis has noted: "Some efforts were made to remove this unnecessary dictum but Taft was adamant." Landis, "Mr. Justice Brandeis: A Law Clerk's View," *Publication of the American Jewish Historical Society*, 46 (June 1957), 472. Authorities differ on the number of pages consumed by each opinion; I have followed the pagination in the *U.S. Reports*.

45. Mason, *Stone*, p. 231.

46. 272 U.S. at 177.

47. 272 U.S. 178 (1926); *Perry v. United States*, 294 U.S. 330 and other cases. Taft wrote of McReynolds's performance in the *Myers* case: "His exhibition in the Court room was such as to disgust Holmes." Mason, *Taft*, p. 227.

48. New York *Herald Tribune*, October 26, 1926.

49. James M. Landis COHC, pp. 37–39.

50. Mason, *Taft*, p. 226. Taft observed: "Brandeis can not avoid writing an opinion in a way in which he wishes to spread himself, as if he were writing an article for the Harvard Law Review."

51. 272 U.S. 240–95, especially at 293–95. The dissents, Stone wrote Taft, "have rather assumed that the people speak only through legislation, forgetting for the moment that the people spoke through the Constitution, and the legislative branch, as well as other branches of the government, have only such powers as were conferred upon it by the Constitution." Stone to Taft, March 29, 1926, Stone MSS, Box 54.

52. *De Lima v. Bidwell,* 182 U.S. 1 (1901) and others.

53. Powell, "Spinning Out the Executive Powers," *New Republic,* 48 (November 17, 1926), 369; *New York Times,* November 7, 16, 1926; Morton Keller, *In Defense of Yesterday* (New York, 1958), p. 181; George B. Galloway, "The Consequences of the Myers Decision," *American Law Review,* 61 (July-August 1927), 481–508; James Hart, "Tenure of Office Under the Constitution," *Johns Hopkins University Studies in Historical and Political Science,* Extra Volumes, New Series, No. 9 (Baltimore, 1930); George Wharton Pepper, *Family Quarrels* (New York, 1931), p. 124; Wilson K. Doyle, *Independent Commissions in the Federal Government* (Chapel Hill, 1939), pp. 23–24.

54. Corwin, *The President's Removal Power under the Constitution* (New York, 1927), p. 3.

55. Stevens to FDR, August 26, 1933, FDRL OF 100, Box 2. For doubt about whether the *Myers* precedent applied to the removal of members of independent commissions, see Huston Thompson MS. Diary, Thompson MSS, LC, April 23, 1933, Thompson MSS, Box 1.

56. Most law journals that committed themselves expressed approval. Doyle, *Independent Commissions,* p. 24; *Illinois Law Review,* 21 (March 1927), 733–36; *Oregon Law Review,* 6 (February 1927), 165–71; *Virginia Law Review,* 13 (December 1926), 122–27; *Michigan Law Review,* 25 (January 1927), 280–87. However, most of the commentators ignored Taft's dictum, and the *Michigan Law Review,* while supporting the Chief Justice's opinion, denied that members of the Federal Trade Commission were now "subject to the President's pleasures or caprice." *Loc. cit.,* at 287.

57. *University of Cincinnati Law Review,* 1 (January 1927), 74–79. Corwin, the chief critic of the decision, went so far as to state that laws like the FTC act were now "void." Corwin, *President's Removal Power,* p. 7. See, too, the discussion in Hart, "Tenure of Office," pp. 369–73, taking off from *Springer et al. v. Philippine Islands,* 277 U.S. 189 (1928).

58. Albert Langeluttig, " 'The Bearing of Myers v. United States Upon the Independence of Federal Administrative Tribunals'—A Criticism," *American Political Science Review,* 24 (February 1950), 65.

59. J. M. Landis COHC, pp. 39–41. Landis added: "My own feelings were a little curious, because I'd been with Brandeis on the dissent in the Myers case, and if I had had an independent opportunity to look at the situation, I would have been on the side of Humphrey. But having the background that I did, I had a feeling that there was a certain amount of precedent that would govern here, and that the answer would be that." Myers, it should be noted, was a first-class, not a "fourth-class," postmaster.

60. Certificate from the Court of Claims, filed January 26, 1935, U.S. Briefs 1934, No. 405.

61. Both arguments are printed in 295 U.S. 604–18 (1935). There is a transcript of Reed's argument in Reed MSS, Box 7.

62. *Washington Post,* May 28, 1935.

63. *Humphrey's Executor v. United States,* 295 U.S. 602 (1935).

64. Joel Paschal, *Mr. Justice Sutherland* (Princeton, 1951), pp. 184–85. It is possible that more than one of these men may have tried to persuade Taft to modify his opinion. Yet their objections were not strong enough for them to have filed a concurrence, let alone a dissent.

A half-year after *Humphrey* was handed down, Stone, who was often indiscreet, told Colonel Donovan, as Donovan noted in his diary: "Taft developed a fantastic idea. He said Taft knew that case was all wrong historically. He, Stone, was new on the Court and, while he had no doubt of the correctness of the decision in the Myers' case, he felt that Taft was all wrong in his history and, particularly, in extending the power of the Executive in the case of all officers. He said he had labored with Taft and got him to take out other paragraphs, but he couldn't get him to take this one out." William J. Donovan MS. Diary, Donovan MSS, U.S. Army Military History Institute, Carlisle Barracks, Pa., November 29, 1935.

The Court, it should be added, did not embrace the extreme view that Congress could limit the President's power to remove purely executive officers. McReynolds, who apparently believed the Court had not gone far enough, concurred in the Sutherland opinion but noted tersely that his dissent in *Myers* had stated "his views concerning the power of the President to remove appointees." 295 U.S. at 632.

65. Cushman, *Independent Regulatory Commissions*, pp. 450–51. See, too, *Columbia Law Review*, 35 (June 1935), 936–38; *Harvard Law Review*, 49 (December 1935), 330–31.

66. Edward S. Corwin, *The President: Office and Powers 1787–1957* (New York, 1957), p. 93.

67. Cushman, *Independent Regulatory Commissions*, pp. 177–213; 445–46.

68. Ibid., pp. 447–48. For the subsequent history of the removal power, see Louis W. Koenig, *The Chief Executive* (New York, 1964), p. 159; Arthur Larson, "Has the President an Inherent Power of Removal of His Non-Executive Appointments?" *Tennessee Law Review*, 16 (March 1940), 259–90; *Morgan v. Tennessee Valley Authority*, 115 F. 2d 990 (6th Circ. 1940); Cert. denied, 312 U.S. 701 (1941); *Wiener v. U.S.*, 357 U.S. 349 (1958); *George Washington Law Review*, 27 (October 1958), 129–32; Corwin, *The President: Office and Powers*, pp. 85–86; Patterson, *Presidential Government in the United States*, p. 153; Doyle, *Independent Commissions*, pp. 30–31.

69. Arthur M. Johnson, "The Federal Trade Commission: The Early Years, 1915–1935," in Joseph R. Frees, S. J. Judd, and Jacob Judd, eds., *Business and Government* (Tarrytown, N. Y., 1985), pp. 168, 180; clippings, David J. Lewis MSS, Duke University, Durham, N. C.

70. Cushman, *Independent Regulatory Commissions*, pp. 222–26.

71. Ibid., pp. 410–15. When the *Humphrey* decision was delivered, Congress was in the process of enacting the Wagner labor bill. After the ruling was handed down, Congress modified the measure to stipulate that the National Labor Relations Board was to be an agent of Congress, not the President. Ibid., pp. 363–66.

72. Cushman, *Independent Regulatory Commissions*, p. 418; *Congressional Record*, 73d Cong., 2d sess., p. 1679.

73. Edgar J. Goodrich, Former Member of the United States Board of Tax Appeals, in *New York Times*, June 2, 1935. See, too, S. Chesterfield Oppenheim, "Federal Trade Commission Silver Anniversary Issue: Foreword," *George Washington Law Review*, 8 (January-February 1940), 253.

74. A. T. Mason, *Brandeis: A Free Man's Life* (New York, 1946), p. 619. See, too, James M. Landis, *The Administrative Process* (New Haven, 1938), p. 115.

75. Felix Frankfurter to Bruce Bliven, June 1, 1935, Frankfurter MSS, Box 25.

76. Humphrey to C. C. Dill, August 18, 1933; Humphrey to Norris, October 4, 1933; Humphrey MSS, Box 1; *Congressional Record*, 73d Cong., 2d sess., pp. 1290–91. Emphasis added.

77. Humphrey to Jerry A. Mathews, September 22, 1933, Humphrey MSS, Box 1.

78. E. Pendleton Herring, "Politics, Personalities, and the Federal Trade Commission," *American Political Science Review*, 28 (December 1934), 1020–21; Herring, "Politics, Personalities, and the Federal Trade Commission: II," *American Political Science Review*, 29 (February 1935), 31. In 1934, administration of the Securities Act was turned over to a newly created agency, the Securities and Exchange Commission.

79. Raymond Moley, *After Seven Years* (New York, 1939), p. 128; Herring, "Politics, Personalities and the Federal Trade Commission: II," pp. 32–33. As early as 1933, Roosevelt had told Secretary of Commerce Daniel Roper, "I'd like to see all the independent commissions brought under the general supervision of Cabinet officers." Early in 1936, he set up a Committee on Administrative Management which described tribunals like the FTC as "a headless 'fourth branch' of the government" that diminished the authority of the President in whom the Constitution invested the executive power. But the Reorganization bill of 1937, which authorized the President either to place these tribunals in a department or to abolish them outright, went down to defeat in 1938, in part because the independent commissions, as rival power centers, were able to rally opposition to it. The chairman of the FTC, in particular, spoke out against it. Richard Polenberg, *Reorganizing Roosevelt's Government* (Cambridge, Mass., 1966); Robert E. Cushman, "Independent Boards and Commissions and Their Relation to the President," typescript, Charles Merriam MSS, University of Chicago, Chicago, Ill., Box 260; Memorandum from H. G. Moulton to Louis Brownlow, March 24, 1937, idem. By 1938, the FTC was one of the agencies exempted from the provisions of the revised bill.

80. Homer Cummings MS. Diary, Cummings MSS, University of Virginia, Charlottesville, Va., May 27, 1935.

81. Felix Frankfurter to C. C. Burlingham, June 9, 1937, Frankfurter MSS, Box 34; Robert H. Jackson, *The Struggle for Judicial Supremacy* (New York, 1941), p. 109. Frankfurter was the author of an opinion in 1958 that reasserted the

Humphrey precedent (*Wiener v. United States,* 357 U.S. 349). One commentator pointed out: "Neither Humphrey nor Wiener actually prevented the President from removing even a quasi-judicial officer. Rather, these cases merely rendered the Government liable for the official's unpaid salary under the general rules of damages." Quoted in Samuel B. Hoff, "The President's Removal Power: Eisenhower and the War Claims Commission Controversy," *Congress & the Presidency,* 18 (Spring 1991), 48. Earlier, Clinton Rossiter had observed, "As the Humphrey case demonstrated and *Wiener v. U.S.* (1958) confirmed, the President can remove just about any official if he wants to badly enough, and the Court will not be able to give the removed man anything more than sympathy and some back salary." Clinton Rossiter, *The American Presidency* (New York, 1960), p. 58.

82. Moley, *After Seven Years,* p. 301; Eugene C. Gerhart, *America's Advocate: Robert H. Jackson* (Indianapolis, 1958), p. 99; Jackson COHC, p. 432. Jackson's allusion to Taft is a bit confusing. It is true that Taft, as Chief Justice, rendered the opinion in *Myers,* but FDR's actual counterpart is not Taft, but Wilson, who fired Myers. Landis later observed: "In those early days of the New Deal, there were some decisions of the Supreme Court of the United States whose sole purpose was to embarrass the President of the United States." Landis COHC, pp. 39–41.

83. Tugwell, *The Democratic Roosevelt,* p. 392. Both here, and in the next quotation, Humphrey is misspelled. For an early statement by a leading constitutional historian in defense of the Court as the guardian of liberty, because of its decision in the *Humphrey* case, see Chicago *Tribune,* June 9, 1935, clipping, Andrew C. McLaughlin MSS, University of Chicago.

84. Joseph Alsop and Turner Catledge, *The 168 Days* (Garden City, N. Y., 1938), pp. 13–14.

85. Flint (Mich.) *Journal,* February 7, 1937, clipping, Prentiss Brown Scrapbooks. I am indebted to Mr. Brown, formerly U.S. Senator from Michigan, whom I interviewed at his home in St. Ignace, Michigan, for permitting me to borrow his scrapbooks and diaries. They were subsequently deposited at the University of Michigan.

86. *Washington Post,* March 6, 1937; Ray Lyman Wilbur to Dr. Arthur Hill Daniels, March 15, 1937, Wilbur MSS, Stanford University, Stanford, Cal. One woman asked: "Is Mr. Roosevelt's venom due to the fact that the nine old men ruled against his injustice in dismissing William E. Humphrey?" Mrs. Barbour Walker to Hon. House of Congress, April 9, 1937, W. W. Ball MSS, Duke University. See, too, Edward H. Neary to Josiah Bailey, n. d. [1937], Bailey MSS, Duke University; Charles W. Tobey to F. T. Wadleigh, February 9, 1937, Tobey MSS, Dartmouth College, Hanover, N. H., Box 78; Frank L. Polk, "Draft (2) Supreme Court Packing Case Opinion," Polk MSS, Yale University, New Haven, Ct., Drawer 86, File 90; New York *Herald Tribune,* May 5, 1937.

87. Tugwell, *Democratic Roosevelt,* p. 400.

4. The Origins of Franklin D. Roosevelt's
"Court-packing" Plan

1. Paul Mallon, "Purely Confidential," Detroit *News*, February 8, April 2, May 21, 1937; Alpheus T. Mason, *Brandeis: A Free Man's Life* (New York, 1946), p. 625; Raymond Moley, *After Seven Years* (New York, 1939), pp. 357–59; Raymond Clapper MS. Diary, February 8, 1937, Clapper MSS, Library of Congress (LC); Frances Perkins, Columbia Oral History Collection (COHC), 7: 128; *Washington Post*, February 13, 1937; *News-Week*, February 13, 1937, p. 9; "America: At Home and Abroad," *Round Table*, 27 (June 1937), 601. This last article also mentioned "an amiable hack politician, Homer S. Cummings." Of Frankfurter, James M. Landis recalled that he "caught hell from him" for supporting the plan. Landis COHC, pp. 49, 302. See, too, Clapper MS. Diary, September 28, 1938; Frank Buxton to William Allen White, June 2, 1937, White MSS, LC, Box 189. For two conflicting recollections of Cohen's role, see Joseph L. Rauh, Jr., "A Personalized View of the Court-Packing Episode," and Warner W. Gardner, "Court Packing: The Drafting Recalled," *Journal of Supreme Court History: 1990 Yearbook of the Supreme Court Historical Society*, pp. 93–103. Rauh has the better of the exchange. His denial of Cohen's role is buttressed by Benjamin V. Cohen to Louis D. Brandeis, July 30, 1937, Thomas G. Corcoran MSS, LC, Box 190. According to one account, some weeks after the plan was announced, a prominent attorney told Ben Cohen, "Everybody in New York thinks you drew the bill," and Cohen replied, "I had nothing to do with it. I never saw or heard of it. I don't like it." C. C. Burlingham to Harlan Fiske Stone, March 12, 1937, Stone MSS, LC, Box 7. When, though, the attorney persisted, "Well, are you against it now?", Cohen answered, "No." Burlingham was reporting on what he had heard from a fellow lawyer. In 1936, Cohen and Corcoran did prepare some material on the Court for Senator Burton K. Wheeler, though the nature of their relationship is in dispute. For Cohen's explanation, see Benjamin V. Cohen to Felix Frankfurter, July 9, 1937, Joseph Lash MSS, Franklin D. Roosevelt Library (FDRL), Hyde Park, N. Y., Box 68.

2. Paul Mallon, "Purely Confidential," Detroit *News*, April 2, 1937; Landis COHC, pp. 44–45; Charles Michelson, *The Ghost Talks* (New York, 1944), pp. 169–70; Eugene C. Gerhart, *America's Advocate: Robert H. Jackson* (Indianapolis, 1958), p. 105; Mark Sullivan in the New York *Herald Tribune*, June 26, 1937; Hiram Johnson to John Francis Neylan, February 26, 1937, Johnson MSS, Bancroft Library, University of California, Berkeley. The least flawed contemporary report is in the *Kiplinger Washington Letter*, February 13, 1937.

3. St. Louis *Star*, June 23, 1930, clipping, Pierce Butler MSS, Minnesota Historical Society, St. Paul, Minn.; Merlo Pusey, *Charles Evans Hughes* (2 vols., New York, 1951), 2: 655–62. One study has noted: "Between 1898 and 1937 the Supreme Court issued some 50 decisions invalidating acts of Congress and about 400 invalidating state laws (as compared to 12 and 125 respectively for the period 1874–98). It seemed as though no progressive social or economic

legislation was constitutionally permissible." Gary L. McDowell, *Curbing the Courts: The Constitution and the Limits of Judicial Power* (Baton Rouge, La., 1988), p. 3.

4. Samuel I. Rosenman, ed., *The Public Papers and Addresses of Franklin D. Roosevelt* (13 vols., New York, 1938–50), 1: 837; James F. Byrnes, *All in One Lifetime* (New York, 1958), p. 65; *New York Times*, February 11, 1937.

5. In the autumn of 1933, Roosevelt received a memorandum stating that of the 266 judges in the federal courts, only 28 percent were Democrats. Homer S. Cummings to FDR, November 8, 1933, FDRL OF 41, Box 114.

6. *New State Ice Co. v. Liebmann*, 285 U.S. 262 (1932).

7. *Public Papers*, 2: 14–15.

8. *Home Building & Loan Ass'n v. Blaisdell*, 290 U.S. 398 (1934); *Nebbia v. New York*, 291 U.S. 502 (1934) at 524. The Court in *Blaisdell* validated a Minnesota mortgage moratorium, and in *Nebbia*, price controls in the New York state milk industry.

9. Homer S. Cummings MS. Diary, Cummings MSS, University of Virginia, Charlottesville, Va., January 17, 1933 (courtesy of Jordan Schwarz).

10. John P. Byrne to FDR, April 18, 1933, FDRL OF 41–A; "News and Comment from the National Capital," *Literary Digest*, January 20, 1934, p. 10.

11. Fletcher to Sullivan, February 28, 1934, Fletcher MSS, LC, Box 16.

12. *Panama Refining Co. v. Ryan*, 293 U.S. 388 (1935); Charles Fahy COHC, p. 148.

13. "New Deal Meets Tests in Supreme Court," *Literary Digest*, January 19, 1935, pp. 5–6. Rexford Guy Tugwell, one of the members of the 1932 Brain Trust and a New Deal official, was a favorite target of the conservative press, in good part because he was known to be an advocate of planning.

14. Arthur M. Schlesinger, Jr., *The Politics of Upheaval* (Boston, 1960), pp. 255–56; *New York Times*, January 15, 1935.

15. Harold L. Ickes MS. Diary, LC, January 11, 1935.

16. Ibid.

17. Brisbane to FDR, February 11, 1935, FDRL OF 41–A, Box 116.

18. Robert Jackson COHC; John M. Blum, *From the Morgenthau Diaries* (Boston, 1959), 1: 126–27.

19. Draft of message, FDRL PSF Supreme Court.

20. *Norman v. B. & O. R. R.*, 294 U.S. 240 (1935), and related cases; Blum, *Morgenthau Diaries*, 1: 130.

21. FDR to Kennedy, February 19, 1935, in Elliott Roosevelt, ed., *F. D. R.: His Personal Letters* (3 vols., New York, 1950), 1: 455.

22. FDR to Angus MacLean, February 21, 1935, FDRL OF 10-F; Norris to Layton Spicher, March 29, 1935, Norris MSS, LC, Tray 27, Box 4. Yet, since the government had been upheld, most of the expressions of dissatisfaction came not from New Deal supporters but from the outraged conservatives, many of whom echoed Justice McReynolds's irate dissent: "Shame and humiliation are upon us now." There is a copy of McReynolds's extemporaneous dissent, with corrections in his handwriting, in McReynolds MSS, University of Virginia,

Charlottesville, Va., Folder H-2. For conservative dismay, see L. E. Armstrong to Willis Van Devanter, February 26, 1935, Van Devanter MSS, LC; James Beck to J. C. McReynolds, April 13, 1934, Beck MSS, Princeton University, Princeton, N. J., Carton 2; Alfred James McClure to Homer Cummings, February 19, 1935, National Archives (NA) Department of Justice 105-42-11; letters in Charles Evans Hughes MSS, LC, Box 157.

23. *Retirement Board v. Alton R. Co.*, 295 U.S. 330 (1935).

24. Thomas Creigh to Paul Shoup, May 7, 1935, Shoup MSS, Stanford University, Stanford, Cal., Box 1; "5 to 4 Against," *Business Week*, May 11, 1935, pp. 7–8.

25. The Court had, of course, angered groups like bondholders by its decisions in the gold cases, but since these elements viewed the Court as a bulwark against social change, they were unlikely to support any movement to limit the Court's powers.

26. D. B. Robertson to FDR, January 22, 1936; P. J. Hasey to FDR, May 6, 1935, NA Dept. of Justice 235460.

27. Cummings to MacLean, May 11, 1935, NA Dept. of Justice 235773.

28. *Schechter Corp. v. United States*, 295 U.S. 495 (1935); *Louisville Bank v. Radford*, 295 U.S. 555 (1935); *Humphrey's Executor v. United States*, 295 U.S. 602 (1935).

29. It is often said that Roosevelt was relieved by the *Schechter* decision, because the NRA had become an intolerable burden. In fact, he believed strongly in the NRA approach, and persisted in later years in trying to revive it. On Roosevelt's indignation at the *Schechter* opinion, see Raymond Clapper MS. Diary, February 24, 1937.

30. Roosevelt wrote: "It is the 'dictum' in the Schechter case opinion that is disturbing because . . . if the 'dictum' is followed in the future the Court would probably find only ten per cent of actual transactions to be directly in interstate commerce." FDR to Henry L. Stimson, June 10, 1935, *Letters*, 1: 484.

31. *Myers v. United States*, 272 U.S. 52 (1926).

32. Landis COHC, pp. 39–41; Gerhart, *America's Advocate*, p. 99.

33. Gerhart, *America's Advocate*, p. 99. "Isaiah" was a familiar term for Justice Brandeis.

34. *Public Papers*, 4: 200–222; *Washington Post*, June 1. 1935.

35. *Washington Post*, June 1, 1935; Stimson to FDR, June 10, 1935, FDRL PPF 20; *Washington Post*, June 1, 1935; cf. Ralph Hayes to Newton Baker, June 8, 1935, Baker MSS, LC, Box 117.

36. Milton to FDR, June 4, 1935, Milton MSS, LC, Box 18. In the Oklahoma ice case, Brandeis had urged tolerance for social experimentation by state governments.

37. *Public Papers*, 4: 222.

38. Moley, *After Seven Years*, p. 307; Schlesinger, *Politics of Upheaval*, p. 288; H. R. No. 7997, Robert Ramsay MSS, University of West Virginia, Morgantown, W. Va.; *Washington Post*, May 29–June 1, 1935.

39. Edward J. Brown to FDR, June 7, 1935; H. M. Stanley to FDR, July 2, 1935, FDRL OF 41-A, Box 116.

40. Moley, *After Seven Years*, p. 307; Rexford G. Tugwell, *The Democratic Roosevelt* (New York, 1957), p. 385; George W. Norris to William A. Ahern, July 10, 1935, Norris MSS, Tray 27, Box 4.

41. Tugwell, *Democratic Roosevelt*, p. 385. For the President's continued concern, see FDR to Armstead Brown, July 6, 1935, FDRL PPF 2669. In a letter marked "Personal," he told the judge of the Supreme Court of Florida: "I am not worrying in any way about 1936, but I am, of course, concerned about future Supreme Court decisions. After all, we do not want to take away State's rights but, at the same time, there are a good many problems which, under modern conditions, can be solved only by Federal action."

42. Breckinridge Long MS. Diary, LC, June 12, June 17, 1935. That same month, the President's son, James Roosevelt, in a speech in Missouri, called for "an earlier determination of the constitutionality of the acts of the Legislature." Carlisle Bargeron, "Along the Potomac," *Washington Post*, June 13, 1935, clipping, John Taber MSS, Cornell University Collection of Regional History, Ithaca, N. Y., Box 62.

43. Schlesinger, *Politics of Upheaval*, pp. 282, 288–89; *Washington Post*, May 29, 1935.

44. Holtzoff, Memorandum for the Attorney General, June 6, 1935; Cummings, Memorandum for Mr. Holtzoff, June 13, 1935; Holtzoff, Memorandum for the Attorney General, June 22, 1935; W. W. Gardner, Memorandum for the Solicitor General, August 15, 1935, NA Dept. of Justice 235773.

45. FDR to Cummings, July 5, 1935; Charlton Ogburn to FDR, August 7, 20, 1935, FDRL OF 142; Schlesinger, *Politics of Upheaval*, p. 453. See, too, Rev. Francis Haas to FDR, October 25, 1935, Haas MSS, Catholic University of America, Washington, D. C. (courtesy of Thomas E. Blantz, C.S.C.).

46. George Creel, *Rebel at Large* (New York, 1935), pp. 291–92.

47. New York *Herald-Tribune*, November 3, 1935.

48. Harold L. Ickes MS. Diary, November 13, 1935.

49. Ibid., December 27, 1935. The Asquith precedent was to be mentioned often during the Court fight. See, for example, Martin J. Lide to Kenneth McKellar, February 16, 1937, McKellar MSS, Memphis/Shelby County Public Library, Memphis, Tenn., Box 229.

50. Harold L. Ickes MS. Diary, December 27, 1935. Roosevelt had sketched out most of this plan at his lunch with Ickes on November 12.

51. Schlesinger, *Politics of Upheaval*, p. 453.

52. *United States v. Butler*, 297 U.S. 1 (1936) at 61.

53. Some of the indignation was aroused by the "windfall" that millers anticipated as a consequence of the decision. Clifford Hope to Chester Stevens, April 21, 1936, Hope MSS, Kansas State Historical Society, Topeka, Kans., Tax (Legis.) folder, Legislative Correspondence, 1935–36.

54. Maurice Daley to Homer Cummings, January 13, 1936, NA Dept. of

Justice 5-36-346; George Thomason to Cummings, NA Dept. of Justice 235773; John W. White to FDR, January 7, 1936, NA Dept. of Justice 5-36-346; W. K. Cochrane to Stephen Early, January 25, 1936, FDRL OF 41-A, Box 120. Governor George Earle of Pennsylvania denounced the Court as "a political body [with] six members committed to the politics of the Liberty League." Address of George H. Earle, January 18, 1935, Earle MSS, Bryn Mawr, Pa., privately held, Speech and News File No. 73.

55. Joe P. Lane to FDR, January 7, 1936, FDRL OF 274, Box 3; S. C. Odenborg to FDR, February 3, 1936, NA Dept. of Justice 235241; John B. Muller to FDR, January 9, 1936, FDRL OF 1-K, Misc. 1936.

56. W. J. Young to FDR, January 7, 1936, NA Dept. of Justice 5-36-346; W. B. Mills to FDR, January 13, 1936; Thomas Duncan to FDR, January 7, 1936; Elmer Graham to FDR, January 7, 1936, NA Dept. of Justice 235773; W. F. Betts to FDR, January 6, 1936, FDRL OF 1-K Misc. 1936; W. H. (Bill) Reed to FDR, January 21, 1936, NA Dept. of Justice 235868. Felix Frankfurter of Harvard Law School was the country's best known commentator on the Constitution; Floyd Olson was the Farmer-Labor governor of Minnesota.

57. Auzias de Turenne to FDR, January 6, 1936, FDRL OF 1-K Misc. 1936; R. W. Sholders to FDR, January 6, 1936, NA Dept. of Justice 5-36-246; Rudolph Isom to FDR, January 13, 1936, FDRL OF 41-A, Box 120.

58. H. B. Sanders to FDR, January 7, 1936, NA Dept. of Justice 5-36-346.

59. *Washington Post*, January 7, 1936.

60. Ibid., January 8, 1936; Charlton Ogburn to FDR, January 9, 1936, FDRL OF 274.

61. Dickinson to George Fort Milton, January 13, 1936, Milton MSS, Box 19.

62. Harold L. Ickes MS. Diary, January 24, 1936.

63. Memorandum, January 24, 1936, FDRL OF 1-K.

64. FDR to Cummings, January 14, 1936; Cummings to FDR, January 16, 1936, FDRL PSF Supreme Court.

65. Cummings to Stone, January 8, 1936, FDRL PSF Justice. Stone responded: "Thank you for your generous note. When one finds himself outvoted two to one he should be humble and perhaps skeptical of his own judgment. But I have a sincere faith that history and long time perspective will see the function of our court in a different light from that in which it is viewed at the moment." For Stone's views, see Alpheus Thomas Mason, *Harlan Fiske Stone* (New York, 1956), p. 417.

66. Schlesinger, *Politics of Upheaval*, pp. 493–94; FDR Memorandum to Homer Cummings, February 24, 1936; FDR Memorandum for Chairman Hatton Sumners, FDRL OF 41, Box 114. During the 1936 campaign, one correspondent wrote the President: "Why not make a campaign on the opinions of Justice Stone? By taking the words of a member of the court itself there can be no justifiable charge of usurpation." Paul Webb to FDR, June 4, 1936, FDRL OF 41-A, Box 116.

67. Cummings to FDR, January 29, 1936, Cummings MSS.

68. Harold L. Ickes MS. Diary, January 29, 1936.

69. Ibid., January 31, 1936. Ickes added: "It happens that I am fully in accord with the President's view on this matter. I believe that this issue will have to be fought out sooner or later and no more important issue has arisen since the Civil War. Naturally, I would like to be in this fight and be a member of the Administration that is carrying it on."

70. Milton to George Foster Peabody, February 10, 1936, Milton MSS, Box 19.

71. Michael Nelson, "The President and the Court: Reinterpreting the Court-packing Episode of 1937," *Political Science Quarterly*, 103 (Summer 1988), 273, drawing upon Stuart S. Nagel, "Court-Curbing Periods in American History," *Vanderbilt Law Review*, 18 (March 1965), 926; Thomas R. Amlie to W. Jett Lauck, March 6, 1937, Amlie MSS, State Historical Society of Wisconsin, Madison, Wisc., Box 6; O. H. Cross to Stanley Reed, January 17, 1936, NA Dept. of Justice 235868.

72. "Legislation by the Judiciary," copy in the George Norris MSS. See, too, Norris to Francis Heney, April 25, 1936, Heney MSS, University of California, Berkeley, Cal. The Norris idea was a familiar one. In January, a Tacoma assessor had written the President: "The extreme penalty is not exacted from the vilest culprit, save on a unanimous verdict. Why should the will of the people be crucified for less?" Fred A. Smith to FDR, January 9, 1936, NA Dept. of Justice 235773.

73. Allen to George W. Norris, February 12, 1936, Norris MSS, Tray 27, Box 4. The anti-New Deal William Randolph Hearst headed the country's most powerful newspaper chain.

74. George W. Norris to Irving Brant, January 11, 1936, Norris MSS, Tray 27, Box 5.

75. *Ashwander v. T. V. A.*, 297 U.S. 288 (1936).

76. David E. Lilienthal, *Journals of David E. Lilienthal* (7 vols., New York, 1964–83), 1: 59; Lilienthal to Felix Frankfurter, February 17, 1936, Lilienthal MSS, Princeton University.

77. Knoxville *News-Sentinel*, February 18–20, 1936, clippings, David Lilienthal Scrapbooks, Lilienthal MSS; George Fort Milton to Francis Coker, February 18, 1936, Milton MSS, Box 19. Cf. Newton Baker to James M. Beck, May 19, 1936, Beck MSS. Earlier in the century, "Mr. Dooley" (Finley Peter Dunne) had written that the Supreme Court followed the election returns.

78. *Jones v. S. E. C.*, 298 U.S. 1 (1936).

79. *Carter v. Carter Coal Co.*, 298 U.S. 238 (1936).

80. Wendell Berge to E. L. Woodcos, May 20, 1936, Berge MSS, LC, Box 10; L. C. Weiss to FDR, May 20, 1936; H. C. Holland to FDR, May 23, 1936; Jan Byrd to FDR, May 20, 1936, NA Dept. of Justice 235773; *Washington Post*, May 20, 1936; John D. Miller to the *New York Times*, May 19, 1936, Miller MSS, Cornell University Collection of Regional History.

81. *Ashton v. Cameron County Water Improvement District No. 1*, 298 U.S. 513 (1936).

82. *Morehead v. New York ex rel. Tipaldo*, 298 U.S. 587 (1936).

83. Tugwell, *Democratic Roosevelt*, p. 391; Mason, *Stone*, p. 438.

84. Harold L. Ickes MS. Diary, June 2, 1936; *Washington Post*, June 2, 1936; *New York Times*, June 7, 1936.

85. James A. Metcalf to FDR, June 3, 1936, NA Dept. of Justice 224196; E. Larkin to FDR, June 4, 1936, FDRL OF 41-A, Box 116; Earl Salley to FDR, June 5, 1936, FDRL OF 274, Box 3.

86. *Public Papers*, 5: 191–92.

87. Louis Boehm to Robert Wagner, June 6, 1936; Clarence V. Tiers to Stephen Early, June 24, 1936, FDRL OF 1871-A.

88. *Detroit News*, June 25, 1936, clipping, Blair Moody Scrapbooks, Moody MSS, Michigan Historical Collections of the University of Michigan, Ann Arbor, Mich.; Cummings to FDR, June 20, 1936, FDRL PSF Justice; Richberg to FDR, June 16, 1936, FDRL PSF Supreme Court.

89. Donald R. Richberg, *My Hero: The Indiscreet Memoirs of an Eventful but Unheroic Life* (New York, 1954), pp. 204–5; Samuel I. Rosenman, *Working with Roosevelt* (New York, 1953), pp. 100–103; Moley, *After Seven Years*, pp. 346–47.

90. Harold L. Ickes MS. Diary, May 22, 1936; Jacob Hayman to FDR, February 24, 1936, FDRL OF 41-A, Box 116. See, too, Stephen Early, Memorandum for the President, May 22, 1936, Bernard Baruch MSS, Princeton University, Princeton, N. J., XXXIX. For a different view, see Henry Wallace COHC, p. 427. The notion that Presidents are able to win approval for legislation only if they have gained a "mandate" in the prior election has something of the smell of the lamp. Roosevelt himself knew well enough that the 1932 results were the consequence of rejection of Hoover, not an endorsement of his ill-defined and sometimes contradictory utterances, but he had gotten through the electrifying enactments of the First Hundred Days nonetheless. A political scientist has argued that "Roosevelt's best strategy was to attack the Court frontally" in the 1936 campaign. Michael Nelson, "The President and the Court: Reinterpreting the Court-packing Episode of 1937," *Political Science Quarterly*, 103 (Summer 1988), 288–93. He is sensitive, though, to the risk in such an approach.

91. *New York Times*, October 8, 1936; James H. Winston to Sterling E. Edmunds, July 30, 1936, copy in Winston to FDR, August 1, 1936, FDRL PPF 1786. See, too, James H. Winston to James Hamilton Lewis, June 24, 1937, Winston MSS, Southern Historical Collection, University of North Carolina at Chapel Hill, N. C., Folder 51; James R. Sheffield to Elihu Root, Jr., February 17, 1937, Sheffield MSS, Yale University, New Haven, Ct., Box 11; Raymond Clapper MS. Diary, August 24, 1937; S. H. Boddinghouse to Daniel Roper, November 6, 1936, FDRL OF 41-A, Box 116; Henry Teigan to C. Schoening, February 16, 1937, Teigan MSS, Minnesota Historical Society, Box 14; Chicago *Tribune*, July 24, 1936, clipping, Frank Murphy Collection, University of Michigan Law School; Frank Gannett to Alexander Falck, March 7, 1936, Gannett MSS, Cornell University Collection of Regional History, Box 16; James H. Winston to FDR, August 1, 1936, FDRL PPF 1786; J. A. Mulhern to New-

ton D. Baker, October 22, 1936, Baker MSS, Box 52; Stephen Duggan to FDR, November 13, 1936, FDRL OF 274; John Robert Moore, "Josiah William Bailey: A Political Biography," Ph. D. dissertation, Duke University, 1965; James Hamilton Lewis to Arthur Vandenberg, September 18, 1936, Lewis MSS, LC; Allen, "Behind the Campaign," *Harper's* (October 1936), p. 476.

92. John H. Clarke to Newton D. Baker, April 6, 1934, January 3, 1936, Baker MSS, Box 60; Detroit *News*, June 2, 1937; Willis Van Devanter to Mrs. John Lacey, January 11, 1933, Van Devanter MSS, Vol. 46; Stanley High MS. Diary, FDRL, October 28, 1936; Ickes, *Diary*, 1: 705; William Lasser, *The Limits of Judicial Power: The Supreme Court in American Politics* (Chapel Hill, N. C., 1988), p. 153. One essay based on assumptions so fallacious that it must have set back quantitative history for a generation contended that it was statistically demonstrable that Roosevelt would have had a vacancy. R. J. Morrison, "Franklin D. Roosevelt and the Supreme Court: An Example of the Use of Probability Theory in Political History," *History and Theory*, 16 (May 1977), 137–46. For a critique, see Baruch Fischhoff, "Intuitive Uses of Formal Models: A Comment on Morrison's 'Quantitative Models in History,' " *History and Theory*, 17 (May 1978), 207–10. In January 1937, a retired Circuit Court judge lamented to Brandeis: "Judges and other pensioners rarely die seasonably." G. W. Anderson to Louis D. Brandeis, January 3, 1937, Brandeis MSS, University of Louisville Law Library, Louisville, Ky., S. C. 19, Folder 1. One table in April 1937 showed that five of the Justices had already exceeded what their life expectancy had been at the time of their appointment. J. P., "Memo for O. K. B.," April 16, 1937, Joseph Pulitzer MSS, LC, Box 76.

It is not clear why the Administration did not move more forcefully to expedite the Sumners bill to make retirement more attractive, though the proposal did encounter considerable resistance in Congress. In the winter of 1935, Rexford Tugwell noted in his diary: "FDR said nothing could make him mad but when I told him the House Judiciary Committee was about to report the bill for Justices' retirement unfavorably, he showed some signs of irritation." Rexford G. Tugwell MS. Diary, FDRL, February 19, 1935. On the early history of this bill, see Alexander Holtzoff to the Attorney General, March 5, 1935, NA Dept. of Justice 235241. For post-election response, see Cummings to FDR, December 29, 1936, FDRL PSF Supreme Court.

93. James C. McReynolds to Dr. Robert P. McReynolds, July 4, 1936, McReynolds MSS; Van Devanter to Dennis Flynn, October 19, 1936, Van Devanter to Mrs. John W. Lacey, November 2, 1936, Van Devanter MSS, Vol. 52.

94. *Time*, March 8, 1937, p. 13.

95. For Roosevelt's belief that he had been snubbed by the Justices in 1936, see the penciled memorandum, "Court story," Harry Hopkins MSS, FDRL, Box 325. The account in Sherwood, *Roosevelt and Hopkins: An Intimate History* (New York, 1948), p. 94, is slightly inaccurate. The whole tale is scoffed at in Merlo J. Pusey, *Charles Evans Hughes* (New York, 1963), pp. 749–50.

96. Minutes in Meyer MSS, School of Industrial and Labor Relations, Cor-

nell University, Ithaca, N. Y., Box 5; W. Jett Lauck to Lucy Mason, January 25, 1937, Lauck MSS, University of Virginia, Charlottesville, Va., Box 163; Arthur N. Holcombe to Emily Sims Marconnier, August 7, 1936; L. B. Boudin to Florina Lasker, October 21, 1936; Report of the Committee of Inquiry to the Board, November 5, 1936, Mary Dewson MSS, FDRL, Box 6. The Dewson papers also contain the original replies.

97. FDR to Charles C. Burlingham, February 23, 1937, *Letters,* 1: 662; Harold L. Ickes MS. Diary, January 10, 1937.

98. Paul Mallon, "Purely Confidential," Detroit *News,* February 13, 1937; *New York Times,* February 12, 1937.

99. Brown to Lucy R. Mason, September 9, 1936, Mary Dewson MSS, Box 6. See, too, Donald Richberg to Raymond Clapper, February 26, 1937, Richberg MSS, LC, Box 2. Advocates of amendments pointed out that the child-labor amendment had been improperly drafted and that the ratification process could involve conventions rather than legislatures.

100. Raymond Clapper MS. Diary, February 8, 1937.

101. Beard, "Rendezvous with the Supreme Court," *New Republic,* September 2, 1936, p. 93; Beard to Nicholas Kelley, August 8, 1936, Mary Dewson MSS, Box 6; Washington *Herald,* March 14, 1937, clipping, Frank Murphy Collection. The most powerful argument for the conviction that Roosevelt should have gone the amendment route is in David E. Kyvig, "The Road Not Taken: FDR, the Supreme Court, and Constitutional Amendment," *Political Science Quarterly,* 104 (Fall 1989), 463–81.

102. *Presidential Press Conferences,* 9: 165–66; Raymond Clapper MS. Diary, February 8, 1937; *Washington Post,* February 13, 1937; Richberg to Clapper, February 26, 1937, Richberg MSS, Box 2.

103. New York *Daily News,* November 4, 1936.

104. John B. McGraw to Stephen Early, December 8, 1936, FDRL OF 274, Box 4; L. L. Wilson to FDR, December 3, 1936, NA Dept. of Justice 235773. See, too, Virgil V. Johnson to FDR, November 13, 1936, FDRL PPF 200, Reelect Cong-J; B. F. Welty to FDR, December 29, 1936, FDRL OF 41, Box 114.

105. San Francisco *Chronicle,* January 11, 1935, clipping; Paul Scharrenberg to FDR, February 15, 1933; Denman to Charles N. Pray, March 18, 1936; Denman to Charles Warren, March 19, 1936; *New York Times,* May 16, 1934; FDR to Homer Cummings, December 19, 1934, FDRL PSF 56; Denman to M. H. McIntyre, March 17, 1936; Denman to FDR, April 25, November 7, 1936, December 21, 1938; Denman to G. Stanleigh Arnold, July 27, 1937, William Denman MSS, Bancroft Library, University of California, Berkeley, Cal.; "Critical Study of United States Trial Courts," *Journal of the American Judicature Society,* 21 (December 1937), 115–16; FDR to Cummings, April 29, 1936, FDRL PPF 336; Denman to FDR, September 5, 1936, FDRL OF 41, Box 114; Denman to Xenophon Hicks, September 30, 1938, Hicks MSS, Box 34; George C. Taylor to Edgar S. Vaught, March 23, 1936, Taylor MSS, Box 1. The papers of

federal judges Hicks and Taylor are both at the National Archives, Southeast Region, East Point, Ga.

106. Edward Keating MS. Diary, Western Historical Collections, University of Colorado, Boulder, Col., November 6, 1936; Homer S. Cummings MS. Diary, November 15, 1936 (italics added); Richberg to FDR, November 16, 1936, FDRL PPF 2418; Louis Wehle to William Bullitt, November 21, 1936, Wehle MSS, FDRL, Box 16. Roosevelt later explained that he "asked two people to put down the result of these studies in black and white. The two people were the Attorney General and the Solicitor General and nobody else." *Presidential Press Conferences*, 9: 163–64.

107. Raymond Clapper MS. Diary, February 8, 1937; Reed, Memorandum for the Attorney General from the Solicitor General, December 19, 1936, NA Dept. of Justice 235773.

108. W. W. Gardner, "Memorandum for the Solicitor General: Congressional Control of Judicial Power to Invalidate Legislation," December 10, 1936, copy in Felix Frankfurter MSS, LC, Box 226; Gardner, "Court Packing," p. 100. My account of the origins of the plan has benefited from reading a challenging eighty-nine-page essay by a Yale Law student, Kevin Leitão. He asserted that the original version of my essay, which in some places rested on the only available source of the time, the contemporary account by Alsop and Catledge, needed to be emended in light of the revelations in the Homer Cummings papers, which were still closed when I published that essay. Leitão had no way of knowing that I had reached that same conclusion after examining the Cummings materials a number of years ago, as well as other collections I consulted subsequently, including the Denman manuscripts in Berkeley. Hence, at many points, my revised essay in this volume is in agreement, more or less, with Leitão's. He, though, concentrates almost all of his attention on the final weeks of the episode, while I believe the outcome must be seen in the context of a long series of developments; gives considerably less weight to FDR's role than I do; brushes aside the significant second Creel interview; and believes that the climactic event was the Gardner memo, which I interpret differently. Nonetheless, my analysis has been sharpened by Leitão's enterprise, and I appreciate his thoughtfulness in sending it to me.

109. Thurman Arnold to Mrs. C. P. Arnold, October 23, 1936, in Gene M. Gressley, ed., *Voltaire and the Cowboy: The Letters of Thurman Arnold* (Boulder, 1977), p. 234. Corwin had helped prepare the Government's brief in the *Carter* case. John Dickinson to Corwin, June 15, 1936, Corwin MSS, Princeton, N. J.

110. Edward S. Corwin, *The Commerce Power versus States Rights* (Princeton, N. J., 1936).

111. Clark to Corwin, August 18, 1936, September 3, 1936, Corwin MSS; Corwin to Lucy R. Mason, September 24, 1936, Mary Dewson MSS, Box 6.

112. Cummings to FDR, December 3, 1936, FDRL OF 41-A, Box 116; Cummings to Corwin, December 3, 1936, Corwin MSS.

113. The proofs are in FDRL OF 41-A, Box 116. Clark argued that Corwin

had underestimated the possibilities of the amendment process. Clark to Corwin, December 11, 1936, and Corwin's reply, December 16, 1936.

114. Cummings to Edward S. Corwin, December 3, 1936; Reed to Corwin, December 3, 1936; Marx to Corwin, December 5, 1936, Corwin MSS, Box 2; Gerald Garvey, "Scholar in Politics: Edward S. Corwin and the 1937 Court-packing Battle," *Princeton University Library Chronicle*, 31 (Autumn 1969), 7–8. The statement was published in *The Nassau Lit.*

115. The exchange is in the Corwin papers. See, too, Garvey, "Scholar in Politics," p. 4.

116. The penciled draft of this letter in the Corwin Papers is undated. The letter could have been sent at any time between December 4 and 16, but December 16 seems highly likely. That same day, Corwin wrote Reed: "I was glad to get your comments on those articles—I believe that my age limit proposal, if adopted, may have considerable effect. It might not get more liberal judges, but it would assure a more rapid replacement of the Bench. Today Jefferson's complaint is well justified: 'Few die and none resign.'—indeed the statement might be made stronger. . . . I believe it could be validly accomplished by an act of Congress." Corwin to Reed, December 16, 1936, NA Dept. of Justice 235868. The section of the Code alluded to deals with the recall to service of retired federal judges.

117. Cummings to Corwin, December 17, 1936, Corwin MSS.

118. Berle, "Law and the Social Revolution," *Survey Graphic*, 22 (December 1933), 594; Charles N. Crewdson to Louis Howe, January 7, 1936, FDRL OF 41-A, Box 116; "Book Lampoons Supreme Court," Statesville (N. C.) *Record*, October 27, 1936, clipping, Drew Pearson MSS, Lyndon B. Johnson Library (LBJL), Austin, Tex., G 201, Box 1; Robert S. Allen LBJL OH, p. 7; Alpheus T. Mason, *William Howard Taft: Chief Justice* (New York, 1964), p. 161.

119. Thomas Reed Powell to William O. Douglas, n. d., Douglas MSS, LC, Box 20; Herbert Hoover to Charles Evans Hughes, February 19, 1937, Hughes MSS, Box 6; James A. Stone to William T. Evjue, March 17, 1937, Stone MSS, Minnesota Historical Society, Box 28; Thomas R. Amlie to Donald A. Butchart, March 6, 1937, Amlie MSS, Box 36; *New York Times*, January 27, 1937. In a debate with Donald Richberg, the former Assistant Attorney General, Seth Richardson, cried, "Those 'nine old men!' I stand aghast at the suggestion that they are cold, inhuman, unsocial and senile." Washington *Star*, October 13, 1936, clipping, Frank Murphy Collection.

120. *Report of the Attorney General for the Fiscal Year Ending June 30, 1913*, p. 5; Homer Cummings and Carl McFarland, *Federal Justice: Chapters in the History of Justice and the Federal Executive* (New York, 1937), p. 531; "What Was the Origin of the President's Supreme Court Proposal?" *United States Law Review*, 71 (September 1937), 488–93.

121. "The Federal Constitution," Shawnee (Okla.) *County Democrat*, August 7, 1936, clipping, FDRL OF 274, Box 4.

122. Homer S. Cummings MS. Diary, January 17, 1937; Robert Jackson COHC; Gardner, "Court Packing," p. 103. Jackson, though, misunderstands

the significance of the McReynolds precedent, and Gardner misremembers details of the episode. Even a man at the Department of Justice who was "one of the half dozen or so people who were in on the secret since December" confessed, "I have been unable to find out whose was the original idea to appoint additional judges. . . . I thought it might have been McFarland, but he disclaims the honor." Abe Glasser to Edward S. Corwin, February 8, 1937, Corwin MSS, Box 2.

123. Drew Pearson and Robert S. Allen, *Nine Old Men at the Crossroads* (Garden City, N. Y., 1936), p. 2.

124. Cummings to FDR, December 22, 1936, FDRL PSF Supreme Court.

125. Creel, *Rebel at Large*, pp. 292–94; George Creel, "Roosevelt's Plans and Purposes," *Collier's*, December 26, 1936, p. 40; Richberg to FDR, November 16, 1936, FDRL PPF 2418.

126. *Hammer v. Dagenhart*, 247 U.S. 251 (1918) at 277.

127. The columnist Dorothy Thompson noted in her diary: "Homer Cummings says it is his conviction that the Constitution is O. K. but not the present interpretation. This is also Beard's contention." Dorothy Thompson MS. Diary, Syracuse University, Syracuse, N. Y., n. d., [1936].

128. *Dred Scott v. Sandford*, 19 Howard 393 (1857); *Pollock v. Farmers' Loan and Trust Co.*, 157 U.S. 429 (1895); 158 U.S. 601 (1895). Cummings was far off in totaling the years that elapsed between these decisions and the ensuing amendments.

129. Homer S. Cummings MS. Diary, December 26, 1937.

130. Raymond Clapper MS Diary, February 8, 1937; Paul Mallon, "Purely Confidential," Detroit *News*, April 2, 1937; Alsop and Catledge, *168 Days*, pp. 31–35. Denman emphasized the importance of the creation of the new office of proctor to ensure that the assignment of judges would be under the direct supervision of the Chief Justice, thereby eliminating the possibility that the Department of Justice could move judges around in order to win favorable decisions for the government. Turner Catledge to Joseph Alsop, October 29, 1937, Alsop MSS, LC, Box 2.

131. By January 5, the bill had reached a fifth draft. "Draft No. 5, January 5, 1937," FDRL PSF Supreme Court. Only at the very end did the draftsmen abandon the conception imbedded in McReynolds's recommendation placing sitting Justices in an inferior position to new appointees.

132. Abe Glasser to Edward S. Corwin, February 8, 1937, Corwin MSS, Box 2; Richberg, *My Hero*, pp. 221–22; Raymond Clapper MS. Diary, January 14, 1938; Hopkins memorandum of conversation with Thomas Corcoran in 1939, in Sherwood, *Roosevelt and Hopkins*, p. 109.

133. Alsop and Catledge, *168 Days*, pp. 43–47; Richberg, *My Hero*, pp. 221–22; Raymond Clapper MS. Diary, January 14, February 8, 1938; Rosenman, *Working with Roosevelt*, pp. 145–50; Homer Cummings MS. Diary, January 30, 1937; *Washington Post*, February 13, 1937; Detroit *News*, April 2, 1937. Two drafts of the message have been retained in the Samuel I. Rosenman MSS, FDRL, "Message to Congress on the Judiciary" folder.

134. Homer Cummings MS. Diary, January 30–February 3, 1937.

135. Raymond Clapper MS. Diary, February 8, 1937, recording an interview with Homer Cummings; Rosenman, *Working with Roosevelt*, p. 155; James Roosevelt MS. Diary, FDRL, February 4, 1937.

136. Raymond Clapper MS. Diary, February 5, 8, 1937; *Washington Post*, February 13, 1937; Ickes, *Diary*, 2: 31; Henry Morgenthau, Jr., MS. Diary, FDRL, February 6, 1937; Edward Rees to William Allen White, n. d., White MSS, Box 186; *Congressional Record*, 75th Cong., 1st Sess., p. 562; Bertrand Snell to Chester C. Bolton, February 5, 1937, Snell MSS, State University College at Potsdam, Potsdam, N. Y., C2.4, Box 1. Clapper's notes on his interview with Early also state: "Steve says that only five people were told of plan by President. He said President wouldn't want him to reveal names but he thought I knew them. Said none was in Congress." Clapper MS. Diary, February 8, 1937.

137. Moley, *After Seven Years*, p. 356; Daniel C. Roper to William E. Dodd, January 6, 1937, Roper MSS, Duke University, Durham, N. C., Box 15; New York *Herald Tribune*, January 7, 1937; William R. Castle MS. Diary, Houghton Library, Harvard University, Cambridge, Mass., January 7, 1937; William M. Colmer, "Congressional Sidelights," Colmer MSS, University of Southern Mississippi, Hattiesburg, Miss., Box 150; Nicholas Murray Butler to James W. Wadsworth, January 20, 1937, copy in Charles D. Hilles MSS, Yale University, New Haven, Ct., Box 211; *Time*, January 18, 1937, pp. 13–14; *New York Times*, January 5, 7, 10, 24, 1937.

138. Paul Mallon, "Purely Confidential," Detroit *News*, February 13, 1937; Mary Dewson to Stanley Reed, December 10, 1936; Dewson to Mrs. Armstrong, n. d.; Elmer F. Andrews to Members of the New York State Minimum Wage Conference, January 26, 1937; Mrs. J. C. Pryer to Mary Dewson, January 11, 1937, Dewson MSS; Alfred M. Bingham to Thomas R. Amlie, January 5, 1937, Amlie MSS, Box 35. Subsequently, Clapper summed up what Cummings had told him: "Didn't know until last minute whether Rvt would go through with it or not." Clapper MS. Diary, February 8, 1937.

139. Breckinridge Long MS. Diary, January 6, 1937.

140. Knutson to Elmer E. Adams, January 11, 1937, Adams MSS, Minnesota Historical Society, Box 42. See, too, Ray Lyman Wilbur to Dr. Arthur H. Daniels, January 8, 1937, Wilbur MSS, Stanford University.

141. Breckinridge Long MS. Diary, January 6, 1937.

142. Raymond Clapper MS. Diary, January 20, 1937.

143. Raymond P. Brandt OH, Harry S. Truman Library, Independence, Mo., pp. 31–32; Homer Cummings MS. Diary, January 24, 1937.

144. Brant to FDR, January 24, 1937, FDRL PPF 2293; *Washington Post*, February 13, 1937; *New York Times*, February 2, 1937; Detroit *News*, February 2, 1937; Mallon, "Purely Confidential," Detroit *News*, February 4, 1937. As early as January 7, the Washington bureau of Scripps-Howard had informed its chain: "An increase in the Supreme Court's membership—'if necessary'—is being considered by the Administration, it was learned today. And President Roo-

sevelt's forthright stand against amendment of the Constitution was interpreted by many as pointing toward an eventual decision to use this big stick." Copy in Raymond Clapper MSS, Box 233. On January 28, Pearson and Allen, in their nationally syndicated column, reported that the President was about to surprise the nation with a request to add six Justices to the U.S. Supreme Court. Since the syndicate required considerable lead time, the item must have been written at least five days earlier. Leo C. Rosten, *The Washington Correspondents* (New York, 1937), pp. 143, 383. Given all of these revelations, it is hard to account for why FDR's message of February 5 came as such a shock.

145. *Washington Post*, February 13, 1937; Raymond Clapper MS Diary, February 8, 1937; Richberg, *My Hero*, p. 222. One of Corwin's former students who had been privy to the scheme since December later wrote him that the message had originally been scheduled for the last week in February. However, when Donald Richberg was brought into the inner council in late January, he strongly recommended publicizing the plan at the earliest possible moment in order to avert a disastrous leak. Abe Glasser to Edward S. Corwin, February 8, 1937, Corwin MSS, Box 2.

146. Raymond Clapper MS. Diary, February 8, 1937.

147. Richberg, *My Hero*, p. 222; *Time*, February 15, March 1, 1937

148. Stanley F. Reed COHC, pp. 21, 24, 150–51, 179–80, transcript, Reed MSS, University of Kentucky, Lexington, Ky.; Reed to the writer, May 14, 1964.

149. James Roosevelt MS. Diary, February 10, 1937.

5. F. D. R.'s "Court-packing" Plan

1. In the first two pages of this essay, I have provided a brief reprise of events described at length in earlier essays so that a reader who turns to this essay first will have sufficient background. *R. R. Retirement Board v. Alton R. R. Co.*, 295 U.S. 330 (1935); Russell W. Galloway, Jr., "The Court That Challenged the New Deal (1930–1936)," *Santa Clara Law Review*, 24 (Winter 1984), 86.

2. *A. L. A. Schechter Poultry Corp. et al. v. United States*, 295 U.S. 553 (1935). That day, too, the Court dealt a personal blow to the President in *Humphrey's Executor v. U.S.*, 295 U.S. 602 (1935).

3. *United States v. Butler et al.*, 297 U.S. 61 (1936); *Carter v. Carter Coal Company*, 298 U.S. 238 (1936); *Morehead v. New York ex rel.* Tipaldo, 298 U.S. 587 (1936).

4. Max Lerner, "The Great Constitutional War," *Virginia Quarterly Review*, 18 (Autumn 1942), 538; Samuel I. Rosenman, ed., *The Public Papers and Addresses of Franklin D. Roosevelt* (13 vols., New York, 1938–50), 5: 191–92. For a defense of the "Old Court," see Richard A. Maidment, *The Judicial Response to the New Deal: The U.S. Supreme Court and Economic Regulation, 1934–1936* (Manchester, Eng., 1991).

5. *Public Papers*, 5: 51–66. The Court bill also provided for certain other changes.

6. Paul Mallon, "Purely Confidential," Detroit *News*, March 17, 1937; Margaret Fowler Dunaway MS. Diary, Early March 1937, Schlesinger Library, Radcliffe College, Cambridge, Mass; A. Roy Moore to John H. Kerr, February 27, 1937, Kerr MSS, Southern Historical Collection, University of North Carolina, Chapel Hill, N. C., Box 9; S. R. Lewis to FDR, February 19, 1937, National Archives (NA), Dept. of Justice 235868; Rochester *Times Union*, February 13, 1937, clipping, Frank Gannett MSS, Cornell University Collection of Regional History, Ithaca, N. Y., Box 2A; Mrs. C. I. Anderson to Merlin Hull, February 19, 1937, Hull MSS, State Historical Society of Wisconsin, Madison, Wis., Box 89; W. C. Cray to John H. Overton, March 21, 1937, Overton MSS, Dept. of Archives and Manuscripts, Louisiana State University, Baton Rouge, La., Box 2; June Beliveau to Theodore Green, April 30, 1937, Green MSS, Library of Congress (LC), Washington, D. C., Box 33; notes for a speech, Dorothy Kirchwey Brown MSS, Schlesinger Library, Folder 14; Beaumont *Enterprize*, February 16, 1937, clipping, Arthur Vandenberg Scrapbooks, Michigan Historical Collections of The University of Michigan, Ann Arbor, Mich.

7. Johnson to John Francis Neylan, March 21, 1937, Johnson MSS, Bancroft Library, University of California, Berkeley, Cal.; Charles O. Andrews to Charles Andrews, Jr., March 2, 1937, Andrews MSS, P. K. Yonge Library of Florida History, University of Florida, Gainesville, Fla., Box 51; Albany (N. Y.) *Knickerbocker News*, February 20, 1937, clipping, Royal Copeland Scrapbooks, Michigan Historical Collections.

8. Stephen Early to FDR, February 8, 1937, Franklin D. Roosevelt Library (FDRL), Hyde Park, N. Y., PSF Supreme Court; Memorandum of Conference with Speaker W. B. Bankhead, February 7, 1937, Lindsay Warren MSS, Southern Historical Collection, University of North Carolina, Box 17; Lawrence Lewis MS. Diary, State Historical Society of Colorado, Denver, Col., February 12, 1937; New York *American*, February 19, 1937, clipping, Royal Copeland Scrapbooks; Joe Hendricks to Wellhorn Phillips, Jr., February 25, 1937, Hendricks MSS, P. K. Yonge Library of Florida History, Box 2; Bert Lord to B. H. Chernin, February 16, 1937, Lord MSS, Cornell University Collection of Regional History.

9. J. F. T. O'Connor MS. Diary, February 15, 1937, Bancroft Library, University of California.

10. Raymond Clapper MS. Diary, LC, February 8, 1937; *Time*, February 15, 1937, pp. 18–19.

11. William M. Fitch to Stanley Reed, February 16, 1937, NA Dept. of Justice 235868; Vyvian Faye Coxon to Joe Hendricks, March 3, 1937, Hendricks MSS, Box 2.

12. A Wisconsin man wrote: "It is now possible, under a five to four decision, for one old man (whose mental and physical powers, as any honest authority will admit, are more than likely to be in process of deterioration) to nullify the acts of 435 congressmen, 96 senators and the President—all duly elected as the government of the people." C. W. Langlotz to Thomas Amlie,

February 12, 1937, Amlie MSS, State Historical Society of Wisconsin, Box 35. See also Henry Ware Allen to the editor, *Washington Post,* May 4, 1937; George Fort Milton to Homer Cummings, March 17, 1937, Milton MSS, LC, Box 20.

13. Josephus Daniels to Frank Gannett, May 11, 1937, Gannett MSS, Box 16; *Congressional Record,* 75th Cong., 1st Sess., p. 307A; Lex Green to C. E. Coomes, February 15, 1937, Green MSS, P. K. Yonge Library of Florida History, Box 27; Thomas R. Amlie to S. A. Jedele, February 12, 1937, Amlie MSS, Box 35.

14. Thomas Reed Powell to William O. Douglas, n. d., Douglas MSS, LC, Box 20; Herbert Hoover to Charles Evans Hughes, February 19, 1937, Hughes MSS, LC, Box 6; James A. Stone to William T. Evjue, March 17, 1937, Stone MSS, State Historical Society of Wisconsin, Box 28; Thomas R. Amlie to Donald A. Butchart, March 6, 1937, Amlie MSS, Box 36; *New York Times,* January 27, 1937; M. A. Hudak to Hughes, April 13, 1937, Hughes MSS, LC, Box 164. For hostility to Hughes, see Chase Osborn to Daniel Willard, December 22, 1937, Osborn MSS, Michigan Historical Collections; Mark Squires to R. L. Doughton, February 10, 1937, Doughton MSS, Southern Historical Collection, University of North Carolina.

15. Nashville *Tennessean,* n. d., clipping in M. H. Berry to Kenneth McKellar, February 10, 1937, McKellar MSS, Memphis/Shelby County Public Library, Memphis, Tenn., Box 202; Al C. Anderson to Merlin Hull, February 12, 1937, Hull MSS, Box 88.

16. *Congressional Record,* 75th Cong., 1st Sess., p. 405A; Edmund P. Grice, Jr., to James F. Byrnes, February 23, 1937, Byrnes MSS, Clemson University, Clemson, S. C. Another Charleston man wrote. "I get a kick out of the hypocritical reverence for the constitution on the part of some of my friends. They often prayed for deliverance from the eighteenth amendment tanked up on a jar of moonshine." Archie P. Owens to the editor, Charleston *News and Courier,* n. d., clipping in Owens to Byrnes, February 21, 1937, idem.

17. *Washington Post,* May 5, 1937; Donald Richberg to Raymond Clapper, February 26, 1937, Richberg MSS, LC, Box 2; Harold Ickes to William Allen White, February 25, 1937, White MSS, LC, Box 186. Ickes was not wide of the mark. A Kansas City attorney who opposed the plan wrote: "The Constitution, by its separation of the trinity of governmental functions, Executive, Legislative and Judicial, vitalized the God concept." W. H. H. Piatt to Robert La Follette, Jr., William Allen White MSS, March 17, 1937, Box 187.

18. "The New Deal versus the Old Courts," *Literary Digest,* February 13, 1937, pp. 5–8; Henry Morgenthau, Jr., MS. Diaries, FDRL, February 15, 1937; Breckinridge Long MS. Diary, LC, February 15, 1937.

19. William B. Mershon to Arthur Vandenberg, February 15, 1937, Mershon MSS, Michigan Historical Collections. See also Merton S. Horrell to Joe Hendricks, February 12, 1937, Hendricks MSS, Box 2; Amy Armour Smith to Rush Holt, March 18, 1937, Holt MSS, University of West Virginia Library, Morgantown, W. Va.; *Constitutional Democracy,* April 5, 1937, copy in Hugh Ike Shott MSS, University of West Virginia Library, Box 38; St. Louis *Post-Dispatch,*

April 11, 1937. Administration supporters replied that the Court matter *had* been discussed in the campaign—by Roosevelt's opponents; hence, the President did have a mandate. Secretary Ickes wrote a Republican editor: "You raised these issues and the people brought in the verdict against you—an overwhelming verdict. Aren't you estopped from saying now that the question of judicial reform was not raised?" Harold Ickes to William Allen White, February 20, 1937, White MSS, Box 186. See also A. F. Whitney to Frank O. Lowden, April 17, 1937, Lowden MSS, University of Chicago Library, Chicago, Ill., Series 5, Box 25, Folder 2.

20. Advocates retorted that the amendment process was too slow; they pointed, in particular, to the protracted odyssey of the failed Child Labor Amendment. One labor leader objected: "Amendments are O.K., except we start to save a kid in a So. Car. cotton mill when she is eight—she is 26 before we get the amendment." George B. Jackson to Joe Hendricks, March 14, 1937, Hendricks MSS, Box 2. See also Breckinridge Long MS. Diary, February 15, 1937.

21. A. M. Savage to John H. Overton, March 16, 1937, Overton MSS, Box 2; W. W. Ball to "Lily," n. d., Ball MSS, Duke University Library, Durham, N. C., July 1936–February 1937 folder; Typescript of address by Joseph E. Ransdell, n. d. [July 1937], Ransdell MSS, Dept. of Archives and Manuscripts, Louisiana State University, Folder 21, Box 3. In the first version of this essay, I emphasized the opposition of Catholic Senators to the plan. I have been persuaded that I overstated that aspect, though I still believe it was important.

22. Vincent P. Smith to Joe Hendricks, March 2, 1937, Hendricks MSS, Box 2.

23. The Vicar to the editor, March 10, 1937, *Washington Post*, March 12, 1937. A Missouri country editor urged: "Let these men serve until they are taken by their maker or resign. . . . They have lived the span of life allotted them by Him, if they live longer it is because He has work for them to do." Raymond Lloyd to James F. Byrnes, February 17, 1937, Byrnes MSS. A North Carolinian assured his elderly Congressman: "I am glad to say that your own constituents do not feel that a man is mentally decrepit at the age of seventy." Waller D. Brown to R. L. Doughton, February 10, 1937, Doughton MSS. Admirers of Justice Brandeis resented the plan as an implied slur at the octogenarian Justice.

24. Richard L. Neuberger, "America Talks Court," *Current History*, 46 (June 1937), 35.

25. Address, March 8, 1937, Station WOR, J. T. Adams MSS, Columbia University Library, New York, N. Y.; Harvey Campbell to Arthur Vandenberg, March 11, 1937, Vandenberg MSS. See also Hugh L. Elsbree to Daniel Reed, October 3, 1958, Reed MSS, Cornell University Collection of Regional History, Box 14; William F. Riley to his father, March 3, 1937, in Riley to Clyde Herring, July 7, 1937, Riley MSS, University of Iowa Library, Iowa City, Iowa, Box 1; Oswald Garrison Villard to Maury Maverick, May 7, 1937, Villard MSS, Houghton Library, Harvard University, Cambridge, Mass. Advo-

cates denied that the Court, and especially the Four Horsemen, had safeguarded the Bill of Rights. Maury Maverick wrote: "If you look at the cases on sedition, espionage and the rest, . . . the courts declared pretty nearly every silly law constitutional during and following the World War. There was not much protection of civil liberties in this country." Maverick to John I. Palmer, January 18, 1937, Maury Maverick MSS, Archives, University of Texas Library, Austin, Tex., Box 5.

26. Virgil Murdoch Rich to Senators Overton and Ellender, February 10, 1937, Overton MSS, Box 2; Edith Dickeymann to James F. Byrnes, n. d., Byrnes MSS.

27. Andrews to Charles Andrews, Jr., February 26, 1937, Andrews MSS, Box 51; Charles O. Andrews to Hamilton Holt, March 10, 1937, Holt MSS, Mills Memorial Library, Rollins College, Winter Park, Fla.; Detroit *News*, February 6, 28, 1937. For other indications of straddling, or concern for public opinion, see F. Ryan Duffy to William B. Rubin, February 11, 1937, Rubin MSS, State Historical Society of Wisconsin, Box 11; J. F. T. O'Connor MS. Diary, February 18, 1937; Portland *Press-Herald*, February 6, 1937, clipping, Wallace White MSS, LC, Box 81; Fred Crawford to H. A. Douglas, March 17, 1937, Crawford MSS, Michigan Historical Collections.

28. Mimeographed press release; Overton to Fayette C. Ewing, February 20, 1937, John H. Overton MSS, Box 2.

29. Karl A. Lamb, "The Opposition Party as Secret Agent: Republicans and the Court Fight, 1937," *Papers of the Michigan Academy of Science, Arts, and Letters*, Vol. 46 (1961); Arthur Vandenberg MS. Diary, February 6, 1937; Herbert Hoover to Frank O. Lowden, February 6, 1937, Lowden MSS, Series I, Box 58, Folder 5; Arthur M. Hyde to Paul Shoup, May 12, 1937, Shoup MSS, Stanford University Library, Stanford, Cal., Box 1. Too much has often been made of the Republican strategy of silence; men such as Vandenberg spoke out after only a brief period of reticence.

30. U.S. Senate Committee on the Judiciary, 75th Cong., 1st Sess., *Reorganization of the Federal Judiciary*, Hearings on S. 1392 (Washington: Government Printing Office, 1937), Part 3, p. 491. Supporters of the plan retorted that if the Court was up to date on its calendar it was only because, ever since the enactment of a 1925 statute, the Court had been refusing to hear cases it should have heard. A federal district court judge from Los Angeles wrote: "I have never seen any logic in catching up with court calendars by shutting off the right to ask for Justice, and that, in plain truth, is just what has been done. It is child's talk to say that the business of the court cannot be apportioned among fifteen so that more and better work can be turned out than through a court of nine." Albert Lee Stephens to William McAdoo, May 21, 1937, McAdoo MSS, LC, Box 435. But see Stanley Reed to FDR, February 26, 1937, FDRL OF 10-F.

31. U.S. Senate, Committee on the Judiciary, *Hearings on S. 1392*, Pt. 4, p. 767.

32. Charles Andrews, Jr., to Charles O. Andrews, March 11, 1937, Andrews MSS, Box 51.

33. F. R. L. to the editor, Detroit *News*, March 2, 1937.

34. *Time*, April 5, 1937, p. 13.

35. *West Coast Hotel Company v. Parrish*, 300 U.S. 379 (1937).

36. The most important case was *National Labor Relations Board v. Jones & Laughlin Steel Corporation*, 301 U.S. 1 (1937).

37. *Steward Machine Company v. Davis*, 301 U.S. 548 (1937); *Helvering v. Davis*, 301 U.S. 619 (1937).

38. Merlo Pusey, *Charles Evans Hughes* (2 vols., New York, 1951), 2: 757, 766–72; Pusey, "Justice Roberts' 1937 Turnaround," *Supreme Court Historical Society Yearbook* (1983), 102–7; Felix Frankfurter, "Mr. Justice Roberts," *University of Pennsylvania Law Review*, 104 (December 1955), 313–16; John W. Chambers, "The Big Switch: Justice Roberts and the Minimum Wage Cases," *Labor History*, 10 (Winter 1969), 44–73; Judith A. Baer, *The Chains of Protection: The Judicial Response to Women's Labor Legislation* (Westport, Ct., 1978), p. 99. See, too, Edward F. Prichard, Jr., to the editor, Boston *Herald*, April 2, 1937, copy in Theodore Green MSS, LC, Box 32.

39. Detroit *News*, April 13, 1937; Thomas Amlie to Mr. and Mrs. E. J. Klema, July 6, 1937, Amlie MSS, Box 39; J. F. T. O'Connor MS. Diary, April 12, 1937; Tom Lewis to William Allen White, March 30, 1937, White MSS, Box 187; Milton to Joseph Greenbaum, April 1, 1937, Milton MSS, Box 20; Emma Guffey Miller, "Speech—Louisville [1937]," Miller MSS, Folder 36, Schlesinger Library, Radcliffe College.

40. Paul Mallon, "Purely Confidential," Detroit *News*, April 13, 1937. At least two Justices did not anticipate that Roosevelt would win so handsomely; a number of Justices might well have believed until that point that they were defending the people against an overbearing tyrant. The election results must have been a jolt. See James C. McReynolds to Dr. Robert P. McReynolds, July 4, 1936, McReynolds MSS, University of Virginia, Charlottesville, Va.; Willis Van Devanter to Dennis Flynn, October 19, 1936; Van Devanter to Mrs. John W. Lacey, November 2, 1936, Van Devanter MSS, LC, Vol. 52. For the conviction that the threat of Court-packing was decisive in changing Roberts's views, see Robert L. Stern, "The Commerce Clause and the National Economy, 1933–1946," *Harvard Law Review*, 59 (May 1946), 681–82.

41. Harlan Fiske Stone to Sterling Carr, May 15, 1937, Stone MSS, LC, Box 8; Thurman Arnold to Fred S. Caldwell, May 17, 1937, in Gene M. Gressley, ed., *Voltaire and the Cowboy: The Letters of Thurman Arnold* (Boulder, Col., 1977), p. 250; Kenneth Culp Davis, "Revolution in the Supreme Court," *Atlantic Monthly*, 166 (July 1940), 92. Some conservatives believed that the Court's reversal had defeated the bill, but that too great a price had been paid. Newton D. Baker wrote: "The change of position by Mr. Justice Roberts is profoundly disturbing and distressing. I think the Court is already saved from the President's proposal, but how much of the old dignity and disinterestedness of the Court will remain as a tradition is a very serious question." Baker to John H. Clarke, June 9, 1937, Baker MSS, LC, Box 60.

42. Edward Corwin to Homer Cummings, May 19, 1937, Corwin MSS,

Princeton University Library, Princeton, N. J.; Raymond Clapper MS. Diary, June 10, 1937.

43. Willis Van Devanter to FDR, May 18, 1937, Van Devanter MSS, Vol. 54; *Time*, May 31, 1937, p. 17; Stephen Tyree Early, Jr., "James Clark McReynolds and the Judicial Process," Ph.D. dissertation, University of Virginia, 1954, p. 102. Three months later Borah wrote: "I made no effort to persuade anyone to get off the Supreme bench. I think I have a fair amount of nerve, but I would not undertake such a job as that." Borah to A. A. Lewis, August 11, 1937, Borah MSS, LC, Box 414. The editor of the Boston *Herald* offered a different explanation: "That is a beautiful little controversy between the President and the C. J. Don't you suppose that Charles the Baptist persuaded Van Devanter to withdraw? Aren't the honors with the Chief Justice to date rather than with the President?" Frank Buxton to William Allen White, June 8, 1937, White MSS, Box 189.

44. *Time*, June 7, 1937, p. 13; Saginaw *Daily News*, April 13, 1937, clipping, Prentiss Brown Scrapbooks; Detroit *News*, May 19, 1937; Frank V. Cantwell, "Public Opinion and the Legislative Process," *American Political Science Review*, 40 (October 1946), 933–35. Senator Brown kindly made his scrapbooks available to me at his home in St. Ignace, Michigan. They have subsequently been deposited with the Michigan Historical Collections. An advocate of the bill wrote: "The resignation of Justice Van Devanter has somewhat altered the situation and it is doubtful if the plan will pass the Senate with[out] some modification." Henry G. Teigan to Ross Blythe, May 20, 1937, Teigan MSS, Minnesota Historical Society, St. Paul, Minn., Box 16. On the same morning that Van Devanter resigned, the Senate Judiciary Committee voted, 10–8, to reject the plan.

45. Raymond Clapper MS. Diary, April 20, May 24, 1937. One White House memorandum concluded: "The President has attained the most difficult of his *objectives*, i.e., the liberalization of the interpretation of the Constitution. He has yet to obtain these two objectives: (a) insurance of the continuity of that liberalism and (b) a more perfect judicial mechanism for giving a maximum of Justice in a minimum of time." FDRL, PSF Supreme Court.

46. Address by Lewis Schwellenbach to Labor's Non-Partisan League, Minneapolis, Minn., April 19, 1937, Schwellenbach MSS, LC, Box 1; Augustus L. and Alice B. Richards to Augustine Lonergan, April 13, 1937, Richards MSS, Cornell University Collection of Regional History; Josephus Daniels to Joseph O'Mahoney, April 7, 1937, O'Mahoney MSS, University of Wyoming Library, Laramie, Wyo.; William McAdoo to Walter Jones, April 1, 1937; McAdoo MSS, Box 433; William Chilton to Roscoe Briggs, April 1, 1937, Chilton MSS, University of West Virginia Library, Box 12; Philadelphia *Record*, April 20, 1937, clipping, Frank Murphy Collection, University of Michigan Law School.

47. Statement of Theodore Francis Green, Green MSS, Box 32. George Fort Milton commented on the Wagner Act decisions: "It would be quite an unsafe thing to depend on the continuance of the present Robertian attachment as an anchor for a new constitutional attitude of the Government. Logically,

Roberts' shift demonstrates so clearly the correctness of the Administration's position that the Constitution is all right; all that was wrong was an uncontemporarily-minded majority of the Court." George Fort Milton to Homer Cummings, April 14, 1937, Milton MSS, Box 20.

48. *Time,* May 21, 1937, p. 9; Holland (Mich.) *Sentinel,* February 16, 1937, clipping, Arthur Vandenberg Scrapbooks; Harold Ball to Joe Hendricks, March 8, 1937, Hendricks MSS, Box 2; George Baldwin to Pat McCarran, June 2, 1937, McCarran MSS, Nevada State Museum, Carson City, Nev., File 672; B. H. Chernin to Bert Lord, February 12, 1937, Lord MSS; M. E. Hennessy, "Round About," Boston *Globe,* clipping, n. d., David I. Walsh Scrapbooks, Holy Cross College Library, Worcester, Mass.; William Gibbs McAdoo to H. Hyer Whiting, March 15, 1937, McAdoo MSS, Box 432. When Senator Green received a monster telegram from members of the Rhode Island bar opposing the plan, he had the signatures analyzed; of those signers who could be identified, 213 were Republicans, seven Democrats. Memorandum, Theodore Green MSS, Box 35. A Baltimore man wrote Senator Byrnes: "On my bended knees, I beg of you not to place the American people at the mercy of a man who seems to have only the interests of the lower classes at heart. . . . Please before it is too late consider the interests of your own class." Anon. to James F. Byrnes, February 19, 1937, Byrnes MSS.

49. Burton K. Wheeler to Amos E. Pinchot, May 24, 1937, Amos Pinchot MSS, LC, Box 60; *Time,* May 31, 1937, p. 18; Lindsay Warren to A. D. McLean, May 23, 1937, Warren MSS, Box 17; New York *Herald Tribune,* June 5, 6, 10, 1937; *New York Times,* June 4, 7, 1937.

50. *Time,* June 21, 1937, p. 15; Clippings, John Garner MSS, Scrapbook 13, Archives, University of Texas, Austin, Tex.; see also *Time,* June 21, 1937, p. 15; Bascom N. Timmons, *Garner of Texas: A Personal History* (New York, 1948), pp. 216–21; Bernard F. Donahoe, *Private Plans and Public Dangers: The Story of FDR's Third Nomination* (Notre Dame, Ind., 1965), p. 49; James A. Farley, *Jim Farley's Story* (New York, 1948), pp. 83–86; Turner Catledge to Joseph W. Alsop, November 11, 1937, Alsop MSS, LC, Box 2; Homer Cummings MS. Diary, June 11, 1937, Cummings MSS, University of Virginia; Breckinridge Long MS. Diary, June 14, 1937; Detroit *News,* June 16, 1937, clipping, Prentiss Brown Scrapbooks.

Garner's departure created a deep rift between Garner and the White House circle. Raymond Clapper noted in his diary that Roosevelt's press secretary, Stephen Early, agreed with him "that Garner is at bottom of a lot of White House trouble now. Early says must be remembered that he is a millionaire and he has his goats and nut trees—is a plantation man." Raymond Clapper MS. Diary, August 3, 1937. See also Joseph Guffey to FDR, July 29, 1939, Guffey MSS, Washington and Jefferson College Library, Washington, Pa.

On the other hand, Senator Bailey was later to confide: "Mr. Garner will not be able to have much influence with those of us who resisted the attack on the Supreme Court. If he was in sympathy with us in that fight we did not find it out. The newspapers have built him up as one who stood out against the

President. He growled a good deal, but in all pinches he appeared to be on the other side." Josiah W. Bailey to Charles D. Hilles, November 30, 1938, Hilles MSS, Yale University, New Haven, Ct., Box 229. Jim Farley believed that Garner was "strongly in favor of the Court plan." Memorandum, March 7, 1937, James A. Farley MSS, LC.

51. U.S. Senate, Committee on the Judiciary, 75th Cong., 1st Sess., *Report No. 711* (Washington: Government Printing Office, 1937), pp. 10, 11, 13, 15, 23; Raymond Clapper MS. Diary, June 14, 1937. Another political column noted: "The fury with which President Roosevelt's fellow Democrats on the Senate Judiciary Committee damned the New Deal's court plan today amazed this politically sophisticated capital. . . . What was not expected was the revelation that a group of Democratic Senators would scourge themselves into an emotional frenzy to denounce a head of their party who had carried 46 States only last November." John O'Donnell and Doris Fleeson, "Capitol Stuff," New York *Daily News,* June 15, 1937, clipping, Royal Copeland Scrapbooks. See, too, Boston *Herald,* n. d., clipping, H. Styles Bridges MSS, New England College, Henniker, N. H., Scrapbook 56.

52. *Washington Post,* June 20, 1937; Alf Landon to Arthur Vandenberg, June 24, 1937, Vandenberg MSS, Personal-Confidential File, Clements Library, University of Michigan; Raymond Clapper MS. Diary, June 23, 1937.

53. William Allen White to David Hinshaw, June 17, 1937, White MSS, Series C, Box 268; R. C. Lindsay to Anthony Eden, June 22, 1937, Public Record Office, London, No. 554E, F.O. 371, 20668 (A4640/542/45).

54. Cleveland *Press,* June 17, 23, 1937; *Time,* June 28, 1937, p. 9, July 5, 1937, pp. 7–8; *New York Times,* June 17, 26, 28, 1937; *Washington Post,* June 17, 26, 27, 1937; Breckinridge Long MS. Diary, June 14, 27, 1937; New York *Herald Tribune,* June 22, 28, 1937; Watertown (N. Y.) *Daily Times,* June 22, 1937, clipping, Royal Copeland Scrapbooks; Lawrence Lewis MS. Diary, June 26, 27, 1937; Detroit *News,* June 28, 1937; Daniel Roper to Key Pittman, June 28, 1937, Pittman MSS, LC, Box 14; Daniel Roper to William E. Dodd, June 30, 1937, Roper MSS, Duke University, Box 15.

55. *New York Times,* June 29, 1937.

56. R. C. Lindsay to Anthony Eden, July 6, 1937, Public Record Office, London, No. 592E, F.O. 371, 20668 (A4931/542/45).

57. Homer Cummings MS. Diary, June 18–July 2, 1937; Stanley Reed, Memorandum for the Attorney General, June 18, 1937, FDRL President's Secretary's File—Supreme Court; Memorandum, June 18, 1937, James A. Farley MSS, LC.

58. Joseph Alsop and Turner Catledge, *The 168 Days* (Garden City, N. Y., 1968), pp. 227–28; Alva Johnston, "White House Tommy," *Saturday Evening Post,* July 31, 1937, p. 6.

59. Alsop and Catledge, *168 Days,* pp. 240–41; *New York Times,* July 3, 1937; Grenville Clark to William H. King, June 29, 1937, Clark MSS, Dartmouth College, Hanover, N. H., Series VII, Box 2; Charles D. Hilles to the Viscount Knollys, July 12, 1937, Hilles MSS, Box 212; W. K. Hutchinson to Alf Lan-

don, July 23, 1937, Landon MSS, Kansas State Historical Society, Topeka, Kan., Box 85; James A. Farley to Claude G. Bowers, July 1, 1937, Farley MSS, LC, Box 5. See, too, *New York Times*, June 5, 1937; George W. Hutsmith to Edward Gluck, June 1 and 4, 1937, Clark MSS, Series VII, Box 2.

60. Colmer, "Congressional Sidelights," Colmer MSS, University of Southern Mississippi, Hattiesburg, Miss., Box 150; Clarence Hancock to Joseph F. Graydon, June 26, 1937, Hancock MSS, Syracuse University, Syracuse, N. Y., Box 1; Kenneth McKellar to Charles T. Pennebaker, July 10, 1937, McKellar MSS, Box 97; Washington *Daily News*, July 6, 7, 1937; Press Herald Bureau, Washington, Portland *Press Herald*, July 7, 1937, clipping, Wallace White MSS, Box 81.

61. Hiram Johnson to Garret W. McEnerney, July 7, 1937, Johnson MSS. Burke's tally ten days before the final vote on the Court bill is in the Frank Gannett MSS, Box 16.

62. *New York Times*, July 4, 6, 1937; H. Styles Bridges to Robert P. Bass, April 7, 1937, Bass MSS, Dartmouth College, Box 46; Hiram Johnson to Garret W. McEnerney, July 7, 1937, Johnson MSS; *New York Times*, July 4, 1937; Portland *Press-Herald*, July 7, 1937, clipping, Wallace White MSS, Box 81.

63. "How to Bust Court Filibuster?" *Business Week*, July 17, 1937, pp. 14–15.

64. *Time*, June 14, 1937, p. 11; J. G. Shoalmire oral history interview of Turner Catledge, Catledge MSS, Mississippi State University, State University, Miss.; Frank R. Kent, "The Great Game of Politics," July 31, 1937, unidentified clipping, Alben Barkley Scrapbooks, Barkley MSS, University of Kentucky, Lexington, Ky.

65. Cleveland *Press*, July 14, 1937; New York *Herald Tribune*, May 16, 1937.

66. Detroit *Free Press*, July 11, 1937; McNary to Mrs. W. T. Stolz, July 10, 1937, McNary MSS, LC, Box 1.

67. Cleveland *Press*, July 14, 1937; *Evening Journal and New York American*, July 14, 1937; *Congressional Record*, 75th Cong., 1st sess., pp. 6787–98; Alsop and Catledge, *168 Days*, pp. 225–26; New York *Herald Tribune*, July 7, 1937; Clapper, "In the Capital," Cleveland *Press*, July 7, 1987; *Time*, July 19, 1937, p. 10; *Time*, July 14, 1937, p. 10.

68. *Congressional Record*, 75th Cong., 1st sess., p. 7144; Alsop and Catledge, *168 Days*, p. 267; Turner Catledge, *My Life and the Times* (New York, 1971), p. 96; *Time*, July 26, 1937, p. 10; New York *Herald Tribune*, July 15, 1987; *New York Times*, July 15, 1937; Dr. Henry J. Rutherford, "Case History," Bernard Baruch MSS, Princeton University.

69. Lex Green to J. H. Scales, July 19, 1937, Green MSS, Box 27; O. Max Gardner to B. B. Gossett, July 16, 1937, Gardner MSS, Southern Historical Collection, University of North Carolina, Box 15; Elmer Ellsworth Adams to Theo Christianson, July 16, 1937, Adams MSS, Minnesota Historical Society, Box 42.

70. Middletown *Times Herald*, July 15, 1937, clipping, Royal Copeland Scrapbooks; Doris Fleeson and John O'Donnell, "Capitol Stuff," Buffalo *Courier Press*, July 16, 1937, clipping, Royal Copeland Scrapbooks; *New York Times*, July 15, 1937.

71. *New York Times*, July 15, 16, 1937.

72. *Washington Post*, July 19, 1937; O. Max Gardner to B. B. Gossett, July 16, 1937, Gardner MSS, Box 15.

73. Washington *Daily News*, July 21, 1937; The Vigilantes and Affiliated Organizations U.S.A. to "Congressman," July 20, 1937, Sam Hobbs MSS, University of Alabama, Tuscaloosa, Ala.

74. Herbert Lehman to Robert F. Wagner, July 19, 1937, Lehman MSS, Columbia University, New York, N. Y.; Detroit *Free Press*, July 21, 23, 1937; Detroit *News*, July 21, 23, 1937, clippings, Prentiss Brown Scrapbooks; interview, Prentiss Brown, St. Ignace, Mich., July 7, 1965; Frank Gannett to J. P. Simmons, July 23, 1937, Gannett MSS, Box 3A; John H. Overton to Richard W. Leche *et al.*, July 22, 1937, Overton MSS; New York *Herald Tribune*, July 21, 1937; *Washington Post*, July 21, 1937; Hiram Johnson to John Francis Neylan, Johnson MSS, July 24, 1937; *New York Times*, July 22, 1937; Homer S. Cummings MS. Diary, August 1, 1937. In September, Herbert Hoover told the White House correspondent of the *New York Times*: "The strategy of silence on the Supreme Court fight was disgraceful. Also it was not effective, for it didn't kill Senator Robinson and that finally lost the Supreme Court proposals." Interview of September 28, 1937, "Black Books," Arthur Krock MSS, Princeton University, Box 10.

75. "Court and Press," *Current History*, 46 (September 1937), 19; Lawrence Lewis MS. Diary, July 22, 1937.

76. Robert Harrison, "The Breakup of the Roosevelt Supreme Court: The Contribution of History and Biography," *Law and History Review*, 2 (Fall 1984), 165–66; David M. O'Brien, *Storm Center: The Supreme Court in American Politics*, Third Edition (New York, 1993), p. 93.

77. Bernard Schwartz, *The Supreme Court: Constitutional Revolution in Retrospect* (New York, 1957); Richard Pacelle, Jr., *The Transformation of the Supreme Court's Agenda from the New Deal to the Reagan Administration* (Boulder, Col., 1991), p. 175. *Wickard v. Filburn*, 317 U.S. 111 (1942); John W. Davis, Columbia Oral History Collection (COHC), Columbia University Library, pp. 165–66.

78. "What the Court Did to Business," *Business Week*, June 5, 1937, p. 17; Frank Gannett to E. A. Dodd, February 5, 1938, Gannett MSS, Box 16. "Economic policy, so far as officialdom is concerned, became a matter of politics, not of constitutional law," one commentator has written. Arthur Selwyn Miller, "The Rise of the Techno-Corporate State in America," *Bulletin of the Atomic Scientists*, 25 (January 1969), 17.

79. Wendell L. Willkie, "The Court Is Now His," *Saturday Evening Post*, March 9, 1940, pp. 71, 74.

80. Robert T. Swaine, *The Cravath Firm* (2 vols., New York, 1948), 2: 455; John W. Davis to L. W. Goodenough, September 24, 1940; Davis to Hon. Herbert Brookes, October 19, 1944, John W. Davis MSS, Yale University, New Haven, Ct., Box 176 (William H. Harbaugh extracts).

81. James McReynolds to Dr. Robert F. McReynolds, October 30, 1937, October 1, 1940, McReynolds MSS; Robert Cushman, "Constitutional Law in 1938–1939," *American Political Science Review*, 34 (April 1940), 249; *Time*, February

3, 1941, pp. 12–13; J. C. McReynolds to John W. Davis, April 12, 1943, Davis MSS, Box 176 (Harbaugh extracts).

82. Robert J. Maddox, "Roosevelt vs. The Court," *American History Illustrated,* 4 (November 1969), 10–11; Arthur A. Ekirch, Jr., *Ideologies and Utopias: The Impact of the New Deal on American Thought* (Chicago, 1969), p. 197.

83. Torbjorn Sirevag, "Rooseveltian Ideas and the 1937 Court Fight: A Neglected Factor," *Historian,* 33 (August 1971), 579; Francis P. Miller to Herbert Claiborne Pell, April 1, 1937, Pell MSS, FDRL, Box 8; *New York Times,* August 22, 1937; Blair Moody in Detroit *News,* August 21, 1937, Blair Moody Scrapbooks, Michigan Historical Collections.

84. Albert L. Warner in New York *Herald Tribune,* February 21, 1937; George Tindall, *The Emergence of the New South, 1913–1945* (Baton Rouge, La., 1967), p. 623; James T. Patterson, *Congressional Conservatism and the New Deal* (Lexington, Ky., 1967), p. 95. The seeds of the coalition had been planted before the Court message. Ralph Flanders to Warren Austin, January 19, 1937, Flanders MSS, Syracuse University, Box 20. See, too, Frank Knox to George H. Moses, July 28, 1937, Moses MSS, New Hampshire Historical Society, Concord, N. H., Box 4.

85. D. W. Brogan, "The Attack on the Presidency," *Fortnightly,* 149 (June 1938), 686, 688; Henry Wallace COHC, p. 464. Brogan somewhat overstated matters; Roosevelt did get through legislation such as the Fair Labor Standards Act. Nonetheless, as one historian has noted, when it became "increasingly evident during the long wrangle over the Court reform bill that the coalition which had elected Roosevelt was in shambles," Congress did not hesitate to cut back funding for the WPA, which among its myriad of enterprises nurtured imaginative arts programs. Jane De Hart Mathews, *The Federal Theatre, 1935–1939: Plays, Relief, and Politics* (Princeton, N. J., 1967), p. 135.

86. Springfield (Mass.) *Republican,* March 14, 1937, clipping, David I. Walsh Scrapbooks; J. B. Hodges to Henry H. Hudson, January 14, 1938, Hodges MSS, P. K. Yonge Library of Florida History, Box 130; Richard T. Ruetten, "Showdown in Montana, 1938," *Pacific Northwest Quarterly,* 54 (January 1963), 19–29; Turner Catledge, *My Life and the Times,* p. 101; "Dean of Capitol Hill," *Columbia College Today* (Fall 1970), p. 55. I am indebted to Professor Ruetten for permission to read his excellent unpublished study of Wheeler. See, too, H. A. Sommers to Urey Woodson, August 5, 1937, Woodson MSS, University of Kentucky, Lexington, Ky.; Lionel V. Patenaude, "The Texas Congressional Delegation," *Texana,* 9 (1971), 14.

87. Josiah Bailey to Jas. R. Morris, April 22, 1937; Bailey to Julian Miller, August 4, 1937, Bailey MSS, Duke University Library, Political File.

88. Donahoe, *Private Plans and Public Dangers,* p. 14; Joseph Leib to James B. Hodges, January 4, 1938, Hodges MSS, Box 130; William B. Hill to Robert W. Winston, March 5, 1937, Winston MSS, Southern Historical Collection, Folder 49; J. E. Bass to John Overton, February 24, 1937, Overton MSS, Box 2; Helen St. Clair to Joe Hendricks, April 17, 1937, Hendricks MSS, Box 2; Walter Parkes to Theodore Green, April 6, 1937, Green MSS, Box 34; N. Y.

Gulley to Josiah Bailey, March 17, 1937, Bailey MSS, Political file. See also Martha Washburn Allin to Henry Teigan, February 13, 1937, Teigan MSS, Box 14; William F. Riley to Clyde Herring, July 7, 1937, Riley MSS, Box 1; B. Agee Bowles to Carter Glass, March 30, 1937, Glass MSS, University of Virginia, Box 377.

89. William Brockway to Burton Wheeler, May 15, 1937, Theodore Green MSS, Box 33; Frank Walker, "My Thoughts on President Roosevelt's Supreme Court Plan," Walker MSS, University of Notre Dame, Notre Dame, Ind.; Albert J. Stafne to Henrik Shipstead, July 23, 1937, Shipstead MSS, Minnesota Historical Society, Box 1. A Minnesota newspaper observed: "The Minnesota Farmer-Labor split was adding evidence of the havoc the court issue is working in party lines and in other previous congressional groupings." Duluth *Herald*, May 13, 1937, clipping, Shipstead MSS, Vol. 22.

90. William Allen White to John Finley, April 29, 1937, White MSS, Box 187; Hiram Johnson to Raymond Moley, March 13, 1937, Johnson MSS; Edward Dickson to Hiram Johnson, August 17, 1937, Dickson MSS, University of California at Los Angeles Library, Los Angeles, Cal., Box 8, Folder 9.

91. A. A. Berle, Jr. MS. Diary, February 20, 1937, Berle MSS (privately held); Robert Dallek, *Franklin D. Roosevelt and American Foreign Policy, 1932–1945* (New York, 1979), pp. 136–37, 140.

92. R. C. Lindsay to Anthony Eden, July 19, 1937, F. O. 371, 20668, No. 648E (A5352/542/45).

93. Hiram Johnson to John Francis Neylan, May 4, 1937, Johnson MSS; Burton K. Wheeler to Robert E. Jakoubek, March 27, 1972 (courtesy of Mr. Jakoubek).

94. Homer S. Cummings MS. Diary, August 1, 1937.

95. Edward S. Corwin, *Constitutional Revolution, Ltd.* (Claremont, Cal., 1941), pp. 112–13.

96. That is not to say that the Court in 1937 was prepared to go as far in the realm of civil rights as it would subsequently. Michael J. Klarman has emphasized that point in "Constitutional Fact/Constitutional Fiction: A Critique of Bruce Ackerman's Theory of Constitutional Moments," *Stanford Law Review*, 44 (February 1992), 789–91. The point is rather that the more expansive reading of the commerce clause by the Roosevelt Court opened the way for the civil rights decisions of the Warren Court with their broad conception of the commerce power.

7. A Klansman Joins the Court

1. Joseph Alsop and Turner Catledge, *The 168 Days*, (Garden City, N. Y., 1938), p. 295. One Senator wrote of "the heat and worry of this long and tedious session." Dennis Chavez to Frederick Hale, Hale MSS, Bowdoin College, Brunswick, Me., August 10, 1937, Hale MSS, Box 1.

2. *New York Times*, August 8, 1937.

3. *Complete Presidential Press Conferences of Franklin D. Roosevelt,* 10: 70–72; Louis Brandeis to Felix Frankfurter, July 30, August 3, 1937, Frankfurter MSS, Library of Congress (LC), Box 28.

4. Homer S. Cummings MS. Diary, August 2, 1937, Cummings MSS, University of Virginia, Charlottesville, Va. See, too, Cummings to Franklin D. Roosevelt, July 29, 1937, August 4, 1937, President's Secretary's File: Supreme Court, Franklin D. Roosevelt Library, Hyde Park, N. Y.; *Washington Post,* August 4, 1937.

5. Raymond Clapper MS. Diary, August 4, 1937, Clapper MSS, LC. See, too, Harold L. Ickes MS. Diary, LC, August 4, 1937. That same day, at the White House, Senator Alben Barkley of Kentucky urged Roosevelt to choose Reed, and, as he and Cummings sat together in a parked car near Barkley's office, the Senator lobbied the Attorney General to support his fellow Kentuckyian. Homer S. Cummings MS. Diary, August 4, 1937.

6. James F. Byrnes to C. C. Wyche, August 10, 1937, Byrnes MSS, Clemson University, Clemson, S. C. Byrnes added that the others being discussed were Stanley F. Reed and Donald Richberg.

7. Cummings MS. Diary, August 11, 1937.

8. Virginia Van Der Veer Hamilton, *Hugo Black: The Alabama Years* (Baton Rouge, La., 1972), p. 275; *News-Week,* August 21, 1937, p. 7; *New York Times,* August 13, 1937.

9. *News-Week,* August 21, 1937, p. 7; *New York Times,* August 13, 1937; Esther Tufty, "Michigan in Washington," *Pontiac News,* August 17, 1937, clipping, Prentiss Brown Scrapbooks, St. Ignace, Mich., subsequently deposited at Michigan Historical Collections, The University of Michigan, Ann Arbor.

10. *The Digest,* August 28, 1937, p. 6. Doubts were raised about Ashurst's argument in Cole, "Mr. Justice Black and 'Senatorial Courtesy,' " *American Political Science Review,* 31 (December 1937), 1113–15.

11. *New York Times,* August 13, 1937. For Burke's attitude, see Edward Burke to James Truslow Adams, August 19, 1937, Adams MSS, Columbia University, New York, N. Y.

12. In April, a former Republican Senator, renowned as the man who had called Western progressives "Sons of the Wild Jackass," wrote, "Senator Walsh of Massachusetts told me at a luncheon party the other day, that there are only three members of the Senate who are really in favor of the President's plan— they being La Follette of Wisconsin, Black of Alabama, and Minton of Indiana. The first two of these are extreme radicals, and the third is very much of a nitwit." George H. Moses to Edward Tuck, April 15, 1937, Moses MSS, Concord Historical Society, Concord, N. H., Box 4. See, too, Hugo L. Black to Charles B. Crow, March 18, 1937, John H. Bankhead MSS, Alabama Department of Archives and Manuscripts, Montgomery, Ala., Drawer 8.

13. Peter Gerry to W. L. Mackenzie King, August 24, 1937. I am indebted to Erik Olssen of Otago College, Dunedin, New Zealand, for this letter from the King papers in Ottawa. In June, Justice Stone had written Felix Frankfurter sardonically, "I shall not be getting much news after I leave here and if anything

new or exciting occurs, like the appointment to the Supreme Court of a man who has legal background and knowledge, do let me know about it." Harlan F. Stone to Frankfurter, June 5, 1937, Frankfurter MSS, LC, Box 105. Black, said a Republican Congressman from Massachusetts, "is an able man but not of a judiciary temperament." Allen T. Treadway, quoted in Holyoke (Mass.) *Daily Transcript*, September 14, 1937, clipping, Treadway Scrapbooks, Stockbridge Public Library, Stockbridge, Mass.

14. Douglas, *Go East, Young Man: The Early Years: The Autobiography of William O. Douglas* (New York, 1974), p. 366; Charlotte Williams, *Hugo L. Black: A Study in the Judicial Process* (Baltimore, 1950), p. 15; Earl Latham, *The Communist Controversy in Washington: From the New Deal to McCarthy* (Cambridge, Mass., 1966), p. 386. See also James Williams Columbia Oral History Collection (COHC), Columbia University, pp. 770–72; Eugene Wilson COHC, pp. 557–58; Washington *Star*, August 18, 1937, clipping, H. Styles Bridges MSS, New England College, Henniker, N. H, Scrapbook 58. For a defense of Black, see Felix Frankfurter to Grenville Clark, December 16, 1937, Clark MSS, Dartmouth College, Hanover, N. H., Series XXV, Box 1. John C. Clifford was particularly helpful in facilitating access to the Clark papers. I am also grateful to Elizabeth Mason for arranging for the photocopying of the materials in the Columbia Oral History Collection and to Esta Sobey for assistance with regard to these and other sources in the Columbia libraries.

15. Newton D. Baker to Ralph Hayes, June 10, 1936, Baker MSS, LC, Box 117.

16. C. E. Ingalls to William Allen White, August 19, 1937, White MSS, LC, Box 191; John Shaw Billings MS. Diary, August 12, 1937, South Caroliniana Collection, University of South Carolina, Columbia, S. C.; Detroit *News*, August 13, 1937, clipping, Blair Moody Scrapbooks, Michigan Historical Collections of the University of Michigan, Ann Arbor, Mich.; *The Digest*, August 28, 1937, p. 6; Chicago *Tribune*, August 14, 1937, clipping, Bertrand Snell MSS, State University College at Potsdam, Potsdam, N. Y., E4, Box 6.

17. Moley, "An Inquisitor Comes to Glory," *News-Week*, August 21, 1937, p. 40.

18. William R. Castle MS. Diary, Houghton Library, Harvard University, Cambridge, Mass., August 12–13, 1937.

19. *Washington Post*, August 13, 1937.

20. Frank Gannett to Howard E. Babcock, August 17, 1937, Babcock MSS, Cornell University, Ithaca, N. Y., C-2 (courtesy of Richard Polenberg); Charles D. Hilles to John E. Jackson, October 25, 1937, Hilles MSS, Yale University, New Haven, Ct., Box 213.

21. Alsop and Catledge, *168 Days*, p. 301; *New York Times*, August 18, 1937; *News-Week*, August 21, 1937, p. 7; *The Digest*, August 28, 1937, p. 6.

22. William P. Harvey to Frank P. Walsh, August 13, 1937, Walsh MSS, New York Public Library, New York, N. Y., Box 99; James A. Farley, *Jim Farley's Story* (New York, 1948), p. 98.

23. *Washington Post*, August 4, 1937; *New York Times*, August 4, 1937, Sep-

tember 18, 1937; John Spargo to the editor, Boston *Herald*, August 7, 1937, clipping, Spargo MSS, University of Vermont, Burlington, Vt.; Raymond Clapper MS. Diary, August 3, 1937; Homer Cummings MS. Diary, August 12, 1937; Bruce Johnstone to Harold L. Ickes, August 5, 1937, Ickes MSS, Box 205. Borah's point had, however, been troubling the Administration for several months. Edward S. Corwin to Homer Cummings, March 2, 1937, and Cummings to Corwin, March 3, 1937, Corwin MSS, Princeton University, Princeton, N. J. Some contended alternatively that Black had been a member of a Congress that had unwittingly created a new office, from which the Constitution barred him. These issues are carefully dissected in McGovney, "Is Hugo L. Black a Supreme Court Justice De Jure?," *California Law Review*, 26 (November 1937), 1–32. See, too, Charles Hall Davis to Harold Knutson, August 19, 1937, Davis MSS, University of Virginia, "Constitution 1937."

24. *New York Times*, August 17, 1937; Norman Thomas to the Committee on the Judiciary, August 16, 1937, National Office files, Socialist Party MSS, Duke University, Durham, N. C. See also Dan T. Carter, *Scottsboro: A Tragedy of the American South* (Baton Rouge, La., 1969).

25. Manchester *Union*, August 17, 1937, clipping, Bridges MSS, Scrapbook 58. See also Hamilton, *Hugo Black*, pp. 277–78.

26. *New York Times*, August 14–18, 1937. For the claim that the *Baltimore Catholic Review* supplied opposition Senators with evidence against Black, see *The Tablet*, September 18, 1937, clipping, Prentiss Brown Scrapbooks. On Black's role in the 1928 campaign, see Alfred E. Smith to Jouett Shouse, October 2, 1937, and Shouse to Smith, October 4, 1937, Shouse MSS, University of Kentucky, Lexington, Ky.

27. *New York Times*, September 13, 1937. Borah wrote a constituent, "Hawley, I do not know of a single iota of evidence to the effect that Black was a Ku Kluxer. He has denied positively that he was and denied it long before this appointment came up." William E. Borah to Jess Hawley, August 16, 1937, Borah MSS, LC, Box 412.

28. Harold L. Ickes MS. Diary, August 18, 1937; *Time*, August 23, 1937, p. 13.

29. Hiram Johnson to Frank P. Doherty, August 23, 1937, Johnson MSS, Bancroft Library, University of California, Berkeley, Cal.

30. Sprigle was later awarded the Pulitzer Prize for his work.

31. Pittsburgh *Post-Gazette*, September 13–18, 1937. Phyllis Wallach kindly photocopied this series of articles for me at the Carnegie Library, Pittsburgh, Pa.

32. Nock, "The Packing of Hugo Black," *American Mercury*, 42 (October 1937), 231–32; Rebecca Hourwich Reyher to Thomas Corcoran, September 23, 1937, Corcoran MSS, LC, Box 190. Roy Howard, head of the Scripps-Howard chain, chewed out one of his columnists for a labored, unpersuasive effort at defending Black. Roy W. Howard to Harry Elmer Barnes, September 2, 1937, Howard MSS, LC, Box 12. See also Frank Gannett to C. Greene,

September 22, 1937, Gannett MSS, Cornell University Collection of Regional History, Ithaca, N. Y., Box 16.

33. *New York Times,* September 15, 16, 1937; J. H. Bankhead to Grenville Clark, September 21, 1937, Clark MSS, Series XXV, Box 1; New York *Journal and American,* September 14, 1937, clipping, Royal S. Copeland Scrapbooks, Michigan Historical Collections. A prominent liberal editor claimed that Borah and other Senators had been informed by Black privately that he was not a member but "left them with a definite understanding that he had been." So the charge that Black, by remaining silent, had deceived the Senate was untrue. Irving Brant to Harold L. Ickes, October 4, 1937, Ickes MSS, Box 205.

34. *New York Times,* September 27, 23, 17, 21, 1937.

35. Ibid., September 27, 23, 1937; Edward L. O'Neill to John O'Connor, September 16, 1937, O'Connor MSS, Indiana University, Bloomington, Ind. Joseph Witherow to Theodore Green, September 13, 1937, Green MSS, LC, Box 32; Memorandum, September 16, 1937, Green MSS. O'Connor overstated matters. A number of Congressmen were noncommittal, and from San Antonio Maury Maverick wired him: "As a Southerner who never belonged to the Klan and who vigorously fought it and helped to eliminate it in my part of Texas, I would just as vigorously oppose the impeachment of Supreme Court Justice Black. Justice Black is an honorable, upright, progressive American and will make an able judge. Appreciate it if this be given to newspapers." Maverick to John O'Connor, September 16, 1937, O'Connor MSS. For early support by a Catholic Senator for Black, see Joseph C. O'Mahoney to Everett Martine, August 14, 1937, O'Mahoney MSS, University of Wyoming, Laramie, Wyo.

36. *New York Times,* September 14, 1937; New York *Post,* September 16, 1937, clipping, Royal S. Copeland Scrapbooks.

37. *New York Times,* September 19, 22, 1937.

38. Ibid., September 26, 1937. See also Ickes, *Diary,* 2: 216–17. For contrary views, see Philadelphia *Record,* September 15, 1937, clipping, Frank Murphy Collection, University of Michigan Law School; Paul Block editorial, clipping, H. Styles Bridges MSS, Scrapbook 60; New York *World-Telegram,* September 14, 1937, clipping, Royal S. Copeland Scrapbooks.

39. Drew Pearson and Robert S. Allen, "Washington Merry-Go-Round," September 21, 1937, clipping, Virginia Durr MSS, Alabama Department of Archives and Manuscripts, Montgomery, Ala.; Ted Morgan, *FDR: A Biography* (New York, 1985), p. 529; Harold L. Ickes MS. Diary, September 19, 1937, "Miscellaneous Pages," Ickes MSS, Box 25. The passage bears the notation, "omit B. V. C." In the printed version, this entry is dated September 25. Ickes, *Diary,* 2: 215–16. Fred Crawford to D. Kinahan, September 23, 1937, Crawford MSS, Michigan Historical Collections; Chase S. Osborn, "Editorial Evidence Piles Up," Osborn MSS, Michigan Historical Collections; Roy O. Woodruff, "Notes and Comments from Washington," attached to letter from Woodruff to Daniel Reed, September 21, 1937, Reed MSS, Cornell University Collection of Regional History, Box 14. Joseph P. Kennedy headed the SEC

and the U.S. Maritime Commission before being appointed by Roosevelt ambassador to the Court of St. James's.

40. H. L. Mencken, "Five Years of Roosevelt," typescript, November 3–6, 1937, Mencken MSS, Dartmouth College; Samuel G. Blythe to Urey Woodson, September 24, 1937, Woodson MSS, University of Kentucky; Drew Pearson and Robert S. Allen, "Washington Merry-Go-Round," September 21, 1937, clipping, Virginia Durr MSS; *Kiplinger Washington Letter*, September 18, 1937, Edward Stettinius MSS, University of Virginia.

41. *New York Times*, September 15, 1937.

42. [London] *Daily Herald*, September 16, 1937; Toledo *Blade*, September 18, 1937, clipping, Clark MSS, Series XXV, Box 1; *Time*, October 11, 1937, p. 50; John Frank, *Mr. Justice Black* (New York, 1949), p. 105; [London] *Daily Mail*, September 16, 1937; *Pall Mall*, September 17, 1937, Green MSS, Box 32; *New York Times*, September 24, 1937; "A Fugitive Justice," New York *Herald Tribune*, September 29, 1937, in "Nicholas Roosevelt Editorials," Scrapbooks, Nicholas Roosevelt MSS, Syracuse University, Syracuse, N. Y., Series V, Box 8. The American press had made headline news of the relationship between the King and the American Mrs. Simpson, to whom he was subsequently married, at a time when the British press could not breathe a word about it. I am indebted to Betsy Wade Boylan of the *New York Times* and to Joseph Frayman of the London bureau of the *New York Times* for material on the British press response.

43. *New York Times*, September 16, 17, 1937; Max Lerner to Felix Frankfurter, October 6, 1937, Lerner MSS, Yale University, New Haven, Ct.; Lerner, "Hugo Black—A Personal History," *Nation*, October 9, 1937, p. 20.

44. Black, "I Did Join the Klan," *Vital Speeches*, October 15, 1937, p. 20.

45. Ibid.

46. William F. Swindler, *Court and Constitution in the 20th Century: The New Legality, 1932–1968* (Indianapolis, 1970), pp. 86–87; New York *Herald Tribune*, October 2, 1937; Boston *Post*, October 2, 1937, clipping attached to letter from Lawrence F. Quigley to George W. Norris, October 2, 1937, Norris MSS, LC, Tray 27, Box 3; Hamilton, *Hugo Black*, p. 296; *New York Times*, October 2, 1937. For a review of editorials on the affair, with bitter attacks on Black, see Chicago *Tribune*, October 3, 1937.

47. *Commonweal*, October 15, 1937, pp. 559–60; *Catholic World*, 146 (November 1937), p. 132; Elizabeth C. Brands to U.S. Supreme Court, Charles Evans Hughes MSS, Box 18. See, too, Reverend Edward Lodge Curran to Louis Brandeis, October 6, 1937, Brandeis MSS, University of Louisville Law School, Louisville, Ky., S. C. 20, Folder 2. The "K. C.'s" were the Knights of Columbus, a Catholic fraternal organization.

48. James A. Farley to Claude G. Bowers, October 9, 1937, Farley MSS, LC, Box 5; interview of James A. Farley with the writer, New York, N. Y., April 24, 1974.

49. Farley, *Jim Farley's Story*, p. 100.

50. Theodore Green to Frank J. Keough, October 11, 1937, Green MSS, Box 32; *New York Times*, October 3, 1937.

51. Homer Cummings MS. Diary, October 4, 1937; *New York Times*, October 2, 1937.

52. William E. Leuchtenburg, "Franklin D. Roosevelt, 'Quarantine' Address, 1937," in Daniel Boorstin, ed., *An American Primer* (Chicago, 1966), pp. 846–56; John Bassett Moore to Otho Nowland, October 12, 1937, Moore MSS, LC, Box 73; Hiram Johnson to Raymond Moley, October 11, 1937, Johnson MSS. Newton D. Baker scouted these stories. "The President has too simple a mind to work out such a solution for the Black problem," he wrote. Baker to Ralph Hayes, October 12, 1937, Baker MSS, Box 117. Roosevelt also took advantage of his trip to Chicago to call on Cardinal Mundelein, an episode that was interpreted as showing the continued good relations of the Administration with the Catholic hierarchy despite the Black affair. J. F. T. O'Connor MS. Diary, October 6, 1937, Bancroft Library, University of California, Berkeley, Cal.

53. V. A. L. Mallet to Anthony Eden, October 12, 1937, F. O. 371, 20668, No. 924E (A 7543/542/45), Public Record Office, London, England.

54. U.S. Supreme Court Journal, October 11, 1937, pp. 4–5; Newton D. Baker to John H. Clarke, October 20, 1937, Baker MSS, Box 60; *New York Times*, October 12, 1937. On the other hand, when, after the opening session ended, Cummings and Reed called upon Black, they found him, far from being perturbed, "in a rather genial and joking mood," Cummings noted. The Attorney General offered to let him have the benefit of their investigation of motions to unseat him, but Black said that, though he appreciated the gesture, he saw no need, because his brethren had been very gracious and there was no reason for worry. Homer Cummings MS. Diary, October 4, 1937. Dickens portrays Christopher Casby "with his hand on one side and a gentle smile, as if he had something in his thoughts too sweetly profound to be put into words." Charles Dickens, *Little Dorrit*, Tauchnitz edition (Leipzig, 1856), 1: 212.

55. C. C. Burlingham to Felix Frankfurter, n. d. [early September 1937], January 12, 1938, Frankfurter MSS, LC, Box 34; *New York Times*, October 27, 1937; Charles P. Curtis, Jr., "How About Hugo Black?" *Atlantic Monthly*, 163 (May 1939), 667–68; Louis L. Jaffe, "The Supreme Court Today," *Atlantic*, 174 (December 1944), 76; *Newsweek*, May 23, 1938, p. 26.

56. *Time*, May 23, 1938, p. 13.

57. Marquis Childs, *Witness to Power* (New York, 1975), p. 38; Marquis Childs COHC, pp. 89–90. Two days before Black took his seat on the Court, Stone wrote John Bassett Moore, "I experienced a kind of melancholy amusement in reading your two notes with reference to the Ku Klux Klan." Harlan Fiske Stone to John Bassett Moore, October 2, 1937, Moore MSS, Box 73.

58. Childs, *Witness to Power*, pp. 38–39; Childs, "The Supreme Court Today," *Harper's*, 76 (May 1938), 581–83; Alpheus Thomas Mason, *Harlan Fiske Stone* (New York, 1956), pp. 451–55, 472–76; Raymond Clapper MS. Diary,

May 11, 1938; Clapper to Hugo Black, May 12, 1938, Clapper MSS, Box 8. For disavowals by Stone and Childs, see New York *Daily News*, May 12, 1938, Stone MSS, LC, Box 73. Learned Hand told an interviewer years later, Black "isn't my idea of what a judge is at all." Learned Hand COHC, p. 88.

59. Hamilton, "Mr. Justice Black's First Year," *New Republic*, June 8, 1938, p. 121; Canham, "The New Supreme Court," *Christian Science Monitor*, Weekly Magazine Section, April 8, 1937, p. 7. See also Irving Dilliard, *One Man's Stand for Freedom* (New York, 1963), pp. 21–24; Green, "Mr. Justice Black Versus the Supreme Court," *University of Newark Law Review*, 4 (Winter 1939), 113.

60. 309 U.S. 227 (1940) at 241. Chief Justice Hughes's biographer has written that Black voted against taking this case when it reached the Court on petition for certiorari. Merlo J. Pusey, *Charles Evans Hughes* (New York, 1963), p. 774. See, too, McElwain, "The Business of the Supreme Court as Conducted by Chief Justice Hughes," *Harvard Law Review*, 63 (November 1949), 18.

61. 311 U.S. 128 (1940).

62. Douglas, "Mr. Justice Black: A Foreword," *Yale Law Journal*, 65 (February 1956), 449–50; Alexander M. Bickel, *Politics and the Warren Court* (New York, 1965), p. 168. Anthony Lewis, the Supreme Court correspondent of the *New York Times*, wrote, "If any member of the Court saw his philosophy become doctrine in fact, it was not the Chief Justice but Justice Black." Lewis, "Earl Warren," in R. Sayler, ed., *The Warren Court: A Critical Analysis* (New York, 1969), pp. 1–2. See, too, Frederic Coudert COHC, p. 44; Allen Wardwell COHC, p. 111. Black, though, concluded that some of his brethren on the Warren Court were overstepping the bounds in their zeal for liberty and equality. He took an "absolutist" position on incorporation of the Bill of Rights not because he believed that judges should be "activist," but for precisely the opposite reason—that a standard was required so that judges, following what he deplored as "the McReynolds due process concept," would not roam freely to impose their will. *Tinker v. Des Moines School District*, 393 U.S. 503 (1969) at 520; James J. Magee, *Mr. Justice Black: Absolutist on the Court* (Charlottesville, Va., 1980), pp. 140–41.

63. Pittsburgh *Post-Gazette*, March 2, 1959, clipping, Virginia Durr MSS; Denver *Post*, n. d. [1963], clipping, International Union of Mine, Mill and Smelters MSS, University of Colorado, Boulder, Col., Box 194.

64. T. S. B. to John C. Watts, February 17, 1969, Watts MSS, University of Kentucky, Lexington, Ky., Box 85; "Hugo Black at 79," Montgomery *Advertiser*, March 2, 1965, clipping, Virginia Durr MSS. See, too, John Stennis, "Washington Report," September 26, 1962, Stennis MSS, Mississippi State University, State University, Miss.

65. "Hugo Black at 79."

66. Ferrer, "On Choosing Justices," *Time*, October 18, 1971, p. 70; *Time*, October 4, 1971, p. 15. These words were jointly applied to Justice John Harlan.

67. *Newsweek*, October 4, 1971, p. 26. "The law," said one admirer, "has lost a kindly giant." John P. Frank, "Hugo L. Black: He Has Joined the Giants,"

American Bar Association Journal, 58 (January 1972), 25. A number of commentators, especially those in Felix Frankfurter's camp, however, deplored what they regarded as Black's "activism." Black's most persistent critic has been Wallace Mendelson. See, especially, "Hugo Black and Judicial Discretion," *Political Science Quarterly*, 85 (March 1970), 35–36. In a probing essay, another writer stated that "Justice Black's constitutional understanding rested on three dubious propositions," but concluded, in more measured language, that "Black shaped the major trends in contemporary constitutional law . . . through the forcefulness, power, and single-minded clarity of purpose of his opinions, rather than through exceptional analytic ability or subtle treatment of the many complexities of constitutional adjudication. . . . Even with all his shortcomings, the power of his opinions is such that it is still accurate to think of the judicial era just ended as that of 'The Black Court.' " Sylvia Snowiss, "The Legacy of Justice Black," *Supreme Court Review 1973*, pp. 196, 250–51. On the other hand, another commentator, who described himself as an ardent admirer, regretted Black's unwillingness to join his colleagues in extending the range of civil liberties beyond a literal reading of the first eight amendments. Norman G. Rudman, "Incorporation Under the Fourteenth Amendment—the Other Side of the Coin," *Law in Transition Quarterly*, 3 (Spring 1966), 141–60.

68. Harold Brayman, *The President Speaks Off-the-Record* (Princeton, N. J., 1976), pp. 318–19.

69. Raymond Clapper MS. Diary, February 13, 1938; Hamilton, *Hugo Black*, p. 302. For continuing dissonance on the Black appointment, see Lee S. Waterman to Margaret Chase Smith, October 11, 1971, Margaret Chase Smith Library, Skowhegan, Me.

70. Frank, *Mr. Justice Black*, p. 12; Daniel M. Berman, "Hugo Black, Southerner: II. The Negro," *American University Law Review*, 10 (January 1961), 35–42; *New York Times*, September 15, 1937.

71. Bertram Wyatt-Brown, "Ethical Background of Hugo Black's Career: Thought Prompted by the Articles of Sheldon Hackney and Paul L. Murphy," *Alabama Law Review*, 36 (Spring 1985), 920–22.

72. For allegations with respect to the violence of the KKK in Alabama, see "Personal and Confidential" memorandum from Douglas Arant to Grenville Clark, September 22, 1937, Clark MSS, Series XXV, Box 1; Cochran, "One Man's Opinion," September 20, 1937, mimeographed, in Naomi Lowensohn to Raymond Moley, October 2, 1937, Moley MSS. Mr. Moley graciously made his papers available to me at his *Newsweek* offices.

73. Hamilton, *Hugo Black*, pp. 84–95; Hugo Black, Jr., *My Father: A Remembrance* (New York, 1975), pp. 52–53; Daniel M. Berman, "Hugo L. Black: The Early Years," *Catholic University of America Law Review*, 8 (May 1959), 103, 108; Daniel Berman, "The Persistent Race Issue," in Stephen Parks Strickland, ed., *Hugo Black and the Supreme Court: A Symposium* (Indianapolis, 1967), p. 79; Harris Warren, *Herbert Hoover and the Great Depression* (New York, 1959), p. 203; Anderson, "Democracy at Work," *Nation*, March 2, 1932, p. 252.

74. Martha Swain oral history interview of Turner Catledge, Catledge MSS,

Mississippi State University, State University, Miss.; Minneapolis *Journal*, November 17, 1937, clipping, Alben Barkley Scrapbooks, Barkley MSS, University of Kentucky; *Congressional Record*, 74th Cong., 1st sess., p. 6532.

75. *Mr. Justice and Mrs. Black: The Memoirs of Hugo L. Black and Elizabeth Black* (New York, 1986), pp. 70, 216.

76. *Presidential Press Conferences*, 10: 210–11; George Tindall, *The Emergence of the New South, 1913–1945* (Baton Rouge, La., 1967), p. 623; *Washington Post*, August 14, 1937; Turner Catledge to Joseph W. Alsop, November 9, 1937, Alsop MSS, LC, Box 2. Charles Michelson was the Democratic party's publicity director. More than thirty years later, Black wrote: "President Roosevelt, when I went up to lunch with him, told me that there was no reason for my worrying about my having been a member of the Ku Klux Klan. He said that some of his best friends and supporters he had in the state of Georgia were strong members of that organization. He never, in any way, by word or attitude, indicated any doubt about my having been in the Klan nor did he indicate any criticism of me for having been a member of that organization. The rumors and the statements to the contrary are wrong." Statement, April 8, 1968, Black to Virginia Van der Veer Hamilton, April 10, 1968, Black MSS, LC, Box 31; Howard Ball, "Justice Hugo L. Black: A Magnificent Product of the South," *Alabama Law Review*, 36 (Spring 1985), 797. Perhaps the conversation took place just as Black remembered it, but historians are unlikely to give a great deal of weight to an *ex parte* declaration made three decades after an event and for which there is no documentary evidence. No one ever claimed that Roosevelt criticized Black, so he was rebutting a straw man; the phrase "some of my best friends" is curious in this context; and the President did not inform Black of his appointment over lunch but at night.

77. For analyses of the impact of the Great Depression and the New Deal on civil liberties and civil rights, see Jerold Auerbach, *Labor and Liberty* (Indianapolis, 1966); Paul Murphy, *The Constitution in Crisis Times* (New York, 1972); Harvard Sitkoff, *A New Deal for Blacks: The Emergence of Civil Rights as a National Issue, the Depression Decade* (New York, 1978).

78. Statement, n. d., Norris MSS, Tray 27, Box 3; *New York Times*, September 23, 1937.

79. *The Digest*, October 16, 1937, p. 7; *Washington Evening Star*, September 21, 1937, clipping, Green MSS, Box 32. See, too, Mitchell Franklin, "The Constitutional Struggle: 1938," *National Lawyers Guild Quarterly*, 1 (December 1938), 358. It is quite likely that the series resulted from the anti-New Deal animus of Sprigle's boss, the publisher Paul Block; that money was paid for information; and that documents were supplied by a resentful Klan official, but none of these considerations is relevant to assessing Black's own behavior.

80. Philadelphia *Record*, August 18, 1937, clipping, Royal S. Copeland Scrapbooks, Michigan Historical Collections. Thaddeus Stevens served not in the Senate but in the House.

81. *The Progressive*, August 21, 1937, clipping, Royal S. Copeland Scrapbooks; *New York Times*, October 3, 1937.

82. *New York Times,* October 10, 1937.

83. Farley, *Jim Farley's Story,* p. 162. See also Detroit *News,* August 12, 1937. On the allegation that Bratton was unacceptable because of his hostility to women, see Emma Guffey Miller to Marvin McIntyre, August 6, 1937, Miller MSS, Radcliffe College, Schlesinger Library on the History of Women in America, Cambridge, Mass., Folder 14.

84. Raymond Clapper MS. Diary, August 14, 1937.

85. Homer Cummings MS. Diary, August 12, 1937; Alsop and Catledge, *168 Days,* pp. 296–307; Alison Bernstein, "Blacklash: The Making of a Supreme Court Justice, 1937," graduate colloquium paper, Columbia University, 1969; Ickes, *Diary,* 2: 83; A. A. Berle, Jr., MS. Diary, September 14, 1937. As a consequence of the opening of the Cummings papers, my account differs somewhat from that in Alsop and Catledge and from the version I originally published. Roosevelt may possibly have been swayed by electoral considerations too. In mid-July, a writer in the Birmingham *News* reported that, though three months before Black seemed safe, his prospects for re-election were now in jeopardy because of his support of Court-packing and wages and hours legislation and because he was "blamed by many for helping mix the concoctions and pour the highballs that made certain labor leaders power drunk and launched them on a jag of sit-down strike disorders." Ralph E. Hurst in Birmingham *News,* July 18, 1937. At that same time, Black himself confided, "Quite a campaign has been started against me in Alabama." Hugo L. Black to William E. Fort, July 19, 1937, Black MSS, LC, Box 28.

86. Hughes had had an earlier stint on the Supreme Court.

87. Felix Frankfurter to C. C. Burlingham, September 1, 1937, Frankfurter MSS, LC, Box 34.

88. Swindler, *New Legality,* p. 127; Williams, *Hugo L. Black,* p. v; Frank, "Justice Black and the New Deal," *Arizona Law Review,* 9 (Summer 1967), 26–58; C. Herman Pritchett, *The Roosevelt Court* (New York, 1948), p. 35; Wallace Mendelson, *Justices Black and Frankfurter* (Chicago, 1961), pp. 24, 29.

89. Pritchett, *Roosevelt Court,* pp. 12–14.

90. *Washington Post,* August 20, 1967, clipping, Virginia Durr MSS.

8. The Constitutional Revolution of 1937

1. V. O. Key, Jr., *The Responsible Electorate* (Cambridge, Mass., 1966), p. 31. See, too, Harry V. Scheiber, "The Condition of American Federalism: An Historian's View," in Frank Smallwood, ed., *The New Federalism* (Hanover, N. H., 1967), pp. 29–35.

2. M. J. Bonn, "America Today: II. The Making of a State," *Spectator,* 158 (January 29, 1937), 162–63. Cf. William E. Leuchtenburg, "The Great Depression," in C. Vann Woodward, ed., *The Comparative Approach to American History* (New York, 1968), p. 302.

3. *Hammer v. Dagenhart,* 247 U.S. 251 (1918).

4. *Home Building & Loan Association v. Blaisdell,* 290 U.S. 398 (1934); *Nebbia v.*

New York, 291 U.S. 523 (1934); Perry v. United States, 294 U.S. 330 (1935); and other "gold clause cases." Earlier in 1935, the Court, 8–1, had invalidated the "hot oil" provisions of the NIRA for improper delegation of power. *Panama Refining Co. v. Ryan,* 293 U.S. 388 (1935).

5. *R. R. Retirement Board v. Alton R. R. Co.,* 295 U.S. 330 (1935).

6. *Schechter Poultry Corp. v. United States,* 295 U.S. 495 (1935).

7. *Carter v. Carter Coal Co.,* 298 U.S. 238 (1936). The Court found fault with the delegation of powers in *Panama, Schechter,* and *Carter.*

8. *Ashton v. Cameron County Water Improvement District No. 1,* 298 U.S. 513 (1936).

9. *Colgate v. Harvey,* 296 U.S. 404 (1935) at 443; *Slaughterhouse Cases,* 16 Wall. 36 (1873). The name is sometimes rendered as Slaughter-House.

10. *Morehead v. New York ex rel. Tipaldo,* 298 U.S. 587 (1936).

11. *United States v. E. C. Knight Co.,* 156 U.S. 1 (1895).

12. *Carter v. Carter Coal Co.,* 298 U.S. 238 (1936) at 304.

13. *United States v. Butler,* 297 U.S. 1 (1936).

14. Edward S. Corwin defined the basic tenets of dual federalism as: "1. The national government is one of enumerated powers only; 2. Also the purposes which it may constitutionally promote are few; 3. Within their respective spheres the two centers of government are 'sovereign' and hence 'equal'; 4. The relation of the two centers with each other is one of tension rather than collaboration." Corwin, "The Passing of Dual Federalism," *Virginia Law Review,* 36 (February 1950), 4.

15. Virginia Wood, *Due Process of Law, 1932–1949* (Baton Rouge, La., 1951), ch. 2.

16. *West Coast Hotel Co. v. Parrish,* 300 U.S. 379 (1937).

17. Roberts had voted to uphold the Washington law prior to the President's message, although the decision was not handed down until afterward. On the much-debated question of whether Roberts switched, the best source is John W. Chambers's persuasive essay, "The Big Switch: Justice Roberts and the Minimum Wage Cases," *Labor History,* 10 (Winter 1969), 44–73, which demolishes Felix Frankfurter's contention, buttressed by a memorandum from Roberts, that Roberts never switched. Frankfurter, "Mr. Justice Roberts," *University of Pennsylvania Law Review,* 104 (December 1955), 313–16. A recent essay both reinforces Chambers's conclusions and goes beyond them. Michael Ariens, "A Thrice-Told Tale, or Felix the Cat," *Harvard Law Review,* 107 (January 1994), 620–76. Ariens comes perilously close to suggesting that Justice Felix Frankfurter forged the Roberts memorandum. For skepticism about the Frankfurter-Roberts version of Roberts's behavior on the minimum wage cases, see Edward A. Purcell, Jr., "Rethinking Constitutional Change," *Virginia Law Review,* 80 (February 1994), 279, 289–90.

There is considerable misunderstanding about the "switch in time" even among able constitutional historians. One scholar sees as the "most important point" of a recent article that it establishes that the conference vote on *West Coast Hotel Co. v. Parrish* preceded FDR's Court message. Eben Moglen, "Toward a New Deal Legal History," *Virginia Law Review*, 80 (February 1994), 265. But that point has been known for decades. Consider the following passage: "There has been a good deal of speculation about why Roberts joined the liberal majority. It is clear that Roosevelt's Court message was not responsible, for the minimum-wage decision was reached before the President sent his message, although it was not handed down until afterwards." William E. Leuchtenburg, *Franklin D. Roosevelt and the New Deal, 1932–1940* (New York, 1963), p. 236n., citing a 1951 source. Another scholar has written, "*Lochner* and its descendants would rule the juridical roost until 1937 when the Court, bearing the marks of Franklin D. Roosevelt's appointments, handed down its decision in *West Coast Hotel v. Parrish.*" Gary L. McDowell, "The Explosion and Erosion of Rights," in David J. Bodenhamer and James W. Ely, Jr., eds., *The Bill of Rights in Modern America: After 200 Years* (Bloomington, Ind., 1993), p. 29. In fact, the decision in *West Coast Hotel v. Parrish* was reached before Roosevelt had made even one appointment.

18. *Sonzinsky v. United States*, 300 U.S. 506 (1937); *Virginian Railway Co. v. System Federation No. 40*, 300 U.S. 515 (1937); *Wright v. Vinton Branch Bank*, 300 U.S. 440 (1937).

19. Robert H. Jackson, *The Struggle for Judicial Supremacy* (New York, 1941), p. 213. Jackson, who would later be named to the Supreme Court, was Assistant Attorney General in 1937.

20. The origins of the cases are discussed lucidly in Richard C. Cortner, *The Wagner Act Cases* (Knoxville, Tenn., 1964).

21. Charles C. Burlingham to William Allen White, April 1, 1937, White MSS, Library of Congress (LC), Washington, D. C., Box 187; Paul Mallon, "Purely Confidential," Detroit *News*, April 7, 1937; Homer S. Cummings MS. Diary, University of Virginia, Charlottesville, Va., June 20, 1935; *Time*, April 26, 1937, p. 15; J. Warren Madden Oral History (OH), School of Industrial and Labor Relations, Cornell University, Ithaca, N. Y., p. 43. See, too, R. C. Lindsay to Anthony Eden, March 30, 1937, Public Record Office, London, Eng., No. 281E, F. O. 371, 20668 (A2561/542/45); Thomas I. Emerson OH, School of Industrial and Labor Relations, Cornell University, Ithaca, N. Y.; Raymond Clapper MS. Diary, April 12, 1937. For the background of the case, see Memorandum, n. d., Lucy Randolph Mason MSS, Duke University, Durham, N. C. The Court had announced the "current of commerce" doctrine, which broadened the government's powers under the commerce clause, in a unanimous opinion by Justice Oliver Wendell Holmes, Jr. in *Swift and Company v. United States*, 196 U.S. 375 (1905).

22. *Washington, Virginia & Maryland Coach Co. v. N. L. R. B.*, 301 U.S. 142 (1937); *N. L. R. B. v. Jones & Laughlin Steel Corp.*, 301 U.S. 1 (1937); *N. L. R. B. v. Fruehauf Trailer Co.*, 301 U.S. 49 (1937); *N. L. R. B. v. Friedman-Harry Marks Clothing Co.*, 301 U.S. 58 (1937); *Associated Press v. N. L. R. B.*, 301 U.S. 103 (1937). Conservatives were startled by the outcome. A former Hoover official wrote in his diary, "I thought the steel case would be decided unanimously the other way." William R. Castle MS. Diary, April 14, 1937, Houghton Library,

Harvard University, Cambridge, Mass. See, too, John Callan O'Laughlin to Herbert Hoover, March 27, 1937, O'Laughlin MSS, Herbert Hoover Archives, Stanford, Cal.; typescript of radio broadcast by Boake Carter, April 12, 1937, Joseph Pulitzer MSS, LC, Box 76.

23. 301 U.S. at 37.

24. Daniel G. Yorkey, "National Labor Relations Cases," *Cornell Law Quarterly,* 22 (June 1937), 568–76; Spurgeon Avakian, "The National Labor Relations Decisions in the United States Supreme Court," *California Law Review,* 25 (July 1937), 593–615; *University of Pennsylvania Law Review,* 85 (May 1937), 733–35. One critic found fault with "all the phoney distinctions which the Chief Justice has since tried to draw between what he said in the Schechter case and what Sutherland said in the Carter case, and what the Chief Justice said later in the Jones and Laughlin case." Edward F. Prichard, Jr. to Edward S. Corwin, April 21, 1937, Corwin MSS, Box 2, Princeton University, Princeton, N. J.

25. *Carter v. Carter Coal Co.,* 298 U.S. 238 (1936) at 303.

26. 301 U.S. at 94, 97, 99.

27. Detroit *News,* April 13, 1937; *Christian Century,* 54 (April 21, 1937), 510. See, too, Address by Lewis Schwellenbach to Labor's Non-Partisan League, Minneapolis, Minn., April 19, 1937, Schwellenbach MSS, LC, Box 1.

28. Raymond Clapper MS. Diary, May 6, 1937. On the government's strategy, see, too, Thurman Arnold to Edward Corwin, October 5, 1936, Corwin MSS.

29. *Steward Machine Co. v. Davis,* 301 U.S. 548 (1937).

30. *Helvering v. Davis,* 301 U.S. 619 (1937).

31. 301 U.S. 619 at 640. In *Butler,* Roberts had endorsed the broad Hamiltonian view of the welfare clause before going on to hold that the AAA's processing tax was invalid.

32. *Carmichael v. Southern Coal & Coke Co.,* 301 U.S. 495 (1937).

33. John R. Schmidhauser, *The Supreme Court as Final Arbiter in Federal-State Relations, 1789–1957* (Chapel Hill, N. C., 1958), p. 176.

34. *Currin v. Wallace,* 306 U.S. 1 (1939) at 14.

35. Schwartz, *Supreme Court,* p. 27. The Court did, nonetheless, retain wide scope in interpreting statutes. That point is stressed in John J. Cound, review of Bernard Schwartz, *The Supreme Court: Constitutional Revolution in Retrospect,* in *Minnesota Law Review,* 42 (May 1958), 1218.

36. Brother E. Adrian Leonard, F.S.C., "Mr. Justice Roberts and the Constitutional Revolution of 1937," Ph. D. dissertation, University of Notre Dame, 1967, ch. 6.

37. Stanley F. Reed, Columbia Oral History Collection (COHC), pp. 275–76.

38. *Mulford v. Smith,* 307 U.S. 38 (1939) at 48; Robert L. Stern, "The Commerce Clause and the National Economy, 1933–1946," *Harvard Law Review,* 59 (May 1946), 692–93; Notes for argument, *Mulford v. Smith,* Robert H. Jackson

MSS, LC, Box 82; Robert Shields to Charles Fahy, November 12, 1942, Fahy MSS, Franklin D. Roosevelt Library, Hyde Park, N. Y., Box 46.

39. It should, though, be noted that the second AAA did not levy a processing tax and imposed marketing quotas rather than direct production quotas. At issue was the commerce power rather than the power to tax for the general welfare. The Court did not state flatly that the commerce clause permitted federal regulation of agriculture until 1955. *Maneja v. Waialua Agricultural Co.*, 349 U.S. 254 (1955) at 259.

40. *Currin v. Wallace*, 306 U.S. 1 (1939) at 10–11.

41. *United States v. Wrightwood Dairy Co.*, 315 U.S. 110 (1942); *U.S. v. Rock Royal Co-operative Co.*, 307 U.S. 533 (1939). See, too, *H. P. Hood and Sons v. U.S.*, 307 U.S. 588 (1939); Ashley Sellers and Jesse E. Baskette, Jr., "Agricultural Marketing Agreement and Order Programs, 1933–1943," *Georgetown Law Journal*, 33 (January 1945), 123; Sotirios A. Barber, *The Constitution and the Delegation of Congressional Power* (Chicago, 1975), pp. 95–96.

42. *Wickard v. Filburn*, 317 U.S. 111 (1942).

43. Robert G. McCloskey, *The American Supreme Court* (Chicago, 1960), p. 185. John W. Davis, the Democratic presidential nominee in 1924 and the country's leading corporation lawyer, later called it "the most ridiculous opinion any man ever put his name to." He added: "*Wickard v. Filburn* is my pet abomination. . . . He's affecting commerce because he doesn't engage in it." John W. Davis COHC.

44. *Polish National Alliance v. N. L. R. B.*, 136 F.2d 185 (CCA 7th, 1943) at 180, quoted in Cortner, *Wagner Act Cases*, p. 189. He made this statement with respect to the expansion of the NLRB's jurisdiction.

45. *Electric Bond & Share Company v. S. E. C.*, 303 U.S. 419 (1938); Robert H. Jackson MS. Autobiography, LC, pp. 45–48.

46. *North American Co. v. S. E. C.*, 327 U.S. 686 (1946); *American Power and Light Co. v. S. E. C.*, 329 U.S. 90 (1946).

47. 327 U.S. 686 at 705. The Court also freed both national and state agencies engaged in regulating utility rates from the tyranny of *Smyth v. Ames*, 169 U.S. 466 (1898). By holding that rate-making had to be based on the "fair value" of the utility property, that ruling had implicated the Justices in functions that properly belonged to legislatures and their agents. For the new doctrines, see *Driscoll v. Edison Light & Power Co.*, 307 U.S. 104 (1939); *Federal Power Commission v. Natural Gas Pipeline Co.*, 315 U.S. 575 (1942); *Federal Power Commission v. Hope Natural Gas Co.*, 320 U.S. 591 (1944).

48. *Alabama Power Co. v. Ickes*, 302 U.S. 464 (1938); *Tennessee Electric Power Company v. T. V. A.*, 306 U.S. 118 (1939); R. L. Duffus, *The Valley and the People* (New York, 1946), p. 68; "Midnight, August 15, 1939—The End of an Era," Scrapbook of clippings from Chattanooga Papers, Tennessee Electric Power Company MSS, Tennessee Valley Authority Library, Knoxville, Tenn., Box 8.

49. *United States v. Appalachian Electric Power Co.*, 311 U.S. 377 (1940). The New River flowed through two states, and a few craft had been dragged

through its shallow reaches. For the odyssey of the case, see "The Story of New River," Judson King MSS, LC, Box 15.

50. Arthur Krock, "Reminiscences," *Centennial Review*, 9 (Spring 1965), 239.

51. 311 U.S. at 426.

52. *Oklahoma ex rel. Phillips v. Guy F. Atkinson Co.*, 313 U.S. 508 (1941).

53. *United States v. Bekins*, 304 U.S. 27 (1938).

54. *Prudential Ins. Co. v. Benjamin*, 328 U.S. 408 (1946) at 433, note 42. See David Fellman, "Ten Years of the Supreme Court: 1937–1947, I. Federalism," *American Political Science Review*, 41 (December 1947), 1148n.

55. *Sunshine Anthracite Coal Co. v. Adkins*, 310 U.S. 381 (1940). The new act did not, however, contain the labor provisions to which the Court had objected in *Carter*.

56. 310 U.S. at 393, 396. Thomas C. Longin, "Coal, Congress and the Courts: The Bituminous Coal Industry and the New Deal," *West Virginia History*, 35 (January 1974), 128.

57. *United States v. Darby Lumber Company*, 312 U.S. 100 (1941).

58. Ibid. at 117, 116, 119.

59. Paul R. Benson, Jr., *The Supreme Court and the Commerce Clause, 1937–1970* (New York, 1970), p. 89. For the pleasure of organized labor in this and other decisions, see American Federation of Labor, "Committee Report on Legal Activities," John P. Frey MSS, LC, Box 13. In a controversial decision thirty-five years later, the Court breathed new life into the Tenth Amendment in *National League of Cities v. Usery*, 426 U.S. 833 (1976). But only nine years later, the Court overturned this ruling. *Garcia v. San Antonio Metropolitan Transit Authority*, 469 U.S. 528 (1985).

60. *Santa Cruz Fruit Packing Company v. N. L. R. B.*, 303 U.S. 453 (1938) at 467.

61. *Consolidated Edison Company v. N. L. R. B.*, 305 U.S. 197 (1938); *N. L. R. B. v. Fainblatt*, 306 U.S. 601 (1939).

62. *A. B. Kirschbaum Co. v. Walling*, 316 U.S. 517 (1942).

63. *Walton v. Southern Package Corporation*, U.S. 540 (1944); *Borden Co. v. Borella*, U.S. 679 (1945); *Martino v. Michigan Window Cleaning Co.*, 327 U.S. 173 (1946).

64. *Case v. Bowles*, 327 U.S. 92 (1946). See, too, *Standard Oil Co. of California v. Johnson*, 316 U.S. 418 (1942).

65. See, e.g., *Southern Pacific Co. v. Arizona*, 325 U.S. 761 (1945); *Hale v. Bimco Trading Co.*, 306 U.S. 375 (1939); *Best v. Maxwell*, 311 U.S. 454 (1940); *McLeod v. Dilworth*, 322 U.S. 327 (1944).

66. Benjamin F. Wright, *The Growth of American Constitutional Law* (Chicago, 1967), pp. 221–22. The book originally appeared in 1942.

67. Bernard Schwartz, *The Supreme Court: Constitutional Revolution in Retrospect* (New York, 1957), p. 28.

68. Michael E. Parrish, "The Great Depression, the New Deal, and the American Legal Order," *Washington Law Review*, 59 (September 1984), 743; Wright, *Growth*, pp. 221–22.

69. *Nebbia v. New York,* 291 U.S. 502 (1934) at 556.

70. *Osborn v. Ozlin,* 310 U.S. 53 (1940) at 62.

71. *Daniel v. Family Security Life Ins. Co.,* 336 U.S. 220 (1949) at 224.

72. *Day-Brite Lighting Inc. v. Missouri,* 342 U.S. 421 (1952) at 423.

73. John A. C. Hetherington, "State Economic Regulation and Substantive Due Process of Law," *Northwestern University Law Review* 53 (March-April 1958), 24–25. See, too, Vincent M. Barnett, Jr., "The Supreme Court and the Capacity to Govern," *Political Science Quarterly,* 63 (September 1948), 354–55.

74. *Milk Control Board v. Eisenberg Farm Products,* 306 U.S. 346 (1939); *Parker v. Brown,* 317 U.S. 341 (1943).

75. *Clark v. Paul Gray, Inc.,* 306 U.S. 583 (1939); *McGoldrick v. Berwind-White Coal Mining Co.,* 309 U.S. 33 (1940). *Nelson v. Sears, Roebuck & Co.,* 312 U.S. 359 (1941); *Caskey Baking Co. v. Virginia,* 313 U.S. 117 (1941); *General Trading Co. v. Tax Commission,* 322 U.S. 335 (1944).

76. *Madden v. Kentucky,* 309 U.S. 83 (1940).

77. *Swift v. Tyson,* 16 Pet. 1 (1842); *Erie Railroad Co. v. Tompkins,* 304 U.S. 64 (1938); Harlan Fiske Stone to Louis Brandeis, March 23, 25, 1938, Stone MSS, LC, Box 73; Erwin Griswold to Stone, May 4, 1938, Stone MSS, Box 15; Felix Frankfurter to Harry Shulman, May 23, 1938, Frankfurter MSS, LC; Stanley F. Reed COHC, pp. 248–49; Harold Leventhal COHC, pp. 321–22; Grant Gilmore, "Legal Realism: Its Cause and Cure," *Yale Law Journal,* 70 (June 1961), 1046–47. See, too, Harlan F. Stone to Frankfurter, April 29, 1938, Frankfurter MSS, LC, Box 105; Stone to Walter Wheeler Cook, Stone MSS, LC, Box 10; Alexander Bickel to Frankfurter, May 7, 1959, Frankfurter MSS, Box 24; J. J. Smith, Jr. to Ross Collins, April 29, 1957, Collins MSS, LC; Tony Freyer, *Harmony and Dissonance: The Swift and Erie Cases in American Federalism* (New York, 1981); John Hart Ely, "The Irrepressible Myth of Erie," *Harvard Law Review,* 87 (February 1974), 693–740. For the application of the same principle to equity cases, see *Ruhlin v. New York Life Ins. Co.,* 304 U.S. 202 (1938); Fellman, "Ten Years," pp. 1149–53.

78. *Connecticut General Life Insurance Co. v. Johnson,* 303 U.S. 77 (1938).

79. *Williamson v. Lee Optical Co.,* 348 U.S. 483 (1955) at 488.

80. C. Herman Pritchett, *The Roosevelt Court* (New York, 1963), p. 168. The book originally appeared in 1948. See, too, Vincent M. Barnett, Jr., "The Political Philosophy of the New Supreme Court," *Journal of Social Philosophy and Jurisprudence,* 7 (January 1942), 117.

81. *I. C. C. v. Railway Labor Executives Association,* 315 U.S. 373 (1942); *First Iowa Hydro-Electric Cooperative v. Federal Power Commission,* 328 U.S. 152 (1946).

82. *Morgan v. United States,* 298 U.S. 468 (1936); 304 U.S. 1 (1938) at 14–15; *Time,* May 9, 1938, p. 14; *United States v. Morgan,* 307 U.S. 183 (1939); 313 U.S. 409 (1941) at 422. Subsequently, some of FDR's appointees concluded that they had carried tolerance of bureaucratic judgments too far. "Expertise can become a monster which rules with no practical limit on its discretion," declared Justice William O. Douglas in 1951. "Absolute discretion, like corruption, marks the beginning of the end of liberty." *New York v. United States,* 342

U.S. 882 (1951) at 884. As Michael Parrish has observed, "Douglas, the heir to Brandeis, sounded very much like Charles Evans Hughes" in his hostility to administrative license. Michael E. Parrish, "The Hughes Court, the Great Depression, and the Historians," *Historian*, 40 (February 1978), 306.

83. *Herndon v. Lowry*, 301 U.S. 242 (1937); McCloskey, *American Supreme Court*, pp. 178–79.

84. *Palko v. Connecticut*, 302 U.S. 319 (1937) at 326–27; *United States v. Carolene Products Co.*, 304 U.S. 144 (1938) at 152, n. 4; *Missouri ex rel. Gaines v. Canada*, 305 U.S. 337 (1938). See, though, Wiley Rutledge to Irving Brant, December 15, 1941, Rutledge MSS, LC, Box 95.

85. Wright, *Growth*, p. 221.

86. *Chambers v. Florida*, 309 U.S. 227 (1940); *Edwards v. California*, 314 U.S. 160 (1941); *Thomas v. Collins*, 323 U.S. 516 (1945); *Bridges v. California*, 314 U.S. 252 (1941); *Senn v. Tile Layers Union*, 301 U.S. 468 (1937); *Lovell v. Griffin*, 303 U.S. 444 (1938). These developments are very well treated in Richard C. Cortner, *The Supreme Court and the Second Bill of Rights: The Fourteenth Amendment and the Nationalization of Civil Liberties* (Madison, Wis., 1981). Numbers of commentators have concluded that the Court eventually, especially in the 1960s, in its zeal for civil liberties took on the characteristics of the pre-1937 Court. One historian has written, "It is fair to postulate that Brandeis would have been pleased at the context of some of the Court's proliberties decisions but horrified by the activist stance adopted by the judiciary." Philippa Strum, *Louis D. Brandeis: Justice for the People* (Cambridge, Mass., 1984), p. 415. For the contention that substantive due process did not die but merely shifted emphases and clients, see Martin Shapiro, "The Supreme Court's 'Return' to Economic Regulation," *Studies in American Political Development*, 1 (1986), 93, and Arthur Shenfield, "The New Deal and the Supreme Court," in Robert Eden, ed., *The New Deal and Its Legacy: Critique and Reappraisal* (Westport, Ct., 1989), p. 170.

87. Tinsley E. Yarbrough, *Mr. Justice Black and His Critics* (Durham, N. C., 1988), p. 53; Donald H. Gjerdingen, "The Future of Our Past: The Legal Mind and the Legacy of Classical Common-Law Thought," *Indiana Law Journal*, 68 (Summer 1993), 764–65. See, too, James W. Ely, Jr., "The Enigmatic Place of Property Rights in Modern Constitutional Thought," in Bodenhamer and Ely, *Bill of Rights*, p. 87; Gjerdingen, "The Future of Legal Scholarship and the Search for a Modern Theory of Law," *Buffalo Law Review*, 35 (Spring 1986), 423n.

In a brilliant bicentennial essay in 1987, the legal scholar Cass Sunstein concluded: "The New Deal . . . produced a radically different constitutional structure. . . . In a time in which the nation celebrates the enormous achievements of the drafters of the original document, it is important to remember the accomplishment of others who have played a role in developing the modern constitutional structure. This category includes not merely the most important Justices of the Supreme Court, but a small group of others who have attained the status of constitutional framers—prominent among them Franklin D. Roosevelt." Cass R. Sunstein, "The Beard Thesis and Franklin Roosevelt," *George Washington Law Review*, 56 (November 1987), 122–23.

In the two decades after 1937, the Court held only four federal statutes unconstitutional, and in none of these was an important regulation of the economy involved. *Tot v. United States*, 319 U.S. 463 (1943); *United States v. Lovett*, 328 U.S. 303 (1946); *United States ex rel. Toth v. Quarles*, 350 U.S. 11 (1955); *Reid v. Covert*, 354 U.S. 1 (1957). The last case was grouped with *Kinsella, Warden v. Krueger*.

88. *Youngstown Sheet & Tube Co. v. Sawyer*, 343 U.S. 579 (1952). The decision nullified an order issued by President Truman directing the seizure and operation of the nation's steel mills in order to head off a strike. The best account of the controversy is Maeva Marcus, *Truman and the Steel Seizure Case: The Limits of Presidential Power* (New York, 1977).

89. It held, for example, that taxicab service at Chicago railroad terminals was not in interstate commerce. *United States v. Yellow Cab Co.*, 332 U.S. 218 (1947). See, too, *Walling v. Jacksonville Paper Co.*, U.S. 564 (1943) at 570; 10 *East Building v. Callus*, 325 U.S. 578 (1945).

90. Thomas Reed Powell, *Vagaries and Varieties in Constitutional Interpretation* (New York, 1956), p. 69.

91. *N. L. R. B. v. Fansteel Metallurgical Corp.*, 306 U.S. 240 (1939) at 252. See, too, Elizabeth Ahern to the editor, *Commonweal*, 39 (March 17, 1939), 575–76; William Allen White to Felix Frankfurter, April 2, 1937, White MSS, Box 187; Chase S. Osborn to George Osborn, March 31, 1937, Osborn MSS, Michigan Historical Collections of the University of Michigan, Ann Arbor, Mich. Reed subsequently denied that the Court in *Fansteel* had outlawed sitdown strikes. At issue, he said, was not the legitimacy of sitdowns but the authority of the board. Stanley F. Reed COHC, pp. 271–72.

92. The Court did, however, sustain extensive delegations of power to both regulatory agencies and private groups. See, e.g., *Opp Cotton Mills v. Administrator*, 312 U.S. 126 (1941).

93. Carl B. Swisher, *The Growth of Constitutional Power in the United States* (Chicago, 1946), p. 229. For a stimulating analysis of the way in which a younger generation of lawyers views the preoccupations of the New Deal era, see Bruce A. Ackerman, *Reconstructing American Law* (Cambridge, Mass., 1984).

94. Peter H. Irons, *The New Deal Lawyers* (Princeton, N. J., 1982), p. 297; *Industrial Union Department v. American Petroleum Institute*, 100 S. Ct., 2844 (1980) at 2886; James O. Freedman, "Delegation of Power and Institutional Competence," *University of Chicago Law Review*, 43 (Winter 1976), 318–21.

95. Alfred H. Kelly and Winfred A. Harbison, *The American Constitution*, Third Edition (New York, 1963), p. 795. At another point they refer to "a limited revolution in the American constitutional system." p. 722. Yet, curiously, they also observe: "The Court executed the most abrupt change of face in its entire history." p. 760. At a later point: "The decisions of the Roosevelt Court in the field of civil liberties worked a revolution in the relation of the

Court to the states and of government in general to the individual hardly less important than the revolution in federalism consummated about the same time." p. 815. In 1994 a historian contemptuously dismissed the conclusion of two generations of scholars that 1937 was a watershed as a "bedtime story." Barry Cushman, "Rethinking the New Deal Court," *Virginia Law Review*, 80 (February 1994), 201–61. He reached that judgment without the benefit of any original research in the papers of the Justices, and, though he argued for approaching the question by examining the internal legal reasoning of the Court, without scrutinizing most of the cases of the era and, in particular, without coping with the arguments of Justices such as Stone who had no doubt there had been a volte-face.

96. *Kentucky Whip & Collar Co. v. Illinois Central Railroad Co.*, 299 U.S. 334 (1937). The Court sustained an act banning shipment of convict-made goods across state lines, although there was nothing harmful about the articles themselves, a distinction that had been insisted on in *Hammer v. Dagenhart*.

97. *Henneford v. Silas Mason Co.*, 300 U.S. 577 (1937).

98. *Stromberg v. California*, 283 U.S. 359 (1931); *Powell v. Alabama*, 287 U.S. 45 (1932); *Norris v. Alabama*, 294 U.S. 587 (1935); *Near v. Minnesota*, 283 U.S. 697 (1931); *Grosjean v. American Press Co.*, 297 U.S. 233 (1936); *Brown v. Mississippi*, 297 U.S. 278 (1936). The last case is scrutinized in Richard C. Cortner, *A "Scottsboro" Case in Mississippi: The Supreme Court and Brown v. Mississippi* (Jackson, Miss., 1986). For the view that 1937 was not a watershed in civil liberties, see John Braeman, *Before the Civil Rights Revolution: The Old Court and Individual Rights* (Westport, Ct., 1988), p. viii.

99. Merlo J. Pusey, *Charles Evans Hughes* (New York, 1963), pp. 768–69. The book first appeared in 1951. The notion that the constitutional crisis of the 1930s derived not from the behavior of the judiciary but from the shortcomings of the New Dealers as legislative draftsmen and as lawyers has proved remarkably enduring. One 1994 article finds this contention convincing because of "the *very large number* of cases during FDR's first term in which the Government lost unanimously or convinced only one Justice of the propriety of its position." Eben Moglen, "Toward a New Deal Legal History," 270 (italics added). In fact, only a single statute, the National Industrial Recovery Act, fits that description. (The only other law struck down in this fashion, the Frazier-Lemke measure, was not a New Deal proposal.) By far the most effective statement of the poor draftsmanship argument is in Peter H. Irons's *The New Deal Lawyers*, a most important contribution. Irons, though, confines his attention to a very few statutes.

100. The Administration took pains to argue that there was no conflict between the Wagner Act and the Court's earlier decisions. Solicitor General Stanley Reed observed: "As you know I do not see any clear inconsistency between Wagner on the one hand and the Guffey or N.R.A. decision on the other. The Wagner decision is based on the right to remedy situations which obstruct or tend to obstruct interstate commerce. The Guffey and the Poultry Code were aimed directly at wages, hours and labor conditions." Reed, Memorandum for

the Attorney General, April 22, 1937, National Archives, Washington, D. C., Dept. of Justice 114-115-2. One historian has noted that "several contemporary commentators . . . doubted that the Wagner Act cases stood for anything broader than the proposition that the labor relations of a productive enterprise that stood astride a current of commerce could be regulated in the national public interest." Barry Cushman, "A Stream of Legal Consciousness: The Current of Commerce Doctrine from *Swift* to *Jones & Laughlin*," *Fordham Law Review*, 61 (October 1992), 154. He asserts, "Many members of Congress sincerely doubted the constitutionality of the Guffey Coal Act but not that of the Wagner Act." Ibid., p. 138. In fact, as the leading authority on the subject emphasized a generation ago, "the central argument [of opponents of the Wagner legislation] was that the bill was unconstitutional" and the legislation was approved by a large margin in good part because "many senators, convinced that the bill was unconstitutional, wished to shift the onus of its defeat to the Supreme Court. They would gain labor's political support while certain that the measure would not take effect because employers would fail to comply until the court declared it void." Irving Bernstein, *Turbulent Years: A History of the American Worker, 1933–1941* (Boston, 1970), pp. 336, 341.

101. Pusey, *Hughes*, p. 767. See, too, Samuel Hendel, *Charles Evans Hughes and the Supreme Court* (New York, 1951), pp. 264–65. Cf. F. D. G. Ribble, "The Constitutional Doctrines of Chief Justice Hughes," *Columbia Law Review*, 41 (November 1941), 1198–99; Alpheus Thomas Mason, *The Supreme Court from Taft to Warren* (Baton Rouge, La., 1958), pp. 104–5; W. Graham Cole, Jr., "The Supreme Court and the New Deal: Change and Continuity," Colloquium essay, Columbia University, 1968. A powerful argument for the consistency of Hughes's views is Paul A. Freund, "Charles Evans Hughes as Chief Justice," *Harvard Law Review*, 81 (November 1967), 4. An argument for continuity is made from a different perspective in Karl E. Klare, "Judicial Deradicalization of the Wagner Act and the Origins of Modern Legal Consciousness, 1937–1941," *Minnesota Law Review*, 62 (1978), 280. Some writers who are impressed by Hughes's consistency also believe that the Court as a whole changed its outlook in 1937.

102. *Houston, East and West Texas Ry. v. United States*, 234 U.S. 342 (1914) at 353–54, 358. See Freund, "Hughes as Chief Justice," p. 37; Robert H. Jackson, "The Judicial Career of Chief Justice Hughes," *American Bar Association Journal*, 27 (July 1941), 410. Jackson and others point to additional earlier opinions by Hughes such as that in the *Minnesota Rate Cases*, 230 U.S. 352 at 398–99.

103. *Madden v. Kentucky*, 309 U.S. 83 (1940); *Colgate v. Harvey*, 296 U.S. 404 (1935); *Slaughterhouse Cases*, 16 Wall. 36 (1873).

104. Raymond Clapper MS. Diary, April 12, 1937. Jackson later declared, "Hughes's vigorous championship of federal power under the commerce clause is reminiscent of Marshall." Jackson, "Judicial Career," p. 410.

105. Parrish, "Great Depression," p. 732. One commentator has said that "the real constitutional crisis" arose not from the conflict between Roosevelt and the Court but from the "disillusion," after Roberts's switch, "that came with the

realization that law was made by the Court." Philip Bobbitt, *Constitutional Fate: Theory of the Constitution* (New York, 1982), p. 28. For yet another perspective on that moment, see Howard Gillman, *The Constitution Besieged: The Rise and Demise of Lochner Era Police Powers Jurisprudence* (Durham, N. C., 1993).

106. *Grovey v. Townsend,* 295 U.S. 45 (1935); *Near v. Minnesota,* 283 U.S. 697 (1931); *Herndon v. Lowry,* 301 U.S. 242 (1937); *Nardone v. United States,* 302 U.S. 379 (1937).

107. Felix Frankfurter to FDR, November 15, 1935, in Max Freedman, ed., *Roosevelt and Frankfurter: Their Correspondence, 1928–1945* (Boston, 1967), p. 294; Parrish, "Hughes Court," p. 290n.

108. Edward S. Corwin, "The Schechter Case—Landmark, Or What?" *New York University Law Quarterly Review,* 13 (January 1936), 185–90; Alpheus Thomas Mason, *The Supreme Court: Palladium of Freedom* (Ann Arbor, Mich., 1962), p. 139.

109. R. Kent Newmyer, "John Marshall," in Kermit L. Hall, ed., *The Oxford Companion to the Supreme Court of the United States* (New York, 1992), p. 526.

110. Bruce Ackerman, "Constitutional Politics/Constitutional Law," *Yale Law Journal,* 99 (December 1989), 491; Richard A. Epstein, "The Mistakes of 1937," *George Mason University Law Review,* 11 (Winter 1988), 11.

111. Wright, *Growth,* p. 200.

112. *Morehead v. New York ex rel. Tipaldo,* 298 U.S. 587 (1936) at 611.

113. Alan F. Westin and C. Herman Pritchett, "The Supreme Court Since 1937," in Pritchett and Westin, eds., *The Third Branch of Government* (New York, 1963), p. 1; Ackerman, "Constitutional Politics/Constitutional Law," pp. 487–88. One scholar has written recently, "President Roosevelt's New Deal marked a fundamental change in American legal and political culture." Cass R. Sunstein, *The Partial Constitution* (Cambridge, Mass., 1993), p. 349.

114. Pritchett, *Roosevelt Court,* pp. 57, 55.

115. *Graves v. New York ex rel. O'Keefe,* 306 U.S. 466 (1939), reversing *Collector v. Day,* 11 Wall. 113 (1870), a doctrine reaffirmed in *New York ex rel. Rogers v. Graves,* 299 U.S. 401 (1937).

116. 8 Wall. 168 (1869); *United States v. South-Eastern Underwriters Assn.,* 322 U.S. 533 (1944). See, too, *Polish National Alliance v. N. L. R. B.,* 322 U.S. 643 (1944).

117. *Smith v. Allwright,* 321 U.S. 649 (1944); *Grovey v. Townsend,* 295 U.S. 45 (1935).

118. 321 U.S. at 669. Cf. Roberts's complaint in *Mahnich v. Southern Steamship Co.,* 321 U.S. 96 (1944) at 113.

119. Quoted in Felix Frankfurter to Harlan Fiske Stone, March 17, 1939, Stone MSS, Box 6; Charles E. Clark to Edward S. Corwin, February 10, 1941, Corwin MSS, Box 1.

120. Norman Silber and Geoffrey Miller, "Toward 'Neutral Principles' in the Law: Selections from the Oral History of Herbert Wechsler," *Columbia Law Review,* 93 (May 1993), 924; Duncan Kennedy, "Toward an Historical Under-

standing of Legal Consciousness: The Case of Classical Legal Thought in America, 1850–1940," *Research in Law and Sociology*, 3 (1980), 6.

121. *Bowers v. Hardwick*, 478 U.S. 186 (1986) at 194–95.

122. Henry J. Abraham, "The Bill of Rights After 200 Years: Some Unfinished Business," *Extensions* (Spring 1993), p. 12; Richard L. Pacelle, Jr., *The Transformation of the Supreme Court's Agenda: From the New Deal to the Reagan Administration* (Boulder, Col., 1991), p. 49; Pritchett and Westin, *Third Branch*, pp. 1–5.

123. McCloskey, *American Supreme Court*, p. 178.

124. Edward S. Corwin, *Constitutional Revolution, Ltd.* (Claremont, Cal., 1941), p. 91. The familiar view that the Court in the Progressive era was monolithically hostile to the State was rebutted in John E. Semonche, *Charting the Future: The Supreme Court Responds to a Changing Society, 1890–1920* (Westport, Ct., 1978), and in Melvin I. Urofsky, "Myth and Reality: The Supreme Court and Protective Legislation in the Progressive Era," *Yearbook of the Supreme Court Historical Society* (1983), pp. 463–78, but their perception has been challenged in turn by Paul Kens, "The Source of a Myth: Police Powers of the States and Laissez Faire Constitutionalism, 1900–1937," *American Journal of Legal History*, 35 (January 1991), 70–98.

125. McCloskey, *American Supreme Court*, pp. 175, 178. One commentator has written: "Whether completely illegitimized or still claiming some modicum of protection as a stepchild, the laissez-faire philosophy as epitomized in the concept of economic liberty is no longer a substantial factor in constitutional interpretation." Paul G. Kauper, *Frontiers of Constitutional Liberty* (Ann Arbor, Mich., 1956), p. 36.

9. The Birth of America's Second Bill of Rights

1. I hasten to add that there has never been so draconian a law. In 1858, however, in North Carolina a man was sentenced to a year in prison for circulating a book hostile to slavery, and the North Carolina Supreme Court sustained the conviction on the ground that it was criminal conduct to disseminate literature that caused "slaves to be discontented and free negroes dissatisfied." *State v. Worth*, 52 N.C. (7 Jones) 488 (1860) at 492; Michael Kent Curtis, *No State Shall Abridge* (Durham, N.C., 1986), p. 31. Individuals could, of course, invoke the bills of rights in state constitutions, but, Curtis maintains, "too often they proved to be paper barriers." Ibid., p. xiii.

2. The other seven of the first eight amendments do not mention Congress. The legal historian Sanford Levinson has asked, "Is there even a canonical text of the Bill of Rights?" He goes on to point out that a liberal and a conservative would have different "maps" of which amendments were embraced by that rubric. Sanford Levinson, "The Embarrassing Second Amendment," *Yale Law Journal*, 90 (December 1989), 637–78. In most commentary, the term "Bill of Rights" has been taken to refer to most of the first eight amendments, but not the Third (on quartering of soldiers), which is regarded as no longer pertinent,

while the Second (on the right to bear arms) has largely been passed over. In an elegant essay, a leading legal scholar has written, "The Second Amendment has generated almost no useful body of law. Indeed, it is substantially accurate to say that the useful case law of the Second Amendment, even in 1994, is mostly just missing in action." William Van Alstyne, "The Second Amendment and the Personal Right to Arms," *Duke Law Journal* (1994), p. 4. On the Ninth Amendment, see Randy E. Barnett, *The Rights Retained by the People* (2 vols., Fairfax, Va., 1989, 1992). A few conservative commentators would find a place for the Tenth Amendment on their "map."

3. *Barron v. Baltimore,* 7 Pet. 243 (1833) at 250–51; Henry Abraham, *Freedom and the Court: Civil Rights and Civil Liberties in the United States* (New York, 1972), pp. 30–31.

4. *Permoli v. New Orleans,* 3 How. 589 (1845) at 609.

5. Henry Steele Commager, *Majority Rule and Minority Rights* (New York, 1943), p. 55.

6. For Hughes's explanation of what he meant by that often-misquoted remark, see Merlo Pusey, *Charles Evans Hughes* (New York, 1963), p. 204. The literature on "original intent" is vast. The basic essay denying that Congress intended to absorb the Bill of Rights is that by Charles Fairman: "Does the Fourteenth Amendment Incorporate the Bill of Rights?" *Stanford Law Review,* 2 (December 1949), 5–139. Fairman wrote in response to Justice Hugo Black's contrary claim in *Adamson v. California,* 332 U.S. 46 (1947) at 71. Fairman finds support in William L. Richter, "One Hundred Years of Controversy: The Fourteenth Amendment and the Bill of Rights," *Loyola Law Review,* 15 (1968–69), 281–95, and in Richard E. Morgan, *The Law and Politics of Civil Rights and Liberties* (New York, 1985), p. 18. Black is rebutted somewhat differently in Frank H. Walker, Jr., "Was It Intended That the Fourteenth Amendment Incorporate the Bill of Rights?" *North Carolina Law Review,* 42 (June 1964), 925–36. The most extensive response to Fairman is Curtis, *No State Shall Abridge,* with an arresting foreword by William W. Van Alstyne. In 1949, an eminent constitutional authority wrote, "From a long study of the debates . . . relative to the 14th Amendment, I am satisfied that those who drafted and those who supported it, clearly intended through it to make the first eight Amendments . . . applicable to the States." Charles Warren to E. S. Corwin, January 25, 1948, Corwin MSS, Princeton University, Princeton, N. J., Box 1. In 1968 in a concurring opinion, Black gave a piece of his mind to Fairman. *Duncan v. Louisiana,* 391 U.S. 145 (1968) at 162. The most reasonable judgment about this controversy may well be that of Roald Mykkelvedt: "Because of the inconclusive nature of the historical record, and the imprecise wording of the Fourteenth Amendment's first section, 'firm ground for its proper construction' has proved exceedingly difficult to locate. Therefore, the Court has had exceptional latitude to develop the meaning of the first section's provisions." Roald Y. Mykkeltvedt, *The Nationalization of the Bill of Rights* (Port Washington, N. Y., 1983), pp. 10–11. The "firm ground" allusion is to Justice Rufus Peckham's opinion in the 1900 case of *Maxwell v. Dow.*

7. *Slaughterhouse Cases*, 16 Wall. 36 (1873); Loren P. Beth, "The Slaughterhouse Cases—Revisited," *Louisiana Law Review*, 23 (April 1963), 492–93.

8. When the Court invoked the privileges or immunities clause to strike down a Vermont tax law in 1935, it encountered widespread criticism for resurrecting a corpse. *Colgate v. Harvey*, 296 U.S. 404 (1935). That ruling survived for only five years. It was overturned in *Madden v. Kentucky*, 309 U.S. 83 (1940). For criticism of *Colgate*, see Alpheus Thomas Mason, *Harlan Fiske Stone* (New York, 1956), pp. 397–99; Felix Frankfurter to Harlan Fiske Stone, December 16, 19, 1935, Frankfurter MSS, Library of Congress (LC), Box 105.

9. In two 1876 rulings, the Court had denied that the Fourteenth Amendment's due process clause embraced either the Seventh Amendment's requirement of jury trials in civil cases or the rights stipulated in the First and Second Amendments of assembly and petition and to bear arms. *Walker v. Sauvinet*, 92 U.S. 90 (1876); *United States v. Cruikshank*, 92 U.S. 542 (1876).

10. Richard C. Cortner, *The Supreme Court and the Second Bill of Rights: The Fourteenth Amendment and the Nationalization of Civil Liberties* (Madison, Wis., 1981), pp. 12–22. I have found Cortner's outstanding book indispensable both for background and for analysis of this and other cases discussed in the essay. Although distinctions have sometimes been drawn between and among words such as "absorb," "nationalize," and "incorporate," I have followed the more usual practice of using the terms interchangeably to avoid repetition.

11. *Hurtado v. California*, 110 U.S. 516 (1884) at 529. As it happened, he did not hang but died of tuberculosis in his cell.

12. *Chicago, Burlington & Quincy Railroad Co. v. Chicago*, 166 U.S. 226 (1897). The decision was significant chiefly in departing from the view in *Hurtado* that "due process" could not include any of the basic rights of the first eight amendments because such a reading would render some of the language of the Constitution superfluous, though the Court never spelled out how its reasoning differed from that in *Hurtado*. Moreover, Justice Harlan never mentioned the Fifth Amendment, despite the efforts of counsel for the railroads to have the case turn on absorption of the just compensation clause of the Fifth Amendment. Seven years earlier, in another railroad case, the Court had taken the first short step toward absorbing the Bill of Rights into the Fourteenth Amendment by broadening the meaning of the due process clause to include substantive as well as procedural protections. *Chicago, Milwaukee & St. Paul Railroad v. Minnesota*, 134 U.S. 418 (1890).

13. Cortner, *Supreme Court*, pp. 29–37; *Maxwell v. Dow*, 176 U.S. 581 (1900). The Court dismissed Maxwell's claims both under the privileges or immunities clause and under the due process clause. It also denied Maxwell's claim that indictment by a grand jury was required by citing *Hurtado*, with no acknowledgment that the Court's reasoning in the more recent case of *Chicago, Burlington & Quincy Railroad* had diverged from that in *Hurtado*, thereby leaving a considerable area of confusion.

14. Cortner, *Supreme Court*, pp. 28–29; Mark A. Graber, *Transforming Free Speech: The Ambiguous Legacy of Civil Libertarianism* (Berkeley, 1991), pp. 31–35;

Henry J. Abraham, "John Marshall Harlan: The Justice and the Man," *Kentucky Law Journal,* 46 (Spring 1958), 469–70. For one conservative judge's openness to an expansive view of the Fourteenth Amendment, see Justice Stephen J. Field's dissent in *O'Neil v. Vermont,* 144 U.S. 323 (1892).

15. Cortner, *Supreme Court,* pp. 38–49; *Twining v. New Jersey,* 211 U.S. 78 (1908) at 98–99.

16. *Malloy v. Hogan,* 378 U.S. 1 (1964). Louis Henkin, however, has pointed out: "It is sometimes said—even by the Justices—that the Court has refused to find that the fourteenth amendment incorporated the fifth amendment's provision that no person shall be compelled to be a witness against himself. In fact, the Court *held* only that the state did not violate due process if it permitted the prosecution to comment on the failure . . . to take the stand." The Court did, though, draw the line on the kind of testimony against oneself involved in coerced confessions. *Brown v. Mississippi,* 297 U.S. 278 (1936). Louis Henkin, "'Selective Incorporation' in the Fourteenth Amendment," *Yale Law Journal,* 73 (November 1963), 81.

17. Louis H. Pollak, "Advocating Civil Liberties: A Young Lawyer Before the Old Court," *Harvard Civil Rights-Civil Liberties Review,* 17 (Spring 1982), 11; David M. Rabban, "The First Amendment in Its Forgotten Years," *Yale Law Journal,* 90 (December 1980), 579.

18. *Patterson v. Colorado,* 205 U.S. 454 (1907) at 462, 464–65; *Hawkins v. Bleakly,* 243 U.S. 210 (1917) at 216; Francis H. Heller, *The Sixth Amendment to the Constitution of the United States: A Study in Constitutional Development* (Lawrence, Kans., 1951), p. 42. See, too, *Jordan v. Massachusetts,* 225 U.S. 167 (1911) at 174; *Fox v. Washington,* 236 U.S. 273 (1915).

19. *Gilbert v. Minnesota,* 254 U.S. 325 (1920) at 343. In contrast to Zechariah Chafee, who read *Gilbert* as indicating that Brandeis favored substantive due process safeguarding of free expression, Robert Cover has written: "The tone seems to me to suggest that, *if* one must have *Coppage v. Kansas,* 236 U.S. 1 (1915), and other horrors in our jurisprudence, *then* surely the principle of those cases justifies extending free speech to the states. But it seems to me that Brandeis is holding back precisely so that it remains possible for him to deny substantive due process altogether." Robert M. Cover, "The Left, the Right and the First Amendment: 1918–1928," *Maryland Law Review,* 40 (1981), 378n., citing Chafee, *Free Speech in the United States* (Cambridge, Mass., 1941), pp. 295–96. *Coppage,* striking down a law forbidding yellow dog contracts, was viewed by progressives as a gross example of the Court's hostility to labor. Brandeis's opinion in *Gilbert* "was only the second occasion on which any member of the Court had maintained in any opinion that the Fourteenth Amendment protected freedom of speech from encroachment by state action," another commentator has observed. "In at least twenty rulings since the passage of the Fourteenth Amendment in 1868, the High Court had upheld the old 1833 rule that the Bill of Rights did not apply to the states." Carol E. Jenson, *The Network of Control: State Supreme Courts and State Security Statutes, 1920–1970* (Westport, Ct., 1982), p. 20.

20. *Prudential Insurance Co. v. Cheek,* 259 U.S. 530 (1922) at 543. "It is clear then," one historian has written, "that for a quarter of a century the Court had readily accepted freedom of contract as a constitutionally guaranteed liberty but had steadfastly refused to give an equal status to freedom of speech, press, assembly, and religion." George W. Spicer, *The Supreme Court and Fundamental Freedoms* (New York, 1959), p. 13. For a different perspective, see Alex B. Lacy, Jr., "The Bill of Rights and the Fourteenth Amendment: The Evolution of the Absorption Doctrine," *Washington and Lee Law Review,* 23 (Spring 1966), 43. Neither *Meyer v. Nebraska* nor *Pierce v. Society of Sisters,* often thought to be stepping stones toward the adoption by the Court of a new attitude, were pertinent to incorporation. *Meyer v. Nebraska,* 262 U.S. 390 (1923); *Pierce v. Society of Sisters,* 252 U.S. 510 (1925). As Philip Kurland has observed, "Probably the most abused citation in the construction of the first amendment is the case of *Pierce v. Society of Sisters.* The case raised no church-state issues; the Court decided no church-state issues. Indeed, no reference to the first amendment is made anywhere in the Court's opinion." Philip B. Kurland, *Religion and the Law: Of Church and State and the Supreme Court* (Chicago, 1962), p. 27. The plaintiffs, he added, drew upon property rights decisions such as the child labor tax case.

21. Lawrence H. Chamberlain, *Loyalty and Legislative Action: A Survey of Activity by the New York State Legislature, 1919–1949* (Ithaca, N. Y., 1951), pp. 9–52; Paul L. Murphy, *The Meaning of Freedom of Speech: First Amendment Freedoms from Wilson to FDR* (Westport, Ct., 1972), p. 80; Benjamin Gitlow, *I Confess: The Truth About American Communism* (New York, 1940), pp. 72, 74. "One wonders," observed the civil liberties attorney Albert DeSilver, in a 1921 review of the Lusk Committee's final report, "what caused the inclusion of the irrelevant statement that Bela Kun's real name is Cohen and that twenty-five of his commissars were Jews." Walter Nelles, *A Liberal in Wartime: The Education of Albert DeSilver* (New York, 1940), p. 179. Gitlow was also indicted for publishing an article by Nikolai Bukharin.

22. Cortner, *Supreme Court,* pp. 57–58, citing Chafee, *Free Speech,* p. 319. Far from being inflammatory, the Manifesto declared, "The revolutionary epoch of the final struggle against Capitalism may last for years and tens of years." Milton R. Konvitz, *Fundamental Liberties of a Free People: Religion, Speech, Press, Assembly* (Ithaca, N. Y., 1957), p. 297. Darrow called the Manifesto the "tamest, the dullest, the most uninteresting document ever submitted," and Louis Pollak has characterized it as "pages of polysyllabic exhortation." Harold Josephson, "Political Justice during the Red Scare: The Trial of Benjamin Gitlow," in Michael A. Belknap, *American Political Trials* (Westport, Ct., 1981), p. 161; Pollak, "Advocating Civil Liberties," p. 9. The Gitlow papers at the University of North Carolina at Charlotte have materials that are important for Gitlow's radical activities, but I found nothing directly pertinent to the case.

23. *Gitlow v. New York,* 268 U.S. 652 (1925) at 666; Charles Warren, "The New 'Liberty' Under the Fourteenth Amendment," *Harvard Law Review,* 39 (February 1926), 432–33. For an exegesis of Sanford's reasoning in *Gitlow,* and a criticism of the dissent by Holmes in which Brandeis joined, see Harry Kalven,

Jr., *A Worthy Tradition: Freedom of Speech in America* (New York, 1988), pp. 150–56.

24. Before the year was out, though, Gitlow had been pardoned by the governor of New York, Al Smith. Indeed, Smith would have freed him sooner, but obligingly agreed to delay a pardon so that the Supreme Court would have an opportunity to rule. Harold Josephson, "The Dynamics of Repression: New York During the Red Scare," *Mid-America*, 59 (October 1977), 143. Gitlow went on to be the Communist party's national vice-presidential candidate in 1928—ironically on a ticket opposed to Al Smith—and then, after a falling out with Stalin, an implacable anti-Communist and paid government informer for the next generation.

25. Cortner, *Supreme Court*, pp. 73–81.

26. *Stromberg v. California*, 283 U.S. 359 (1931) at 368; Joseph Mosnier, "Free Speech and the Red Flag: An Examination of *Stromberg v. California*," seminar paper, University of North Carolina at Chapel Hill. The Court divided 7–2, with McReynolds and Butler in the minority. A few writers place the dividing line four years earlier with *Fiske v. Kansas*, 274 U.S. 380 (1927). See, for example, John Raeburn Green, "The Bill of Rights, the Fourteenth Amendment and the Supreme Court," *Michigan Law Review*, 46 (May 1948), 869. Most commentators, however, regard *Fiske* as too slender a reed. Brandeis's eloquent statement on behalf of civil liberties in a case decided earlier that same year took the form of a concurrence upholding the conviction of a California woman who had been sentenced to fourteen years in San Quentin for attending a meeting of the Communist Labor Party, though at the convention she had supported using the ballot to achieve change and though she ended her relation with the group shortly afterwards. *Whitney v. California*, 274 U.S. 357 (1927) at 377.

27. The most extensive account of *Near* is Fred W. Friendly's lively *Minnesota Rag* (New York, 1981). The passages quoted appear on pp. 31, 32, and 45–48 and in Nat Hentoff, *The First Freedom: The Tumultuous History of Free Speech in America* (New York, 1981), p. 200. But see, too, John E. Hartmann, "The Minnesota Gag Law and the Fourteenth Amendment," *Minnesota History*, 27 (December 1960), 161–73, and the excellent analysis by Paul L. Murphy, "*Near v. Minnesota* in the Context of Historical Developments," *Minnesota Law Review*, 66 (November 1981), 95–160.

28. Cortner, *Supreme Court*, p. x.

29. Hyman Berman, "Political Antisemitism in Minnesota During the Great Depression," *Jewish Social Studies 1976*, 38 (1976), 248–49; *State ex rel. Olson v. Guilford*, 174 Minn. 457 (1928); 179 Minn. 40 (1929). "If there be any menace to the freedom of the press," said the *Christian Science Monitor*, "it is a menace which comes from the unscrupulous within the ranks of the profession." "The War on the Minnesota Law," *Literary Digest*, February 1, 1930, in Lamar T. Beman, ed., *Selected Articles on Censorship of Speech and the Press* (New York, 1930), p. 215.

30. The American Civil Liberties Union offered to represent Near, but it was displaced by McCormick, who headed a key committee of the American Newspaper Publishers Association.

31. *Near v. Minnesota*, 283 U.S. 697 (1931) at 707. For Hughes's achievements, see Merle William Loper, "The Court of Chief Justice Hughes: Contributions to Civil Liberties," *Wayne Law Review*, 12 (Spring 1966), 535–95.

32. Klaus H. Heberle, "From Gitlow to Near: Judicial Amendment by Absent-Minded Incrementalism," *Journal of Politics*, 34 (May 1972), 458–83. See, too, David P. Currie, "The Constitution in the Supreme Court: Civil Rights and Liberties, 1930–1941," *Duke Law Journal* (November 1987), 809. Curiously, not even the ACLU, despite its role in *Gitlow*, appeared to grasp the historic importance of the case.

33. *Hamilton v. Regents of the University of California*, 293 U.S. 245 (1934).

34. *Powell v. Alabama*, 287 U.S. 45 (1932) at 71–73. The facts in the case are graphically set forth in Dan T. Carter, *Scottsboro: A Tragedy of the American South* (Baton Rouge, La., 1969). For analyses of the case, see William M. Beaney, *The Right to Counsel in American Courts* (Ann Arbor, Mich., 1955), pp. 151–57, and Yale Kamisar, "Equal Justice in Criminal Procedure," in Kamisar, Fred E. Inbau, and Thurman Arnold, *Criminal Justice in Our Time*, ed. A. E. Dick Howard (Charlottesville, Va., 1965), p. 56.

35. *Grosjean v. American Press Co.*, 297 U.S. 233 (1936); *Brown v. Mississippi*, 297 U.S. 278 (1936); *Johnson v. Zerbst*, 304 U.S. 458 (1938); *Betts v. Brady*, 316 U.S. 455 (1942). Cardozo's opinion in *Palko v. Connecticut*, 302 U.S. 319 (1937) is confused on this question. On a related matter, the right to confront witnesses, see *Snyder v. Massachusetts*, 291 U.S. 97 (1934). This subject is well covered in Heller, *Sixth Amendment*, pp. 124–26.

36. *De Jonge v. Oregon*, 299 U.S. 353 (1937) at 364.

37. *Palko v. Connecticut*, 302 U.S. 319 (1937) at 323–27.

38. Robert Fairchild Cushman, "Incorporation: Due Process and the Bill of Rights," *Cornell Law Quarterly*, 51 (Spring 1966), 484; Green, "Bill of Rights," pp. 871, 876.

39. *Cantwell v. Connecticut*, 310 U.S. 296 (1940) at 303; Cortner, *Supreme Court*, pp. 100–108; Kurland, *Religion and Law*, p. 54. Some thought that the Court, in subsequent Jehovah's Witnesses cases, went too far in upholding the rights of that sect to proselytize. In the spring of 1943, Felix Frankfurter wrote his fellow Justice Robert Jackson: "If one religion must call another a 'whore,' at least let them confine such manifestation of the Fatherhood of God and the Brotherhood of Man to their own temples and tabernacles, and not turn one's house into a scene of coercing and hating." Frankfurter to Jackson, April 9, 1943, Frankfurter MSS, LC, Box 69. Subsequently, a distinguished constitutional historian, Paul Freund, stated, "The Court here has acted virtually as a legislative drafting bureau for municipal authorities. . . . While the privilege of righteous peaceful aggression has thus been sanctified, the privilege of private belief and of security from intrusion has been qualified." Paul A. Freund, *The Supreme Court of the United States: Its Business, Purposes, and Performance* (Cleveland, 1949), pp. 40–41.

40. *Everson v. Board of Education*, 330 U.S. 1 (1947). The religious provisions of the First Amendment have two aspects. *Cantwell* concerned the right to "free exercise," *Everson*, the ban on "establishment of religion." The latter decision

dealt with a New Jersey law authorizing reimbursement of parents for bus fares paid by children attending private schools, including Catholic parochial schools. Justice Black declared: "The First Amendment has erected a wall between church and state. That wall must be kept high and impregnable. We could not approve the slightest breach." But then, surprisingly, he added, "New Jersey has not breached it here." Four Justices dissented, including Robert Jackson, who wrote, "The case which irresistibly comes to mind as the most fitting precedent is that of Julia who, according to Byron's reports, 'whispering "I will ne'er consent,"—consented.' " See Wilber G. Katz, *Religion and American Constitutions* (Evanston, Ill., 1964), pp. 64–73; William H. Marnell, *The First Amendment: The History of Religious Freedom in America* (Garden City, N. Y., 1964), pp. 186–89; Theodore Powell, *The School Bus Law: A Case Study in Education, Religion, and Politics* (Middletown, Ct., 1960), pp. 37–43; Dallin H. Oaks, ed., *The Wall Between Church and State* (Chicago, 1963).

41. The emphasis on civil liberties was strengthened by the emergence of the "preferred position" doctrine in *United States v. Carolene Prods. Co.*, 304 U.S. 144 (1938) at 152 n. 4. See Louis Lusky, "Footnote Redux: A *Carolene Products* Reminiscence," *Columbia Law Review*, 82 (October 1982), 1093–1105.

42. Cortner, *Supreme Court*, pp. 139–51; *Adamson v. California*, 332 U.S. 46 (1947). The accused's full name was Admiral Dewey Adamson. "Admiral" was not a title but his first name.

43. Ibid. at 62, 66. See, too, Felix Frankfurter, "Memorandum of 'Incorporation' of the Bill of Rights into the Due Process Clause of the Fourteenth Amendment," *Harvard Law Review*, 78 (February 1965), 746–83; Mark Silverstein, *Constitutional Faiths: Felix Frankfurter, Hugo Black, and the Process of Judicial Decision Making* (Ithaca, N. Y., 1984).

44. *Adamson v. California*, 332 U.S. 46 (1947) at 71–72, 89, 123–24.

45. *Wolf v. Colorado*, 338 U.S. 25 (1949); Jacob W. Landynski, *Search and Seizure and the Supreme Court: A Study in Constitutional Interpretation* (Baltimore, 1966), pp. 126–34; Fred P. Graham, *The Self-Inflicted Wound* (New York, 1970), pp. 39–40.

46. *Ciucci v. Illinois*, 356 U.S. 571 (1958); Leonard G. Miller, *Double Jeopardy and the Federal System* (Chicago, 1968), p. 8.

47. David Fellman, *The Limits of Freedom* (New Brunswick, N. J., 1959), p. 49. The Court, however, indicated that there were limits to what it would tolerate when it was confronted by a case in which a drug suspect was convicted on the basis of morphine capsules that were extracted by the forcible administration of an emetic after the handcuffed suspect had been taken to a hospital. *Rochin v. California*, 342 U.S. 165 (1952). For requirement of a public trial, see *In re Oliver*, 333 U.S. 257 (1948).

48. Cortner, *Supreme Court*, pp. 179–88; *Mapp v. Ohio*, 367 U.S. 643 (1961) at 660.

49. *Robinson v. California*, 370 U.S. 660 (1962). I have drawn upon the vivid account of the case in Cortner, *Supreme Court*, pp. 188–93.

50. Anthony Lewis, *Gideon's Trumpet* (New York, 1964); Laura Kalman, *Abe Fortas: A Biography* (New Haven, Ct., 1990), p. 181.

51. *Gideon v. Wainwright*, 372 U.S. 335 (1963). Less than a decade later, a unanimous Court extended the *Gideon* principle to misdemeanor cases that could result in conviction. *Argersinger v. Hamlin*, 407 U.S. 25 (1972). For the consequences of *Gideon*, see David Fellman, *The Defendant's Rights Today* (Madison, Wis., 1976), pp. 215–18; William W. Van Alstyne, "In Gideon's Wake: Harsher Penalties and the Successful Criminal Appellant," *Yale Law Journal*, 74 (March 1965), 606–39; and David L. Bazelon, "The Realities of *Gideon* and *Argersinger*," *Georgetown Law Journal*, 64 (March 1976), 811–38.

52. *Malloy v. Hogan*, 378 U.S. 1 (1964). See, too, *Murphy v. Waterfront Commission of New York Harbor*, 378 U.S. 52 (1964).

53. *Miranda v. Arizona*, 384 U.S. 436 (1966).

54. *Pointer v. Texas*, 380 U.S. 400 (1965) at 403.

55. *Washington v. Texas*, 385 U.S. 812 (1966); Graham, *Self-Inflicted Wound*, p. 28.

56. *Klopfer v. North Carolina*, 386 U.S. 213 (1967); Joseph Mosnier, "Demise of an 'Extraordinary Criminal Procedure': Klopfer v. North Carolina and the Incorporation of the Sixth Amendment's Speedy Trial Provision," M. A. essay, University of North Carolina at Chapel Hill; Daniel H. Pollitt, "Legal Problems in Southern Desegregation: The Chapel Hill Story," *North Carolina Law Review*, 43 (1965), 689–767; John Ehle, *The Free Men* (New York, 1965). In 1905, the Court had said, "The right of a speedy trial is necessarily relative. It is consistent with delays and depends upon circumstances." *Beavers v. Haubert*, 198 U.S. 77 (1905) at 87. For subsequent developments, see *Barker v. Wingo*, 407 U.S. 514 (1972); Charles P. Schroop, "Sixth Amendment—Right to a Speedy Trial—A Balancing Test," *Cornell Law Review*, 58 (January 1973), 399–415. One commentator has observed, "The Court's concern with criminal procedure can be understood only in the context of the struggle for civil rights." A. Kenneth Pye, "The Warren Court and Criminal Procedure," *Michigan Law Review*, 67 (December 1968), 256.

57. Cortner, *Supreme Court*, pp. 246–62; *Duncan v. Louisiana*, 391 U.S. 145 (1968). "Parish" is Louisiana nomenclature for "county." The Plaquemines despotism is dissected in Glen Jeansonne, *Leander Perez: Boss of the Delta* (Baton Rouge, La., 1977).

58. *Benton v. Maryland*, 395 U.S. 784 (1969) at 795–96.

59. Furthermore, as one writer noted, "the Court, when it did hold that a right of the first eight amendments applied to the states, began to say that the whole right applied and not just part of it. Usually, this . . . step took the form of . . . praising a particular Bill of Rights guarantee and then asking (with not a little horror at the thought) 'can we permit this right to be diluted or debased?' with a predictable 'no' being the answer. The Court often also considered it 'incongruous' for one standard to apply to state courts and another in federal courts." Christopher Wolfe, *The Rise of Modern Judicial Review: From Constitutional Interpretation to Judge-Made Law* (New York, 1986), p. 270. For a thoughtful criticism of this practice, see Henry J. Friendly, "The Bill of Rights as a Code of Criminal Procedure," *California Law Review*, 53 (1965), 929–56.

60. As one commentator has written, if the Seventh Amendment were fully

incorporated in the Fourteenth Amendment to mandate trial by jury, whenever requested, in every civil case where more than twenty dollars was at stake, "it is not difficult to imagine what this requirement might impose on the legal system." James J. Magee, *Mr. Justice Black: Absolutist on the Court* (Charlottesville, Va., 1980), p. 122. The Court also balked at compelling the states to impanel grand juries, probably because doing so would occasion large and needless expense, and as a consequence *Hurtado* was one of the few precedents not reversed. It also has not absorbed the Third Amendment's ban on quartering troops in private homes, the "excessive bail" feature of the Eight Amendment, or the guarantee in the Second Amendment of the right to bear arms, though in recent years a number of commentators have argued for the incorporation of this feature of the Second Amendment. See, especially, Stephen B. Halbrook, *That Every Man Be Armed: The Evolution of a Constitutional Right* (Albuquerque, N. M., 1984) and Robert J. Cottrol and Raymond T. Diamond, "Public Safety and the Right to Bear Arms," in David J. Bodenhamer and James W. Ely, Jr., *The Bill of Rights in Modern America: After 200 Years* (Bloomington, Ind., 1993), pp. 72–86. Moreover, not even in *Benton* did the Court, in so many words, embrace Black's view that the Fourteenth Amendment incorporated all of the Bill of Rights. Indeed, it has never done so.

   61. *Newsweek,* May 25, 1987, p. 66.

Index